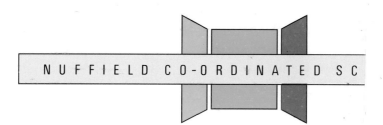

NUFFIELD CO-ORDINATED SC

PHYSICS

Published for the Nuffield–Chelsea Curriculum Trust by
Longman Group UK Limited

General Editors,
Nuffield Co-ordinated Sciences
Geoffrey Dorling
Mark Ellse
Andrew Hunt
Grace Monger

Author and General Editor, Physics
Geoffrey Dorling

Advisers, Physics
Mark Ellse
E. J. Wenham

Other contributors, Physics
Alan Boyle
Iain Hall
Philip Poole

The Nuffield–Chelsea Curriculum Trust wish to acknowledge their debt to the many contributors to earlier Nuffield Science schemes and also, particularly, to Tim Hickson of King's School, Worcester and Brenda Jennison of the Department of Education, University of Cambridge for their help in the early stages of the project.

They are also grateful for the help given to the editor by Alan Boyle who helped and advised throughout the project, Mary Whitehouse who read and commented on all of the first draft of the pupils' book, and Pamela Rivaz who did so much to make the final text more readable.

The Trust are also indebted to the Headmaster and Governors of Wymondham College, Norfolk, for their willing support in releasing the editor from his duties at the College during the development of the project.

Longman Group UK Limited
Longman House, Bunt Mill, Harlow, Essex CM20 2JE, England
and Associated Companies throughout the World.

First published 1988
Colour edition 1992
Second impression 1994
Copyright © The Nuffield-Chelsea Curriculum Trust 1988, 1992

Illustrations by
Peter Edwards, Hardlines and Chris Ryley
Cover illustration by Plus 2 Design

Filmset in Times Roman
Printed in Hong Kong
SWT/02

ISBN 0 582 09396 1

The Publishers' policy is to use paper manufactured from sustainable forests.

Contents

Acknowledgements

AEA Technology 3.19b
Allsport 4.9, 7.23, 8.1a and b

BBC Engineering 15.21
Barnaby's Picture Library 12.7c, 12.19, 14.12
Black & Decker 18.22
Catherine Blackie 1.5a, 2.1, 2.2, 2.22b, 7.9, 9.26, 11.3, 11.9, 12.3, page 212, 13.11, 16.25, 16.26, 17.26b, 18.34
Paul Brierley 21.9
British Aerospace 6.7a, 6.26, 6.27
British Nuclear Fuels 12.11

CEGB page 243, 11.29
CERN 3.26a
CMB Aerosols 2.19
Caradon Everest 9.16a
J. Allan Cash Ltd 0.5
Bruce Coleman 0.2, page 9, 1.4, 8.16, 11.1, 12.1, 12.2, 12.30, 14.1, 16.15a and b
Collections 1.15b, 1.19, 6.11
Creda 15.25

Geoffrey Dorling 9.7, 9.17, 11.24, 12.20, 16.24, 20.16

Energy Efficiency Office 8.8
Mary Evans Picture Library 3.28

Ferranti International 20.22
Ford 8.10b, 18.1

GEC 8.10a, 11.29
GEC-Marconi 21.13
Sally and Richard Greenhill 5.5, 7.1, 9.18, 9.20, 10.2, 10.17, 12.4
Griffin & George 1.25, 16.14

HMS Naval Base, Portsmouth (British Crown copyright, reproduced with the permission of The Controller of Her Britannic Majesty's Stationery Office) 6.14
Philip Harris 4.8
Philip Harris/Kodansha 7.11, 7.20
Michael Holford 21.3a, 21.4, 21.14a
Honda 8.20
Hozelock 6.15b
Hutchison 10.9

Institution of Civil Engineers 1.3

JET 12.18a, 12.18b

King's College, London, AVSU 7.13, 20.1b, 20.2, 20.4, 20.6, 20.8, 20.10, 20.12a and b, 20.25, 20.27

London Electricity 9.3
London Transport Museum 16.1

M.O.D. Crown Copyright (reproduced by permission of The Controller of Her Majesty's Stationery Office) 15.20
Magic Circle 5.21
Mansell Collection 10.8a, 10.23, 11.31, 17.25
Maplin Electronics 21.7
Maunsell 1.18b
Keith Moseley 0.8, 1.5c, 3.11, 4.6, 4.10, 4.17, 5.4, 5.13, 5.14, 6.10, 6.17, 6.21, 6.22, 6.23, 6.31, 9.22, 11.7, 12.5, 15.17, 15.24b, 16.8, 16.9, 19.5, 20.24, 21.12, 21.17
Mullard 19.2

National Centre for Alternative Technology 12.28
National Power 11.10, 11.14
The Natural History Museum page 11
The Nobel Foundation 0.6
Nuclear Electric 18.38
Nuffield-Chelsea Curriculum Trust 1.2

Orbik Electronics 11.30

Philips 15.24a, 17.26a
Philips CED Publicity 21.14b
Philips Components 19.2
Pilkington 13.10
Pirelli Cables 13.9a and b
Potterton Myson 20.14
Eileen Preston 11.2

Retna 19.14a and b
Rex Features page 65, 6.1, 6.5, 6.25, 12.7a, 12.21, 15.30, 17.1
Estate of Mrs J. C. Robinson 4.2

Rockwool Ltd 9.10a and b, 9.14
Rolls-Royce 6.28
Ann Ronan 10.8b, 18.25
Rover 8.6
Royal Society 2.15, 5.12, 10.11a and b, 10.14
Rutherford Appleton Laboratory 3.26b

STC Telecommunications 13.9a and b
Professor S. Salter 12.22
Scala 4.4, 10.3
Science Museum 8.10c
Science Photo Library 0.3, 3.9, 3.19a, 6.15c, 6.20, 7.2, 7.26, 7.27, 10.8c, 11.5, 12.9, 12.15, 12.26, 12.27, 12.29, 15.1, 15.6, 15.9, 15.19, 17.2, 17.3, 18.25, 19.13, 21.18, 21.19a and b
Scotrail 1.17
Scottish Power 12.25
Shell page 129
Silva 18.6
Singer 20.23a
Smiths Industries Environmental Controls 16.30
Sony 21.27
Stannah Lifts 8.2
Still Moving Picture Company 1.1a

Telefocus 21.5, 21.11a and b, 21.23
Teltron 19.3a and b
Times Newspapers 0.7
Topham 12.16
Transport and Road Research Laboratory 6.4

UKAEA 3.19b
Unilab 9.25, 11.18, 19.11

Vauxhall 6.7b

Walk Fund 17.34
Dave Waterman 7.15
Whirlpool 2.21
David Woodfall/NHPA 11.4

Zanussi 20.23b
Zefa 0.1, 0.4, 1.1b, 1.5b, 7.8, 11.15, 11.33, 12.7a, page 209

Introduction

What is science?

Before you can join in and be a scientist you need to know something of what scientists have already discovered and how they do their work. All the people pictured in figures 1 to 5 are scientists. What is special about being a scientist? What do scientists do and how do they do it?

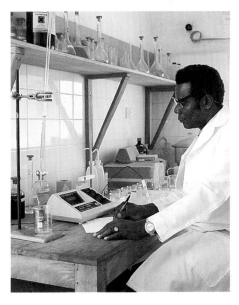

Figure 1 (above)
Investigating the properties of a laser beam.

Figure 2 (above centre)
Cleaning oil from the feathers of jackass penguins.

Figure 3 (above right)
Checking for evidence of insect damage to trees weakened by acid rain.

Figure 4 (right)
Testing rope.

Figure 5 (far right)
Technician at a film laboratory in Nigeria.

Figure 6
The Nobel medal, which is given to the winners of the annual prizes for physics, chemistry, medicine, literature, and the promotion of peace. The awards are made from the bequest of Alfred Nobel, the Swedish inventor of dynamite, who died in 1896. The prize has been awarded to several of the people mentioned in this book, including Marie Curie, Albert Einstein and Ernest Rutherford.

Some people compare being a scientist with playing a game. It can be great fun but it is also very competitive. Many scientists want to be first to publish new results and theories so that they will win awards and be remembered for their work. Scientists, like sports professionals, need plenty of training and have to work hard for success.

Often scientists work in teams and enjoy the excitement of working out ideas and making discoveries as a group. Members of a team play the game according to agreed rules. One of the rules in the game of science is that the results of experiments are not accepted until they have been published and checked by other scientists. The editors of science journals send new articles to "referees" to make sure that they are written according to the rules and are fit to print.

Science helps us to make sense of the world we live in. Every day we experience regular patterns: the Sun rises each morning, sugar always dissolves in water, plants wilt without water. This gives us a sense of order which lets us make predictions: the Sun will rise tomorrow morning, the next spoonful of sugar will dissolve in a cup of tea, the rubber plant will die if we forget to water it.

So scientists look for order in what they observe. To see order, they must first make observations and take measurements. In this way they collect much information about the world we live in. They look for patterns in their knowledge.

For example, meteorologists are scientists who study the weather. They record huge numbers of measurements of air pressure, rainfall, temperature and windspeed. The measurements are not taken at random. Meteorologists have theories about which are the important readings to take. Computers are programmed according to these theories to process the mass of data.

We see one way of making a pattern out of all the facts about the climate every time we watch a weather forecast on television. The lines on the weather map have been worked out from all the measurements and satellite observations.

Once scientists have found patterns it becomes possible to make predictions. Some predictions are very reliable. Astronomers can predict the movement of the planets and comets very accurately. Sometimes the predictions are less certain as you know if you have ever been misled by a weather forecast.

As they are collecting facts and looking for patterns scientists also seek explanations. Why is the world as it is? Why do things behave in the way that they do? Inventing theories to explain what we know is an important part of science.

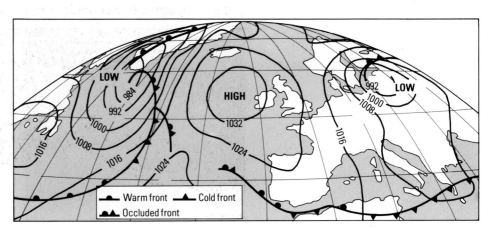

Figure 7
Weather maps like this are published in newspapers.

As you study this science course, you will see for yourself some of the things which scientists have already found. We will be taking you on a "conducted tour" to give you firsthand experience of what scientists have discovered.

While on this tour you will be taught some of the practical skills needed to use scientific equipment and methods. Learning skills needs practice as you will know if you play a musical instrument or are learning to type. The practice may not always be enjoyable but it is necessary.

If you have ever been a tourist on holiday you will know that it can be interesting – at least for a time. However, in the end being a tourist is not as interesting as living your own life where you belong. So it is with science.

To understand science you need to have experience of asking questions and planning investigations. You have to be involved in experiments where the answer is not known in advance. We hope that by the end of this course you will have had several opportunities to join in and be a scientist using your knowledge and skills to carry out investigations.

The law of springs

We shall start this course by describing an investigation that you have probably already carried out. We shall think carefully about what you did so that you can understand what "carrying out an investigation" means.

"If I pull on this spring it stretches!" So it does! But that's not doing anything scientific – no more than striking a note on a piano is playing a piano or plucking a string on a guitar is playing the guitar.

"What happens if I pull a bit harder? Oh! it stretches some more." "How much more does it stretch?" "If I double the 'pull' will I double the 'stretch'?" "I could do an experiment to find out." Now that is starting to "do science".

You may have made an investigation into the behaviour of springs earlier in science, but have you thought out the various steps you had to take in order to do it satisfactorily? The pictures that follow show you the steps you probably took when you made this investigation. All scientists have to follow similar steps whenever they investigate something.

Investigating the behaviour of springs

First of all you will probably stretch some springs with your hands, feeling the force needed to extend the spring. These **observations** are important before you can go on to the next step in your investigation.

Next you need to **plan** your investigation, thinking about what you are going to measure. For example, are you going to measure the overall length

Figure 8
This pupil is investigating the behaviour of a spring.

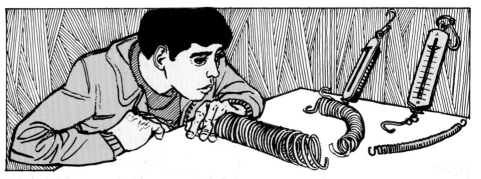

Figure 9
Planning.

of the spring or just the increase in length? You will need to think about how big the quantities are that you are going to measure and choose appropriate pieces of equipment to do this.

The next step is to make the **measurements**. In this case you will need to measure the amount the spring is stretched for each force that you use to stretch it. You will also need to measure the force.

Figure 10
Measuring.

You will need to **select** relevant observations. Once the spring has become permanently stretched, measurements of the force and the amount the spring stretched may not fit in with previous observations.

Figure 11
Selecting relevant observations.

Now you will want to **display** your results in such a way that you can spot any relationships between them. The usual way to do this is to use a **table** or a **graph**, though some results are best displayed as a **bar chart**, as you will see in Chapter **P9**.

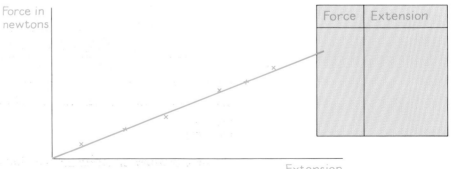

Figure 12
Displaying results.

You will look at your results to see whether they fall into any simple **pattern**, and perhaps try to express this mathematically in words or symbols. Patterns of this sort are called **laws** in physics.

As a scientist you will ask yourself how this result fits in with other, **related** things you know in science. This is what we mean by the word **explanation** in science.

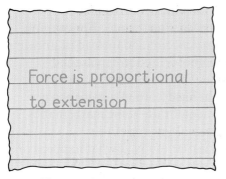

Figure 13
Finding a pattern.

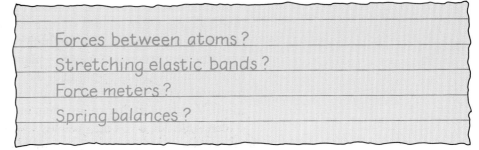

Figure 14
Relating it to other things.

It is important to record your work for others to read and also to be able to read and understand other people's similar experiments. This is all part of **communication** between scientists and others.

Figure 15
Communicating.

Once the law has been established, it can be used to make **predictions** and to **solve problems**.

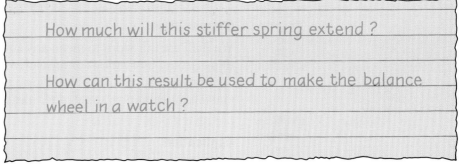

Figure 16
Predicting.

These pictures illustrate the fact that to "do science" properly you have to have some **skills**: like being able to use measuring instruments, being able to plot graphs, being able to read instructions, being able to write reports.

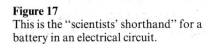

Figure 17
This is the "scientists' shorthand" for a battery in an electrical circuit.

Writing reports and reading instructions often means being able to understand special symbols – a sort of "scientists' shorthand". For example you will see in Chapter **P**16 how to draw electrical circuits. Instead of drawing a picture of a battery every time, a special symbol is used to represent it (figure 17).

Sometimes you have to use skills you might have learned outside science. You may have to construct a piece of equipment, or use some mathematics.

But these skills are not all you call on when making a scientific investigation. Often an idea starts from looking carefully at what happens or is to be seen around you – something we refer to as **observation**. Then there are "thinking processes" as well – **planning** and **selecting the right apparatus** (and often this means thinking of the **sizes** of the things you are going to measure). You have to look at your results **critically**, and think what they mean. You may try to explain them in terms of science you already understand. Then you may use the result of your investigation to predict some other event or to solve a problem.

These are important skills and processes. You will not necessarily use them all in every experiment you do. Sometimes for example the experiment may be only a matter of making observations. There will be nothing you can measure. To learn to use these skills, you need to use them throughout your work. Often it will be obvious to you when you are using one of these skills – for example, if you draw a circuit diagram, plot a graph, or make a report on what you have done.

But you will only learn to recognize some of the other important skills by thinking carefully each time you do an experiment about what you are doing. To help you, when one of the skills or processes is used in the work of this book you will often find the appropriate word in the margin. Here are the skills and processes we shall emphasize:

Observation

This is the skill we use when we have to notice carefully what is happening in a particular experiment.

Measurement

This is an important skill that we use when we are trying to find patterns of behaviour.

Interpretation

We shall use this word to mean any activity that involves trying to find new things from observations or measurements. "Interpretation" may mean "making a deduction", or "making a prediction", or "relating observations and measurements to some other ideas in physics".

Application

Planning

Planning is a very important part of any scientific investigation. Before making measurements, and often before making detailed observations, you must decide what it is you want to do and what you hope to gain from the investigation.

More about physics

Physics is about making connections. If we stretch a piece of wire or a rubber band we find it behaves in the same way as a coiled spring. When different things behave in the same way we ask, "Why? What connects their similar behaviour?" The trouble is we quickly find ourselves talking about atoms and the forces between them, and the topic soon seems very remote from the springs we first experimented with.

But these connections make physics a very powerful "thinking tool". It can enable us to solve many problems. It can make sense of things that did not make sense before; and we can apply these new ideas to do things we could not do before. Once we understood why springs, pieces of wire and rubber bands behaved in the same way we could invent new materials to do old jobs in better ways.

If finding connections can seem to take us very quickly away from the real problems which started us off, so can many of the investigations in physics. These often take place in laboratories using special equipment. Both the ideas and the experiments can often seem only remotely connected with the world we live in.

In this book we shall try to keep your world in mind. Rather than starting with the ideas in physics – that is the "connections" – we shall start with some of the things physics has helped to create. We shall study these and try to understand them. We shall look at different things which behave in similar ways, so that at the end you should be able to see the connecting ideas behind them. In doing so, you will have many opportunities to make your own investigations and use some of these ideas to solve problems.

As you progress you will find that physics alone does not provide enough ideas or knowledge to solve all these problems. Often you will find you need ideas from your work in chemistry and biology and maybe ideas from other sciences as well. And more and more you will find that these other sciences need ideas from your work in physics.

A connecting theme

There are many connections between the events we see in the physical world. Some of these connections cover so many different events that they acquire names of their own – like "force" and "electricity". You will meet many of these connecting ideas (or *concepts* as they are called) in this course. But one idea runs throughout the whole of the course. This is the idea of *energy*, and in particular the transfer of energy.

Co-ordinated Sciences

This is a Co-ordinated Sciences course. You may have seen the word *co-ordinated* used elsewhere. What do you think this newspaper story means?

> "Police carried out a *co-ordinated* raid on ten warehouses in the London area last night. As a result fifteen people were arrested and are being held for questioning."

To be *co-ordinated* the raid must have been carefully organised. Each person in the police team knew exactly what was happening elsewhere and when it was happening. That is what we and your teachers have tried to do with this science course.

You have different books for Biology, Chemistry and Physics, but the separate parts of the course have been carefully co-ordinated so that ideas you meet in one subject can be used in another. For example you will need to use ideas about energy in all your sciences. You will learn about energy first in Physics. When you come to use energy ideas in Biology and Chemistry, your teachers will know and expect to use what you have learned in Physics.

To help you make the most of this co-ordination we have included a large number of cross references in each of the books. For example when you first come to the subject of X-rays in Chemistry you will be reminded that you can find out more about the wavelength of X-rays in your Physics book. You are also told that chemists use X-rays to investigate structure in a way which is quite different from the use of X-rays in biology.

Sciences are only a part of your school timetable. Your work in this course will also have links with other subjects such as mathematics, design and technology, and geography. You should be on the look out for opportunities to take advantage of these links.

Using this book

You will find that this book is divided into five topics. A topic is a label that connects many similar bits of the physical world. Unfortunately topics have to be invented; the world does not conveniently organize itself as we might like! So you will find that your work in Physics does not proceed chapter by chapter through the book. For example Chapters **P**1 and **P**2 are about atoms and molecules. You will probably need to read these early on in your course. Chapter **P**3 is also about atoms – so it is part of the same topic. But it is really no good reading Chapter **P**3 until you know a bit about electricity which comes later in the book.

When you finish the course, however, you may find it helpful to read the book straight through. Then you may see new "connections" which you had not realized were there before – like visiting familiar places in a city, or well-known trees on a farm, but going there by different routes.

You will find too that it is not necessary to read all of a chapter in order to get the general idea of what its subject is about. Look at the cartoon on page 69. Physics is rather like a book of good cartoons. You can flick through it quickly, having a laugh at each one. But good cartoons repay careful study! Often funny things are happening in the background or one corner that you had not noticed at first. It is the same with physics – in every topic there are things you may not notice at first. It is well worth having a closer look.

Within each chapter you will often be guided as to how to study the chapter at different levels. If you feel that all you need is to get the general idea of the topic then you can miss out several parts of the chapter. The more you want to get out of it, the more you will find to read and to do.

Summary

All of the following words have been used somewhere in this introductory chapter. Write a sentence or two about each one.

experiment	**communication**	**symbol**
prediction	**explanation**	**concepts**

Topic **P1**   **Matter**

What this topic is about

This topic is about the nature of materials. It does not deal with the reasons why one substance differs from another – for example, why iron differs from aluminium. That is a matter for chemistry, and your work in chemistry will help you understand such differences.

We are interested here in large-scale differences. What are the properties of solids that make them useful for building? Why can a substance be a solid, a liquid or a gas? When and how does a solid change to a liquid, or a liquid to a gas? What are atoms and molecules? Are they made from something else? This will lead us finally to radioactivity and the nature of atoms.

Unless you have reached the end of your course in science, do not try to read all this topic at once. To understand some of the ideas in Chapter **P3** you will need to have learned more about electricity, forces and energy. However, when you come to revise, you may find it helpful to read all of this topic in one go, to see how scientists' ideas about matter "hang together".

You will already know some things about atoms and molecules and the way they can build up solids, liquids and gases. Before starting on this topic, here are the ideas you should already have met.

What you should already know about matter

- A **solid** is a material which retains its shape, with no need for a container. Solids resist attempts to change their shape or size. Some solids occur naturally with symmetrical shapes; these are called crystals.
- **Liquids** are "runny". While keeping their volume, they will flow to cover the bottom of any container in which they are placed.
- **Gases** can go everywhere. They fill any container in which they are placed.

All of these properties of matter can be understood by assuming that matter is built up from atoms and molecules. The atoms and molecules themselves cannot easily be broken up, squashed, expanded, or in any way changed. There is evidence to suggest that atoms and molecules are in a constant state of motion. This "movement" energy (called *kinetic* energy) increases as the temperature of a substance increases.

The atoms and molecules in **solids** are packed closely together, held in place by forces between them. These atoms and molecules can vibrate, but the kinetic energy is not sufficient to cause them to break apart. The atoms and molecules in **liquids** are also close together, but they have sufficient energy for molecules (tightly-bound groups of a few atoms) to move about so that they can slide over each other in any direction. This is how a liquid can easily change shape.

The molecules in **gases** have so much energy that they have broken away from the forces trying to hold them together. The only things stopping the molecules moving right away from each other are the sides of the container.

The atoms and molecules which make up matter are very small. Ten thousand million of them, placed side by side, would only be about one metre long. Ten million of them placed side by side would only occupy a length equal to one of the millimetre divisions on your ruler!

Atoms and molecules in chemistry and physics

We said earlier that this topic is not much concerned with the differences in the nature of individual substances – the differences which make oxygen unlike iron or water, for example. This is a matter for chemistry. Chemical differences between substances show that the atoms and molecules from which they are made are **different**. You will learn in chemistry about:

- **atoms** (the "building bricks" of matter),
- **molecules** (which are tightly bound groups of a few atoms)
- and **ions** (which are electrically charged atoms, or groups of atoms).

Often the term "particle" is used in physics to mean **either** an atom **or** a molecule. In this book we shall use the proper terms "atom" or "molecule" when referring to particular substances. For example, we shall speak of molecules of oxygen and atoms of iron.

Sometimes, however, we shall want to refer simply to the fact that all solids, liquids and gases are made of individual specks of matter. It will not be important whether these are atoms **or** molecules. Then we shall use the term "particle" to refer to them. It will always be made clear to you when the word "particle" is used in this way.

Chapter **C2** in your Chemistry book will make the difference between atoms and molecules clearer to you.

Some revision questions

Figure 1
A crystal of calcite.

1 Describe an experiment that suggests that particles of air are always moving.

2 Figure 1 shows a crystal. Suggest how the particles that make up a crystal could be arranged to make such a symmetrical shape.

3 Suppose a very powerful microscope were able to enlarge an oxygen molecule, contained in a box 10 cm long, until the oxygen molecule was 1 cm across.
a How big would the box have become in comparison?
b Which of the following sizes is nearest to the length of the box?
  A   The width of an average house.
  B   The length of Britain.
  C   The diameter of the planet Earth.
  D   The distance from the Earth to the Moon.

4 Describe an experiment you may have seen or may have done to estimate the size of an oil molecule.

5 "Brownian motion" is the name given to the "shimmering" motion of smoke particles in air, seen under a microscope. Here are three explanations that might be given for this motion. Write a sentence about each, saying whether you think the explanation is right or wrong.
a The motion is due to convection currents in the air.
b The smoke particles get hot and they vibrate.
c The smoke particles move because they are kicked around by the moving air molecules.

6 It would be much easier to see larger particles than smoke particles, but if you were to hang a ping-pong ball up in a room in which there were no draughts it would not be seen to move at all. Why do you think this is?

7 Each of the following statements could refer to a solid, a liquid, or a gas. Make up a table with three columns headed "SOLID", "LIQUID" and "GAS", and write the letter referring to each statement in the appropriate column:

A   The molecules bump into each other and the walls of the container.
B   Ice is an example.
C   Mercury at room temperature is an example.
D   The substance will spread over the bottom of the container.
E   The molecules have enough energy to overcome completely the forces trying to hold them together.
F   Milk is an example.
G   If it is heated sufficiently it will turn into a liquid.
H   Nitrogen at room temperature is an example.
I   If it is cooled down it turns into a liquid.

Chapter P1   Building bridges successfully
The strength of solids

*This chapter looks at the strength of solids and the way they can withstand forces. You can get a basic understanding of these ideas by working through section **P1.1** to section **P1.3**. You will then have done enough to be able to make a survey of bridges using Worksheet **P1C**, and to understand something of their construction. If you follow this route, you should also read the first paragraph of section **P1.4**.*

*If you have time to do more, you can make an investigation into cantilevers using Worksheet **P1B** and learn more about the forces involved in section **P1.4**.*

*Finally, for those who work very quickly, the extension topics in section **P1.5**, at the end of the chapter, fill in a few gaps left in sections **P1.3** and **P1.4**.*

P1.1   Structures

Life on another planet is often a part of science fiction stories. But what is the first clue that space travellers in such stories have that a newly discovered world is inhabited by **intelligent** beings? More often than not it is the discovery of some structure or building.

The word *structure* is used to refer to any construction which is large and immobile, like a house, an office block, or a multi-storey car-park.

*Structure is a word also used in chemistry to describe the way atoms are arranged. You will find this explained in Chapter **C5** of your Chemistry book.*

Some of the most impressive structures in the world around us are bridges. Figure 1.1 shows photographs of two famous bridges built very close to each other. Try to answer the questions about them on the next page.

Figure 1.1a (below left)
Road bridge over the River Forth.

Figure 1.1b (below right)
Rail bridge over the River Forth. The road bridge can be seen in the background.

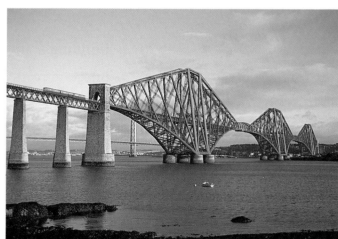

1a One is a rail bridge and the other is a road bridge. Do you think one has to be stronger than the other? Give a reason for your answer.
b In what ways do the two bridges differ from each other?

2 Make a list of the forces that a bridge has to be able to withstand.

Bridges have to be built to withstand all the forces that are expected to act on them. Occasionally engineers have been unsuccessful in their predictions of these forces. Figure 1.2 shows what happened to a bridge across the Tacoma Narrows in the USA when the bridge was subjected to some unexpected vibrations in quite a moderate wind. In 1879, a railway bridge across the River Tay collapsed when a train was crossing it in gale-force winds.

Figure 1.2
The collapse of the bridge across the Tacoma Narrows, USA, on 7 November 1940.

Building a model bridge

Bridges are costly to build and engineers go to a great deal of trouble to build them safely and yet use the minimum amount of material. Try to build your own model bridge to achieve a given strength using the smallest amount of material. You will find details of such a challenge in Worksheet **P1A**. Your bridge has to be single span, of width 30 cm, and must be able to carry a load of 20 N in the middle. Describing what your bridge must be like gives you your *design criteria*. Your task is to meet these design criteria using the least material you can.

You may be asked to carry out this project in the laboratory in a limited time, or you can try it at home.

Thomas Telford

Figure 1.3
Thomas Telford (1757–1834).

One of the most famous bridge builders and engineers of the nineteenth century was Thomas Telford (figure 1.3). Born in 1757, the son of a Scottish shepherd, his most famous construction is the road bridge which crosses the Menai Straits between North Wales and Anglesey. The bridge carries the A5 road which connects London with the port of Holyhead in Anglesey (figure 1.4). This port has been an important point of departure for travellers to Ireland for centuries. But until Telford constructed the road bridge, travellers had to be carried across the Straits by ferry.

Figure 1.4
Telford's suspension bridge across the Menai Straits, opened in 1826.

Although Telford designed several bridges which still stand, his fame lies in the revolution he brought to bridge building. The bridge across the Menai Straits is a *suspension* bridge. When it was built, this method of bridge building was still in its infancy. The first such bridge of any note to be built in Britain had been opened in 1820 and had a span of 91 m. Telford's bridge had a span almost twice as big (174 m), and this showed the possibility of spanning rivers and valleys never before possible. The suspension bridge across the Menai Straits was opened on January 30, 1826. Over 160 years later, Telford's bridge is still carrying the A5 across the Straits. But now there are even longer suspension bridges. For example the one across the Humber Estuary, opened in 1981, has a central span of almost 1300 m (figure 1.19).

P1.2 Balanced forces

The important thing about a bridge is that it has to support both itself and the people, cars and trains that may cross it, without collapsing. We say that the bridge is in *equilibrium*. The pictures in figure 1.5 (on the next page) show some other things in equilibrium. In each case the Earth pulls down on the object with a force that we call the object's *weight*. The object remains where it is because another force balances the pull of the Earth.

Figure 1.5a
Pendant lamp.

Figure 1.5b
Crane lifting a large load.

Figure 1.5c
Climbing a rope.

3 For each of the pictures in figure 1.5 say what is providing the force that balances the pull of the Earth on the suspended object.

4 Suppose a mass of 1 kg is suspended by a string from a hook in the ceiling of a room. Design an experiment to show that the string pulls **up** on the 1-kg mass with the same force as the Earth pulls **down** on it.

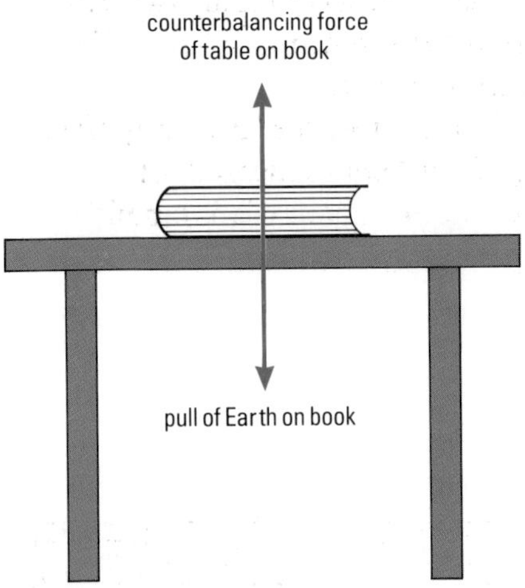

When an object is prevented from moving because it rests on another object (like the book on the table in figure 1.6) there has again to be a force to balance the pull of the Earth. In the case of the book on a table, the table provides this force on the book. How do strings, tables and bridges provide this force – the force that prevents the book falling to the floor, or the car to the river bed? The next section investigates this.

counterbalancing force
of table on book

pull of Earth on book

Figure 1.6
A book resting on a table. The downwards pull of the Earth on the book is balanced by the upward push of the table on the book.

P1.3   Changing shape

When you tried to build your model bridge, you probably found that the problem was not so much one of your bridge **breaking** under load as one of it **bending** too much. The bridge probably tended to collapse in the middle. It is of course very important that this does not happen in a real bridge.

If a bridge is to remain in equilibrium under a load (or simply its own weight), its structure has to produce a force which counterbalances the load. The load is transferred to the surrounding ground on which the piers of the bridge are built. This means that the structure of the bridge is acted on by pairs of forces which, although balanced out, are trying to **squash**, **stretch**, or **bend** it (figure 1.7). Of course these forces may be so big that they actually **break** the material. Designers of bridges have to take care to specify materials that will withstand much bigger forces than are likely to occur.

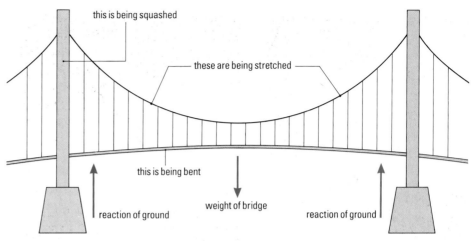

Figure 1.7
Some of the forces acting on a suspension bridge.

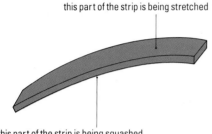

Figure 1.8
A bending beam. The bottom half of the beam is being squeezed together, while the top half is being stretched.

Bending, stretching and squashing

Whenever materials are bent, stretched or squashed, the atoms from which they are made are either pulled apart or squeezed together. When a strip of wood or steel is bent, it is being squeezed and stretched at the same time. Some of the atoms are being dragged apart, while others are being forced closer together. The diagram in figure 1.8 helps to explain this.

There are two important ways of describing the behaviour of materials when acted upon by pairs of forces.

Strength

A material is strong if a large force has to be used to break it. Materials can be described as **strong** or **weak**. For example, a bar of steel is roughly twice as strong as a bar of aluminium of the same cross-sectional area. That is why steel saucepans do not dent as easily as aluminium ones.

The strength of a material can also depend on the **way** the force is applied. For example a concrete pillar may be strong if it is being squeezed (or compressed), but very much weaker if it is stretched. If you tried to build a bridge of concrete, like the one shown in figure 1.9, you would find the

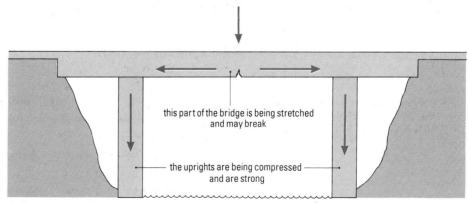

Figure 1.9
This concrete bridge would collapse because the bottom part of the bridge is being stretched. One way of overcoming this problem is to re-inforce the concrete with steel.

concrete pillars could support the weight of the bridge, but the cross piece would be very weak. This is because any force on it will bend it, and the part of the concrete being stretched may break.

The strength of steel does not vary in this way, so steel is often embedded in the concrete if stretching, or *tension*, forces are involved. Concrete with steel embedded in it is called *re-inforced concrete*.

Flexibility

The flexibility of a material describes how much change of shape takes place under a particular force. Figure 1.10 shows a strip of paper, a strip of wood and a strip of steel, all of the same size, fixed to the edge of a table. A small mass is hung on the end of the wood and steel strips. The steel strip hardly bends at all. The wood bends a little. The paper bends a great deal. We describe these differences by saying that the steel is **stiff**, but that the paper is **flexible**.

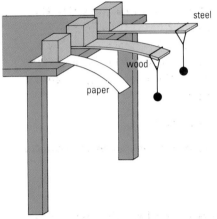

Figure 1.10
Steel is a stiff material, while paper is flexible. The flexibility of wood lies somewhere between these two materials.

5 Materials can be described in each of the following ways:
   A   Strong and stiff
   B   Strong and flexible
   C   Weak and stiff
   D   Weak and flexible.
Use the key above to classify each of the following:
   steel
   rubber
   concrete (in compression)
   glass
   wood
   paper
   bone

6a Find out how arches are used to support materials like brick or concrete which easily break when stretched.
b Bone needs similar support in your body. Find out from Chapter **B**10 of your Biology book how arches are used in skeletons to give strength.

Concrete and steel are both stiff materials, and so are very useful for building bridges. Used in the right way, both can make very strong structures.

Force and extension

In the introduction we described an investigation you will have made into the behaviour of springs. In this investigation, you found that the amount a spring stretches depends in a simple way on the size of the stretching force. And when that stretching force was removed, the spring returned to its original length.

Proportionality

The amount a spring stretches is called its extension (figure 1.11a). When you plotted a graph of force against extension you probably found that the points

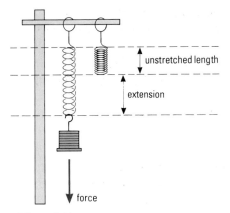

Figure 1.11a
Stretching a spring.

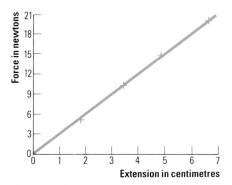

Figure 1.11b
Force plotted against extension for a spring.

formed a straight line, like the graph in figure 1.11b. If you made your measurements carefully you will also have found that this line passes through the point (0,0). This means, of course, that if no stretching force is applied to the spring the extension is zero.

Look again at figure 1.11b. The spring used in this experiment extends by 1 cm when stretched by a force of 3 N. To extend the spring 2 cm requires a stretching force of 6 N. Twice the stretching force produces twice the extension. How much force is needed to stretch the spring 3 cm? The graph shows that the force needed is 9 N.

These results mean that we can show how the extension is related to the force in another way. To produce an extension of 1 cm, a force of 3 N is needed; to produce an extension of 2 cm, a force of 6 N is needed. In each case, the size of the force (measured in newtons) is **three times** the size of the extension it produces (measured in centimetres). We can write down an equation to find the force from the extension:

force (in newtons) = 3 × extension (in centimetres)

If we use the symbols F for force and x for extension, we can write down this formula in symbols:

$$F = 3x$$

When two quantities are related by a simple equation like this, they are said to be *proportional* to each other. If a graph is plotted of the two quantities, it will always be a straight line passing through the point (0,0).

The same result applies to all springs, but of course the number to multiply the extension by in order to find the force is not always 3! For stiff springs, this number will be much larger, because you need a much **larger** force to produce the same extension. Very flexible springs will have a smaller number. Usually we represent this number by the letter *"k"* and call it the *spring constant*. So a formula which applies to **all** springs is:

$$F = kx$$

We state this result by saying that for springs, extension is proportional to force. When the result of an experiment can be expressed in a simple way like this, the result is referred to as a *law*. In this case it is named after Robert Hooke, the man who discovered it, and it is called Hooke's Law.

Being careful over units

You may have noticed that we were careful to say in our example that the size of the extension is multiplied by 3 if the extension is measured in centimetres and the force in newtons. If we had chosen to measure the extension in different units – say metres – we would have had to use a different number to find the force in newtons. If the extension had been measured in metres, every 3 N increase in force would have increased the extension by 0.01 m. So to find the size of the force from the size of the extension, you would have to multiply the extension by 300. The result of the experiment would then have been written as:

force (in newtons) = 300 × extension (in metres)

To avoid misunderstandings, you should always be careful to say what units are being used in your measurements.

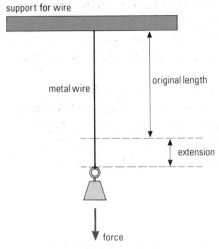

support for wire

metal wire

original length

extension

force

Figure 1.12
Stretching a metal wire.

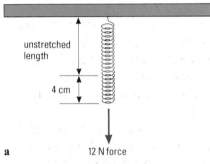

unstretched
length

4 cm

a   12 N force

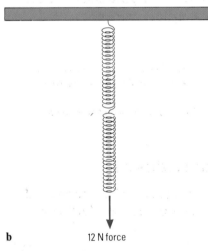

b   12 N force

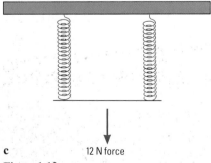

c   12 N force

Figure 1.13
Identical springs in series and in parallel.

Using Hooke's Law

You must be careful how you use such laws. You probably found out in your own experiment that if too much force is applied to a spring, the extension is **not** the same as this law would predict. Very few laws can be applied without exception, and you have to learn from experience when and when not to use them. In the case of Hooke's Law, it can usually only be applied up to a certain maximum force for each spring.

The importance of Hooke's Law, however, is that it does not **just** apply to springs. Figure 1.12 illustrates an experiment in which a metal wire is being stretched by the load attached to its end. A graph of force plotted against extension gives a straight line for a large part of the range of forces that the wire will withstand before breaking.

Over that range of forces for which the extension is proportional to force, we also find that if the force is removed, the wire returns to its original length. This is also true for many materials, such as rubber, even when the extension is not proportional to the force. Materials which return to their original length after they have been stretched are called *elastic*.

If the forces get very big – close to the breaking force – the extension is no longer proportional to the force. When this happens, the wire becomes permanently stretched. It will not return to its original length if the force is removed. You can learn more about the behaviour of metals under big forces at the end of this chapter.

*It is not only metals and other man-made materials that are elastic. The muscles in your body are elastic. This is a very important property of which you will find out more in Chapter **B**10 of your Biology book.*

---

7 The spring in figure 1.13a extends 4 cm when stretched with a force of 12 N.
a How far will it stretch under a force of 6 N?
b What force would have to be applied to stretch the spring 3 cm?
c Karen says these results must mean that if the spring is stretched with 36 N force, the spring will extend 12 cm. Jill says she thinks that may well not be correct.
    i Why does Karen predict the extension will be 12 cm?
    ii Why does Jill think that Karen's prediction may not be correct?
d The springs shown in figures 1.13b and 1.13c are identical to the one in figure 1.13a. Predict the extension produced in each case when a load weighing 12 N is hung on the springs.

Robert Hooke

Robert Hooke, whose name is remembered through his "law of springs", was not a professional scientist in the sense we use the word today. Today, a professional scientist is one who is paid for working as a scientist and has laboratories and equipment provided for her or him. Isaac Newton (see section **P**5.3) was probably one of the few professional scientists working at the same time as Hooke. Robert Boyle, whose name is remembered in Boyle's gas law, was another contemporary. Boyle had a large private income and did not need to "work for a living".

Robert Hooke was employed as an architect by the City of London and was responsible for much of its rebuilding after the "Great Fire" in 1666. He used to meet regularly with other such amateur scientists as Christopher

Wren and Robert Boyle in London coffee houses to discuss science. Hooke seems to have been on very bad terms with Newton. He felt that Newton and others used his ideas in their work and claimed **his** discoveries as their own. So when he discovered the Law of Springs he published it in code so no one else could say it was theirs!

Hooke also invented the balance spring used in watches – a direct application of his work with springs. The king in Hooke's day was Charles II. The King was himself a keen amateur scientist, and he founded the Royal Society as a "club" for scientists. Robert Hooke became its first secretary. Today, the Royal Society is one of the most distinguished and famous scientific societies in the world.

Atoms and Hooke's Law

Many materials, in the form of bars and wires, stretch so that their extension is proportional to the applied force. Experiments show that the same is true when such materials are squashed or compressed. The more you squash the materials, the greater the force you need to do it.

If materials, such as steel, behave as Hooke's Law describes, this could mean that the atoms which make up steel have forces between them that get bigger as they are pulled apart or pressed together, just like the forces in springs. This is how steel structures can resist loads placed on them. They distort a little under the load so the atoms move apart or move closer together. As a result the force between the atoms increases and the steel is able to resist the forces placed upon it (figure 1.14).

Of course, there is a limit to how big these forces between atoms can get. If the atoms are squeezed together too hard, they may start to slide over each other without providing any more resisting force. If they are pulled too far apart they will be unable to provide any opposing force and the material breaks.

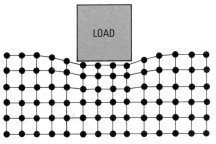

Figure 1.14
The atoms of the metal column are pushed closer together. The force between the atoms increases, so supporting the load on the column.

*The way metals behave when forces act upon them is only one of a number of properties that metals share. You will learn more about metals and their properties in Chapter **C7** of your Chemistry book.*

*At this point you could go on to read the first paragraph of section **P1.4** and then do the investigation into bridges described in Worksheet **P1C**.*

An investigation into the behaviour of cantilevers

A cantilever is the name given to any bar which is anchored at one end and has to support a load at the other (figure 1.15a). Some modern bridges are

Figure 1.15a (below left)
The diving board is a cantilever which bends due to the weight of the diver.

Figure 1.15b (below right)
A cantilever bridge carrying the A45 across the River Orwell at Ipswich.

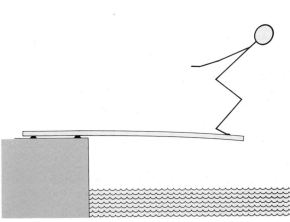

often constructed as pairs of cantilevers which meet in the middle. The bridge which carries the A45 across the River Orwell (figure 1.15b) is a good example of such a construction. So too is the rail bridge across the River Forth in figure 1.1.

It is possible to work out how a cantilever behaves under bending forces from a knowledge of how the material from which it is made behaves under stretching and squeezing. However, this can be very difficult. It is much easier to do an experiment to find out. Worksheet **P1B** describes an investigation you can do into the way a cantilever behaves under bending forces. A lot can be learned about the design of cantilever bridges from these simple experiments.

Tubes and boxes

Bridges have to be stiff as well as strong if they are not to wave about in the breeze! Your investigation into cantilevers may have shown you that bending becomes more and more of a problem the longer you make the cantilever. Of course, the cantilever could be made so that it bent less by making it thicker. But this makes it heavier. A long thick cantilever may not be strong enough to support its own weight.

One way in which structures can be made stiff yet light is to turn them into *tubes*. Remember how flexible the piece of paper was in figure 1.10. If that same piece of paper were turned into a tube, you would find that it was much stiffer (figure 1.16a). You can try this for yourself. Light but stiff bridges can be built from steel which has been fashioned into square section tubes called box girders (figure 1.16b). The modern Tay bridge is built from steel box girders in 42 spans over a total length of 2210 m (figure 1.17).

Plant stems are made of tubes. This helps them to withstand the bending forces of wind, rain and passing animals, despite the flexibility of the sheets of cellulose from which they are made. The bones of birds are hollow for a different reason. Their skeletons need to be stiff and strong, yet light enough to be borne in the air.

*You can learn more about the structure of plants and animals in Chapter **B10** of your Biology book.*

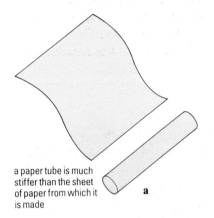

a paper tube is much stiffer than the sheet of paper from which it is made

a

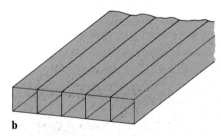

b

Figure 1.16
a Paper tube.
b A box-girder construction.

Figure 1.17
The railway bridge across the River Tay. This bridge is constructed from box girders.

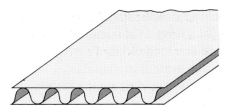

Figure 1.18a
The construction of corrugated
cardboard.

Figure 1.18b
A corrugated bridge lining. Structures
such as these are stiff and strong.
Engineers can put them in place very
quickly.

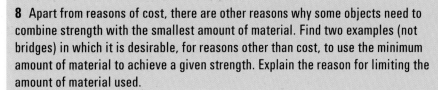

8 Apart from reasons of cost, there are other reasons why some objects need to combine strength with the smallest amount of material. Find two examples (not bridges) in which it is desirable, for reasons other than cost, to use the minimum amount of material to achieve a given strength. Explain the reason for limiting the amount of material used.

9 Why do you think engineers use square boxes instead of cylindrical tubes for bridge construction?

Another way of achieving stiffness is shown in the construction of corrugated cardboard (figure 1.18a). A similar process is now being used to build some bridges (figure 1.18b). The corrugated shape enables engineers to build large, yet light sections which can be quickly fixed in place. This is important when building bridges over railways, for example, which cannot be closed for very long.

P1.4 Suspension bridges

Figure 1.19
The bridge across the Humber estuary. This is one of the longest suspension bridges in the world.

Bridges may be supported by resting them on blocks (or *piers* as they are called), but it is quite common today to suspend them as well. One of the bridges in figure 1.1 is built in this way. So was Telford's bridge across the Menai Straits. The weight of the bridge platform is supported by vertical chains (as you can see in figure 1.1a), but they in turn are being held up by a cable which is not vertical. Engineers who design bridges need to know how much force the main cables will have to withstand in order to support the bridge. Figure 1.20 shows a simple arrangement of supports which could be used to investigate this.

supporting
force

supporting
force

pull of Earth on mass

Figure 1.20
The weight of the load is supported by the
forces in the two strings.

10 How could you measure the force in figure 1.20 supplied by the two supporting strings which keep a load in equilibrium?

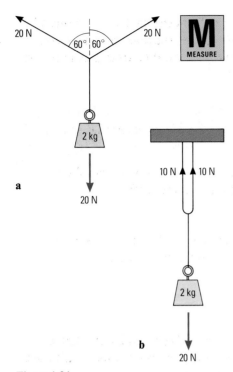

Figure 1.21
a A load of 2 kg supported by two strings both at 60° to the horizontal.
b The same load supported by two vertical strings.

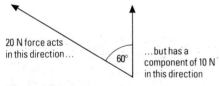

Figure 1.22
The component of a force of 20 N in a direction 60° to its own.

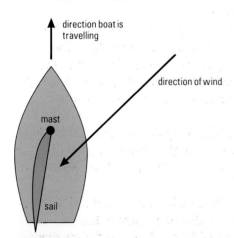

Figure 1.23
The force of the wind acting on the sail of a yacht sailing "into the wind".

One way to measure the forces is to replace the attachment points of the supports with pulleys and then run the support strings over them. The counterbalancing force can be provided by either a load of known weight or a force meter. You may see this experiment demonstrated. In a similar experiment in which the support strings made an angle of 60° to the vertical, it was found that the force in **each** support was 20 N in order to counterbalance a weight of 20 N (figure 1.21a). If the same two supports were vertical, the force provided by each was found to be only 10 N, as you would expect (figure 1.21b). This is a very important result – as much for physics as for bridge builders! It means that the bigger the angle the support has to make with the vertical, the more force it has to exert to support any particular load.

*The remainder of this chapter takes these ideas a little further. It is possible to finish this chapter now by going on to the summary and doing Worksheet **P**1C. Your teacher will advise you which you should do.*

Vector quantities

In order to build a bridge safely it is not enough to know what forces it has to withstand. It is also necessary to know in what direction the supporting forces are acting. Quantities which can only be described in full by both a direction and a size are called *vector* quantities. A force is a vector quantity.

The experiment in which we measured the force needed to support a mass of 2 kg showed that the supporting strings had to pull with a force of 20 N **each** to support the mass. Yet if the strings had been vertical, the force in each would only have been 10 N.

When the strings are arranged as shown in figure 1.21a, the 20 N force in each provides only 10 N in the vertical direction. Vector quantities are always like this. Because they act in a particular direction, their effect in other directions is always less. The effect they have in some other direction than their own is called the *component* of the vector. In this case we say that a 20 N force has a component value of only 10 N in a direction of 60° to its own direction. This is illustrated for you in figure 1.22.

> **11** It is because a force can have components in various directions that a dinghy (a small yacht) can sail **into** the wind. When the wind hits a sail, it causes a force to act perpendicular to the sail.
> **a** Copy the diagram in figure 1.23 and draw in the direction of the force of the wind on the sail.

If there were nothing to prevent it doing so, the dinghy would drift in the direction of the force on the sail. However, dinghies have a *centre board* (a sort of keel that can be lowered into the water when sailing into the wind) that helps stop the dinghy drifting sideways.

> **11b** Draw two **components** of the force acting on the sail: one acting from back to front of the dinghy; the other acting sideways, at right-angles to the first component.
> **c** How does the centre board give a force that helps prevent the dinghy drifting sideways?

The only unbalanced force is the one acting from the back to the front of the dinghy. This drives the dinghy forwards. To get the maximum force on the sail, the mast should be vertical. However, the wind tends to push the boat over.

11d How do people who sail dinghies keep the mast as near to the vertical as possible when sailing into the wind?

12 There are two component directions in which the size of the component of any force is zero, whatever the size of the force. What are those directions?

In the next section you will find a drawing method that can be used for finding the size of the component value of any force in any direction.

Summary: looking at bridges

Make a survey of the bridges near where you live. Try to understand how their construction is related to their age, their purpose and the materials used. Worksheet **P**1C can help you with the details of the survey.

The rest of this chapter looks a little more closely at **components** *and investigates what happens to metal wires when they are stretched to breaking point. It is not essential to the rest of the course and your teacher will advise you whether you should read it.*

P1.5 More about components and metals under force

Finding the component of a force by drawing

To show how this can be done, we will take the particular example quoted earlier of a 20 N force acting in a direction of 60° to the vertical and find the value of its component in a vertical direction.

Step 1: Draw two lines at an angle of 60° to each other. One line (OA in figure 1.24a) represents the direction of the force and the other (OB) the direction in which you want to find its component. It helps if you can draw the lines so that it is easy to visualize which is which. In this case, the line OB in the direction of the component has actually been drawn in a vertical direction. Label the lines.

Step 2: Mark off a length OX (figure 1.24b) along the line OA, proportional to the magnitude of the force. To do this you will need to choose a suitable scale. In this case, making 1 cm represent 2 N should be about right (figure 1.24b).

Step 3: Draw a line from X, perpendicular to OB, to cross OB at Y (figure 1.24c). The length OY is then proportional to the magnitude of the component of the 20 N force in a direction of 60° to OA. If you follow these steps you should find (to within the errors of your drawing) that OY is 5 cm long and thus represents a force of $5 \times 2 = 10$ N.

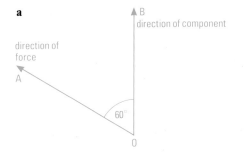

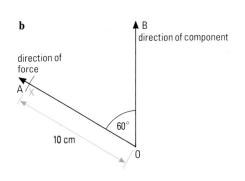

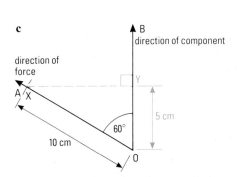

Figure 1.24
Using a drawing to find the component of a force.

The behaviour of a metal under force

MEASURE

On page 20 you read that metals do not increase in length in proportion to the stretching force (or *tension*) right up to the point at which they break. A knowledge of the behaviour of metals under tension up to their breaking point is important in many branches of applied science, and special equipment, known as a *tensometer* (figure 1.25), is used to investigate it.

Figure 1.25
A tensometer. This is a piece of equipment used to investigate the way the extension of a material varies with the force stretching it.

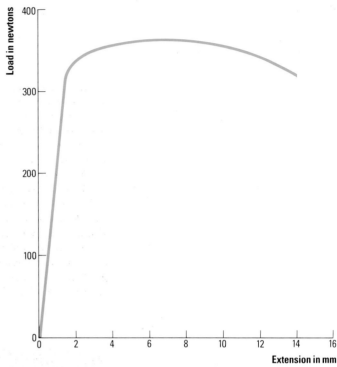

Figure 1.26
A graph of force plotted against extension for a 2-metre length of aluminium wire. The wire had a cross-sectional area of 1 mm².

The graph in figure 1.26 shows a force–extension graph for a 2-m long aluminium wire of cross-sectional area 1 mm².

13 The following questions refer to the graph in figure 1.26.
a Up to what force is the extension proportional to the applied force?
b What is the maximum force that can be applied to the wire?
c Why would it be dangerous to apply such a force to the wire?

For the range of forces for which the extension is proportional to the force, the wire returns to its original length when the force is removed – just like an elastic band. For this reason the metal is said to behave **elastically** in this region. For greater forces, the metal deforms much more easily, and if the force is removed, the metal no longer returns to its original length but remains permanently stretched. The metal is said to have behaved **plastically**. It is this property that enables metals to be drawn out into wires and beaten into new shapes. It is of course very important that the forces on metal structures (such as bridges) are never so great that a part of the metal starts to deform plastically.

Cooking food quickly
Molecules in motion

This is not the first time you will have met the idea that the atoms and molecules which make up substances are in continuous motion. This chapter starts by looking at a pressure cooker; something that was often in use a few years ago, but less frequently so today. To understand how it works you will soon have to go back to exploring the properties of "particles in motion". The first experiments use marbles in a tray to show how the idea of "particles in motion" can be used to explain many things about solids, liquids and gases. You may have done these experiments before and be quite confident about the ideas they show. If so, do not spend too long on them but go on quickly to the section called "The kinetic theory of matter".

Section P2.2 on Boyle's Law will help in completing your understanding of the pressure cooker. You should then go on to the section on evaporation (section P2.3), and finally you should have time to do at least part of the work on gas pressure and temperature.

If you are unfamiliar with the idea of "particles in motion" then you will find it best to spend more time on Worksheet P2A. When you have completed section P2.1, you may find it easier to go straight to section P2.3 on evaporation. You can end the chapter by doing some work on gas pressure and volume (section P2.2), leaving out section P2.4 entirely.

P2.1   Solids, liquids and gases

The pressure cooker

In figure 2.1 some vegetables are being cooked in an open pan on a stove. In figure 2.2, the same vegetables are being cooked in a pressure cooker. Pressure cookers are much more expensive than ordinary saucepans. But many people buy pressure cookers because food can be cooked more quickly in them than in an open pan.

Figure 2.1
Cooking using an open saucepan.

Figure 2.2
Cooking using a pressure cooker.

Pressure cookers cook more quickly because they make the boiling water and the steam, in which the food is cooked, hotter than normal. The hotter the water, the faster the food cooks. But how is it that the water is hotter inside a pressure cooker? Does pressure have anything to do with it? How is temperature related to pressure? These are some of the questions we shall answer in this chapter.

Changing solids to liquids and liquids to gases

Imagine you have some cold water in an open saucepan. To change it to a gas (steam), you have to first raise its temperature. The same thing is true if ice ("solid" water) is changed to a liquid. In the low temperature of the freezing compartment of a refrigerator, the ice stays solid. Out in a warm kitchen, the temperature of the ice rises and it changes to a liquid. As you will see in Chapter **P**10, raising the temperature of something means transferring energy to it. This means that the atoms and molecules which make up matter are able to take up energy. How can taking up energy also change a substance from a solid to a liquid, or a liquid to a gas?

The simplest way to explain this is to imagine that the atoms and molecules are continually moving. The diagrams in figure 2.3 illustrate experiments you can do with marbles in a tray. The tray is tilted slightly so that the marbles run down to one edge. The marbles can then be given varying amounts of energy by just shaking the tray. With little movement, the marbles keep together in the bottom part of the tray. They shake down into a regular pattern just like the atoms in a crystal. They have too little energy to move far from these fixed positions (figure 2.3a).

With more shaking, the pattern starts to break up. The marbles remain in the bottom of the tray, but now they have enough energy to move past each other (figure 2.3b). The marbles are now behaving like the molecules in a liquid.

With even more vigorous shaking, the marbles break free from each other. Only the edge of the tray stops them flying away (figure 2.3c). The marbles are now behaving like the molecules in a gas. With this simple equipment it is possible to show some other properties of solids, liquids and gases as well. You should try these for yourself. Worksheet **P**2A will help in suggesting some of the things you can do.

Figure 2.3
Imitating the behaviour of solids, liquids and gases using a tray of marbles.

a

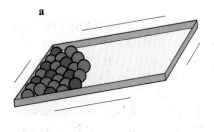

solid

b

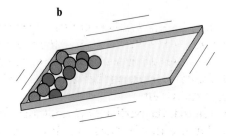

liquid

c

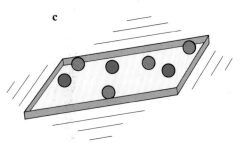

gas

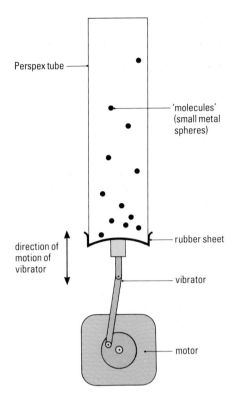

Perspex tube

'molecules' (small metal spheres)

direction of motion of vibrator

rubber sheet

vibrator

motor

Figure 2.4
Another experiment to imitate the behaviour of a gas. The particles are kept in motion by the vibrator.

Figure 2.4 shows another piece of equipment that demonstrates some of the properties we would expect to find in atoms and molecules in motion. You may well have seen it working. Although more elaborate and impressive than the "marbles in a tray", it is in fact no better at showing the way moving atoms and molecules will behave.

The kinetic theory of matter

This picture of matter made up of *particles* (atoms and molecules) which are in constant movement is called the *kinetic theory*. "Kinetic" means "motion": we use the same word in "cinema" ("moving pictures"), but the letter "k" has become a letter "c". We use the word again in "kinetic energy" which means the energy of moving bodies.

In the following sections we shall investigate how the kinetic theory can help to give us explanations of several properties of solids, liquids and gases. The "moving particles", which we imagine make up solids, liquids and gases, are sometimes atoms (as in solids such as iron or aluminium) and sometimes molecules (as in a liquid such as water, or a gas such as oxygen). In this chapter it does not matter to us whether these "particles" are atoms or molecules. So we shall often simply refer to them as "particles".

The movement of particles is not enough **on its own** to explain why substances are sometimes solids, sometimes liquids, and sometimes gases. With the marbles in a tray, the force of gravity tended to keep the marbles at the bottom of the tray. Shaking the tray made the marbles move: they gained kinetic energy. When the marbles had little kinetic energy, the force of gravity kept the marbles in the bottom of the tray. When the marbles had a great deal of kinetic energy, gravity had little influence on their behaviour.

In Chapter **P**1, the strength of solids showed that there were strong forces holding the atoms or molecules of solids together. To change solids to liquids and liquids to gases, energy has to be transferred so that the atoms or molecules can move apart from each other, working against these forces of attraction.

Our picture of a **solid** is of particles (atoms or molecules) arranged in a regular pattern, like the repeating patterns of a wallpaper. But the pattern in a solid is spread out in three dimensions. The particles are held together in the pattern by strong forces which give the solid its strength. You may see a model of a solid like that in figure 2.5. The balls represent the particles and the springs represent the forces that tie the particles together.

You will find a further explanation of the way **models** *can be used to represent groups of atoms in Chapter* **C**5 *in the Chemistry book. The ball-and-spring model is used again in that chapter, but only when the forces between atoms act in definite directions. In this chapter the ball-and-spring model is meant to show no more than how particles in a solid can have energy without losing their positions.*

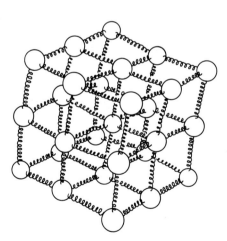

Figure 2.5
A model of a solid. The polystyrene spheres, which represent the atoms of a solid, are held in place by the springs. The particles can vibrate but cannot move very far.

The particles in a **solid** are constantly vibrating (moving to and fro) in various directions. The hotter the solid, the more energetic the vibrations become. If the solid is heated enough, the vibrations may become so energetic that the particles cannot stay in their well-ordered arrangement. This is what happens when a solid melts.

In a **liquid**, the particles are not much further apart; but they are less firmly locked in position by the forces between neighbours. A liquid can flow when we pour it. This shows that the particles must be able to slip past each other.

In **gases**, the movement of the particles has become so energetic that the forces between them are not enough to hold the particles together. Then the particles move freely, constantly bumping into each other and their surroundings.

---

3 The last four paragraphs describe what happens to the atoms or molecules ("particles") when a solid changes first to a liquid and then to a gas. Now start with a gas. Describe what happens to the particles as it changes first to a liquid and then to a solid.

It is not good science, however, to make up a picture like this if all it will do is explain the things we **want** it to explain. We should ask what further use we can make of it. If we can put our picture to use – to let it make predictions and help us to make new measurements – then it will be useful.

Such a "thinking" model is a *theory* to sum up and develop our knowledge. The kinetic theory is such a "thinking" model about matter.

---

4 Try using the kinetic theory to explain each of the following:
a Gases can exert pressure.
b A gas exerts a greater pressure when it is squeezed into a smaller volume.

More about liquids changing to gases

At a particular temperature, different molecules in a glass of water will have different energies. The molecules continually bump into each other. As a result some slow down and others speed up. But if the temperature of the water does not change, the **average** energy of all the molecules stays the same.

Think of the molecules near the surface of the water. These are also continually bumping into each other. A few molecules may gain enough energy to escape from the water surface into the space above. This is called *evaporation* (figure 2.6). It is because liquids (and even solids) evaporate, that you can **smell** them.

The vapour collects above the liquid. Here, the moving vapour molecules will collide with each other and with the nearby air molecules. Some will slow down. If they happen to be close to the liquid at this time, they may be "recaptured" by the liquid. If there is enough vapour above the liquid, molecules may be returning to the liquid as fast as they are leaving it and the liquid will seem to stop evaporating. When things are "balanced" in this way, they are said to be *in equilibrium*. In Chapter **P**1, the forces on a bridge had to be balanced if the bridge was to remain in equilibrium. This equilibrium of a liquid and its vapour is a different sort of equilibrium – instead of there being no change at all (as when a bridge stands across a river), change is taking place but in two directions at once, so the changes "balance out" (figure 2.7). You will find some other examples of this sort of equilibrium in question **6**.

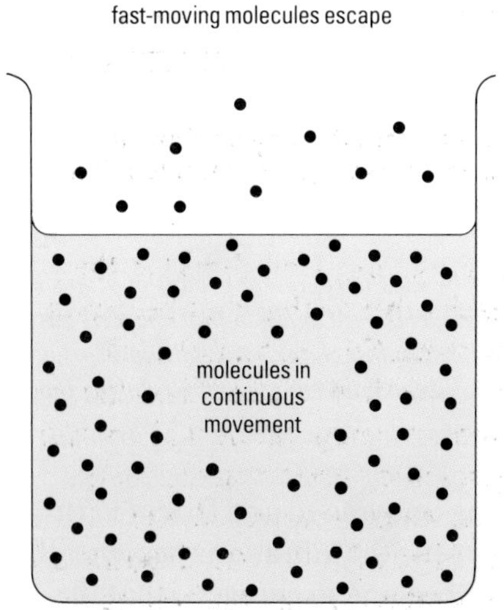

fast-moving molecules escape

molecules in
continuous
movement

Figure 2.6
Evaporation of a liquid. Fast-moving particles near the surface of the liquid have enough energy to overcome the attraction of their neighbours and escape into the air above.

---

5 What is the effect on the evaporation of a liquid of:
a raising the temperature of the liquid?

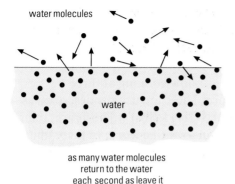

water molecules

water

as many water molecules
return to the water
each second as leave it

Figure 2.7
A liquid and its vapour in equilibrium.
When the number of particles leaving the
water each second is equal to the number
returning to the water each second there is
no overall loss of liquid.

5b blowing across the surface of the liquid and removing the vapour as quickly as it
is formed?

6 Explain each of the following:
a the number of people shopping in a particular supermarket is constant despite the
fact that people are coming and going all the time
b before people made extensive use of fossil fuels, the amount of carbon dioxide in
the atmosphere was constant despite the fact that animals and plants were continually
producing it in respiration. (See Chapter **B**3 in the Biology book.)

Of course molecules well below the surface of the water are continually
bumping into each other as well, and some will gain a lot of energy in this
way. But they cannot escape because the other water molecules around them
are crowded in by the pressure of the air above the water surface.

If the temperature of the water is raised, the average energy of the
molecules increases. Eventually they have so much energy that even the
molecules well below the surface can overcome the buffeting of their
neighbours and so escape. When this happens, the water is said to *boil*.

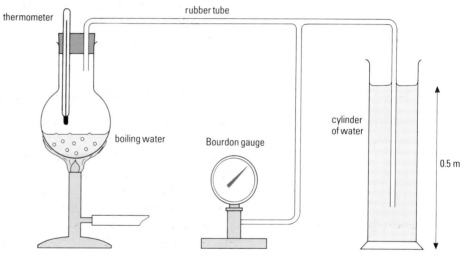

thermometer

rubber tube

boiling water

Bourdon gauge

cylinder
of water

0.5 m

Figure 2.8
An experiment to show how the boiling-point of water rises when the pressure above it
increases. The pressure over the boiling water is increased by lowering the rubber tube into
a tall jar of water.

When the boiling-point has been reached, any energy transferred to the
liquid goes into freeing the molecules from each other so that they become a
gas. The liquid temperature does not rise any more. So you cannot cook
vegetables in water any more quickly in a hot oven than you could on the top
of a stove. Once the water reaches boiling-point, its temperature will not rise
any further. All the energy transferred to it goes into vaporizing the water.

However, if the pressure of the gas above the water is increased, the
temperature at which the water boils will rise. Figure 2.8 shows a diagram of
an experiment you may have seen that demonstrates the way the boiling-
point changes with the pressure above the liquid. A higher pressure above the
liquid means that molecules need more energy to escape from the other water
molecules which crowd in around them.

In a pressure cooker (figure 2.9), the steam from the evaporating water is
not (at first) allowed to escape. So as more and more steam molecules crowd

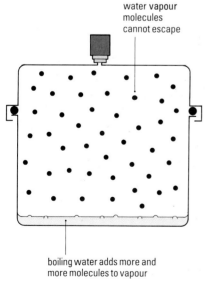

water vapour
molecules
cannot escape

boiling water adds more and
more molecules to vapour

Figure 2.9
Water boiling in a pressure cooker.

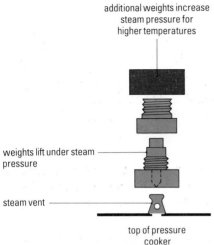

additional weights increase
steam pressure for
higher temperatures

weights lift under steam
pressure

steam vent

top of pressure
cooker

Figure 2.10
The control valve on a pressure cooker.
When the pressure in the cooker reaches a
pre-set value, the control valve allows
steam to escape.

Pressure	Temperature in °C
1 atmosphere (normal)	100
1.3 atmosphere ("LOW")	109
1.7 atmosphere ("MEDIUM")	115
2.0 atmosphere ("HIGH")	122

Figure 2.11
The boiling-points of water at three
pressure cooker settings.

into this space, the pressure over the water increases. This increase in pressure raises the temperature at which the water can boil.

Of course there has to be a *control valve* so that once the required pressure and temperature have been reached, the extra steam can escape from the saucepan (figure 2.10). Most pressure cookers allow cooking at three pressures above normal atmospheric pressure. These are usually described as "LOW (5 lbs)", "MEDIUM (10 lbs)" and "HIGH (15 lbs)". The figures refer to units of pressure which are no longer used in scientific work. In these units "15 lbs" refers to normal atmospheric pressure. This means that the pressure inside a pressure cooker with the control valve set to HIGH is **twice** the normal atmospheric pressure.

7 Normal atmospheric pressure, in scientific units, is approximately 100 kN/m² (1 kN (pronounced "kilo-newton") = 1000 N). What pressures inside the pressure cooker correspond to the three settings "LOW", "MEDIUM" and "HIGH"?

The table in figure 2.11 gives the temperatures at which the water boils for the three pressures usually available.

8 If the pressure above water falls below normal, the boiling-point of the water falls. Explain why mountaineers in the Himalayas find it impossible to "cook" eggs by boiling, high up the mountainside.

*You could go on to section **P2.3** on evaporation at this point and leave out the work on pressure and volume until later in the unit.*

P2.2   **Pressure and volume**

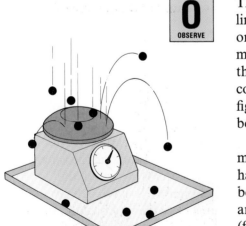

O
OBSERVE

Figure 2.12
An experiment to show how
bombardment by particles produces a
force.

The pressure in a pressure cooker is raised by squeezing more gas into a limited space. This property of gases has been known for many years. It was one of the first properties to suggest that a gas might consist of swarms of moving molecules constantly colliding with each other and with the walls of their container. In the kinetic model of a gas, pressure is produced by the collisions of the moving particles with the container walls. The diagram in figure 2.12 shows a demonstration you may have seen that shows how particle bombardment can produce a force.

We will now use this model to see how it is that crowding up the gas molecules produces more pressure on the walls of the container. Suppose you have air (or any other gas) in a box. You could attach a pressure gauge to the box of gas and read the pressure (figure 2.13a). Now suppose you put more and more molecules into the box until there are twice as many as before (figure 2.13b).

When there are twice as many molecules as before, what pressure would you expect? With twice as many molecules to bombard the walls, you might expect double the pressure. But all that the pressure gauge shows is a doubling of the number of molecules **"at the place it measures"**. And we can

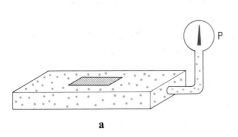
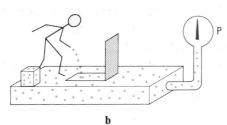
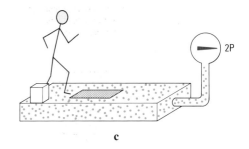

a   b   c

Figure 2.13
Increasing the number of particles in a box
can increase the pressure in it. In these
drawings, a microscopic person is
imagined to be putting particles in the box
from a supply alongside.

produce double the number of molecules at any point without putting in extra
molecules. We simply push the end wall of the box in, like a piston, to make
the volume half as big. The pressure gauge would still show double pressure
in the same way (figure 2.14).

Now we have got a prediction from our theory: **Halving the volume would
double the pressure**. Is this true?

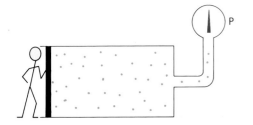

Figure 2.14
These drawings show how decreasing the
volume occupied by the gas can achieve
the same effect as in figure 2.13 of
increasing the pressure in a box.

Robert Boyle

Robert Boyle's name was mentioned in the last chapter; you may remember
that he was a friend of Robert Hooke and lived at the same time as Isaac
Newton. Coming from a wealthy family he was able to spend most of his life
doing experiments in science. He was particularly fascinated by the behaviour
of gases. He knew that a few years earlier Torricelli, an Italian scientist, had
done a number of experiments with air. Torricelli had poured mercury into a
long tube, which was sealed at one end. He filled the tube with mercury and
then turned it upside down so that the open end of the tube stood in a bowl of
mercury (figure 2.16). Torricelli noticed that the mercury in the tube did not
run into the bowl, but remained standing. The height of the column of

Figure 2.15
Robert Boyle (1627–1691).

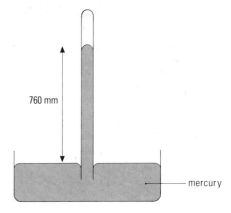

Figure 2.16
A diagram of Torricelli's experiment
which led him to suggest that the air
around us exerts a pressure big enough to
support a column of mercury 760 mm high.

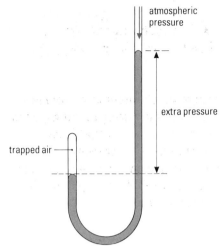

Figure 2.17a
Robert Boyle's method of finding the relationship between the pressure and the volume of the gas. He increased the pressure on the gas in the lefthand side of the tube by adding more mercury to the open tube on the right.

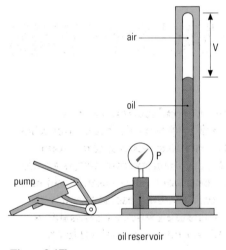

Figure 2.17b
Modern apparatus that can be used to find the relationship between the pressure of a gas and its volume.

Pressure of gas, in kN/m²	Volume of gas, in cm³
100	44
130	34
160	28
200	22
230	19
260	17
300	15

Figure 2.18
A table of readings which relate the pressure of the gas to its volume. These results were obtained using equipment similar to that shown in figure 2.17b.

mercury was never greater than about 760 mm, no matter how long the tube. You may have seen a similar experiment done in your science lessons. Torricelli said that the reason the mercury column stayed up was because it was supported by the air outside the tube, pressing down on the mercury in the bowl.

In Boyle's time, many scientists could not accept Torricelli's explanation of the behaviour of the column of mercury. They said that something as light as air could never produce enough force to hold up something as heavy as mercury. But Boyle was sure Torricelli was right, and he carried out a number of experiments to show that air could produce a force big enough to support a column of mercury. It was while he was doing these experiments that he discovered the way the pressure of a fixed mass of air could be increased by decreasing its volume.

Robert Boyle used a piece of equipment very like that shown in figure 2.17a. He compressed the air in the end of the J-tube by adding mercury to the open limb. He could thus work out the pressure on any volume of gas enclosed by the mercury by adding to the atmospheric pressure the extra pressure exerted by the mercury in the right-hand limb. You can do a similar experiment using the equipment shown in figure 2.17b. As we shall see later, change in temperature can also affect pressure. It is therefore important in these experiments that the temperature of the gas does not change.

All of these experiments show that the prediction made by the kinetic theory is correct.

9 What do you think is meant by saying that ''air is light'' but that ''mercury is heavy''?

The next question analyses some results (tabulated in figure 2.18) that have been obtained using apparatus shown in figure 2.17b. If you find using numbers rather difficult, you could omit this question.

10 The table in figure 2.18 gives some results obtained using equipment similar to that shown in figure 2.17b. The pressure of the gas has been measured in kN/m². (1 kN/m² = 1000 N/m². Normal atmospheric pressure is 100 kN/m².) The first few questions show how we can test these readings to see if they follow Boyle's Law.
a With a pressure of 100 kN/m², the volume of air was measured to be 44 cm³. Using Boyle's Law, what would you **expect** the volume of air to be if the pressure on it is raised to 200 kN/m²?
b What would you expect the volume to be if the pressure is **reduced** to 50 kN/m²?
c You should have found the volume in **a** to be 22 cm³, because doubling the pressure will halve the volume. In **b**, the volume should have been 88 cm³, because halving the pressure doubles the volume. Now, multiply the first volume by the corresponding pressure. Repeat this for each of the volumes you have worked out. What results do you get?

If you have done the arithmetic correctly, you should have found the value 4400 in each case. This is one of the consequences of Boyle's Law – for a fixed mass of gas at a constant temperature, the product (pressure × volume) is a constant. In symbols PV = constant.

The trouble with tests of this sort is that things which ought to be constant never are exactly so. This may be due to uncertainties in taking readings, or to some other reason. It is better to plot a graph. You may know that if the product of two quantities is a constant, then one of them is **inversely proportional** to the other. This means that P is inversely proportional to V. In other words, P is proportional to $1/V$. So the graph of P plotted against $1/V$ should be a straight line passing through the point (0,0).

*You can find out more about plotting graphs in Chapter **P4** and Chapter **P17**.*

Figure 2.19
Some of the wide range of products now sold in aerosol cans.

P2.3 Making use of evaporation

Aerosol sprays

Figure 2.19 gives some idea of the wide range of products that are now available in aerosol cans. The fact that the boiling point of a liquid rises when pressure is applied to it is put to very good use in these aerosol cans. Some substances have a boiling point which, under atmospheric pressure, is a little below normal air temperature. Under such conditions the substance will be a gas. But if its pressure is raised, its boiling point is raised also. If the new boiling point is above normal room temperature the substance turns into a liquid. A substance with such a boiling point is used as a *propellant* in an aerosol spray can.

A diagram of a cross-section through an aerosol spray can is shown in figure 2.20. The substance to be sprayed – which could be a paint, a hair spray or a deodorant – is mixed with the propellant while it is in liquid form. The mixture is sealed inside the can. At room temperature some of the propellant vaporizes and the pressure in the can rises. This raises the boiling point of the propellant above room temperature and the propellant stops boiling.

When the push button on the top of the can is pressed down, a valve is opened and a mixture of the spray material and the liquid propellant is forced out of the can by the pressure of propellant gas in the container. Under normal air pressure, the propellant vaporizes, leaving a spray in the form of a **mist** of fine droplets. When the push button is released, more of the propellant left in the can vaporizes and the spray can is ready to use again.

By using a propellant that does not mix with the material, this material can be ejected as a fine stream, rather than as a mist. A more viscous (thicker) liquid and a wider nozzle can produce a foam (as in shaving cream or hair-styling mousse).

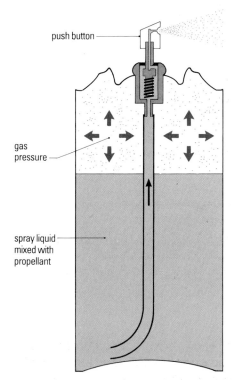

push button

gas pressure

spray liquid mixed with propellant

Figure 2.20
A cross-section of an aerosol can.

*You can find out more about mists and foams in Chapter **C**9 "Foams, emulsions, sols and gels" in the Chemistry book. You may like to try Worksheet **P2B** which deals with aerosol sprays in more detail and asks some questions about them.*

Evaporation and cooling

If you have ever used an aerosol spray can for any length of time (for example, painting with an aerosol paint) you may have noticed that the can gets quite cold to the touch.

When the spray is used some of the propellant inside the can vaporizes and so makes up the slight reduction in pressure there. But only the fastest-moving molecules, with enough energy to overcome the forces of attraction between the molecules, will leave the liquid. This leaves the remaining molecules with **less** average energy between them than they had before, and that means a colder liquid.

To understand this, imagine 100 people standing on the platform of a railway station. All of them would like to catch a train to London. Let us imagine that they have £500 between them, and that the fare to London is £10. If the £500 is evenly divided, each person would have £5 and no one would be able to go to London.

But suppose the money is not evenly divided. Let us imagine that twenty people have £10 each. The remainder have £300 divided between them, but no one has as much as £10. The average money carried by each person is still £5. So here is the situation:

Number of people	Total money	Average, per person
100	£500	£5

Of these 100 people, we have:

20	£200	£10
80	£300	£3.75

When the train comes in, 20 people can afford the fare so they get on the train. This leaves 80 people on the platform with only £300 between them: an average of £3.75 per person. Because those with most money have gone off on the train, the average money of each person left is lower.

It is like this with the molecules in the spray can. The most energetic molecules escape, so the average energy of those left behind is smaller.

As the can is now colder than the surroundings, energy is transferred from the warmer surroundings to the can and eventually more molecules have enough energy to vaporize.

> **11** You can now apply the ideas in this section to explain each of the following:
> **a** In winter a pond will freeze over much more quickly on a windy day than on a still day at the same air temperature.
> **b** Wet hands feel colder than dry hands.

Evaporation and body temperature

The cooling produced by evaporation is an important part of the body's temperature control system. Try licking your fingers and waving your hand in the air. Can you feel the cooling effect? Why is it more noticeable if you move

Figure 2.21
A refrigerator.

your hand than if you hold it still? You will find out more about this in Chapter **B**12 in the Biology book.

Refrigerators

The cooling produced by vaporization is put to good use in a refrigerator (figure 2.21). Figure 2.22 shows how it works. The pump compresses an easily-liquefied gas and forces it through the pipes on the lefthand side of the diagram, and then through the valve. The pressure on the righthand side of the valve is much lower, so the liquid vaporizes as it passes through the valve. The gas reaches the pump again and is compressed, turning back into a liquid. You should be able to work out how a refrigerator operates by answering question **12**.

12 This question refers to the operation of the refrigerator drawn in figure 2.22.
a When the liquid passes through the valve the pressure drops and the liquid vaporizes. What will happen to the temperature of the gas?
b What, as a result, will happen to the temperature in the container through which the gas passes?
c The pump compresses the gas and it turns back to a liquid. What will happen to the temperature of the liquid?
d What will happen to the temperature of the pipes through which the liquid passes?
e What will happen to the temperature of the room in which the refrigerator stands?

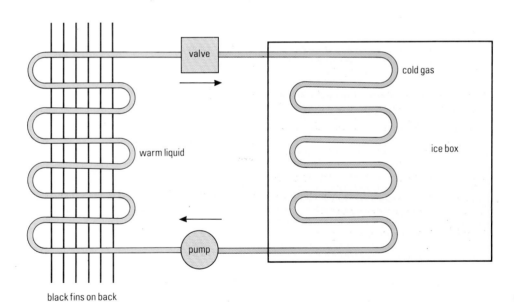

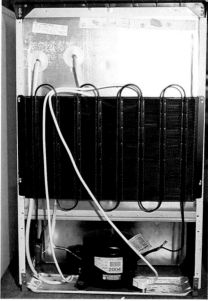

Figure 2.22a (above left)
The working parts of a refrigerator.

Figure 2.22b (above right)
The back of a refrigerator showing the cooling pipes. Why are the pipes painted black?

You will see from this that the contents of the refrigerator (through which the low pressure gas passes) get colder; while the pipes on the outside of the refrigerator through which the higher pressure liquid passes, get warmer. You will find these pipes on the back of the refrigerator. Feel them to see how warm they are. The liquid and gas together transfer energy from inside the refrigerator to the outside. But we have to spend energy in driving the pump to make this happen. In fact, we always have to provide energy to do such things.

13 In their instructions, manufacturers always say that you must leave room at the back of the refrigerator for a free flow of air. Why do they give this instruction?

If you have not so far looked at the relationship between the pressure of a gas and its volume (section P2.2) you should return to this now. The last section looks at the relationship between the pressure and temperature of a gas. Your teacher will advise you whether you should do the work of this section.

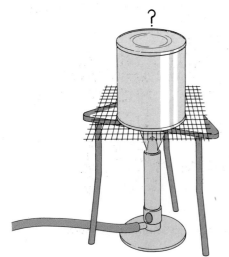

Figure 2.23
An experiment which shows in a spectacular way the increase in the pressure of air when heated in an enclosed space.

P2.4   Pressure and temperature

In this section we shall look at the way changes in the temperature of a gas can change its pressure. What happens to the pressure of air when it is heated? The answer is "nothing", if the sample is open to the atmosphere! If you heat a sample of air or another gas in a loose plastic bag it will just increase in volume. It remains at atmospheric pressure.

But what happens if you do not let the air expand but keep its volume constant? You may have seen a demonstration in which a can with a tightly-fitting lid is heated (figure 2.23). This shows in a spectacular way how the pressure in a tin can rises if the temperature of the gas inside it is raised. (Do not try this experiment yourself. Without care it could be dangerous.)

14 When the temperature of a gas in a closed container is raised, the pressure inside the container rises. Give **two** reasons why the kinetic theory predicts that the pressure of the gas will rise.

Raising the temperature of a gas can raise its pressure, if it cannot fully expand. Experiments can also show that increasing the pressure of a gas can raise its temperature. This is put to good use in the diesel engine, described in question **16** and shown in figure 2.24.

15a A rise in temperature of the gas means that the molecules are travelling more quickly and have more energy. Where does this energy come from?
b (This question is HARD!) Why is the temperature rise so much greater if the compression takes place rapidly?

The diesel engine

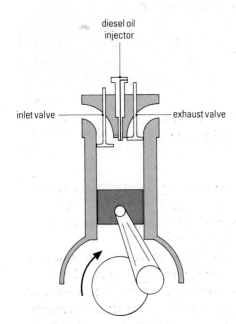

Figure 2.24
One cylinder of a diesel engine.

16 There are no spark plugs in a diesel engine. Instead, diesel oil is sprayed into the air in the cylinder that has just been rapidly compressed by the piston.
a What happens to the temperature of the gas in the cylinder when it is compressed?
b What do you think happens to the diesel oil when it enters the cylinder?
c Why is the piston then driven outwards again?

A relationship between pressure and temperature

You may have seen or tried the experiment illustrated in figure 2.25. You can try it for yourself using Worksheet **P2C**. Pairs of readings of temperature and pressure are taken at various water temperatures from cold to boiling point. If you have not tried this experiment yourself you can do question **17** which gives you some readings taken from a similar experiment.

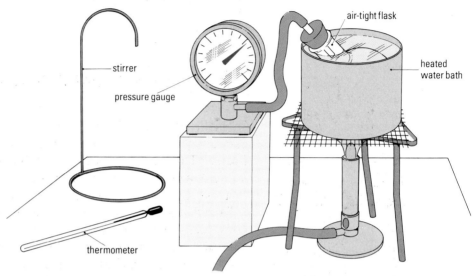

Figure 2.25
An experiment to investigate the way the pressure of a gas changes with temperature.

17 This question refers to the equipment shown assembled in figure 2.25.
a Describe how you would take a set of readings like those shown in **c** below.
b Why is it important to hold the water at each temperature for a minute or two, with constant stirring, before taking the pressure reading?
c Here is a set of readings someone obtained from such an experiment.

Thermometer reading in °C	Pressure gauge reading in N/m²
0	100 000
25	110 000
50	118 000
75	127 000
100	136 000

Plot a graph of these readings. Plot the temperature on the horizontal (or *x*) axis, starting at 0; plot the pressure on the vertical (or *y*) axis, also starting at 0.

You should have found, either in an experiment of your own, or using the results in question **17**, that the graph of pressure against temperature is a straight line. Simple relationships like this are always exciting discoveries because it is quite easy now to make some further discoveries!

First of all you will notice that pressure is **not** proportional to temperature, measured in °C, as the graph line does not pass through the origin. That is, the pressure is **not** zero at 0°C. And neither should you expect it to be – the air is still pushing against the walls of your house even when the air temperature is well below 0°C! But the straight line shape does raise a very interesting possibility. What if it were produced backwards until we reached a

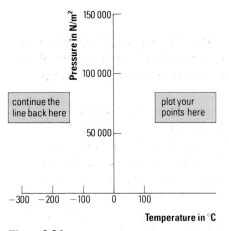

Figure 2.26
How to draw your axes when plotting a graph of pressure against temperature in question **18**.

temperature at which the pressure **was** zero? It looks as though it is possible to do that.

> **18** Replot the readings of pressure and temperature given in question **17c** on a new set of axes drawn as shown in figure 2.26. Draw the best straight line you can through your points. At what temperature does your graph suggest that the pressure of the gas would become zero?

It is impossible to imagine how a gas could possibly have a pressure less than nothing! So these results suggest that this low temperature at which the pressure of a gas is zero is the lowest it is possible to reach: it is called *absolute zero*.

Of course we have made all sorts of assumptions in finding this temperature. We do not know if we ought to extend the straight line backwards in this way; perhaps we ought not to. Certainly air could not remain a gas right the way down to a temperature as low as the one you will have found. It would become first a liquid and then a solid. But scientists often like to ask "Suppose it did" questions. "Suppose air did remain a gas right down to absolute zero, what would have happened to the molecules if it exerted no pressure?"

You can probably see that the answer to this question is that the molecules would not be moving at all. So absolute zero corresponds to the temperature at which the molecules of matter have stopped moving around.

More careful experiments support this idea. If absolute zero really is the temperature at which the molecules of matter stop moving around, then we ought to get the same temperature no matter how much air we use, no matter what pressure it is when we start the experiment and no matter what gas we use. This is just what we **do** find in practice.

All of these experiments give a value of $-273\,°C$ to "absolute zero".

The Kelvin scale of temperature

Because there is a temperature ($-273\,°C$) below which we cannot go, it might seem a good idea to relabel all our temperatures starting from absolute zero. To do this we have just to add "273" to all the temperatures in $°C$. This has never been done for day-to-day temperature measurements, but scientists use such a scale a great deal: it is called the Kelvin scale of temperature and the symbol K (which stands for "kelvin") is used for it. Temperature **differences** are no different on the Kelvin scale from those on the $°C$ (or Celsius) scale. The two scales simply take a different point for zero. This means that while we say that water freezes at $0\,°C$ or $273\,K$, the temperature **difference** between melting ice and boiling water is $100\,°C$ or $100\,K$. Figure 2.27 shows, in diagrammatic form, the range of temperatures which have become commonplace in science.

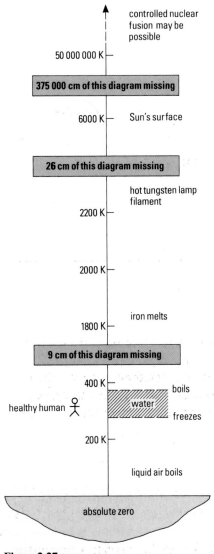

Figure 2.27
A diagram showing the wide range of temperatures.

> **19** What are the following temperatures on the Kelvin scale?
> **a** The boiling point of water
> **b** Human body temperature ($37\,°C$)
> **c** The boiling point of liquid oxygen ($-183\,°C$).

Making risky guesses

Look back at what you have done. When you continued your graph on down to find absolute zero, you were making a risky guess that the behaviour of air would stay the same. Continuing beyond all measurements like that is called *extrapolation*.

Extrapolation is always a risky business, trusting or pretending that what you have observed continues on and on. Did the Sun rise in the east this morning? Did it rise in the east yesterday? Did it rise in the east many a morning before that? Are you willing to **extrapolate** these observations into the future and say that you are **sure** the Sun will rise in the east tomorrow? Are you **quite sure**?

Sometimes graphs are used by scientists and engineers to work out what a reading would be between a pair of measured points. This process is called *interpolation*. Carefully done, it is safe, but it does not develop new science. The difference between interpolation and extrapolation is shown in figure 2.28.

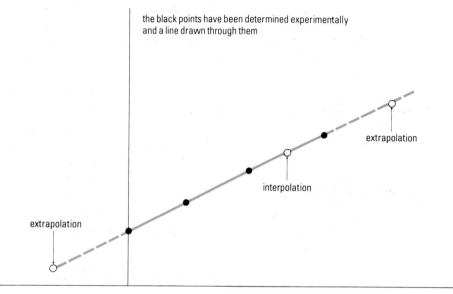

Figure 2.28
Extrapolation and interpolation.

Although extrapolation is risky, it is the way in which some of the great discoveries have been made. Scientists guess what may happen if they continue our knowledge into an unknown region; then they try to test their guess by experiment. Sometimes these experiments lead them in quite a new direction of knowledge. Extrapolation is risky but sometimes very fruitful; interpolation is safe but dull!

Summary

The following passage summarizes the main ideas in this chapter. Copy out the passage, filling in the blanks with either a word or phrase from the list at the beginning of the passage. (There is only one word or phrase to each blank; the words are not listed in the order you will need to use them, and you may use any word more than once.)

Boyle	Celsius	decrease	double
energy	evaporation	fall	gas
halve	increase	Kelvin	kinetic
liquid	Newton	not change	particles
pressure	rise	solid	temperature
volume	zero		

If we imagine the particles (atoms or molecules), from which substances are made, to be in a continual state of motion, we can understand why it is that many substances can be changed from solid to _____ and then to gas by heating them. This picture of matter as moving particles is called the _____ theory.

In solids and liquids the energy associated with the moving particles is not enough for them to break away from the forces binding the particles together. In a _____, the particles move freely and their energy is so great that we can often ignore the forces which in a _____, or a _____, bind the particles together.

Not all of the particles have the same _____. In a liquid, those with most energy escape to become a gas. This process is called _____. It results in a _____ in the temperature of the liquid, if it is unable to make up the energy lost with the evaporating particles from elsewhere.

The pressure of a gas enclosed in a container depends on the number of _____ in the container and on how fast they are moving. Squeezing the gas, or putting more _____ in the container, will raise the pressure.

For a fixed mass of gas at a constant temperature, halving the volume will _____ its pressure. This is an example of _____'s Law.

Raising the temperature of the gas will _____ the speed of the particles. Raising the temperature will also _____ the pressure of a gas. If the gas is cooled down the pressure will _____. At a temperature of $-273\,°C$ the speed of the particles is zero. This temperature is called absolute zero. The scale of temperature starting from this point is called the _____ scale.

Radioactivity
The structure of atoms

*Understanding radioactivity is not easy; but knowing some things about radioactivity is not so difficult. Section **P3.1** links radioactivity to some ideas you may already have about atoms, molecules and ions. It is not essential to understand this if you are prepared to accept that radioactive materials give off radiations that can break up other atoms. You could then read the first paragraph of section **P3.1** and go on to section **P3.2**.*

P3.1   Radiation from atoms

What do you think of as soon as someone mentions the word "radioactivity"? Probably the word "dangerous" is not very far from your thoughts. And yet the radiation we call radioactivity is as **natural** as the radiation from the Sun. Worksheet **P3A** lists some of the things some people might say about radioactivity. Some of them are true; others are false. Write down your own views of each of the statements in the worksheet. Look at them again at the end of your work on radioactivity and see whether you still agree with your answers.

Pulling atoms and molecules apart

If enough energy is transferred to the molecules of a substance, the molecules can be pulled apart into smaller pieces such as atoms. Because of its energy, a **flame** contains many such molecular pieces. You may have seen an experiment like the one shown in figure 3.1. The power supply is a very

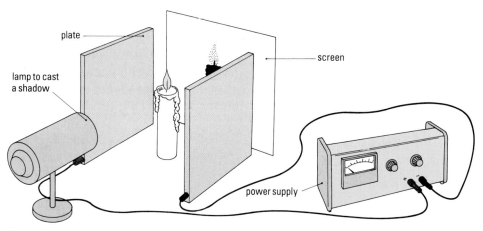

Figure 3.1
An experiment to show the presence of ions (charged particles) in a candle flame. (In the diagram, the power supply has not yet been switched on.)

high-voltage electricity supply which makes the plates electrically charged. The candle flame can be seen to spread out between the plates.

> **1a** We believe there are positively and negatively charged particles in the candle flame. What observation is made in the experiment just described that helps to support this idea?
> **b** Make a diagram of the plates connected to the power pack with a candle in between. Add some arrows to the diagram to show which way (i) a positively charged particle and (ii) a negatively charged particle will be pulled by the plates.
> **c** What is the correct name for an electrically charged particle that consists of only one atom, or a small group of atoms?

Heating is not the only way in which molecules can be broken up. Atoms and molecules are electrically uncharged, so they are called *electrically neutral*. But the experiment with the candle flame shows that the pieces into which molecules are broken are often electrically charged. This suggests that atoms and molecules contain charged particles. As an atom or molecule is electrically neutral, there is as much positive charge in it as there is negative charge. When broken into pieces, however, some bits may have more of one sort of charge than the other (figure 3.2).

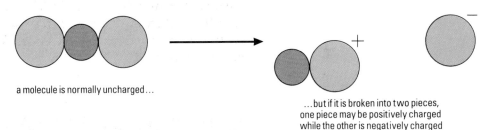

a molecule is normally uncharged…

…but if it is broken into two pieces, one piece may be positively charged while the other is negatively charged

Figure 3.2
Ions produced by the break-up of a molecule.

Electrical forces can be made to act on these charged particles in atoms and molecules and so break them up. One way of doing this is to use the Van de Graaff generator shown in figure 3.3. As the generator is "charged up", nothing is seen to happen at first. Then, suddenly there is a loud "crack", and a spark passes between the top of the generator and the metal ball on the right of the diagram. This metal ball is connected by a wire to the base of the generator.

The electrical forces produced by the generator have helped the air molecules to break up into charged particles (which we call *ions*). These charged particles have carried the charge away from the top of the generator, and in doing so have produced the spark.

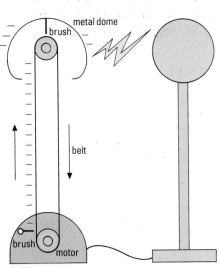

Figure 3.3
Sparks produced by the high voltage generated by a Van de Graaff generator.

> **2** Here are two everyday examples of sparks produced by electrical forces.
> **a** The spark plug in an internal combustion engine "sparks" by having a high voltage put across it.
>   **i** Find out what the purpose of the spark is.
>   **ii** Find out what part of the car engine produces the high voltage.
> **b** Lightning is a natural "spark". Find out how it is produced.

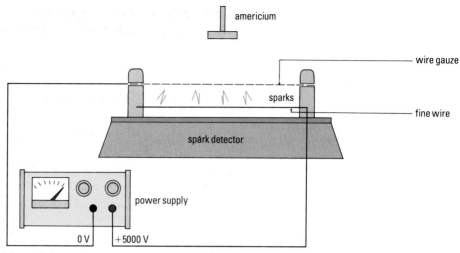

Figure 3.4
A spark detector. The air is ionized by the radiation from the americium radioactive source.

You will probably have seen a demonstration of the experiment illustrated in figure 3.4. A high voltage is placed across the gauze and the wire. But the voltage is not quite high enough to produce a spark on its own.

When a piece of *americium* (a man-made element a little heavier than *uranium*) is brought close to the gauze, sparks pass to the wire below. The americium emits a radiation which breaks up some of the air molecules into ions. These then allow the spark to pass. Many other substances including radium, thorium and uranium can also do this. We say that such substances are *radioactive*.

P3.2 Ionizing radiation

All the radiations from radioactive substances can transfer energy to other atoms and molecules, causing them to break up into electrically charged fragments. As we have seen, these charged fragments are called ions. So the radiation from radioactive substances is frequently called ionizing radiation.

In the experiment illustrated in figure 3.4, the energy carried by the

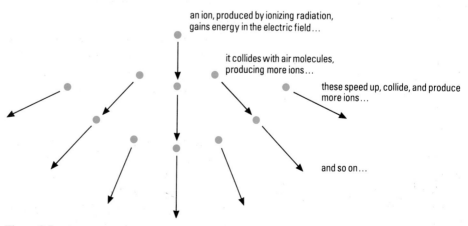

Figure 3.5
A single ion producing a cascade of ions in an electric field.

radiation from americium ionizes only a few air molecules. But due to the strong electric force between the wire and the gauze, these ions gain more energy from the electrical supply. They then collide with other molecules with enough energy to produce more ions (figure 3.5, on the previous page). This cascade of ions produces the spark which you see and hear.

You will find out more about ions and their relation to atoms and molecules in Chapter C5 and Chapter C18 of your Chemistry book.

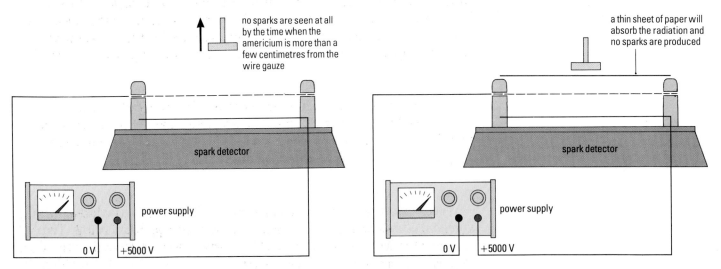

Figure 3.6 (above left)
An experiment to show the limited range in air of the radiation from an americium source.

Figure 3.7 (above right)
Using a spark detector to show how the radiation from an americium source is absorbed by a thin sheet of paper.

Figures 3.6 and 3.7 show two more experiments that can be done with americium and the "spark detector" first shown in figure 3.4. The first experiment shows how the ionizing radiation producing the sparks can be stopped by a few centimetres of air. The second shows that the same ionizing radiation can be stopped by a thin sheet of paper.

If the experiment shown in figure 3.7 is repeated using sheets of thin tissue paper, you will find that one or two sheets do not stop the ionizing radiation entirely. As more sheets are added, fewer and fewer sparks are produced in the spark detector.

The greater the ionizing power of the radiation, the more sparks are produced every second. It would be quite difficult to measure this ionizing power by counting sparks. Instead we could measure the electric current that flows when the ionizing radiation ionizes the air between the gauze and the

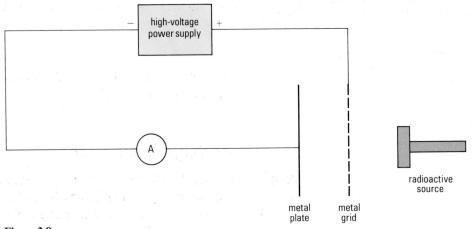

Figure 3.8
Using a sensitive ammeter to measure the ionization produced by a radioactive source.

wire. Figure 3.8 shows an experiment that will do this. The current does not transfer enough energy to produce sparks in this case, but the reading on the ammeter shows how much ionization is being produced by the radiation.

If the experiment shown in figure 3.7 is repeated using this apparatus, it is easy to see how the reading of the ammeter falls as the number of sheets of paper covering the radioactive source is increased.

3 A manufacturer of tissue paper needs to make sure that the paper he produces is of a constant thickness. If he makes it too thick, he wastes paper; if he makes it too thin, it is not strong enough to do its job. How could he use a radioactive source and the sort of equipment shown in figure 3.8 to control the thickness of the tissue paper?

It is very important to realize that the radiations from radioactive substances almost never make other things radioactive when they come in contact with them. It is only in exceptional circumstances that this could happen.

4 Suppose someone saw the experiment shown in figure 3.7 in which radiation from americium is stopped by a sheet of paper. They might say to you that they believed the paper had become radioactive. Invent an experiment that might be done to prove to them that the paper was in fact not radioactive.

If ionizing radiation does not make other things radioactive, what happens to its energy? The energy is first transferred to the pieces of molecules and ions that it has produced. These, however, rapidly recombine to form fast-moving neutral molecules. Collisions between these molecules and others nearby spread out this energy into the surrounding material and produce a rise in its temperature. As the energy carried by the radiation is now widely spread out over many atoms and molecules, the rise in temperature is usually very small.

However, by using a sufficient quantity of a radioactive material, it is possible to get a rise in temperature high enough to drive a small electrical generator. A generator of this sort was left on the Moon to provide power for several scientific experiments (figure 3.9). Such generators are also used deep down in the ocean to provide the energy amplifiers need in transatlantic telephone cables.

Figure 3.9
An electricity generator that uses a radioactive source for its "fuel".

5 What do you think are the special advantages of electrical generators "powered" by a radioactive material?

The Geiger–Müller tube

The spark detector is not a very sensitive detector of ionizing radiations. You may see an experiment in which another substance, a form of *strontium*, known to be radioactive, is brought close to the detector. No sparks are seen. To show that this form of strontium emits ionizing radiations, a different detector (called a Geiger–Müller tube) is needed.

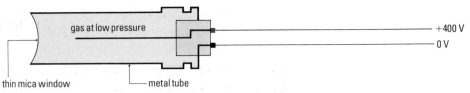

Figure 3.10
A diagram of a Geiger–Müller (G–M) tube.

The Geiger–Müller tube (frequently called a Geiger tube or G–M tube) works in much the same way as the spark detector. A drawing of one is shown in figure 3.10. A voltage of around 400 V is applied between the metal tube and the central wire. Ionizing radiation passes through the end of the tube covered by a thin layer of mica. This lets in the radiation, but not the air. Inside the tube is a gas at a very low pressure. Ions, formed in this gas by the radiation, easily travel to the metal case or the central wire, making an electric current.

Tubes such as these are very sensitive and will respond to the smallest degree of ionization. The tubes do not produce a visible spark. The short burst of electric current that passes through the tube in response to ionization has to be recorded by another electronic instrument. This device is called a *counter*. You can see one pictured in figure 3.11.

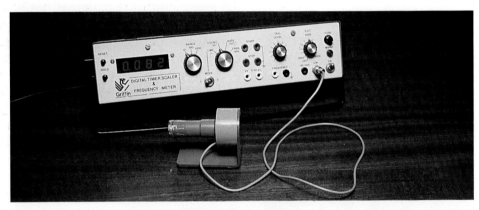

Figure 3.11
Using a G–M tube, connected to a scaler, to detect ionizing radiation from a radioactive source.

The ionizing radiation from strontium and cobalt

Radioactive strontium and radioactive cobalt are two man-made forms of strontium and cobalt. Special forms of elements that are radioactive are called *radioactive isotopes* (or *radio-isotopes* for short). Neither of these isotopes has any effect on a spark detector, but radiations from both are detected by a Geiger tube.

The radiation from radioactive strontium will travel further in air than the radiation from americium. You may remember, also, that the radiation from americium could be stopped by a thin sheet of paper. It takes several millimetres of aluminium sheet to stop the radiation from radioactive strontium. Radiation from radioactive cobalt penetrates even further through matter, and is only stopped by lead blocks several centimetres thick.

These experiments show that there are differences between the ionizing power of the radiations from different radioactive elements. There are also differences in the distance that these radiations can travel through other substances.

P3.3   What is background radiation?

When a Geiger tube is used you will notice that it continues working even when a radioactive source is nowhere near it. This is caused by radiation called *background radiation*. Background radiation is produced partly by "cosmic rays" which come to us from the Sun and our galaxy, and partly by naturally-occurring radioactive substances in the Earth's crust. The ionizing level of this radiation varies greatly from one part of the Earth to another – largely depending on the type of surrounding rock. For example, granite rocks are much more radioactive than limestone.

As far as anyone knows, background radiation has always bathed the Earth, like sunlight. This fact enables us to use the strength of background radiation to measure the likely dangers from man-made ionizing radiations.

P3.4   Why are ionizing radiations dangerous to people?

Although ionizing radiation carries little energy, it is able to penetrate matter and break up atoms or molecules well below its surface. It is this property which can make ionizing radiation dangerous to people. The radiation can damage molecules within living cells. The damage may not be important, even if it occurs, because the cells in our bodies are constantly being renewed. However, the more ionizing radiation a person experiences, the more cells there are that will be damaged. If too many cells are damaged in this way, the results can be unpleasant and even fatal.

Ionizing intensity

When ionizing radiation breaks up atoms and molecules it transfers energy to them. The strength of any one ionizing radiation is given by the energy it transfers to each kilogram of substance. Radiation "doses" received by people are measured in sieverts (symbol, Sv). 1 Sv is 1 joule per kilogram. The table in figure 3.12 shows the radiation doses received during various types of exposure to ionizing radiation.

Type of exposure	microsievert
1 working for a month in a uranium mine	1 000
2 wearing a radioactive luminous watch for a year (now not very common)	30
3 exposure to fallout in Britain from nuclear bomb testing in 1959	350
4 having a chest X-ray	200
5 watching television for a year	10
6 radiation from a brick house, per year	750
7 radiation from nuclear power stations for a year	10
8 maximum dose allowed to general public from artificial sources, per year	1000
9 typical dose received by a member of the general public in a year from all sources	2500
10 maximum dose allowed to workers exposed to radiation per year	50 000

Figure 3.12
Average radiation "doses" from a number of common sources of ionizing radiation.

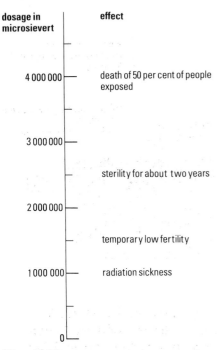

dosage in microsievert	effect
4 000 000	death of 50 per cent of people exposed
3 000 000	
	sterility for about two years
2 000 000	
	temporary low fertility
1 000 000	radiation sickness
0	

Figure 3.13
The effects of exposure to high levels of ionizing radiation.

6a Make a bar-chart of the radiation doses shown in figure 3.12.
b One simple way of protecting people from a radioactive source is to keep them at a distance from it. Explain how it is that distance alone can reduce the ionizing intensity.
c Why do you think that workers exposed to radiation are permitted much greater doses of ionizing radiation than the population as a whole?

At much higher levels of exposure, ionizing radiation can be harmful. The chart in figure 3.13 shows some of the effects of intense ionizing radiation.

7a According to the diagram in figure 3.13, are the present levels of radiation to which the public are exposed likely to be harmful?
b Again referring to figure 3.13, which part of the human organism is most likely to be affected by ionizing radiation? Give a reason for your answer.
c Why do you think that international regulations are most concerned with the total dose of ionizing radiation received **up to the age of 30?**

P3.5　Are all ionizing radiations the same?

We have already seen that ionizing radiations from different radioactive substances do not all behave in the same way.

1 They differ in their ability to ionize materials through which they pass.
2 They differ in the distance they can travel through air (figure 3.14).

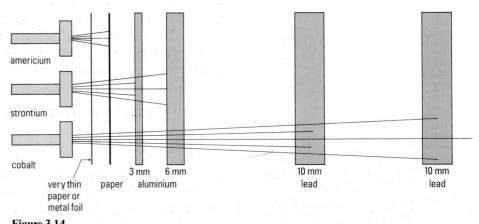

americium

strontium

cobalt

very thin paper or metal foil　paper　3 mm　6 mm aluminium　10 mm lead　10 mm lead

Figure 3.14
The ionizing radiations from different radioactive sources may differ significantly in both their range in air and their ability to pass through other materials.

Passing ionizing radiation from radioactive strontium through a magnetic field

You may see a demonstration of the experiment illustrated in figure 3.15. The small sample of radioactive strontium gives off ionizing radiation, but this is

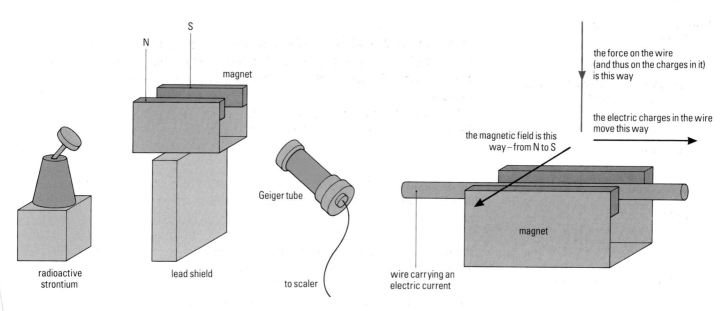

Figure 3.15 (above left)
An experiment to show the way the radiation from a strontium–60 radioactive source can be bent by a magnetic field.

Figure 3.16 (above right)
The direction of the force on an electric current flowing through a magnetic field.

stopped from reaching the Geiger tube directly by the blocks of lead. A magnet is placed so that its magnetic field crosses the path of the radiation. With the magnet arranged as shown, the Geiger tube picks up the ionizing radiation, but if the magnet is turned round so that its field is in the opposite direction, the Geiger tube fails to pick up any radiation. It seems as if the magnetic field is bending the ionizing radiation **round the lead blocks**.

What does this tell us about the ionizing radiation from radioactive strontium? In Chapter **P**18, we see that magnetic fields are able to move wires through which an electric current is flowing. In Chapter **P**16, we see that an electric current is a flow of electric charge along a wire. Putting these two facts together, it seems that magnetic fields give a sideways force to moving charges (figure 3.16). In Chapter **P**19 there is further evidence for this. In that chapter we explore some of the properties of electron beams. Electron beams are streams of charged particles. These streams of charged particles can also be deflected sideways by a magnetic field.

These facts suggest that the ionizing radiation from strontium is itself a stream of charged particles. The direction in which the radiation beam is turned by the magnetic field shows us that the ionizing radiation from strontium is a stream of **negatively-charged** particles.

The ionizing radiation from americium

It is difficult to do similar experiments with the ionizing radiation from americium because it does not travel far in air. It is possible to make the path of the particles emitted by radioactive americium visible, in a *cloud chamber*. If the cloud chamber is placed in a strong magnetic field and the field is made perpendicular to the path of the particles, the tracks are seen to be curved as shown in figure 3.17. The results from such an experiment show that this ionizing radiation also consists of a stream of charged particles, but this time the particles are **positively** charged and have a mass almost 7000 times **greater** than those emitted by radioactive strontium.

Figure 3.17
The results of an experiment designed to show that the radiation from an americium source can also be bent in a magnetic field.

8a If the trails left by radiation from strontium were made visible in the same way and the magnetic field was in the same direction, which way would their path bend?

8b If the particles from the strontium source travel through the magnetic field at the same speed as the particles from the americium source, will the path of the particles from strontium be more curved or less curved than the path of the particles from americium?

Radiation from radioactive cobalt

Similar experiments with the ionizing radiation from radioactive cobalt show that the radiation carries no charge. (The path of the radiation is not changed by a magnetic field.) It has been shown that this radiation is a **wave** – one in the same "family" as light. But the wavelength of light is about 10 000 000 times longer than the wavelength of this radiation!

The "family" of ionizing radiations

The only "family characteristic" of ionizing radiations is their ability to ionize material through which they pass. Apart from this, they are very different from each other.

How many more radiations are there which can be called "ionizing radiations"? The only commonly occurring ones are X-rays – waves of a wavelength about 10 000 times longer than the radiation from radioactive cobalt. Each of the three ionizing radiations we have already encountered has a name. The ionizing radiation from americium is called *alpha radiation* and it is made up of *alpha particles*. That from radioactive strontium is called *beta radiation* and it is made up of *beta particles*. The radiation from cobalt is called *gamma radiation*. All ionizing radiation from naturally-occurring radioactive materials is one of these three types.

9 Copy out and complete the table in figure 3.18 which summarizes the properties of the three types of radiation.

Name of radiation	Range in air	Radiation absorbed by	Particle or wave	Charge
alpha	?	thin paper	particle	?
?	50 cm	6 mm aluminium	?	negative
gamma	several metres	?	?	none

Figure 3.18
Some of the properties of different ionizing radiations.

Making use of ionizing radiations

Using Worksheet **P3B**, you can now start your own investigation into the use we make of ionizing radiations. You may see a film or video which will illustrate how these radiations are being put to life-saving use in hospitals. You will also see how they can be used in many places in industry and in scientific research.

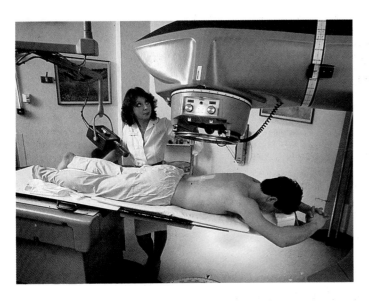

Figure 3.19
Some of the many uses of radioactive materials.
a (left) Radiotherapy treatment.
b (right) Searching for faults in a jet engine.

Radioactive chemicals have also been used in chemistry to find out what happens in many reactions. Similarly, in biology they have helped in investigations into the chemical reactions that take place in plants and animals (see Biology, section **B**8.2). The pictures in figure 3.19 show some of the uses made today of radioactive materials.

P3.6   How long do substances stay radioactive?

When radioactive atoms give off alpha or beta radiation they lose tiny particles of matter. You would expect the atoms remaining to be different. Radioactive atoms do not stay permanently the same, as atoms of ordinary copper or nitrogen do. They are unstable, and when they suddenly break up and fling out a particle such as an alpha particle, they become atoms of a **different** chemical element.

Sometimes the new atoms are not themselves radioactive. This means that as time passes there are fewer and fewer radioactive atoms (figure 3.20). When a radioactive atom loses an alpha or beta particle it is said to decay. When we use the word "decay" in this way we do not mean quite the same thing as when we say a dead tree *decays*. All the word means when talking of

Figure 3.20
The decay of radioactive atoms with time.

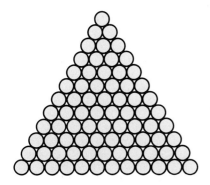

To begin with, all the atoms are radioactive.

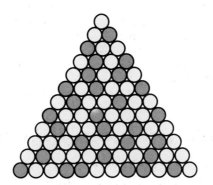

After some time, some of the atoms decay to become stable atoms. There are now fewer radioactive atoms, so the activity of the material is reduced.

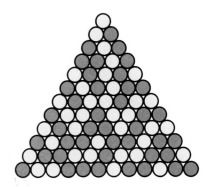

After a further period, more radioactive atoms have decayed. There are now even fewer radioactive atoms left and the activity of the material is even smaller.

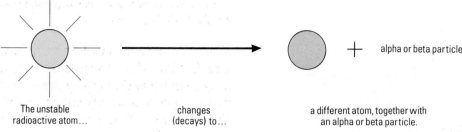

The unstable
radioactive atom...

changes
(decays) to...

a different atom, together with
an alpha or beta particle.

Figure 3.21
The decay of an unstable atom to another atom. This new atom may itself be unstable and decay in turn.

radioactivity is "change". The phrase "radioactive decay" is a shorthand way of saying "the radioactive atom emits a particle and changes to another atom" (figure 3.21). The number of radioactive atoms decaying each second in a sample of radioactive material is called the material's *activity*. So activity is measured in **decays per second**. An activity of 1 decay per second is called 1 becquerel (symbol, Bq).

Activity is not the same as the **ionizing ability** mentioned in section P3.4. The ionizing ability of the radiation depends on the activity of the source it comes from, but it also depends on many other things as well.

10 The ionizing ability of some ionizing radiation is measured by the number of ions it can create per second in a small mass of material. Write down as many other factors as you can think of that might affect the ionizing ability of the radiation from a radioactive source.

The time it takes a radioactive material to decay is quite unaffected by any "outside" changes. Experiments have been done to see whether the time it takes a radioactive material to decay can be changed by raising or lowering its temperature, or combining it with other elements – or in fact anything you can think of! None of these changes has ever been found to have any affect on the rate of decay of the radioactivity of a substance.

11 A fortune could be made by the first person to find a way of **increasing** the rate of decay of radioactive materials. Why do you think this is so?

Radioactive clocks

The decrease in the activity of a radioactive material with time has been used in recent years to find the date of many events that took place in the past. Here is one method that uses the minute radioactivity found in natural carbon.

All material that is either living, or has once lived, contains carbon. By a stroke of good fortune, a tiny proportion of this carbon is naturally radioactive. Although its radioactivity declines with time, new quantities of radioactive carbon are always being created high up in the atmosphere by cosmic rays. This means that a known mass of **living** material always contains a constant and unchanging amount of radioactive carbon (figure 3.22).

*You can find out more about how organisms continually gain and lose carbon in Chapters **B**3 and **B**9 of your Biology book.*

When the material dies, however, the radioactive carbon is locked up inside it and then its radioactivity does decrease because it is not being replenished. It is by comparing the activity of radioactive carbon locked up inside dead material (such as wood) with the activity of the same carbon in living material that the "age" of the material can be worked out. To be able to do this, however, it is necessary to know how the activity of a radioactive substance changes with time.

Figure 3.22
Using radioactive decay as a "clock" to measure the time since a tree died.

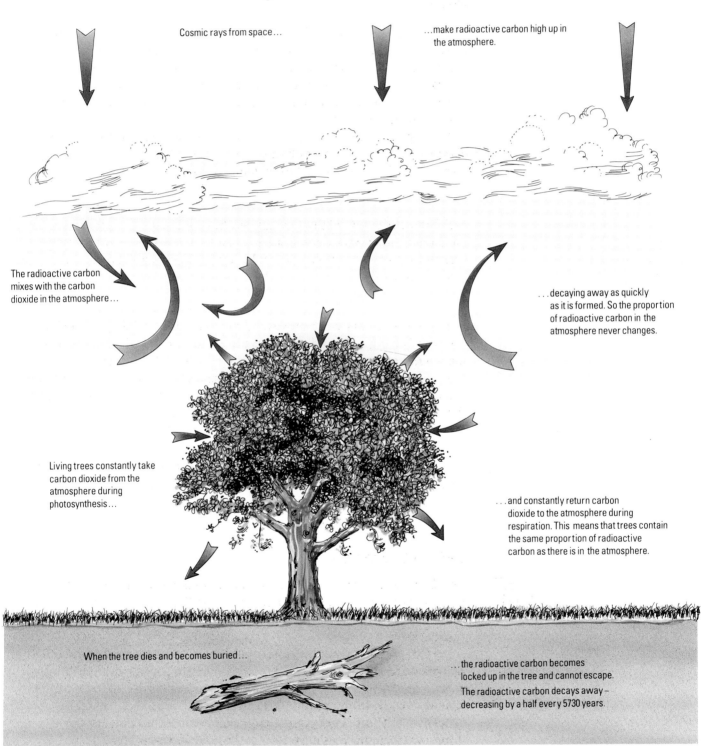

Cosmic rays from space…

…make radioactive carbon high up in the atmosphere.

The radioactive carbon mixes with the carbon dioxide in the atmosphere…

…decaying away as quickly as it is formed. So the proportion of radioactive carbon in the atmosphere never changes.

Living trees constantly take carbon dioxide from the atmosphere during photosynthesis…

…and constantly return carbon dioxide to the atmosphere during respiration. This means that trees contain the same proportion of radioactive carbon as there is in the atmosphere.

When the tree dies and becomes buried…

…the radioactive carbon becomes locked up in the tree and cannot escape. The radioactive carbon decays away – decreasing by a half every 5730 years.

Measuring radioactive decay

You may see a demonstration of the experiment illustrated in figure 3.23. The experiment measures the decay of a radioactive element called protactinium.

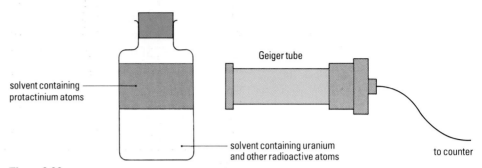

Figure 3.23
An experiment to measure the decay and half-life of radioactive protactinium.

12 Find out where protactinium is in the Periodic Table.

The protactinium used in this experiment is produced from the decay of uranium. Uranium is a naturally-occurring radioactive element which decays to produce a form of radioactive thorium. This in turn decays to produce radioactive protactinium which is a rare element. Because radioactive protactinium is being created as quickly as it is decaying, the quantity in any sample of natural uranium remains constant. In this experiment, the protactinium is separated chemically from the uranium so that you can watch it decay.

The activity of the protactinium is measured, using a G–M tube connected to a *counter* or a *rate-meter*. A rate-meter (shown in figure 3.11) is a counter which automatically records how many pulses a G–M tube produces every second. This reading is often referred to as the "count rate". The count rate recorded by the rate-meter can be taken every ten seconds. If a counter is used instead, the total number of counts is recorded every ten seconds. You can find the average count rate during each successive ten-second period from these readings.

You will find that the count rate continues to fall for several minutes after the start of the experiment, but will then fall no further. This is because the count rate recorded by the rate-meter is now entirely due to background radiation and the radioactive substances in the rest of the bottle. The "total background" can be measured by taking the average count rate over the next five minutes.

If this "total background" is subtracted from the earlier readings, then you will have a count rate that depends **only** on the decaying protactinium. This corrected count rate is proportional to the activity of the protactinium.

You can plot your own graph of the changing activity of the protactinium either from results obtained for you in class, or using the table of results from a similar experiment given in figure 3.24. When analysing your results you have to be very careful to allow for ionizing radiations which are escaping from the nearby uranium solution and creating a constant, but high, "background". The background radiation readings have already been subtracted from the readings given in the table in figure 3.24.

Time from start in seconds	Counts per 10 s	Time from start in seconds	Counts per 10 s	Time from start in seconds	Counts per 10 s
5	75	105	12	205	5
15	48	115	18	215	8
25	49	125	10	225	10
35	44	135	2	235	10
45	41	145	14	245	9
55	32	155	12	255	10
65	47	165	2	265	0
75	41	175	15	275	0
85	27	185	8	285	5
95	27	195	9	295	6

Figure 3.24
Results from an experiment on the decay of radioactive protactinium.

13 Use either the results given in the table in figure 3.24 or results from an experiment you may have seen.
a Plot a graph of count rate against time.
b Draw a **smooth curve** on your graph to follow the readings as closely as possible.
c The line gives the way the **average activity** of the protactinium varies with time. How much time passes before the average activity of the protactinium has dropped to one half of its value at the beginning of the experiment?
d How much time passes before the activity of the protactinium has dropped to one quarter of its value at the beginning of the experiment?
e Now choose another starting point on your graph – say about 30 s after the first reading. How long does it take the average activity to drop by one half **of this reading?**

The time taken for the activity of the substance to decrease by one half is **always** the same, no matter where you start. This is a remarkable property of radioactive decay. This length of time is called the *half-life* of the radioactive element.

14 What is the half-life of protactinium according to your results?

How long, then, does it take for the element to have completely decayed? This, you can see, is an unanswerable question!

15 Suppose the half-life of a particular radioactive substance is 60 s, and its measured activity is 512 decays per second from the instant a clock is started.
a What would you expect the activity to be 60 s later?
b What would you expect the activity to be 120 s after the clock was started?

Every 60 s the activity of the radioactive material is reduced by a half. Eventually there will be only a few radioactive atoms left. Figure 3.25 (on the next page) gives a table of the half-lives of a range of common radio-isotopes. Some are very long indeed and can only be measured indirectly by finding out the likelihood of any one radioactive atom decaying.

Element	Half-life	Notes
Carbon–14	5730 years	Occurs naturally in the atmosphere. Basis for carbon dating.
Sodium–24	15 hours	Artificial radio-isotope of sodium. Used medically.
Phosphorus–32	14.3 days	Much used as a tracer in plant research.
Cobalt–60	5.3 years	Artificial. Used extensively for radio-therapy in hospitals.
Strontium–90	28 years	Used in school work.
Iodine–131	8 days	Dangerous product of nuclear reactions (but note short half-life).
Radium–226	1600 years	The common form of natural radium.
Uranium–238	4.5×10^9 years	Commonest form of uranium.
Plutonium–239	24 000 years	Artificial and used in nuclear power industry.

Figure 3.25
The half-lives of some common radioactive materials. The number after the name of each element gives the number of protons and neutrons in the nucleus. Elements which also exist in a stable form have a different number of neutrons.

The way a radioactive material decays is related to the way atoms decay at random. The relationship between random decay and half-life is developed after the summary to this chapter. You could omit it without harming your understanding of this chapter.

P3.7   The structure of the atom

The discovery of radioactivity helped revolutionize our ideas of the structure of the atom. Even before then, Faraday and other nineteenth-century scientists had realized that atoms could become electrically charged.

Experiments by the famous English physicist J. J. Thomson showed that there was a speck of matter, even smaller than an atom and carrying a negative charge, which could be separated from atoms. This was called an *electron*. It is these particles which make up the current of electric charges in most electric circuits. You can learn more about electrons in Chapter **P**19.

Finding out about the structure of atoms

The discovery of radioactivity by the French scientist Henri Becquerel in 1895 soon led scientists to suspect that atoms might themselves be built up from other particles. Another famous scientist, Ernest Rutherford, started a series of experiments in which alpha particles were used like bullets to probe the inside of atoms.

Rutherford's work is of great importance to modern physics. He was the first to use the idea that matter could be investigated by firing particles at it. This is still the main method used today. But instead of relying on natural radioactivity to provide the "bullets", huge machines called "particle accelerators" (figure 3.26) are used.

This is a very exciting and interesting piece of physics, but it uses ideas that are really beyond this course. You will certainly learn about Rutherford's work and about particle accelerators if you go on to do more physics. For now, we will simply describe what scientists have found out about the atom. You should remember, however, that this description is the result of a lot of careful experiments and observation.

Figure 3.26a (above left)
Particle accelerators at CERN, Geneva.
These accelerators are underground, but
their shape can be seen as the rings in this
aerial photograph.

Figure 3.26b (above right)
Inside a particle accelerator at the
Rutherford Appleton Laboratory. The
main accelerator, called a synchrotron, is
on the left of the picture. The tube on the
right injects particles into the synchrotron.

A modern picture of the atom

What emerged from Rutherford's work was a picture of the atom very
different from the solid, snooker-ball picture that scientists once had.
Rutherford showed that the atom is largely empty space! Nearly all its mass is
concentrated in a tiny *nucleus* which carries a positive charge. Surrounding
this nucleus is a cloud of *electrons*. The nucleus is only $\frac{1}{10\,000}$ the diameter of
an atom.

16 Suppose you were trying to build a scale model of an **atom** and you intended to
use a table-tennis ball to represent the **nucleus**. (A table-tennis ball is about 4 cm in
diameter.) How big would your model have to be? Do you think this is a sensible size?

It is this protective cloud of electrons that makes the atom seem so solid.
The energy of chemical reactions and the collisions of atoms in gases, liquids
and solids are far too little to make much of a "dent" on this cloud of
negative charge.

Atoms are electrically neutral because the positive charge on the nucleus
exactly balances the negative charge of the electron cloud. If atoms gain or
lose one or two electrons (and they can do this quite easily) they become
electrically charged. We then call them *ions*.

The electrons are not scattered at random through the cloud. The way they
are arranged has an important bearing on their chemical properties. You will
learn more about this in Chapter **C**18 in your Chemistry book.

neutron

proton

Figure 3.27
The nucleus of an atom. It is important to
remember how small this is. If you were to
draw in the rest of the atom, the outside
edge would be 10 000 cm from the centre
of this drawing – that is 100 m away.

The nucleus

Further investigation has shown that the nucleus itself is made of two even
smaller particles. They are called *neutrons* and *protons*. These two particles
are almost identical in all respects except one – the proton is positively
charged while the neutron is uncharged (figure 3.27).

Figure 3.28
Marie and Pierre Curie at work in their laboratory. Marie Curie's work led to our present understanding of radioactivity.

The proton carries a charge equal in size to that of the electron. Hydrogen, the lightest of all the elements, has a nucleus that consists of a single proton. Heavier elements have nuclei made up of protons **and** neutrons.

The nuclei of some atoms easily break up. This is what causes them to be radioactive. We have seen that radioactive materials may give off alpha, beta and gamma rays. The investigations of Ernest Rutherford and many other scientists, such as the famous Polish scientist Marie Curie (figure 3.28), have led to a better understanding of radioactivity. Their work shows that:

- *alpha particles* consist of two protons and two neutrons, bound tightly together
- *beta particles* consist of high-energy electrons.

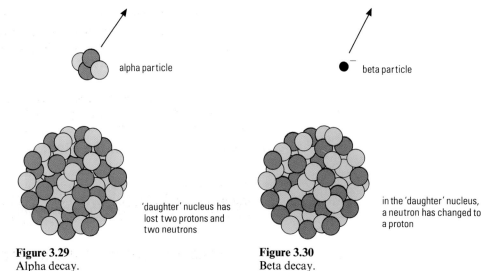

Figure 3.29
Alpha decay.

Figure 3.30
Beta decay.

When a radioactive nucleus emits an alpha particle it loses two neutrons and two protons (figure 3.29). What happens when a radioactive nucleus emits a beta particle is a little more mysterious. There are **no** electrons in the nucleus of an atom. Instead, what happens is that a neutron turns into a proton plus an electron. The electron has so much energy that it "explodes" out of the nucleus (figure 3.30).

You will learn a lot more about the structure of atoms and the way the nucleus is built up from protons and neutrons in Chapter **C**18 of the Chemistry book.

Summary

The following passage summarizes the main ideas in this chapter. Copy out the passage, filling in the blanks with either a word or phrase from the list at the beginning of the passage. (There is only one word or phrase to each blank; the words are not listed in the order you will need to use them, and you may use any word more than once.)

air	protons	all	aluminium	lead
element	ionizing	half	waves	steady
paper	reacting with	particles	neutrons	nucleus

Radiation from radioactive atoms transfers energy to air by _____ the air molecules.

There are three common types of ionizing radiation called alpha radiation, beta radiation and gamma rays. Alpha and beta radiation both consist of streams of _____ while gamma rays are _____.

Alpha radiation can be absorbed by a thin sheet of _____. A sheet of _____ must be a few millimetres thick to stop beta radiation. Gamma rays can be absorbed by many centimetres of _____.

In the process of radioactive decay the atoms change into a new _____. The half-life is the time for _____ the atoms to decay. Rutherford suggested that most of the mass of an atom is concentrated in a tiny _____ which is itself made up from _____ and _____.

Finally, look again at the answers you gave to Worksheet **P3A**. Do you still agree with your previous answers? Give your reasons for any change in your views. You might like to discuss them with other people in your class.

*The last section looks at another aspect of radioactive decay – called **randomness** – and shows you how this is related to radioactive decay and half-life. It is more difficult than the rest of the chapter. Your teacher will advise you whether or not to read it.*

P3.8   Random events and radioactive decay

What do we mean by "random events"?

You will have seen a Geiger tube connected to a counter. A counter responds to each burst of ionization that occurs within the Geiger tube. You may have noticed that the counter shows the bursts of ionization arriving irregularly.

Suppose the Geiger tube is set up to record the radiation produced by radioactive strontium. If you count the number of "radiation bursts" produced every minute over a period of, say, 10 minutes, you will see that, compared with the average number, you get little variation. But if you make a similar count over, say, 5 seconds, you will find that, compared with the average, you get a great deal of variation from one period to the next. The table in figure 3.31 shows some such results.

Number of Geiger tube pulses in 60 seconds	Number of Geiger tube pulses in 5 seconds
257	16
258	22
239	25
249	20
262	15
265	15
230	22
232	17
249	22
255	18
	10
	18

Figure 3.31
The number of pulses from a Geiger tube close to a radioactive source.

17a Use the results displayed in the lefthand column in figure 3.31 to calculate the average number of counts (bursts of ionization) made by the Geiger tube every minute.
b Using the average result calculated in **a**, predict the number of counts that the Geiger tube would make in 5 seconds.
c The righthand column in figure 3.31 shows the number of counts actually recorded by the Geiger tube each 5 seconds, over a period of one minute. Suppose you were asked to **predict** the number of counts in (i) the next minute and (ii) the next 5 seconds. Explain, with a reason, which prediction you would expect to be the most accurate.

Each burst of ionization is produced by the emission of a beta particle by a radioactive strontium nucleus. Over a reasonably long period of time it is possible to predict with some accuracy how many bursts will occur. But over short periods there is a considerable variation in the number of bursts of ionization occurring. This means that there is considerable variation in the number of beta particles emitted by the radioactive source over a short period of time. These variations are "smoothed out" to a steady and predictable number over a long period of time.

This sort of irregularity is very common in everyday life. To take an example, consider the possibility of there being a fire in your home. House fires are unpredictable for an individual. You may never have one; the chances are you never will. On the other hand some unlucky person will have one tomorrow. You cannot tell who. Things which occur in this irregular and unpredictable way are called *random events*.

Because a fire at home is a random, or chance, event householders insure themselves against any possible damage from one. Insurance companies protect householders against fire and yet make a profit. The reason they can do this is because it is **not important to them** whether you or your neighbour have a fire today, tomorrow or next month. The important thing to them is the average number of household fires, over the country as a whole, in a year. Despite the fact that you cannot predict when, or if, a particular householder will have a fire, the total number of household fires in a year over the whole country can be predicted very accurately. So the insurance company knows exactly what to charge someone so that they are protected from damage if they are unlucky enough to have a fire themselves.

Suppose a particular company insures five million homes against fire and "pays out" on 100 claims in the course of a year. The company can predict with some certainty that it will have to pay out on 100 claims next year. Another way of expressing this fact is to say that there is a chance of 1 in 50 000 that any one householder will have a fire in one year.

The total number of fires expected
= chance of a house having a fire × number of houses insured

$$= \frac{1}{50\,000} \times 5\,000\,000$$

$$= 100$$

Of course, chance does not "average out" so well if the number of houses insured is smaller, or the number of fires in only one month is considered.

18a Suppose the insurance company only insured one million homes. For how many fires might the insurance company expect to have claims during one year?
b Would you be surprised if the company had several more or several fewer claims than you predict in a year?
c How many claims might the company expect to receive in a month?

What answer did you give to part c? If you worked it out arithmetically you will have got the answer "1.67 claims". But the company cannot have a **fraction** of a claim! You might guess that the most likely number of claims is 1 or 2.

The point being made here is that the number of insurance claims made may be different from that predicted. That is because each fire is a random, or chance, event. You may be able to see, or to guess, that you are more likely to be wrong if your prediction is for a small number of claims.

Radioactive decay is like this. It is a random occurrence, ruled by chance. By measuring the number of beta particles given off by a known number of radioactive strontium atoms over several minutes, we can work out the chance of one atom giving out one beta particle in a time of one second. We can then use this to predict how many beta particles will be given off by any other group of strontium atoms, over any other time interval. But this prediction will only be accurate if the number we predict is quite large.

A game with dice

We can make a model of radioactive decay using dice – or any cubes which have one face distinguished from the others. The face marked "D" in figure 3.32 will represent a **D**ecaying atom.

Suppose we have 120 such cubes and we shake them up and throw them over the bench. This could represent 120 radioactive atoms. Each cube that comes up with a "D" on top represents an atom which decays during the time of the "throw".

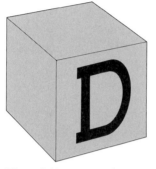

Figure 3.32
The wooden cube used in a game to represent radioactive decay.

19a How many cubes would you expect to come up with a "D" on top?
b If you take away the cubes with a "D" on top, you will be left with the "atoms" which did not decay during the time of that throw. How many cubes (or "atoms") would this leave undecayed?
c Suppose you collect up the undecayed "atoms", shake them up and throw them again. How many would you **expect** to come up with a "D" on top? (Round the number to the nearest whole number.)
d How many would this leave "undecayed"?
e Complete the table in figure 3.33.
f Plot a graph of the number of "atoms" left "undecayed" at the end of each throw against the number of the throw. Plot the throws along the horizontal axis and the number of "atoms" vertically. Draw a smooth curve through the points.

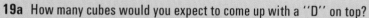

Throw number	0	1	2	3	4	5	6	7	8	9
Number of "D"s	–	20	17							
Number left	120	100								

Figure 3.33
How to lay out the table for question **19**.

You now have a graph of the way you would expect the number of atoms to change with time, **if the model is correct**. Of course this is not quite what you would find in practice, because the effect of "chance" means that at any one time your throw may be more or less than the number you expect to get. To see the effect of chance, you will have to do an experiment with 120 cubes (small wooden ones of about 1-cm side are excellent) or you can use dice – in which case you will have to agree that one number (say the five) represents a decayed atom. If you use wooden cubes, one side must be marked in some way – perhaps with a "D".

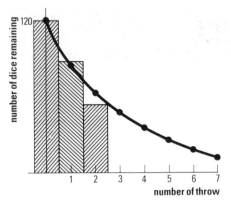

Figure 3.34
Making a graph of the results of the dice game and comparing it with the graph you might expect to get.

Make successive throws of the dice or cubes.

1 Remove the ones which represent the decayed atoms after each throw.
2 Count the remaining dice or cubes.
3 Plot the number of dice or cubes remaining after each throw as a **bar chart** on top of the graph you plotted in question **19** (see figure 3.34).

You should find that the graph line you drew in question **19** is a fairly good average or "trend" line for the results you get by throwing the dice or cubes.

Half-life

Look at the results you get for the expected number of cubes or dice remaining after each throw (question **19**).

> **20** How many throws would it take to reduce the expected number of dice remaining to 60?

It is of course usually meaningless to talk of a **fraction** of a throw, but in our model a **throw** is like a particular **interval of time** in the decay of radioactive atoms. We can certainly divide up intervals of time into smaller intervals; so in this sense we **can** talk of fractions of a throw.

> **21a** How many throws does it take to reduce the expected number of dice or cubes from 60 to 30?
> **b** How many throws does it take to reduce the expected number of dice from 50 to 25?
> **c** Does it always take the same number of throws (and fraction of a throw) to reduce the expected number of cubes or dice by one-half?
> **d** Explain why this is like the behaviour of radioactive decay.
> **e** What is the "half-life" of the cubes or dice, measured in throws (and fraction of a throw)?

If you were to mark **two** faces of the cubes – or take out dice showing a four or a five – the number of cubes or dice would go down more quickly. The "half-life" of the cubes would be shorter. The half-life is shorter because there is **more chance** of the "atoms" decaying. This is the same with real radioactive atoms – the greater their chance of decaying, the shorter the half-life of the substance.

For a given number of atoms, the **greater** the chance of decay, the **greater** is the number decaying at any one time. This means that for two radioactive substances with equal numbers of atoms to begin with, the one with the shorter half-life has the greater activity. This is why the radioactive waste from nuclear reactors only stays very radioactive for a short time. The most radioactive material decays the most quickly.

Topic P2   Force and motion

This topic is about motion and how it can be changed. Chapter **P4** looks at the way we describe and measure motion. You will learn how to measure *time* and *distance*. You will find out how *velocity* and *acceleration* are used to describe the different sorts of movement we find in the world around us.

More often than not, movement involves *forces*. In Chapter **P5**, you will meet two theories about how force and motion are linked together, and you will have the chance to invent your own experiments to decide which theory is best.

Energy is another idea that you will have met already in connection with motion. In Chapter **P6** you will find out that energy is another useful way of describing and understanding changes in motion. In that chapter you will meet an entirely new idea called *momentum*. This is very useful when it comes to describing how things like rockets and jet engines work – as well as why it is so easy to fall in the water when you step off a boat!

Finally, in Chapter **P7**, we shall have a brief look at *gravity* – the force that keeps us on the Earth's surface. Unlike more familiar forces, gravity seems to act even when we are not touching the Earth. But understanding gravity can be important if you are a "sky-diver" or an astronaut.

Learning to do physics

In the introduction to this book you will have seen that physics (and any other science) is much more than a list of facts. It involves finding out about the world we live in. If you are to understand the things scientists say, then it is important to understand how they work. In this topic you will meet a number of important things that scientists often assume when they work at their job. You will also have the chance to try out several of the skills they use.

In Chapter **P4**, you will use *graphs* to represent motion. Graphs are used a great deal in physics to display the way things are related to each other. They help us to see patterns in results. You have already seen the importance of *straight-line graphs* in Chapter **P1**.

In Chapter **P5** you will have to think carefully about what scientists do when they make *theories*. You will have an opportunity yourself to test two rival theories about motion and to see which is best. There will be another opportunity to test out theories in Chapter **P10**.

In Chapter **P7** another general idea comes up – *predictability*. You will learn what we mean when we talk about "predicting things" when you study the effect of gravity in that chapter.

What you should already know about force and motion

You are not expected to have made many investigations into motion in any of your earlier work in science. But you should have had some experience of using *forces*. This is no more than you have already needed in order to understand Chapter **P1**.

If you have already worked through Chapter **P8**, you will know that you are expected to understand a few things about energy before this course begins. You may like to read the introduction to the topic on energy (page 130) just to see what ideas you should be familiar with.

You ought to have seen in earlier science studies how energy is transferred when changes take place. Moving objects have energy – we call it *kinetic energy*. If motion changes, energy must be transferred.

Work is the main way we have of measuring energy transfers. Often, when energy is transferred, we can feel a force acting. Work is equal to the force acting multiplied by the distance it moves. This tells us how much energy is transferred. Energy and changes in energy are both measured in *joules* (J).

Since all of this revision is covered in the introduction to the topic on energy, there are no revision questions here. If you have not yet started the energy topic, this might be a good time to try the revision questions in the introduction to that topic.

Speed, velocity and acceleration

P4.1   Measuring time

Do you know that "marathon races" are run in memory of a famous battle in Greek history? About 490 B.C. an Athenian soldier ran from Marathon to Athens to tell his fellow countrymen that their enemies, the Persians, had been defeated.

Figure 4.1
The modern marathon is named after an unknown Greek soldier who ran from Marathon to Athens in 490 BC. We have no idea how long he took to make the run.

We do not know how long it took that soldier to take the news to Athens because clocks, as we know them today, had not been invented. The Greeks had things for measuring time, such as water clocks and burning candles, but these could not be moved from place to place while they were working in the way a modern clock or watch can.

Of course, there is another way the Greeks might have measured how long the unknown Greek soldier took over his famous run. They could have written down the time of day he set out from Marathon and the time of day he arrived in Athens. This is the way you usually know how long a journey takes. If someone says to you, "How long did it take you to get to school today?", you would probably say something like, "Well I set out at eight o'clock and got here at half-past eight – so that is half-an-hour." The Greeks had sundials that they could use to find the time of day, but they were not much use in cloudy weather. In any case, whatever happened, no one knows how long the soldier took on his run.

Time can mean one of two things. It can mean the **time of day** – as when we say, "I always have breakfast at half-past seven." Or it can mean a **time interval**, as we do when we say, "It takes ten minutes to get down to the shops." In science when we "measure time", the thing we are measuring is a time interval.

We use clocks for measuring time; but usually we think of clocks as giving us the time of day. So we shall call something used for measuring a "time interval", a *timing device*.

Inventing a timing device

In the past, there have been many other timing devices apart from water clocks, candles and sundials. The Greeks were well known for inventing things. Can you explain to a friend how a water clock or a candle can be used for timing? Can you invent a timing device yourself? Worksheet **P4A** gives you some suggestions about how a group of you can invent your own timing

Figure 4.2
Timing devices can become very complicated!

device to measure a time interval of two minutes as accurately as possible.

Your timing device could be a water clock, a burning candle or some kind of sand clock. Perhaps you can think of something different from these suggestions.

Early clocks

Who made the first clock? History books are not very clear about this, but clocks like those we use today were being built in France in the fourteenth century. They had hour and minute hands, but they could not be used to make accurate measurements of very small time intervals. The first accurate timing device that could be used in this way was invented in 1581 by an Italian medical student named Galileo. He discovered that a swinging pendulum always took the same time to come back to its starting point no matter how far it swung.

Figure 4.3
The Italian scientist, Galileo Galilei, was the first to discover the regularity of a swinging pendulum as he watched the lamps swinging in Pisa Cathedral.

You can try this out for yourself by tying a small mass to a piece of string about one metre long. This discovery led to the production of pendulum clocks and scientists had their first reliable timing device.

Galileo Galilei

Galileo was born in Italy in the year 1564. Although he began his studies as a medical student, he became a very famous mathematician, physicist and astronomer. Much of our modern science comes from his discoveries and inventions. It was as a student in 1581 that he first observed the movement of the hanging lamps in the great cathedral in Pisa as they swung in the breeze.

In a slight breeze they travelled slowly and only a small way. In a stronger breeze they travelled much faster and over a greater distance – but they always took the same time to complete the swing, no matter how far, or fast, they moved.

He used this discovery to make a swinging pendulum that could be used for measuring the pulse rates of sick people. He called it a "pulsilogium". Galileo later went on to do experiments to find out what made things move. He was also interested in the way gravity – the pull of the Earth – affected things. He invented the thermometer and built one of the earliest telescopes.

Figure 4.4
Galileo Galilei (1564–1642).

Measuring time intervals

A pendulum was set up in a laboratory. Ten pupils were asked to measure how long it took to make ten swings. (One "swing" of a pendulum is one complete to-and-fro motion. This is illustrated for you in figure 4.5.)

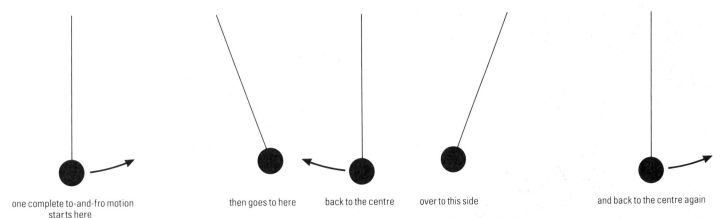

one complete to-and-fro motion starts here

then goes to here

back to the centre

over to this side

and back to the centre again

Figure 4.5
One swing of a pendulum.

They each used a stop-clock and the times they recorded are displayed on the diagram in figure 4.7.

1 Look at the diagram in figure 4.7.
a Why didn't the pupils all get the same time for ten swings of the pendulum?
b Which result was obtained by the largest number of pupils?
c How many pupils obtained that result?

Figure 4.6 (below left)
Timing the swing of a pendulum with a stop clock.

Figure 4.7 (below right)
Ten different timings of the same pendulum.

In mathematical terms, the most common result obtained when making repeated measurements of the same thing is called the *mode*.

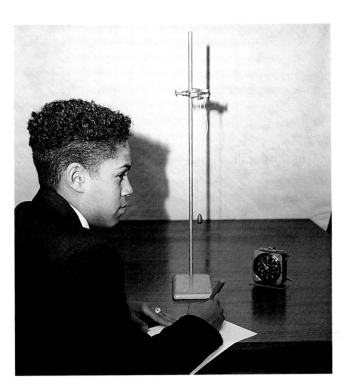

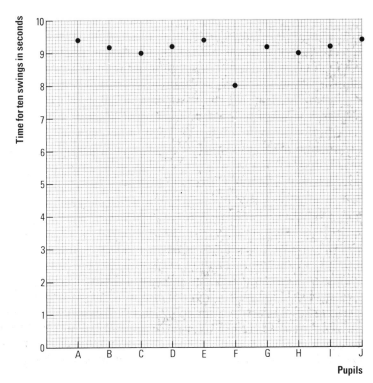

Whenever a number of measurements are made of the same thing (like the swing of this particular pendulum), there are always small differences between the measurements. This is so whether the measurements are made by one person or by several. The small differences between one measurement and another are called *errors of measurement*. The word "error" means something different in science from the way we use it in everyday speech. In everyday use, "error" means "mistake" – something we try to avoid! In science, "errors of measurement" cannot be avoided entirely. In timing a pendulum, errors of measurement can arise from the precise point at which the stop-clock is started and stopped as not everyone will do it at the same moment. They can also arise from differences between clocks (if different stop-clocks are used). You may be able to think of some more. The most **accurate** measurements are ones in which the errors are as small as you can make them.

Sometimes you find that one or two measurements differ from the mode by a much larger amount than all the others. This usually means that a **mistake** has been made. Mistakes in timing a pendulum could arise from reading the stop-clock wrongly, counting the swings wrongly, missing off half a swing at one end, and so on. Again, you can probably think of some more. Measurements that are very different from most of the others should be thought about carefully and possibly taken again.

Average times

The pupils who took part in the experiment were asked to work out the *average* time for the ten swings of the pendulum. See if you can work out the average of a set of results. Add them all up and divide by the number of results taken. In mathematical terms this is called the *mean* of the results. To work out the "average time" of the pupils' results we would carry out the following calculation.

$$\text{average time for ten swings} = \frac{\text{total of all times recorded}}{\text{number of readings taken}}$$

4c Do you think the "odd" result should have been included in the average? See what difference you get by working out the average from (i) all ten results and (ii) the nine "close" results only.
d What does this suggest you should do before working out the average of some results from an experiment?

When working out the average of some readings you must always be very careful not to make your answer look more accurate than it really is. Suppose three pupils timed ten swings of a pendulum and recorded 8.1, 8.0 and 8.3 seconds for their answers. If you work out the average of these results on your calculator you would get the answer 8.1333 ... seconds. But you can see from their measurements that the pupils' clocks would only time to one-tenth of a second. So once the average has been worked out, you should "round it" to the nearest tenth of a second as well. In this case, the average time should be written down as "8.1 seconds".

5a Why is it important to take more than one measurement when carrying out an experiment?
b How would you work out the average of several measurements?
c In an experiment the following timings, in seconds, were recorded. Work out the average time for the experiment.

5.4	5.2	5.4	5.5	5.3
5.1	5.5	5.3	5.4	5.2

6 Joan made a pendulum which took 25 seconds to make ten swings. She then timed 100 pulse beats with it and found that they took 40 complete swings.
a How long does it take for her pendulum to make one complete swing?
b How long does it take to complete 40 swings?
c What is her pulse rate per minute (that is, the number of pulse beats made in every minute)?

Modern timing devices

It was difficult to measure time accurately in ancient Greece, but now we can measure time intervals as short as one-tenthousandth ($\frac{1}{10000}$) of a second (or less) in the school laboratory. You should try to gain some practice in using timing devices. Worksheet **P4B** will help you.

7 Here is some research for you to do. Find out as much as you can to write one paragraph about each of the following.
a Sundials.
b Water clocks.
c Hour glasses.
d Analogue watches.
e Digital watches.
f Atomic clocks.

Figure 4.8
An electronic timer.

P4.2   Speed and velocity

Figure 4.9
A 3000-metre race in progress.

Today, timing runners is no longer a problem. It is easy to measure how long they took, but how can we work out how fast they were running?

We could say that they were running at a fast speed or perhaps a slow speed, but what would be fast to a long-distance runner may be slow to a sprinter. We need to have a way of comparing the speed of one runner with another. So we say:

$$\text{speed} = \frac{\text{distance travelled}}{\text{time taken}}$$

Average speed

If a marathon runner had completed 14 kilometres in the first hour of the race then we would say that his average speed was 14 kilometres per hour. We write this as 14 km/h.

The "/h" is a way of writing "per hour". It tells us that to find the speed we must **divide** the distance travelled by the time taken.

Does this mean that he must have kept running at this speed for the whole of the first hour? This would have been very difficult to do. He may, at times, have dropped his speed as low as 12 km/h when going up hills and, perhaps, accelerated to 16 km/h when coming down them. But because he covered a total of 14 kilometres in one hour we say his **average speed** was 14 km/h.

$$\text{average speed} = \frac{\text{total distance travelled}}{\text{total time taken}}$$

8 A walker travels 6 kilometres in one hour. What is his average speed in
a km/h
b m/s?

9 How far will a train travel in three minutes if its average speed is 80 km/h?

10 How long will it take a car to travel 160 km from Gloucester to London if it does so at an average speed of 60 km/h? (Give your answer in hours and minutes.)

11 An athlete's trainer kept a note of the distance she covered during each ten-minute period of a training run. The distances are given in the chart below.

Time in minutes	0 to 10	10 to 20	20 to 30	30 to 40	40 to 50
Distance in km	2.5	2.0	1.8	1.5	2.2

a Work out the athlete's average speed for each ten-minute period.
b What is the athlete's average speed for the whole of the training run?
There are two ways you could do this:
  i Add up all the average speeds you have just found and divide by five.
  ii Divide the total distance run by the total time taken.
Use both methods and compare the two results. Are they the same?

12 Look at the two lists below. Match the moving object in one column with the appropriate value of its estimated speed in the other.

Moving object		Average speed in km/h	
A	Marathon runner	1	28 800
B	Mini car	2	110
C	Satellite in orbit round Earth	3	36
D	Racing car	4	360
E	Sprinter	5	15
F	Panther	6	90

13 Estimate how long it takes for light to travel from the Sun to the Earth if the speed of light is 300 000 km/s.

Measuring average speed

We can measure the average speed of objects in the laboratory with the help of the timing devices that we used in the earlier part of the unit (Worksheet P4B). The second part of this worksheet gives you some practice in working out average speeds from the results you have already taken.

Speed or velocity?

In physics, we do not use the term "speed" very often. "Speed" may tell us how fast or slow an object is moving, but it does not tell us in which direction the object is moving. If we wish to include the direction we should use the term *velocity*.

Velocity is speed in a stated direction.

On a certain part of the M4 motorway, two cars could be travelling from Bristol to London with the same **speed** of 90 km/h and the same **velocity** of 90 km/h due east. (90 km/h is approximately 56 miles/hour.) If, however, one was heading for Bristol and the other was heading for London then, although their speeds could still be the same, their velocities would be different – one would be 90 km/h due east and the other 90 km/h due west. You must always give the **direction** when you state the velocity of an object. A moving object can have a constant speed but a changing velocity if it changes direction.

Figure 4.10
A dynamics trolley passing through a light beam. An electronic timer records how long it takes the card fixed to the trolley to pass through the beam.

We can now write:

$$\text{average } \mathbf{velocity} = \frac{\text{total distance covered in a given direction}}{\text{total time taken}}$$

The relationship between velocity (and speed) with distance and time is often quoted in symbols as:

$$v = s/t$$

where *v* is the velocity or speed of the object
  s is the distance it has travelled
  t is the time it has taken.

When an object moves with the same velocity all the time, we say that it is moving with a *uniform*, or *constant*, velocity. When the velocity of a moving object is constant, then its average velocity is equal to its actual velocity.

*The remainder of this section looks more closely at velocity as a vector quantity and asks some more questions. You could omit this and go straight on to section **P4.3**.*

Velocity is a vector quantity

The work on forces in Chapter **P1** introduces the idea that there are many quantities in physics that have a direction associated with them. Force was one such quantity. Now we can see that velocity is another.

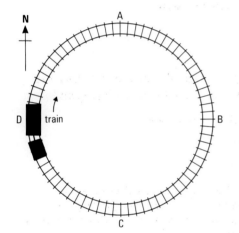

Figure 4.11
A model train running round a track.

> **14** A swimmer swims at a speed of 2 m/s in still water. If he swam in a river which had a current of 1 m/s, what would be his velocity if he
> **a** swam with the current
> **b** swam against the current?
>
> **15a** What is the difference between speed and velocity?
> **b** A model train travels at a constant speed of 3 cm/s around the track illustrated in figure 4.11. What is the train's velocity at points A, B, C and D?

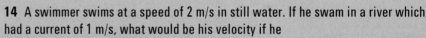

P4.3   Distance–time graphs

We can often get a better idea of how moving objects are behaving if we construct graphs of their motion rather than examine lots of numbers in a table. Putting information in this form can sometimes allow us to examine, or even compare, performances at a glance.

Consider the case of three cars, moving from a standing start, travelling as fast as they can for five seconds. The distance in metres that they travelled from the starting point was measured and is recorded in figure 4.12a.

Although figure 4.12a is quite a simple table it is not easy to compare the performance of the cars. However, if we were to draw graphs of how the cars travelled (putting distance, in metres, on the vertical axis and time, in seconds, on the horizontal axis) we could produce a more easily understood picture as shown in figure 4.12b (opposite). These graphs are called distance–time graphs.

Time, in seconds	Car P	Car Q	Car R
0	0	0	0
1	23.5	18.2	7.5
2	42.7	36.4	17.0
3	59.0	54.6	30.0
4	70.5	72.8	47.0
5	80.5	91.0	74.5

Figure 4.12a
Distances travelled by three different cars in five seconds.

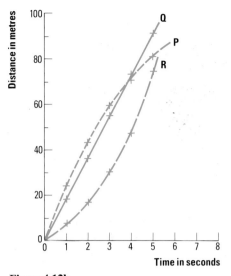

Figure 4.12b
Graph of the distances travelled by the three cars plotted against time.

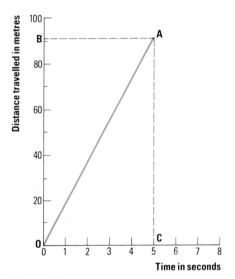

Figure 4.13
Graph of the distance travelled by car Q plotted against time.

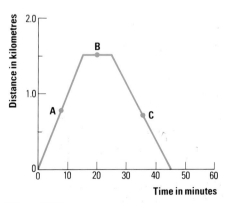

Figure 4.14
Graph showing someone's midday walk for question **17**.

Calculating the average speed

Let us examine the performance of car Q in greater detail. Look at the graph in figure 4.12b. The graph line for car Q is a straight line. If you look up the distances travelled by car Q in figure 4.12a you will see that the car covered the same distance (18.2 m) during each second of its journey. This means that car Q was travelling at a steady (or **constant**) speed. If something is travelling at a constant speed, its distance–time graph will always be a straight line.

We can easily calculate the speed of the car from the graph:

$$\text{speed} = \frac{\text{total distance covered}}{\text{total time taken}}$$

On the graph in figure 4.13 the total distance travelled by car Q is shown by OB. The total time taken by the car to travel this distance is shown by OC. So we can now write:

$$\text{speed of car Q} = \frac{\text{OB}}{\text{OC}} \text{ in scale units}$$

But OB is the same distance as AC, so we can also write

$$\text{speed} = \frac{\text{AC}}{\text{OC}}$$

You should be able to recognize that AC/OC is the slope of the line OA – in other words, the gradient of the graph line. So, on a distance–time graph:

speed is equal to the slope, or gradient, of the graph line.

Plotting a distance–time graph

*Displaying measurements in the form of graphs and then getting new data from them is an important skill in physics. Worksheet **P4C** takes you step by step through the plotting of a distance–time graph for a racing car and shows you how to work out its speed. If you feel confident about doing this, however, you can go straight on to the next questions.*

16a Draw a distance–time graph for the athlete in question 11.
b Calculate, from the graph, the average speed of the athlete in each 10-minute period.
c Calculate, from the graph, the athlete's average speed for the complete training run.
d How do your answers compare with those that you obtained originally?

17 The diagram in figure 4.14 shows a distance–time graph for a person on a midday walk. Make a copy of the graph and then work out the person's average speed at points A, B and C on the graph. Give your answers in km/h.

18 The graph lines for cars P and R in figure 4.12b are curved.
a Describe what is happening to the speed of each of these cars during the first 5 seconds of their journeys.
b How would you find the speeds of cars P and R 2 seconds after the start of their journeys?
c If you can, find the speeds of cars P and R 2 seconds after the start. (These are called the instantaneous speeds of the two cars 2 seconds after the start.)

Speed–time graphs

"Speed–time" graphs are another way of investigating the performance of a moving object. They can often give us more information than a distance–time graph. Look at the examples in figure 4.15. We can even calculate from these graphs how far the object has moved. This is taken up in section **P4.4**.

> **19** Make sketches of graphs representing the variation in speed with time for each of the following:
> **a** a sprinter running a 100 m race
> **b** a trolley running down a slope
> **c** a cyclist on a journey along a main road.

Figure 4.15
Four different sorts of speed–time graph.

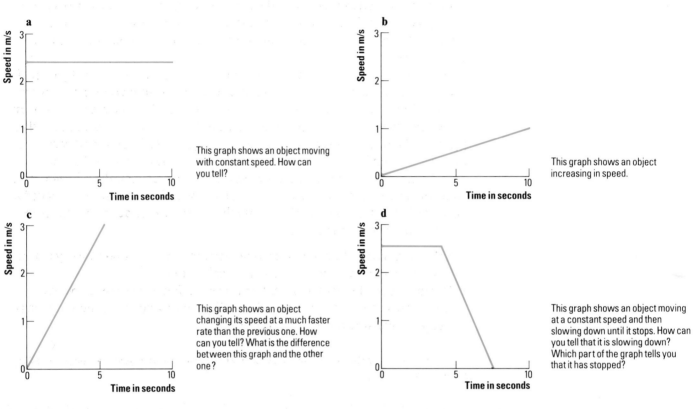

a This graph shows an object moving with constant speed. How can you tell?

b This graph shows an object increasing in speed.

c This graph shows an object changing its speed at a much faster rate than the previous one. How can you tell? What is the difference between this graph and the other one?

d This graph shows an object moving at a constant speed and then slowing down until it stops. How can you tell that it is slowing down? Which part of the graph tells you that it has stopped?

P4.4   Acceleration

When a moving object increases its speed we say that it is *accelerating*. The data in figure 4.16 shows the way the speed of an ambulance, moving in a straight line, changes with time as it moves away from a standing start.

Speed, in metres per second	0	3	6	9	12	15	18
Time, in seconds	0	1	2	3	4	5	6

Figure 4.16
The variation of speed with time for the start of an ambulance's journey.

We can see that its speed increases by 3 m/s every second. This means it has an acceleration of 3 metres per second every second. (You will often find this written as "3 m/s²".)

In physics however, the term "acceleration" is used to mean more than just change in speed; it means change in velocity.

$$\text{acceleration} = \frac{\text{change in velocity}}{\text{time taken for the change}}$$

The difference between speed and velocity was discussed in section **P4**.2. Velocity is speed in a stated direction. If the **direction** of motion of a moving object is changing we also say that it is accelerating. This means that something like a moving car can be accelerating even if its speed is not changing! You may think this a very strange use of the word "accelerate". In Chapter **P5** you will see that a force is always needed to accelerate something. Forces are needed as much to make changes in direction as they are to make changes in speed. That is why acceleration takes on this wider meaning in physics. Acceleration is a vector quantity, like velocity. It has a direction as well as a size.

In this book we shall limit ourselves to studying motion in a **straight line**. In such cases, where there is no change in direction, the acceleration of a moving body is simply the rate of change of speed with time. If a body is increasing in speed, the direction in which it accelerates is the direction in which the body is moving. If a body is slowing down (decreasing its speed) then the direction of the acceleration is opposite to that in which the body is moving. This is usually expressed by making the acceleration a negative number. Sometimes, when dealing with motion in a straight line, a negative acceleration is called a deceleration, but in this chapter we use the word "acceleration" to mean an increase **or** a decrease in speed.

- When a moving object changes its velocity at a constant rate we say that it is moving with *uniform*, or *constant*, acceleration.
- When an object moves with uniform acceleration in a straight line, its average speed is equal to the average of its *starting* and *final* speeds. This is its speed **mid-way** through its acceleration.

*If you are not sure of the meaning of the word "rate" you will find an explanation on page 133 in Chapter **P8**.*

> **20a** Calculate the average speed of the accelerating ambulance from the data in figure 4.16.
> **b** How long does it take for the ambulance to reach that speed?

Many car manufacturers try to sell their cars by telling prospective customers how fast their cars accelerate. Worksheet **P4D** asks you some questions about this.

Measuring acceleration

Earlier in this chapter you saw how electronic timing devices could be used to help measure the speed of moving objects in the laboratory. In a similar way, measurements of time and distance can be used to help find accelerations. Worksheet **P4E** gives you the details of how to do this.

Figure 4.17
Measuring the speed of a trolley as it runs down a ramp.

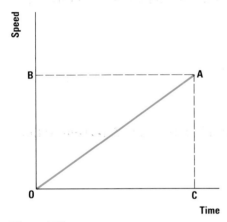

Figure 4.18
A graph of speed against time for a car
moving with a constant acceleration.

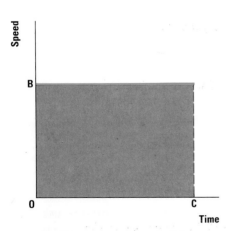

Figure 4.19
Speed–time graph for a car travelling at a
constant speed.

The speed–time graph again

Speed–time graphs were used in section **P4.3** to show how the speed of an
object was changing. Speed–time graphs can be used not only to find the
acceleration of an object whose speed is changing, but also to find the total
distance travelled.

The speed–time graph of a car moving with a constant acceleration from a
"standing start" is shown in figure 4.18. We can easily calculate the
acceleration from the graph.

$$\text{Acceleration} = \frac{\text{change in speed}}{\text{time taken to change}}$$

On the graph the change in speed is shown by OB. The total time for this
change to take place is shown by OC. The acceleration is thus given by $\dfrac{OB}{OC}$
but, as OB is the same as AC, the acceleration is also given by $\dfrac{AC}{OC}$.

But $\dfrac{AC}{OC}$ is the slope of the graph line. Thus for a speed–time graph of a
body moving in a straight line:

acceleration is equal to the slope, or gradient, of the graph line.

Calculating distance travelled from a speed–time graph

Speed–time graphs can also be used to find the distance travelled by a moving
object in a particular period of time. Figure 4.19 shows the speed–time graph
of a car travelling at constant speed. Suppose we want to know how far the
car travels in a time represented by the distance OC on the graph.

The speed of the car is equal to the length OB on the graph. The distance
travelled can be written as

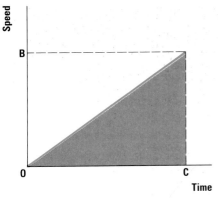

Figure 4.20
Speed–time graph for a car travelling with a constant acceleration. The area shaded under the graph line is equal to the distance the car travels in the time OC.

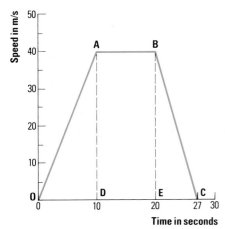

Figure 4.21
Speed–time graph of a car undergoing an acceleration and braking test.

distance travelled = average speed × time taken
= OB × OC

OB × OC is equal to the **area** of the shaded rectangle on the graph. So, for this particular speed–time graph, the total distance travelled is equal to the area under the graph. The graph in figure 4.20 shows a similar car moving with a constant **acceleration**. In this case

$$\text{the average speed} = \frac{OB+0}{2} = \frac{OB}{2}$$

$$\text{distance travelled} = \text{average speed} \times \text{time taken}$$

$$= \frac{OB}{2} \times OC$$

This is equal to the area of the shaded triangle. So again, the distance travelled is equal to the area under the graph.

The area under all graphs can be broken down into a series of triangles and rectangles. So we deduce that no matter what the shape of the graph the area under the graph is equal to the distance travelled.

A practical example

Figure 4.21 shows the way the speed of a sports car varied with time during an acceleration and braking test. Here are three problems that can be solved using the graph.

1 the acceleration during the first 10 s
2 the acceleration during the last 7 s
3 the total distance travelled.

1 Acceleration during the first 10 s

The car is accelerating from O to A. Acceleration from O to A is given by the gradient (or slope) of the line OA.

$$\text{Gradient} = \frac{AD}{OD}$$

$$= \frac{40 \, \text{m/s}}{10 \, \text{s}}$$

$$= 4 \, \text{m/s every s}$$

So, acceleration during first 10 s = 4 m/s every second.

2 Acceleration during the last 7 s

Acceleration from B to C is given by the gradient of the line BC.

$$\text{Gradient} = -\frac{BE}{EC}$$

$$= -\frac{40 \, \text{m/s}}{7 \, \text{s}}$$

$$= -5.7 \, \text{m/s every second}$$

The slope of the graph line between 20 s and 27 s is negative, so the acceleration is a negative quantity as well. This means that the car is *losing* speed. In other words it is slowing down.

3 Total distance travelled

The total distance travelled is the distance travelled while the car speeded up plus the distance travelled at constant speed plus the distance travelled while the car slowed down. We shall work out each of these distances separately.

distance travelled while speeding up
$= $ area under graph from 0 to 10 s
$= $ area of triangle OAD
$= \frac{1}{2} \times AD \times OD$
$= \frac{1}{2} \times 40\,m/s \times 10\,s$
$= 200\,m$

distance travelled at constant speed
$= AD \times DE$
$= 40\,m/s \times 10\,s$
$= 400\,m$

distance travelled while slowing down
$= \frac{1}{2} \times BE \times EC$
$= \frac{1}{2} \times 40\,m/s \times 7\,s$
$= 140\,m$

so total distance travelled
$= 200\,m + 400\,m + 140\,m$
$= 740\,m$

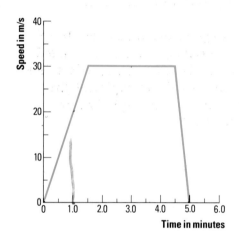

Figure 4.22
A graph of the speed of a particular train plotted against time as it travels between two stations.

21 The speed–time graph in figure 4.22 represents the motion of a train as it travels between two stations.
a During which time interval was the train
 i speeding up
 ii slowing down
 iii moving at a constant speed?
b What was the speed of the train after
 i one minute
 ii 3 minutes
 iii 4.5 minutes?
c Calculate the initial acceleration of the train.
d Calculate the final acceleration of the train.
e What is the distance between the two stations?

22 Use the following data to draw a speed–time graph for a short journey on a motorcycle.

Velocity, in m/s	0	10	20	20	20	20	0
Time, in s	0	30	60	90	120	150	180

Use the graph to calculate:
a the initial acceleration of the motorcycle
b the final acceleration of the motorcycle
c the total distance travelled by the motorcyclist.

We shall be looking again at acceleration in Chapter **P7** "Rising and falling".

Summary

The following passage summarizes the main ideas in this chapter. Copy out the passage, filling in the blanks with either a word or phrase from the list at the beginning of the passage. (There is only one word or phrase to each blank; the words are not listed in the order you will need to use them, and you may use any word more than once.)

acceleration	constant	direction	distance
gradient	scalar	string	swing
time	variable	vector	velocity

The speed of an object is found by dividing the _____ travelled in a given time by the time taken. It is not possible to measure speed unless there is an accurate method of measuring _____ intervals as well as distance.

The pendulum was used in the first accurate clocks. The important behaviour of a pendulum is that the length of time taken by each swing of a particular pendulum does not depend on the length of its _____.

To give the velocity of an object it is necessary to state not only its speed but also the _____ in which its is moving. Velocity is a _____ quantity.

The speed of an object can be found from a graph of the distance it travels plotted against the time taken. If the body is travelling at a _____ speed, the graph will be a straight line and its speed will be the _____ of that line.

If a graph of the way an object's speed changes with time is plotted, the object's _____ can be found from the gradient of the graph. The area under the graph gives the total _____ travelled.

Controlling motion
The effect of unbalanced forces

Police find body by empty house

Has 'Melsham Murderer' struck again?

Police are investigating the discovery of a body in the garden of an empty house in the middle of the busy town of Melsham. A police spokesman said that the body was that of a man, dark haired and believed to be about 25 years old.

At the time of his death the man was wearing a track-suit and running shoes. Mud stained shoes and trousers and the track-suit badge suggest that he was a member of Melsham Athletics Club out on a training run.

While death from natural causes has not been ruled out, police are working on the theory that this may be another victim of the 'Melsham Murderer'.

Figure 5.1
A newspaper report of a crime.

P5.1   What makes things move?

Have you ever asked yourself why things move? To keep a bicycle moving on a level road you have to pedal. Pedalling can be hard work. If you stop pedalling, your bicycle stops as well. But not every movement seems to take so much effort. Why do the planets keep moving around the Sun? What keeps the Earth spinning? To answer questions like these, scientists have to be a bit like detectives. Suppose you read the report shown in figure 5.1 in a newspaper.

To solve this crime (if there has in fact been a crime!) the police will need more facts. But the report suggests that already they are linking this "case" with a number of other deaths.

Figure 5.2
The police discover the body of an unknown man by a deserted house.

1 Imagine you are the detective in charge of this case.
a The death of this man may not be the result of a crime. What other causes for his death can you think of?
b Do you think it is a good idea to try to link his death with the other unsolved murders? Give one disadvantage to your investigation of doing this and one advantage.
c Assuming his death has been caused by someone else, what other evidence would you now look for?

When scientists are faced with a problem like "Why do things move?", they have to work in a similar way. They look for more evidence – something we call *making observations*. But at the same time they may have some ideas about what answer they will eventually find – just as the police detectives had some ideas about who had killed the man.

Understanding motion

When, in the story above, the body of the man was first discovered by the police, they had two possible *theories* about his death. It could have been from "natural causes" or he could have been killed by someone. Their first task was to find out if one of these theories was more likely than the other. How would you set about doing this? The easiest way is to find out if one theory **cannot** be right. For example, if they find a bullet wound in the middle of the man's chest, it is unlikely (to say the least!) that he died from natural causes.

On the other hand, this may not mean someone else killed him. Getting rid of one theory does not necessarily solve the crime.

When we think about our own experience of moving from place to place, it seems obvious that we have to make an effort to keep moving; or if we don't, something else, like a petrol engine, makes the effort for us. It is observations such as these that lead to our first theory about motion:

Figure 5.3
This person was clearly shot.

Theory 1

To keep a thing moving, it has to be pushed or pulled. Without force there is no motion.

A theory is an explanation. The trouble with "explanations" is that they often **ask** as many questions as they **answer**. For example, air molecules are continually moving. What keeps them moving? Spacecraft orbit the Earth without the use of engines. What keeps them moving? Do things moving at different speeds need different forces? Do different things moving at the same speed all need the same force?

> **2** Can you think of some more questions and problems that this theory suggests to you? Discuss this with your friends and write down your ideas.

Galileo, the Italian scientist you read about in the last chapter, found some of these questions so difficult to answer that he came up with a different theory about motion.

Theory 2

Once a thing is moving, it will stay that way. All forces do is change its motion.

What could be more different from theory 1 than that? Of course it solves some of our earlier problems. Air molecules and spacecraft keep moving because there is nothing to stop them (unless they bump into something). But now we have some other questions to answer. What stops my bicycle moving if I stop pedalling? Why do cars continue to burn petrol even if they run at a steady speed?

You probably think you know the answer to this. "Friction" is the answer, you say! But what is friction? If it is a force that slows things down, is it always the same size? Can the force of friction be reduced? If it is reduced, do moving things travel further before coming to rest? Would you expect them to?

When detectives want to understand more about how or why things happen, they will look for more clues. In the same way, scientists set up experiments in order to look for clues to increase their understanding. With more evidence it might be possible to decide between the two theories. Worksheet **P**5A gives you some help in setting up an investigation into motion to help decide between these two rival theories. You may already have your own ideas about which one is correct, just as a police detective may mutter to himself "That was no accident!" But what you have to do is to convince others that one theory is better than the other.

Figure 5.4
Investigating the effect of forces on the motion of a block of wood.

Doing experiments

Your own experiments may have convinced you that the second theory is the best. "Friction" seems a good explanation for why we have to work hard to keep things moving in our everyday world. But the first theory was accepted for many hundreds of years as being the best explanation.

Why was this? There are several reasons, but one is to do with having the equipment to do experiments. Today, police detectives are greatly helped in their investigations by forensic scientists. Forensic scientists are people who apply scientific knowledge and equipment to the solving of crimes. Blood stains can be analysed and classified. This can often help in the identification of people. (You will find out more about blood groups in your Biology book Chapter **B**8, section **B**8.7.)

In a similar way, you are helped in your investigations by having accurate timing devices to measure motion. The lack of an accurate timing device was one of the difficulties Galileo had in doing his experiments on motion.

P5.2   What stops things moving?

We started the last chapter with the story of a Greek soldier running from Marathon to Athens with the news of the Greeks' victory over the Persians. Sadly, after giving the news, he is said to have collapsed and died of exhaustion. If the Greeks had invented bicycles as well as timing devices, he might well have survived the journey by having short rests as he "free-wheeled" after building up speed.

Figure 5.5
Cycling is an easier and quicker way of getting from place to place than walking or running.

Imagine that you are "free-wheeling" on a bicycle along a level road and that you wonder how far you can travel before you have to start pedalling again. What things might be slowing you down?

3a Make a list of all the things that you can think of that are slowing your bicycle down and will eventually bring you to a halt.
b Have the things in your list anything in common?

You should realize that all the things in your list exert a *force* against the forward motion of your bicycle. The most important forces are *friction* and *air resistance* (which is itself a form of friction).

4 Have another look at your list to see how many of the things on the list can be put under one of the two headings "friction" or "air resistance".

If we could eliminate these two forces, how far do you think your bicycle would now travel? How would you then describe your speed – is it constant or changing? The answers to these questions may help us to understand something about why objects keep moving.

The force of friction

You probably investigated friction when you did experiments to decide between the rival theories of motion. Worksheet **P5B** gives some more experiments with friction that you can try.

5 Friction is a very common force. Whenever one object slides over another object friction tries to stop the movement. Think about the way solids are made up from atoms and molecules and see if you can suggest where the force of friction comes from.

6 One way of reducing friction is to lubricate the two surfaces in contact. Why does this work?

7a Why is it easy to slide on ice?
b How is friction reduced in the joints between the bones in our body?
c How do ball bearings reduce friction in the moving parts of a machine?
d What do we mean when we refer to something as streamlined?
e Some animals are streamlined. Name several that are and say why it is an advantage to them.
f How does a parachute use air resistance as it carries a person gently to earth?
g How do animals use friction in order to move?

8 Make a list of instances where friction is useful.

9 Describe what might happen in your home if all the forces of friction were eliminated.

*You can find out more about the joints in your body in Chapter **B**10 of your Biology book.*

P5.3   Aristotle, Galileo and Newton

The two theories of motion that you have investigated were not invented just to give you something to do! The first theory was the one most people accepted for hundreds of years. It has come down to us from the Greek civilization of over 2000 years ago.

The Greek ideas about motion were written down by a famous philosopher, called Aristotle, who was born in 384 B.C. Their theories of motion are almost certainly much older than this, however. The Greeks said that there must be three **different** types of motion:

● The motion of things that we push around on the surface of the Earth.
● The motion of things that fall towards the Earth.
● The motion of the Sun, Moon, and stars.

As they considered these three motions to be quite different, they could have different theories to explain each one. If you think this is a very odd thing to do, you will learn, if you do more physics, that scientists do just the same sort of thing today! The Greeks thought that an object on the Earth's surface needed a force to keep it moving over that surface.

Figure 5.6
The Greeks believed that falling motion was different from horizontal motion. When the arrow left the bow, they believed the air kept pushing it, while at the same time the arrow moved to the earth because this was its natural place.

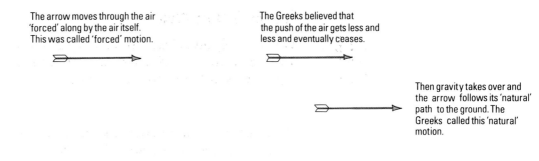

The arrow moves through the air 'forced' along by the air itself. This was called 'forced' motion.

The Greeks believed that the push of the air gets less and less and eventually ceases.

Then gravity takes over and the arrow follows its 'natural' path to the ground. The Greeks called this 'natural' motion.

The work of Galileo and Newton

A modern-day Aristotle would not need to suggest that a different type of matter is needed to explain the motion of the planets. We now have "Earth-made" rockets and satellites which behave in exactly the same way as these celestial bodies.

Thanks to the work of Galileo Galilei and Isaac Newton we can now use just one explanation to explain the behaviour of moving objects. Even though you have been investigating friction and motion yourself, it may still appear very odd to believe that if there were no forces at all, a moving object would just keep on moving. To see that this makes sense, we will look at some experiments very similar to those Galileo did.

Suppose we have a smooth track (a piece of curtain track will do) and bend it into a curve. Now we let a smooth ball run down the track (figure 5.7). The ball will run down one side and up the other. It will come to rest for a moment and then run down again.

Figure 5.7
A ball bearing rolling down a track made from curtain rail.

10a Where will the ball come to rest first? Will it be as high up the other side as it started, or higher, or lower?
b What will happen to the ball after that? Describe what happens to the ball until it finally stops moving.

Now we shall do what is called a "thought experiment". A "thought experiment" is one that we cannot actually do, but one where we can imagine what will happen. Imagine that we have a smooth, **friction-free** track that could be bent to any shape, and a small ball that would run along the track. You should imagine also that there is no air resistance.

We will now release the ball again on our imaginary track. It rolls down one side and up the other.

11a Why is this a "thought experiment"? Why, in other words, can't we do it?
b Where does the ball now come to rest before rolling down again? (Perhaps you think the ball won't stop! But remember it only has a certain amount of energy when it starts out. This energy will only take it so far up the other slope.)
c What happens to the ball as it rolls down again and then up the first side?

Figure 5.8
In this diagram the slope of the track is greater on the left than it is on the right.

Now what would happen if we gave the track on the righthand side a little less slope (figure 5.8)? How high would the ball now rise if it had been released from the same point on the lefthand side?

Figure 5.9
The slope on the right is made less steep.

Figure 5.10
Now the track on the righthand side is
horizontal. How far will the ball travel
along this righthand side of the track now?

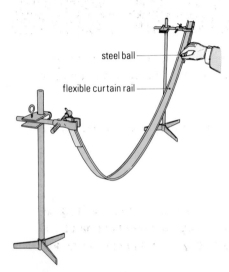

steel ball

flexible curtain rail

Figure 5.11
This is a diagram of a piece of equipment
you may see that illustrates Galileo's
experiment.

Figure 5.12
Isaac Newton (1642–1727)

Now think of the track being even less steep on the righthand side (figure 5.9). Does the same thing still happen?

Now let us imagine the righthand side of the track to be horizontal (figure 5.10). What can we say this time? How far will the ball travel?

In the last experiment, the ball does not reach the same height from which it started, so it will go on (in our thought experiment) for ever. In fact as the ball's height no longer changes, its speed will not change either.

Galileo was the first scientist to try this experiment. He used a series of highly polished wooden planks and showed that only friction prevented the ball, once it was released, from rising up the second incline to its original height. You may well see a demonstration of a modern form of Galileo's experiment (figure 5.11).

By getting others to think about these experiments he was able to convince them that an object, once in motion, would continue to move at an unchanging speed. In other words constant speed in a straight line needs no force.

This was the great breakthrough in thought which allowed Isaac Newton to produce his laws of motion.

Isaac Newton

Isaac Newton was born in Woolsthorpe, near Grantham, the same year that Galileo Galilei died. When he was a boy he did not show much interest in his studies. In his early days at Grantham grammar school he was bottom of the class! However, he became determined to beat the boy that had been bullying him. Eventually he did so, with both his fists and his brains, until at last he was top of the class.

He started his working life as a farmer, to please his mother. He soon lost interest in the job, spending much time at his favourite occupation – studying mathematics. His mother decided that farming was not the life for her son. She sent him to Cambridge University. In only a few years he had become a professor of mathematics and known to the world as an unparalleled genius. By the time he was 30 years of age he had explained how a spectrum was formed from a beam of white light and had invented a reflecting telescope.

At the age of 45 he published one of the most famous science books ever written. In this book he expanded upon the scientific breakthrough that Galileo had made and explained Aristotle's "three different types of motion".

Later in his life he was appointed Master of the Mint and was elected to Parliament twice. He was elected President of the Royal Society in 1703 and re-elected every year until his death in 1727.

It was many years after his death before his true genius was fully realized. Newton was one of the greatest theoretical scientists who have ever lived. His theories and experiments form the basis of many of our modern concepts of physics. A statue was erected in his honour in Grantham. The house in which he lived is now open to the public.

Frictionless motion

Galileo had tried to show that, in the absence of any forces, a moving object would continue to move at a constant speed. However, in the sixteenth century it was not possible to devise experiments which could eliminate such forces as friction and air resistance and so demonstrate the truth of his theories. Today, we can do experiments in which these conditions are almost

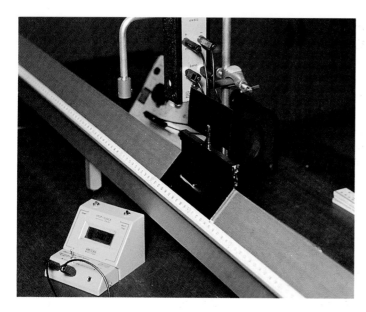

Figure 5.13 (above left)
A linear air track. Air track vehicles can move along the track with almost friction-free motion.

Figure 5.14 (above right)
Pucks on a glass table. A small piece of solid carbon dioxide is placed underneath each puck. The solid evaporates and the pucks are supported by a cushion of gas.

achieved. Figures 5.13 and 5.14 show two pieces of equipment which give almost frictionless motion. In both cases, the moving objects are "balanced" on a cushion of gas, like a hovercraft.

Worksheet P5C describes some experiments with (almost) friction-free motion that you may either be able to do yourself, or see demonstrated.

Balanced forces

The two experiments in Worksheet **P5C** should make you more willing to accept Galileo's theory that, if all the forces acting on a body are balanced, then an extra force is not necessary to keep an object moving at a constant speed.

How do we explain the forces we need to keep everyday things moving? Suppose we want to slide a table from one side of the room to the other. To do this, we have to push it. As we do so it starts to move and, very soon, it reaches a constant speed.

But Galileo's law of motion tells us that no force is needed to keep something moving at a constant speed. This means that once the table is sliding at a steady speed across the room, the force on it, in the direction the table is moving, is zero.

There are in fact **two** forces trying to change the table's movement. One is the force of friction, which is in the opposite direction to that in which the table is moving. The other force is us, pushing. If the force with which we push the table and the force of friction are equal in size, they will balance each other. The total force on the table in the direction it moves **is** zero.

There are two ways the force on a moving body can be zero. **Either** there is no force at all, **or** the forces are balanced. The table will carry on moving until we stop pushing. When that happens, only friction now acts on the table and it slows down. Once it is at rest, friction ceases to act. The table remains at rest because the forces on it are again balanced. (Some of you may have realized that the muscular push and the frictional force are not the only forces acting on the table. We have ignored the weight of the table. Are we safe in doing this? Is the weight of the table also balanced by some other force? This is something we considered in Chapter **P1**, when we were considering bridge building.)

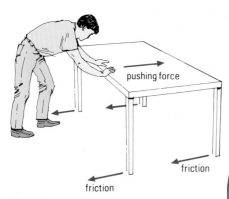

Figure 5.15
The forces acting horizontally on this table are balanced and so, once moving, the table moves forward at a steady speed. Of course the forces acting in the vertical direction are also balanced.

Changing the speed of something is not the only thing a force can do. A force is also needed if the direction of motion is changed. When all the forces acting on a moving object are balanced, it not only keeps moving at a steady speed, but also in an unchanging direction.

Isaac Newton summarized Galileo's observations in his "First Law of Motion":

Every body continues to move with a constant speed in a straight line, or remains stationary, unless there is an unbalanced force acting on it.

12 The following list describes objects moving at a constant speed in a straight line. For each object describe the forces, if any, that are acting on it, and state if these forces are balanced or unbalanced.
a A parachutist in free-fall before her parachute has opened.
b The same person after her parachute has opened.
c A hovercraft crossing the Channel.
d A man pushing a supermarket trolley full of groceries.
e A team of polar explorers pulling a sledge.
f A piece of debris in deep space.
g A paddle-boat crossing a lake.

P5.4   What if the forces are unbalanced?

So far we have only considered motion under the action of balanced forces. What if the forces become unbalanced? What effect will this have on the motion of a moving object?

It is time for another "thought" experiment! This one is about a girl on a sledge. Because it is a "thought" experiment we can make several assumptions. We can assume that each person pulling the sledge exerts an equal force, and that the sledge never reaches a steady speed.

Let us imagine that the sledge is being pulled across a snow-covered field by a boy who can just exert sufficient force to overcome the frictional force between the sledge and the ground (figure 5.16).

How would you describe the motion? By now you should realize that as the forces on the sledge are balanced, it will be moving forward at a constant speed.

What if another friend joins them and decides to help pull the sledge? The forces acting on the sledge will become unbalanced as there will now be a greater forward pull than the "holding back" effect of the frictional forces.

Figure 5.16 (below left)
A girl on a sledge being pulled across snow. The force of friction that the boy has to overcome to keep the sledge moving at a steady speed is quite low.

Figure 5.17 (below right)
When several people pull the same sledge, the girl and the sledge accelerate.

Will the sledge keep moving forward at the same constant speed as before? Newton's First Law of Motion tells us that if the forces are balanced, the sledge will keep moving forward at a constant speed. If they become unbalanced, it seems likely the sledge will increase its speed.

You should remember from the last chapter that when an object is changing its velocity we say it is *accelerating*. If an unbalanced force acts on the sledge it will accelerate. What happens if a third, and then a fourth friend helps to pull the sledge? Experience suggests that the sledge changes speed even more quickly. That is, its acceleration increases.

*You can test this out for yourself by trying the first experiment in Worksheet **P**5D. If you go on to do more work in physics you will find that there is a law linking the size of the unbalanced force and the acceleration it produces. We shall not bother with this law (called Newton's Second Law of Motion) here.*

We can summarize these ideas by saying:

> The greater the unbalanced force that acts on an object the greater the acceleration that will be produced.

The effect of mass

Have you ever helped to push a car when it would not start? You may have thought that hard enough, but what if you were asked to push something as large as a lorry? This would be a lot harder to push as there is a lot more of it!

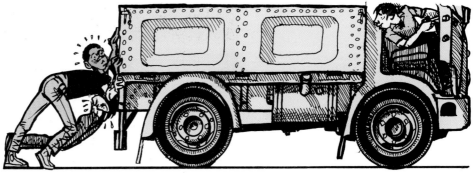

Figure 5.18
Getting a lorry to move by pushing it is a great deal harder than getting a car to move. This is partly due to more friction, but also because the lorry has a greater mass.

Figure 5.19 (below left)
A team of people pulling a sledge will cause the speed of the sledge to increase.

Figure 5.20 (below right)
A similar team pulling a sledge with two people on it will also cause the speed of the sledge to increase, but not so quickly as in figure 5.19.

We say that the lorry has a much greater *mass* than the car! Does the mass of the moving object affect the size of the acceleration that a constant force would produce on it? To answer this question we need to go back to our "thought" experiment about the sledge.

We will assume that one boy can exert just enough force on the sledge to balance the frictional forces between the sledge and the snow and keep the girl

moving with a constant velocity. We will also assume that the force of friction between the sledge and the ground stays the same throughout the experiment.

If we wish to investigate the effect of increasing the mass on the sledge then we must arrange for a large enough force to pull the sledge throughout our experiment. Let us arrange for a team of nine people, all capable of exerting the same muscular force, to pull the sledge. We have already said that the first one is pulling to balance the frictional force. The other eight will give the sledge an acceleration that is much greater than we would get with just one extra person pulling.

How would the acceleration be affected if another person climbed onto the sledge (figure 5.20)? The sledge will now be much harder to accelerate as the mass on it has increased. We can summarize these ideas by saying:

> Under the action of a constant force, the greater the mass of a body the smaller its acceleration will be.

You can test this out for yourself by doing experiment 2 on Worksheet P5D.

---

13 Copy and complete the following sentences, choosing the correct phrase from those underlined.
a If the forces moving an object forwards are increased, its acceleration <u>increases/decreases/stays the same</u>.
b If the mass of a moving object is increased, it needs <u>more/less/the same</u> force to give it the same acceleration.

14 Suppose you pull a large mass and a small mass with the same force. Which will have more acceleration? Why?

15 Find out the masses of different sorts of vehicles (for example, fire engines, cars, buses and motor bikes) and use the physics you have learned to explain why they have different accelerations from a standing start.

Mass and inertia

We know that an unbalanced force will cause an object to accelerate. We have already seen that the size of the acceleration will depend upon the mass of the object to which the force is being applied. Any object with a small mass is easy to accelerate; an object with a much larger mass is much harder to accelerate.

This "unwillingness" to start moving is the property of all objects. It is called the *inertia* of the object. The word "inertia" comes from the Latin word meaning laziness. An object of low inertia (in other words low mass) is much easier to accelerate than an object with a larger inertia (larger mass).

Perhaps you have seen the magician's trick where a tablecloth can be quickly pulled from underneath a full table. Why do the cups, saucers, plates, knives and forks remain on the table after the tablecloth has been pulled from underneath them? You might like to discuss this amongst yourselves. You could try this trick for yourself, but do not use fragile crockery if you do! "Tricks" do not always work first time.

You can investigate for yourself how difficult it is to start things moving. The experiments are described in Worksheet P5E. They should be quite fun to perform and should give you a greater understanding of what we mean by inertia.

Figure 5.21
This "trick" depends on the property of inertia. The tug of the cloth on the objects on the table causes the objects to move only a small way before the friction of the table brings them to a stop again.

16 Explain what is meant by the "inertia" of an object and describe an experiment to illustrate your meaning.

17 Explain:
a why it is dangerous to jump from the platform of a moving bus,
b why it is important to wear a seat-belt when in a moving vehicle,
c why we seem to be thrown to the outside of a car when it is going round a corner.

18 Explain, in terms of force, inertia and acceleration, why it is easier to "push-start" a car that has stalled than a lorry in a similar situation.

Summary

The pictures in figure 5.22 show a car travelling along a road on five separate occasions. For each of the pictures, say whether the driving force of the engine is greater than, equal to, or less than the combined force of air resistance and friction.

Give **two** reasons why the driving force of the engine in picture 5 will be greater than the driving force in picture 1.

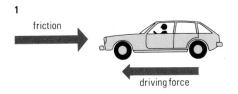
this car is travelling at a steady speed of 10 m/s

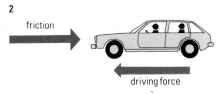
this car is also travelling at a steady speed of 10 m/s

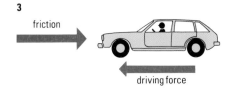
this car is slowing down (decelerating) from a speed of 10 m/s

Figure 5.22

this car is travelling at a steady speed of 20 m/s

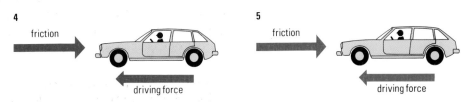
this car is accelerating from a speed of 20 m/s.

Chapter P6 Crashes and bangs
Kinetic energy and momentum

P6.1   Motorway madness

Accidents on motorways can have quite horrific consequences. These accidents and the resulting injuries are caused by rapidly moving, and often quite massive, vehicles being brought to an unexpected halt. The forces that are involved in these collisions can be very great.

Figure 6.1
This picture shows the consequence of the large forces involved when bodies of large mass collide at high speed.

Let us compare the damage that would be caused by the following vehicles if they were brought to a sudden halt in a motorway accident.

- a car travelling at 25 m/s
- an identical car travelling at 30 m/s
- a coach travelling at 25 m/s

It is quite likely that more damage will be caused by the car travelling at 30 m/s than by the one travelling at 25 m/s.

What about the coach? How much damage will this cause as it is brought to a halt? It has a much greater mass than either car. Does this matter? Will it be harder or easier to stop than the car moving at the same speed? Why is this so? How would this affect your attitude if you were the driver of the coach?

You should be able to see that the mass and velocity of the vehicles are two important factors that we must consider when we are studying safety on motorways.

P6.2 Stopping safely

The stopping distances shown in figure 6.2 have been published by the Department of Transport. They refer to a good car, with good brakes, on a dry road, driven by an alert driver. If the road is wet, or slippery, then the car will need a greater distance in which to stop. Poor brakes and worn tyres will also affect the "stopping distance".

Compare the stopping distances for cars travelling at 30 miles per hour and cars travelling at 50 miles per hour. The faster car is travelling at **less than** twice the speed of the slower car. Yet its stopping distance is **well over** twice as great.

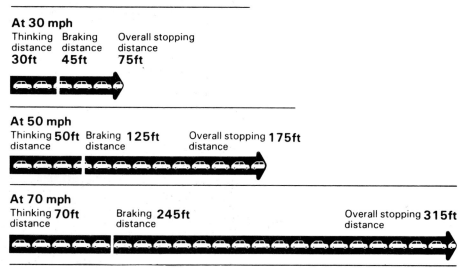

The distances shown in car lengths are based on an average family saloon

Figure 6.2
This table is published by the Department of Transport and shows the shortest stopping distances for cars travelling at different speeds.

You can see that there is a part of the chart called the "thinking distance". For each of us there is always a short time between seeing that something has to be done and actually moving our muscles to do it. It takes time for the message to go into the brain and out again to the muscles. This time is called the *reaction* time. For a normal, healthy person it is about half a second. It is less than this for young people, and more for people who are old. If a person is tired or has been taking some sorts of medicine then the reaction time can be longer than normal. It can be **much** longer for a person who has been drinking alcohol.

You can find out more about the effects of alcohol on the body in Chapter B11, section B11.10, in your Biology book.

1 Look again at the stopping distance chart. What is the thinking distance for the driver of a car travelling at 30 miles per hour?

Measure this out either in your classroom or laboratory, or outside. This is the distance a car, moving at 30 miles per hour, will travel before its driver can react to an emergency.

Drivers are always advised to leave an adequate distance between themselves and a car travelling in front of them. This distance allows for the "thinking time" of a driver between seeing the car in front brake and putting on his own brakes.

2 Drivers are usually advised to leave one car's-length separation for every 10 miles per hour of speed. Does this advice seem sensible when compared with the table in figure 6.2?

The "stopping distances" published in the Highway Code are still given for speeds in miles per hour (or "mph" as it is often shortened to). This is because in Britain "miles per hour" are still used as the unit for road speeds both in everyday speech and in making laws for road use. In the rest of Europe, the unit for road speed is the kilometre per hour (abbreviated to "km/h"). In the next question road speeds are given in km/h. It is easy to convert speeds in mph to km/h; 10 mph is the same as 16 km/h.

In this question you will also find the term "braking distance". The braking distance is the distance a car moves on **after** the brakes have been applied. So "stopping distance" = distance car moves while driver is thinking + "braking distance".

3 Here are some figures for the braking distance of a family car with just the driver travelling in it.

Speed, in km/h	40	50	60	80	100
Braking distance, in m	8	12.5	18	32	50

a Look at the distances for 40 km/h and 80 km/h. Do they suggest a pattern to you?
b Look at the distances for 50 km/h and 100 km/h. Do they suggest the same pattern? How can you tell?
c (*Harder*) Do all the figures fit the same pattern?
d These measurements were made under test conditions. The test driver was driving with good brakes and tyres, on a dry surface. What differences would you expect in normal, everyday driving? Explain your answer.

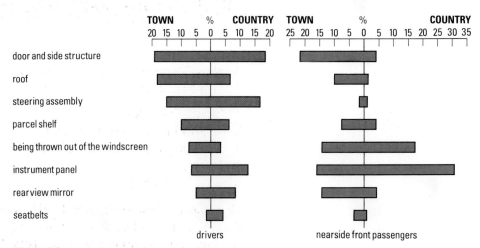

Figure 6.3
A chart showing the parts of a car and the kinds of impact that cause injuries to car drivers and their passengers.

4a Suppose the car in question **3** is now heavily loaded with passengers and luggage. How will the braking distances be affected?
b Make a commonsense guess about the new braking distances.

5 The chart in figure 6.3 shows you which parts of a car, or which kinds of impact, cause injuries to people in the front seats.
a Which impact causes the most injury to drivers?
b Which impact causes the least injury to drivers?
c Which impact causes the most injury to front seat passengers?
d Which impact causes the least injury to front seat passengers?

6 Quite often dummies are used to test certain features of a car so that these features can be made safer.
a What features do you think could be tested in this way?
b What safety equipment could be tested using dummies?
c Make a list of things you would include in a **safe** car.
Explain why you would include each item you mention.

7 Many car manufacturers now use safety as a selling point in their advertisements. Collect four or five brochures and see if the claims are sensible and worth paying for.

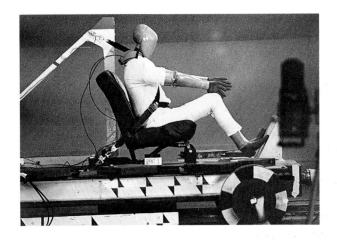

Figure 6.4 (below left)
A dummy on a test rig used for investigating the effect of road accidents.

Figure 6.5 (below right)
This picture shows the damage that can be done to a vehicle involved in a road accident.

P6.3   A road safety investigation

The best way of reducing injuries is to reduce the number of accidents that happen. There are many factors that affect the number of traffic accidents. Here is a list of them.

1 Speed of vehicles
2 Conditions of brakes and tyres
3 Road surface, including ice and snow
4 Effect of fog
5 Effect of alcohol
6 Age of driver
7 Number of vehicles on the road
8 Type of road user
9 Type of vehicle
10 City or country area

Over the next few weeks you should collect facts about some of the items in the list. You may be asked to write a report on the items you have chosen. Alternatively, a group of you could divide up the list between you. Eventually you could make a group report recommending what could be done to reduce accidents on the roads.

P6.4   Force and change in motion

Figure 6.6
This picture should remind you that an unbalanced force changes motion.

We have seen in Chapter **P5** that whenever an unbalanced force acts on an object a change will occur in its motion. It may change its speed or simply change its direction, but one thing we can be sure of is that its motion will change.

In this chapter we shall see if there is any way in which we can predict the changes of motion that take place when unbalanced forces act on an object.

In your investigation into the motion of the sledge in Chapter **P5** you may have seen that the acceleration of the sledge depended on two things:

1 the size of the unbalanced force that was acting on the sledge
2 the mass of the sledge.

Figure 6.7
a (left) A Tornado air defence jet.
b (right) A Vauxhall saloon car.

There are many things engineers have to be told before they can design an engine for vehicles as different as cars and jet aircraft. When designing the engine of a car they will need to know what its top speed is to be, how many passengers it is to hold, and so on.

8 Imagine that you have to provide some design criteria to engineers for a new car. Write down a list of things they would need to know before they could start designing the engine needed for the car.

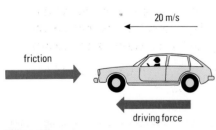

Figure 6.8
This car is travelling at a steady speed of 20 m/s. The driving force exactly balances the force of friction opposing the motion.

If you have already looked at the long problem at the end of Chapter **P8** on the top speed of a car, you will know how it is possible to work out the power needed from the engine. In Chapter **P8** we said that when a car is travelling at a steady speed all the energy transferred by the engine goes into warming up the surroundings. None is transferred to motion because the speed is not changing.

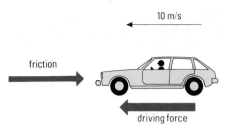

Figure 6.9
The force of friction on the same car as in figure 6.8 is smaller when the car's speed is only 10 m/s. If the driving force is unchanged, the two forces are unbalanced and the car's speed will increase.

Figure 6.10
A linear air track being used to investigate the kinetic energy of a moving vehicle.

Chapter **P**5 showed another way of looking at the same idea. When a car is travelling at a steady speed there is no unbalanced force acting on it (figure 6.8). The force provided by the wheels on the road exactly balances the combined force of friction between tyres and road and air resistance. All of the work being done each second by the engine transfers energy to the surroundings, warming them up.

But what happens if the speed of the car is changing? The force of friction acting against the car decreases as the speed decreases. At speeds below its top speed, a car engine can provide a force greater than that needed to overcome friction. There is now an unbalanced force acting on the car and the car speeds up (figure 6.9).

How quickly a car is to increase its speed may be one of the things an engineer needs to know. Remember, energy has to be transferred to increase the speed of a car.

Kinetic energy

The energy of motion is very important. We need to know as much as possible about it if we are to study the movement of cars, rockets, gas molecules and other moving things. The energy of motion which is associated with so many different moving things is usually known as *kinetic energy*.

You can use Worksheet **P**6A to investigate the way a moving trolley gains energy when its speed increases. You may also see some experiments demonstrated with an air track. Figure 6.10 shows an air track carrying an air track vehicle. This equipment can be used to find out how the kinetic energy of a moving vehicle depends on its mass and its speed.

Summarizing the results of the experiments

Experiments like the ones you may have done can measure the energy of a moving vehicle. These experiments show the following two points.

1 The kinetic energy is proportional to the mass of the vehicle. To see what this means, imagine you have two cars, one with a mass of 700 kg and the other with a mass of 1400 kg. If both are travelling at the same speed, the car with a mass of 1400 kg will have twice the energy of the 700-kg car.

9 Suppose a lorry with a mass of 3500 kg is travelling at the same speed as the 700-kg car. How much energy will it have compared with that of the car?

2 The kinetic energy is proportional to the **square** of the vehicle's speed. To see what this means, imagine that two 700-kg cars are travelling along the road, one at 15 m/s and the other at 30 m/s. Experiments show that the car travelling at 30 m/s has **four times** the energy of the car travelling at 15 m/s.

This last result is a surprising one. It means that differences in speed have more effect on kinetic energy than differences in mass.

10 A car is travelling along a road at 10 m/s. It is passed by an identical car travelling at 30 m/s. How much more kinetic energy has the faster car than the slower one?

11 A car of mass 1500 kg, travelling at 30 m/s, passes a slow-moving lorry. The lorry is moving at 15 m/s and has a mass of 4500 kg. Which vehicle has the greater kinetic energy? Explain how you worked out your answer.

The next piece of work shows you how to find the energy in joules of a moving object. You could omit this and go on to the section on car safety belts.

These experimental results only show us how the kinetic energy of something depends on its mass and its speed. But what if we wanted to know how to work out the kinetic energy of a moving object in joules? Further work (that you will do if you go on to more physics studies) shows that:

kinetic energy (in joules) $= \frac{1}{2} \times$ mass (in kg) $\times$ [speed (in m/s)]^2

We can use this to find out the energy of the 1500-kg car in question **11**.

$$\text{kinetic energy} = \frac{1}{2} \times 1500 \text{ kg} \times (30 \text{ m/s})^2$$
$$= \frac{1}{2} \times 1500 \text{ kg} \times 900 \text{ (m/s)}^2$$
$$= 675\,000 \text{ J}$$

12 Transferring energy makes things happen. In each of the following a change in speed is part of the energy transfer. In each case say where the energy is transferred **from** and where it is transferred **to**.
a throwing a cricket ball
b catching a netball
c firing a catapult
d launching a rocket into space
e accelerating away from the traffic lights in a car.

13 Calculate the kinetic energy of
a a 1-kg ball thrown at 5 m/s
b the same ball thrown at 10 m/s
c a 20-kg shot thrown at 5 m/s
d a 10-kg shot thrown at 5 m/s
e a 1000-kg ambulance travelling at 72 km/h
(Be careful about the units you use for speed in **e**. If the kinetic energy is to be in joules, then the speed must be in metres per second.)

Car safety belts

We can now try putting these facts about kinetic energy to some practical use. A car safety belt is meant to bring its wearer safely to a stop in a collision.

If a car is brought quickly to a stop, the driver and passengers will continue to move forwards with the original speed of the car until they too come to a stop. Without a safety belt, the force bringing them to a stop comes from their collision with the part of the car in front of them.

14 Passengers in a car accident are often said to be "thrown forwards". Explain whether this is an accurate description of what really happens to them.

Figure 6.11
Putting on a car safety belt.

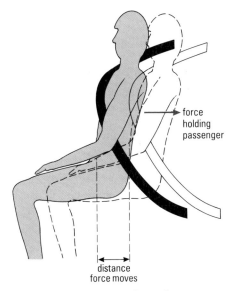

force
holding
passenger

distance
force moves

force holding passenger × distance force moves
= energy transferred from passenger in coming to rest

Figure 6.12
This picture shows how energy is
transferred to the seat belt in bringing a
moving passenger to rest in a car.

A safety belt is designed to provide the force needed to bring the wearers to rest **before** they collide dangerously with the car itself. In most cars, the driver can move forward no more than about 50 cm before coming into contact with the steering wheel. (This allows for the fact that the car itself slides forward a bit during the collision.)

If a car stops suddenly, as in a collision, the seat belt has to be able to stop the driver moving within a space of 50 cm (or 0.5 m). In coming to rest, the kinetic energy of the driver is transferred to the seat belt by stretching it.

The next few paragraphs show how we can find out how strong a seat belt needs to be. You could omit this if you wanted to and go on to the next section. However, the "working out" is quite easy as long as you take some figures "on trust". There is a question at the end (question 15) which lets you check the figures used.

The speed of a car at the moment of collision is usually much less than the speed at which the car was originally travelling. Let us suppose that a car is travelling at 10 m/s on impact (that's a speed of just about 22 miles per hour). The mass of an average person is about 65 kg.

A 65-kg person travelling at 10 m/s has a kinetic energy of about 3000 J.

This is the energy that must be transferred to the seat belt. The energy transferred to the seat belt can be worked out by multiplying the average force it exerts by the distance it stretches.

It is this energy which must equal 3000 J:

energy transferred = force × distance moved

In this case, 3000 J = average force of belt (in newtons) × 0.5 m

so, average force $= \dfrac{3000 \, \text{J}}{0.5 \, \text{m}}$

$= 6000 \, \text{N}$

The pull of the Earth on a 65-kg person is about 650 N. So 6000 N is nearly ten times the wearer's weight! You can see that seat belts have to be quite strong.

15 If you know how to work out kinetic energy in joules, check for yourself that a 65-kg person travelling at 10 m/s has an energy of about 3000 J.

16 Car seat belts have to be able to cope with many different conditions that might be met in an accident. For each of the following situations, say whether the force a seat belt would have to exert would be smaller than, larger than, or the same as the value worked out above.
a The seat belt was used by someone whose mass was only 40 kg.
b The seat belt had to restrain someone in a car which had a speed on collision of 20 m/s.
c The seat belt restrained someone in a collision in which the car itself slid forward 1 m before coming to rest.

17 Car seat belts are meant to restrain car occupants in the event of an accident. This means that someone wearing a seat belt may not be able to move around easily on the seat.
To overcome this problem, manufacturers now fit *inertia-reel* belts. These allow someone wearing such a belt to move easily. But in an accident, the belt holds the wearer fast. Find out how inertia-reel safety belts work.

18 Imagine you are a scientist working for a manufacturer of seat belts. You are given some new material which might make good seat belts. Plan an investigation to see whether it would be suitable for this purpose. You should think of all the properties such a material should have – there may be more than those mentioned above.

(*Harder!*) How strong should it be? Remember we have only worked out the average force needed to stop someone travelling at 10 m/s in an accident. The seat belt material may act like a spring, applying more and more force as it stretches.

Braking distances

In question **3** you looked for a pattern linking braking distances with the speed of a car. You probably noticed that a doubling of the car's speed increased the braking distance by **four** times. Let's see if we can understand this pattern in terms of the energy transfers taking place during braking.

You have already seen from experiments on the energy of a moving vehicle that doubling a car's speed means increasing its energy four times. When a car is brought to rest using its brakes, the driver exerts a **braking force** throughout the entire braking distance. This transfers the kinetic energy of the moving car to the surroundings, warming them up slightly.

The energy transferred to the surroundings is equal to the braking force × braking distance. This must equal the kinetic energy the car loses:

kinetic energy transferred = braking force × braking distance

Suppose that one car is travelling at 10 m/s while an identical one is travelling at 20 m/s. The kinetic energy of the faster car is four times that of the slower car. To bring them both to rest, the braking force × braking distance of the faster car is also four times that of the slower car.

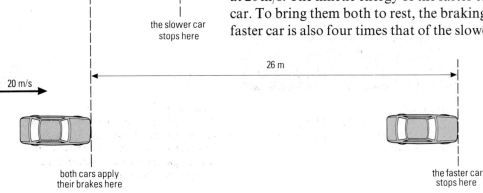

Figure 6.13
The two cars in this diagram are identical and are being brought to rest by the same braking force. The faster car travels much further than the slower one in coming to rest.

If the two cars exert the **same** braking force, then the faster car will travel four times the distance in coming to rest. This is exactly the pattern you should have found in question **3**. You should be able to see from these results why the braking distance goes up four times when the car speed only doubles.

19 Use the same argument to compare the braking distances of two identical cars, one travelling at 10 m/s and the other at 30 m/s.

20 The braking distance for a car travelling at 40 km/h on a dry day is 8 m. Suppose that on a wet day a car's braking force is only one-quarter its value on a dry day.
a What effect will this have on its braking distance?
b At what speed should a driver travel, to have a braking distance of 8 m on such a day?

Figure 6.14
Guns in fighting ships of two hundred years ago would roll back on their wheels when the gun was fired.

P6.5 Recoil

If you have ever fired an air-rifle, you will know how the rifle "kicks" back against your shoulder when it is fired. This backwards kick is called *recoil*. It means the same as when the word "recoil" is used in an everyday sense. If you read in a book that, "The boy recoiled at the sight of the snake", you know it means that he stepped, or moved backwards, away from it. When a gun recoils it moves backwards, away from the direction in which the bullet is fired. Figure 6.14 shows the sort of guns used on board ship in Nelson's time. Great care had to be taken when firing guns like these. As the cannon ball left the barrel, the gun would roll back on its wheels – and anyone who got in its way did so at his own peril!

Figure 6.15 shows several similar examples. You may all have experienced stepping off a small boat as in figure 6.15a. As you try to step ashore, the boat moves backwards, away from the shore. Unless you are very careful, this can lead to you getting wet.

Figure 6.15a
A person stepping ashore from a boat. The boat will move backwards as the person steps forward.

Figure 6.15b
A rotating water sprinkler. The sprinkler spins in the opposite direction to the water leaving the nozzles.

Figure 6.15c
The launch of the space shuttle *Discovery*, which is taken into orbit using rockets. The rockets are driven upwards by the exhaust gases which leave the motors in the opposite direction.

The lawn sprinkler in figure 6.15b spins in one direction as water is forced out in the other. In space, rockets fly by driving hot gas from their engines. The gases move one way: the rocket moves the other. Rockets and jet engines both use recoil to propel themselves through the air. Worksheet **P6B** gives you some experiments to do to investigate recoil.

*Try to do experiment 1 in Worksheet **P6B** before continuing with this chapter.*

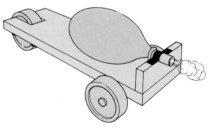

Figure 6.16
A trolley with an inflated balloon attached will move forward in the same way as a rocket.

Figure 6.16 shows you the trolley and balloon you used in experiment 1 in Worksheet **P6B**. You probably found out that the speed the trolley moved along the runway depended on its mass. The bigger the mass, the slower the speed. The speed of recoil seems to depend on the size of the mass recoiling.

*Now try experiment 2 in Worksheet **P6B**.*

OBSERVE

Is there a "law of recoil"?

In experiment 2, you were able to investigate recoil in more detail by allowing two trolleys to "explode" apart. Using the photo-electric timers you first used in Chapter **P4**, you will have measured the speed with which both trolleys recoiled from each other. For each "explosion" you were asked to work out the number you got by multiplying each trolley's mass by its speed. Were you able to find a "pattern" in the results?

It is possible to repeat these experiments using the air track shown in figure 6.17. The force pushing the air track vehicles apart comes from magnets fixed on their ends.

Figure 6.17
A linear air track in use in an investigation into recoil. Great care has to be taken to ensure that both vehicles are released simultaneously. Think how you could do that.

21a Why is an air track likely to give more accurate results than the trolleys?
b If you have already done some work on magnets, explain how the magnets on the ends of the vehicles must be arranged if the vehicles are to "explode" apart.

When an experiment like this was done using an air track, the result shown in figure 6.18 was obtained.

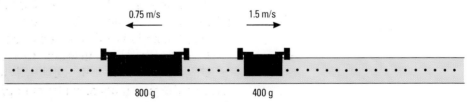

Figure 6.18
The recoil of two air track vehicles. The recoil force is provided by a pair of magnets mounted on the ends of the air track vehicles.

22a Multiply the mass of each vehicle by its speed.
b What can you say about the results?

Did your experiments give the same result? We can summarize these results with the following statement. When two bodies, starting at rest, "explode" apart from each other:

[mass of body 1] × [speed of body 1] = [mass of body 2] × [speed of body 2]

We could call this result the "law of recoil".

How fast does an air-gun recoil when fired?

We can now put this law to some use to work out the speed of recoil of an air-gun when it is fired. Figure 6.19 shows a pellet being fired from an air-gun. Suppose that a pellet has a mass of 1 g and travels at a speed of 200 m/s.

mass of pellet × speed of pellet = 1 g × 200 m/s

The "law of recoil" which we have found experimentally tells us that the mass of the gun × speed of recoil of gun must **also** equal 200 g m/s (say this as "two hundred gram metres per second").

Suppose the gun has a mass of 1000 g. Then we can say that:

$$1000 \text{ g} \times \text{speed of gun recoil} = 200 \text{ g m/s}$$

$$\text{So speed of recoil} = \frac{200 \text{ g m/s}}{1000 \text{ g}}$$

$$= 0.2 \text{ m/s}.$$

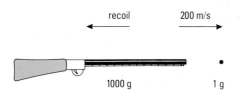

Figure 6.19
A pellet fired from an air-gun. The air-gun recoils backwards as the pellet leaves the barrel.

23 Now try the "recoil" law out for yourself. Suppose you leap ashore from a 100-kg boat (perhaps a silly thing to do!). You leap off at 2 m/s. If your mass is 50 kg, at what speed does the boat move away from the shore?

Introducing momentum

Multiplying the mass of a moving body by its speed gives something that is clearly important in understanding and using recoil. But it is not just the speed that is important. When two bodies recoil apart, they travel in opposite directions.

Speed in a particular direction is called velocity (see Chapter **P4**). So perhaps it is mass × velocity that we ought to be considering.

The mass × the velocity of a moving body is called its *momentum*. The size of the body's momentum is its mass × its speed, while the direction is the same as the body's direction of motion.

Using the word "momentum" we can now describe the recoiling air-gun in another way. The "law of recoil" tells us that the momentum of the bullet, as it leaves the gun, is equal in size but opposite in direction to the momentum of the recoiling air-gun.

24 Explain, as if talking to a friend, why this new statement of the "law of recoil" is the same as the previous one.

25 What is the name given to quantities which have direction as well as size?

Jet aircraft and rockets

Rockets travel by expelling burning gas from engines at their rear. The ignited fuel turns to a high pressure gas which is expelled at high velocity from the rocket engines. The rocket gains momentum equal in size to the momentum of the gases expelled from the engine, but in the opposite direction (figure 6.20). But this is not a single "explosion" like a bullet from a gun: the rocket engine continues to expel gases after the rocket has begun moving. The rocket continues to gain momentum equal in size to that of the hot gases coming from the engine. So instead of travelling at a steady speed, the rocket gets faster and faster all the time the engines are operating.

You can experiment with this idea yourself. Try blowing up a balloon and releasing it without tying up the end (figure 6.21). The balloon flies round the room. As the air rushes out of the balloon, forced to do so by its own high pressure, it gains momentum. So the balloon flies off the opposite way, gaining more and more momentum until the air in the balloon is exhausted.

You may see some more spectacular demonstrations of this. The carbon dioxide "rocket" in figure 6.22 is a small cylinder of compressed carbon dioxide gas attached to a wire. When a hole is punched in the end, the "rocket" travels at great speed along the wire.

The "water rocket" in figure 6.23 contains water and air. The pressure of the air inside the "rocket" is increased using a pump. When it is released the rocket sails up into the air, gaining considerable height, before falling back to earth. The pressure of the air drives out the water, which gains momentum. So the rocket itself gains an equal amount of momentum in the opposite direction.

Figure 6.20
The launch of *Apollo 13* from the Kennedy Space Centre, Florida. This was one of the spacecraft that was sent to the Moon.

Figure 6.21
Releasing a blown-up balloon.

Figure 6.22
A model "rocket" made from a capsule containing compressed carbon dioxide gas.

26 Explain why the carbon dioxide rocket gains much more speed than the blown-up balloon.

27 If the water is left out of the "water rocket" but the air is pumped up to the same pressure as normal, the performance of the rocket is most disappointing! (Try it and see.) Why should the rocket launch be so unsuccessful if there is only air at high pressure inside the rocket?

28 (*Hard!*) You might think from question **27** that the more water you put in a water rocket the better. Try it! You will be disappointed. If the rocket contains a lot of water, the "launch" is as disappointing as if it contained too little water. Explain why a water rocket, almost filled with water, will not perform well.

The next section looks a little more closely into how rockets work, and makes a few calculations. Read and try to understand as much as you can, but it is not essential to understand the calculations.

How do rockets work?

Water rockets work by throwing out a large mass of water from the back. The water gains momentum as it is pushed out of the back of the rocket. The rest of the rocket therefore gains momentum equal in size to that gained by the water, but in the opposite direction. This is all any rocket does; it ejects material in a steady stream in one direction and the rest of the rocket moves forward in the other (figure 6.24).

How fast the rocket eventually travels depends on how much momentum its motors give to the material that it throws out backwards. This can create a problem for rocket engineers. For a spacecraft to be able to go into Earth-orbit it has to gain a very high speed – about 8000 m/s. (That is a speed of approximately 5 miles **per second**.) Suppose the spacecraft has a mass of 10 000 kg (that is, 10 tonnes). The spacecraft has to gain a momentum of 10 000 kg × 8000 m/s – a total of 80 000 000 kg m/s. This means that the gases expelled by the rocket motors have to gain at least as much momentum as that, but in the opposite direction.

Figure 6.23
A "water rocket". This home-made version is made from a plastic lemonade bottle.

Gases carry off momentum in this direction…   and the rocket gains an equal momentum in this direction.

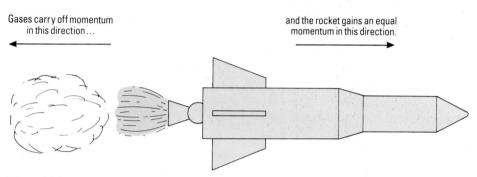

Figure 6.24
How a rocket moves forward.

The speed with which the gases leave the rocket motors depends on the energy transferred to them by the chemical reaction of burning. (Burning is discussed in Chapter C13.) The highest speed with which gases can leave the rocket motor is about 4000 m/s – this is only about half the speed the space-craft has to reach. The momentum gained by the expelled gases is found by multiplying their mass (which is the mass of the fuel burned) by their speed.

momentum of the gases = mass of fuel (in kg) × 4000 m/s

The momentum gained by the spacecraft (plus the rocket and rocket motors) is the same as this, but in the opposite direction. As we have already seen, the size of this momentum needed by the spacecraft is 80 000 000 kg m/s. (Note the way the answer has been rounded to two significant figures. This is because none of the data on which it was based has been given to more than two significant figures.) We can write:

mass of fuel (in kg) × 4000 m/s = 80 000 000 kg m/s

$$\text{so, mass of fuel} = \frac{80\,000\,000 \text{ kg m/s}}{4000 \text{ m/s}}$$

$$= 20\,000 \text{ kg}$$

This means the spacecraft must carry a mass of fuel almost double its own mass. And the problem is worse than this!

- The fuel is carried in containers which are useless once empty. But they have taken up some of the valuable forward momentum.
- The unused fuel also takes up valuable forward momentum before it is itself used.

To allow for this, the engineers have to pack in more fuel – which means bigger containers and more fuel to carry. This means even more wasted momentum. In fact, even using the multi-stage rockets described below, as much as 90 per cent of the launch-mass of a rocket may be fuel.

Multi-stage rockets

One way to overcome the problem of mass of fuel is to make the rocket up from several rockets linked together (figure 6.25). When one rocket has done its job it is discarded, leaving the others to carry the spacecraft further up into the sky, at ever greater speed.

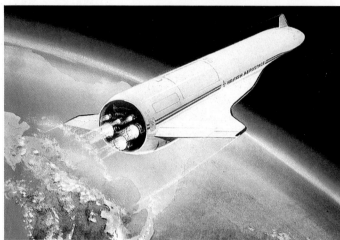

Figure 6.25 (above left)
The Vostock spaceship with its carrier rocket. Rockets such as these consist of several different rockets fixed together. Each rocket is discarded as soon as its fuel has been used up.

Figure 6.26 (above right)
This is a model of a new air-breathing rocket that may one day make space travel much cheaper than it is today.

Rockets have to be able to operate in empty space. This means that they have to carry their fuel **and** the oxygen needed to burn it. So far no rockets have been able to use oxygen in the atmosphere to burn the fuel because they cannot collect it quickly enough. Some rockets, such as that shown in figure 6.26, are being developed which can make use of atmospheric oxygen for some of their journey from the Earth.

Such space vehicles will be much cheaper to operate than present day rockets. The energy transferred from fuel by each Apollo rocket has been worked out. It would take all the water falling over Niagara Falls four years to transfer the same amount of energy. Many people ask whether we can really afford to use so much energy to put rockets into space.

Jet aircraft

Jet engines propel aircraft through the sky in the same way that rocket motors are able to propel rockets and their spacecraft. However, jet engines have no need to carry their own oxygen.

Figure 6.27
Jet aircraft use engines that operate in much the same way as rocket motors. This is a picture of the BAe 146 made by British Aerospace for airports with short runways. It is also designed to be much quieter than earlier jet aircraft.

Jet engines burn a form of petroleum very like domestic paraffin. Air is taken in at the front of the engine and is driven into a smaller space by a pump called a *compressor*. The fuel is burned with this air in special *combustion chambers*.

The burning of the fuel in air causes the gases to get hot and their pressure rises. They rush out at the back of the combustion chambers through a hole (called a *vent*) in the back of the engines. On the way out they drive a *turbine*.

The turbine acts like a windmill and drives the compressor pumps at the front of the engine. Figure 6.28b shows how a jet engine works.

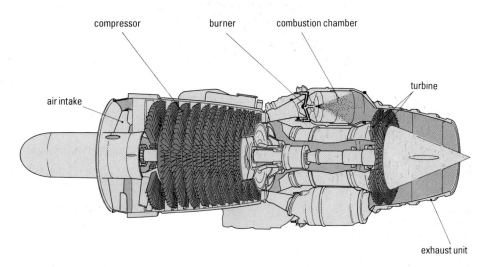

Figure 6.28a (above left)
The "insides" of a jet engine.

Figure 6.28b (above right)
A sectional diagram of a jet engine.

The high temperatures and pressures inside jet engines mean that great care has to be taken in the selection of materials used to build them. You can find out more about the properties of metals in Chapter C7 of your Chemistry book.

The next questions ask you some things about rockets and jet engines. You will be able to answer some of them by re-reading the last section carefully.

29 Some high speed jet aircraft can fly at 2000 km/h. How much faster is a spacecraft in Earth-orbit moving?

30 In describing the problems of launching spacecraft it was stated that the gases expelled by the rocket motors would have to gain **at least** as much momentum as the spacecraft gains. In fact they have to gain quite a lot more. Can you think of some reasons why the gases have to gain more momentum than the spacecraft needs? (Some of the reasons are given earlier in the chapter.)

31 What is the function of each of the following parts of a jet engine:
a compressor,
b combustion chamber,
c turbine?

32 Why have jet engines no need to carry their own oxygen?

33 Why do you think the air is compressed in a jet engine before it passes into the combustion chamber?

34 To drive a jet airliner through the air, hot gases have to be expelled at high speeds by the engines. It is this high speed that makes the engines so noisy. Recently new engines have been developed called turbo-fan engines. These giant engines are able to take in much bigger quantities of air every second.

34a What are the advantages of using turbo-fan engines on passenger aircraft?
b What are the advantages and disadvantages of building airports well away from urban areas?

35 Do you think there is any likelihood of rockets being used for passenger transport?

36 Draw a "time-line" extending from 1960 to the present day. Mark on this line all of the important things that have happened in the exploration of space and the dates on which they happened. You should include such things as the first manned spaceflight, the first walk in space, the first landing on the Moon, etc.

The final section of this chapter shows how momentum can be used more widely. It considers what happens when one moving body collides with another and shows that here too the idea of momentum is a useful one.

It is not essential to the rest of the course that you work through this section. Do it if you have time and have understood the earlier work.

P6.6   Can we make more use of the idea of momentum?

If one car collides with another, it is most unlikely that they both come immediately to rest. In collisions, speeds are shared (figure 6.29). But what determines the speeds objects have after making a collision? The question is an important one, because many changes of motion take place in this way. Here are some examples.

- The pressure a gas exerts on the walls of its container is due to the collisions of the gas molecules with the walls.
- The path of a tennis ball is changed by a collision between the ball and a tennis racket. Similar collisions will change the paths of footballs, cricket balls, golf balls, and so on.

At the beginning of this chapter we looked at the differences in damage occurring in road accidents when vehicles of different masses travelling at different speeds were involved. It became clear that mass and velocity might both be important.

Worksheet **P6C** describes experiments you can do to investigate what happens when one moving vehicle collides with another.

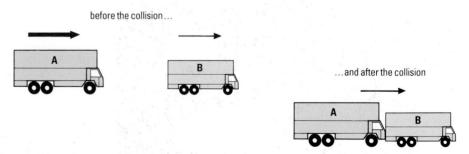

Figure 6.29
If toy lorry A collides with toy lorry B, then, after the collision, lorry A moves more slowly than before, but lorry B moves more quickly.

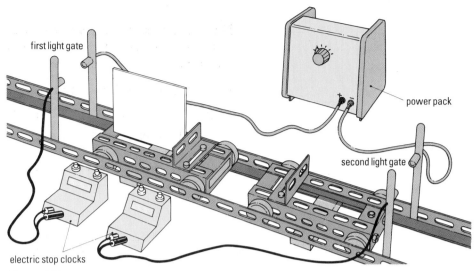

first light gate

power pack

second light gate

electric stop clocks

Figure 6.30
Using dynamics trolleys to investigate collisions.

In each case you should set one or more trolleys into motion and allow them to collide with and stick to some more trolleys which are at rest before the collision. (The worksheet explains how you can do this.) For each experiment you do, you should work out the momentum of the trolleys **before** the collision takes place and the momentum of the trolleys **after** the collision takes place.

Some more collisions

The air track, which you may have seen demonstrated earlier, can be used to experiment with collisions as well. In this case there is little friction between the colliding vehicles and the track.

Do the colliding air track vehicles behave in the same way as the trolleys did in your investigation? The next question gives you some results found in a set of experiments. In each case, one of the air track vehicles was at rest before the collision, and so had no momentum. After the collision, the two vehicles stuck together and moved in the same direction.

Figure 6.31 (below left)
An air track can also be used to investigate collisions.

Figure 6.32 (below right)
This diagram shows two air track vehicles before and after a collision. The needle and plasticine ensure that the two vehicles stick to each other after the collision.

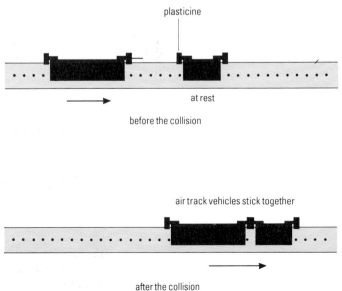

plasticine

at rest

before the collision

air track vehicles stick together

after the collision

Before collision

Mass of first vehicle in kg	Speed of first vehicle in ms⁻¹	Mass of second vehicle in kg	Speed of second vehicle in ms⁻¹	Total momentum before collision
0.4	0.29	0.4	0	
0.4	0.25	0.2	0	
0.4	0.23	0.8	0	
0.8	0.17	0.4	0	
1.2	0.24	0.4	0	

After collision

Mass of first vehicle in kg	Speed of first vehicle in ms⁻¹	Mass of second vehicle in kg	Speed of second vehicle in ms⁻¹	Total momentum after collision
0.4	0.15	0.4	0.15	
0.4	0.16	0.2	0.16	
0.4	0.077	0.8	0.077	
0.8	0.11	0.4	0.11	
1.2	0.18	0.4	0.18	

Figure 6.33
Speeds and masses of air track vehicles that have collided and stuck together in the way shown in figure 6.32

37 Figure 6.33 shows the speeds and masses of air track vehicles before and after collision. In each case the second vehicle was at rest before the collision.
a Copy out and complete the table to show the total momentum of both vehicles before the collision and the total momentum after the collision.
b How would you summarize the results of this experiment?

These experiments show how useful the idea of momentum is. In this case, one of the vehicles has some momentum before it collides with the other. The momentum is shared between the two vehicles by the collision. The total momentum before the collision is the same as the total momentum afterwards. If you do more work in physics you will find that this is an important and general law.

The next question goes back to road accidents and gives you an opportunity to try out the "momentum idea" on two colliding road vehicles.

38 A Mini car of mass 600 kg is involved in a collision with a lorry of mass 2400 kg and they move on together after the collision. Assuming the unlikely fact that neither driver uses his brakes, what is the velocity of both after the collision if
a the car, moving at 10 m/s, collides with the stationary lorry
b the lorry, moving at 10 m/s, collides with the stationary car?
c Use your results to suggest what differences might possibly be expected in the attitudes of car drivers and lorry drivers to the possibility of having accidents.
d Do you think one sort of driver has a greater responsibility than the other?
e Would there be any difference to your answers if one of the vehicles was a passenger-carrying coach with a mass at least as great as that of the lorry?

The conservation of momentum

Whenever moving objects are in collision, the outcome can always be expressed in the way you have found in your own experiments. The total momentum of all the colliding objects is the same after the collision as it was before. In other words the total momentum is unchanged by the collision. It is always like this and there are no exceptions we know of.

The rule is referred to as the *conservation of momentum*. It is a very important one, for there are few rules in physics that seem to have no exceptions! What does the word "conservation" mean? We often use the word, nowadays, to describe our efforts in protecting certain animals or plants which are in danger of becoming extinct. We try to prevent their number declining.

When we use the term "conservation' in physics it means rather more than this. When we say that momentum is conserved we mean that it **stays the same**. It neither increases, nor decreases. You must be careful how you use this law. Momentum will be transferred from any moving object to another if the two objects interact by exerting forces on one another. If you do not remember this it might appear that in some cases momentum is **not** conserved when you expect it to be.

Here is an experiment you can do for yourself. Stand on a large trolley or on roller skates near a wall and push on it with your hands (figure 6.34). What happens? Of course you move away from the wall.

Figure 6.34
A girl on roller skates pushing herself away from a wall.

Figure 6.35
Two girls on roller skates pushing against each other.

Now try the same experiment, but this time push against someone else on roller skates or a trolley. What happens when you push now? You both move away from each other. In figure 6.35, Susan moves due to the force with which Sharon pushes on her; Sharon moves due to the force of Susan pushing on her. Susan and Sharon both change their motion because they *interact* with each other. When we say two objects interact we mean that they are influencing each other's behaviour. We use the same word in biology when we talk of an organism *interacting* with its environment. We mean that the environment and the organism are influencing each other in some way.

If any pair of objects interact in any way, they may transfer momentum. That is why you have to be careful when using the law of conservation of momentum.

Suppose a trolley is given a push and moves across a table. As it does so, it slows up and comes to rest. What has happened to the momentum of the trolley? It hasn't vanished. If you think it has, then you may have forgotten that there is a lot of friction between the trolley and the table. This friction allows the trolley to **interact** with the table and so with the Earth on which the table rests. The momentum the trolley had is transferred to the Earth via friction. The momentum of the Earth is increased by the amount the trolley has lost.

39 Why is it impossible to measure the momentum the Earth must have gained?

40 When the gun described in section **P6.5** recoils, it carries momentum equal and opposite to the momentum gained by the cannon ball. Soon the gun comes to rest. What has happened to the gun's momentum?

Summary

Here are the beginnings of five sentences, labelled **A** to **E**. Below these you will find the ends of five sentences labelled **a** to **e**. Match up each beginning with the correct ending.

A Multiplying the mass of a vehicle by its velocity . . .
B Braking force, but not kinetic energy . . .
C The kinetic energy of a car as well as the braking distance . . .
D Stopping distance of a car . . .
E The momentum of a moving vehicle . . .

a . . . equals thinking distance + braking distance.
b . . . increases four times if its speed is doubled.
c . . . gives the vehicle's momentum.
d . . . doubles if its speed is doubled.
e . . . is measured in newtons.

41 Give two everyday examples of each of the following: kinetic energy, recoil and energy transfer.

Chapter P7 Rising and falling
The force of gravity

P7.1 What goes up must come down?

One of the striking things about events in physics is their *predictability*. When we say something is predictable we mean that we can say what will happen before the event. Fortune tellers try to predict the future. Anyone who "does the football pools" tries to predict the results of next week's football matches. You may have tried to predict things yourself – like tomorrow's weather or the result of your last science test! If you have, you will know how easy it is to be wrong.

Most things in life are unpredictable. We would find life very dull if things were always predictable. If someone behaves in a way we thought they would, someone else may well say "Typical!" in a scornful voice. But the things physics deals with seem to be very predictable. For example, the Sun rises every morning. We can predict with certainty not only that it will rise tomorrow morning, but also the exact time it will do so.

Many other things happen in the world around us with such certainty that everyone seems to know of them as a "Law" of physics. One of these has to do with gravity. Almost everyone has heard the phrase, "What goes up must come down", but does it?

1 Perhaps you have a friend who has not heard the phrase, "What goes up must come down". Write down in a few lines what you think the phrase means. (The best way to do this is to give one or two examples.)

Figure 7.1 (below left)
Playing with a ball in a playground.

Figure 7.2 (below right)
A rocket leaving its launch pad. Will this come down again in the same way as a ball thrown upwards?

Look at figures 7.1 and 7.2. The people playing with the ball are only too aware of the fact that "What goes up, comes down". If the ball is thrown

straight up into the air, it will eventually stop rising and fall down again. The harder it is thrown upwards, the further it will rise. But it always comes down.

But what about the rocket in figure 7.2? Does that **always** come back? You may well know that a successful rocket launch depends on the rocket **not** coming back – at least not all of it.

In this chapter we shall try to find out a bit more about falling. In doing so, you may also understand why it **is** possible to send rockets into space so that they don't fall back to Earth.

Falling

When a ball is thrown into the air, it rises upwards from the Earth at first, and then falls back. To study what is happening it is best to separate out the "falling" bit from the "rising" bit. So we shall start by looking at what happens to a ball that is held up above the ground and then dropped.

Try it for yourself. Just before you let the ball go, it is at rest in your hand. After you let it go it falls downwards and hits the ground at some speed.

When we studied forces in the last chapter, we found that if an unbalanced force acted on something, it *accelerates*. When a ball falls to the ground it accelerates downwards. It must have done, since it was at rest in your hand, yet it was moving when it hit the ground.

This, on its own, tells us that an unbalanced force was acting on the ball once it left your hand. This force we call the pull of the Earth, or *gravity*.

*The next section goes into a bit more detail about the force of gravity, and introduces the idea of a **force field**. It is not essential to work through this section in order to understand the rest of the chapter. You could omit it and go on to section **P**7.2 "Finding out more about gravity".*

Force fields

Science fiction writers love force fields. These are always invisible barriers put up in space, which for some reason or other the enemy cannot get through.

Forces that people can feel yet cannot see always seem to be mysterious. The forces that you met in Chapter **P**5 were all pushes and pulls. You could usually see who or what was exerting the force. Think of the desk being pushed across the room (figure 7.5). You could see the boy pushing the desk. The desk moved because he pushed against it. We cannot see the friction acting on the desk, but we know it acts where the desk touches the floor.

We feel we can understand friction by thinking about the atoms and molecules rubbing against each other. All these forces, whether we can see

ball is at rest here

the ball accelerates as it falls

ball is moving downwards here

Figure 7.3
A ball accelerating downwards under the force of gravity.

Figure 7.4
Force fields are often used in science fiction cartoons as an invisible defence against the enemy.

Figure 7.5
Some of the forces acting on a table as it is pushed along the floor.

them or not, are *contact* forces. The pushing or pulling is being done through the contact between atoms and molecules.

But gravity is more mysterious. The ball is affected by the pull of the Earth when it is above the Earth. There is no contact between the Earth and the ball – yet there is a force on the ball, and it accelerates towards the Earth if you let it go.

> **2** Describe another force that acts in the same way. That is, a force which is caused by something some distance away from the object affected.

Apart from gravity, you will meet two other similar forces in other chapters in this book. The first is the force between *electric charges* (Chapter **P**16). Two charges exert forces on each other, despite the fact that they are separated from each other – in other words, not in contact. The second is magnetism (Chapter **P**18). Magnets can exert forces on each other. Again, they do not have to be in contact to do this.

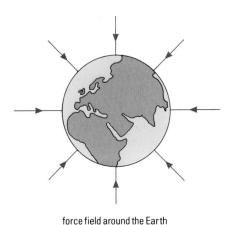
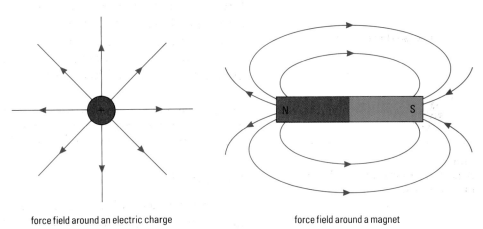

force field around the Earth   force field around an electric charge   force field around a magnet

Figure 7.6
Drawings showing the force fields surrounding the Earth, an electric charge and a bar magnet.

The regions around the Earth, around an electric charge or around a magnet where the influence of the forces can be felt are all called force fields. So, in fact, force fields are not a bit of science fiction at all!

If the force you are studying is gravity, the force field is called a *gravitational field*.

> **3** What do you think are the special names given to the force fields round an electric charge and a magnet?

P7.2   Finding out more about gravity

It takes less than a second for a ball to reach the ground from a height of one metre. This is a very short space of time in which to find out how the speed of the ball changes. To do this we shall use *multiflash photography*.

When you take a photograph of something (your house, for example) a lens makes an image of the house on a film in the back of the camera.

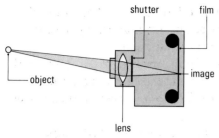

Figure 7.7
How a camera forms an image on a film.

Figure 7.8
A picture of a moving object taken outdoors.

Figure 7.9
A photograph taken indoors using flash. The flash of light lasts so short a time that it "freezes" most movements.

The light forming this image is let into the camera for only a fraction of a second, through the camera shutter (figure 7.7). Because the light only falls on the film for a brief instant, you can quite successfully photograph moving objects, such as the cat jumping over a stream in figure 7.8. The shutter "freezes" the movement because it is open for such a brief time.

If you drop a ball and press the shutter of your camera at the right moment you could get a picture of the falling ball on the film.

If you want to take a photograph of your pet indoors, you would have to use "flash". A photographic flash light gives a very brief flash of light. This light bounces off your pet and makes an image on the film.

When you take a picture in this way, you can hold the camera shutter open for quite a long time and still not get a blurred picture of something that is moving. The light making the picture comes from the flash which lasts a very short time indeed. If you take photographs yourself, you may have noticed how "sharp" flash pictures are. That's because the flash lasts such a short time that even your unsteady hands do not get a chance to ruin the picture!

Now for multiflash photography: to take multiflash photographs we use a *stroboscope* containing a lamp that flashes on and off. Have you been in a disco where lights that flash on and off are used? Have you noticed what other people look like under such lights? They appear to be moving in jerky, puppet-like movements.

4 Write a few lines explaining why people seem to be moving with jerky movements if you watch them under flashing lights.

In the stroboscope there is a lamp which flashes on and off in a regular way. You can alter the rate at which it flashes. For this experiment, it is usual to set it flashing at a rate of 20 flashes every second. The time each flash lasts is very short indeed – much less than one-thousandth of a second.

Figure 7.10 shows how we can arrange a camera and a stroboscope to photograph a falling ball. The room in which the photograph is taken must be quite dark. The shutter on the camera is opened and held open. The flashing light is switched on and someone drops the ball in front of the camera. As soon as the ball hits the ground, the camera shutter is closed.

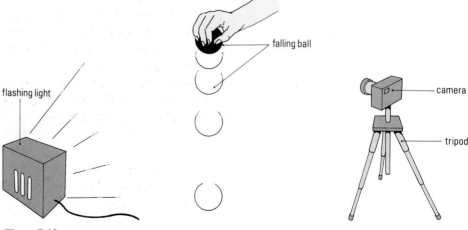

Figure 7.10
Taking a multiflash photograph.

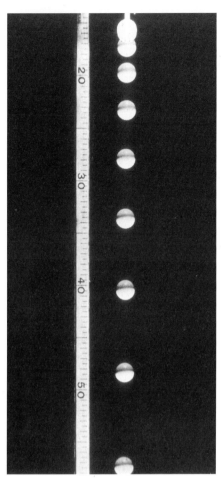

Figure 7.11
A multiflash photograph of a falling ball.
(The length scale is marked in centimetres.)

It is best to have something soft for the ball to fall on to, so that it doesn't bounce up. The bouncing effect can produce some very interesting pictures, but they would confuse what we want to see at the moment.

When the film from the camera is developed and a print is made, it will look something like the one shown in figure 7.11. You will notice that a length scale has been photographed at the same time. This is so we can measure how far the ball falls.

Each picture of the ball was taken by the camera when one flash of the stroboscope lit up the ball.

5 The stoboscope used in taking this photograph produced 30 light flashes each second.
a How far apart in time is each photograph of the ball from the next one?
b From the look of the photograph, would you say that the ball is falling at a steady speed, slowing down, or speeding up? Give a reason for your answer.

The next question shows you how we can get even more information about the force of gravity from the photograph. This question is harder than the last one, but it shows that the force of gravity is a constant, unchanging force near the surface of the Earth. If you are prepared to accept this fact, you can miss out this question and go on to the next section which shows you how to make your own record of a falling mass.

6 You can find out much more about the motion of the falling ball by plotting a graph of its speed against time. Here is how to draw the graph.
a Draw some graph axes on graph paper so that you can plot speed on the y-axis (vertical axis) and time on the x-axis (horizontal axis). Your time axis should be divided up into $\frac{1}{30}$ second intervals. Your speed axis will have to allow you to plot the largest speed of the falling ball.
b Select two neighbouring images of the ball near the top of the photograph and measure the distance between them. Use the scale on the photograph to do this.
  You now know how far the ball fell in $\frac{1}{30}$ second near the top of its fall.
c Work out the average speed of fall of the ball at this point.
d Plot this speed on your graph at the point where time equals 0 seconds. This is the starting point of your graph.
e Now measure the distance the ball fell during the next $\frac{1}{30}$ second. Work out the average speed of the ball.
  This is the average speed of the ball during the next $\frac{1}{30}$ second. You should find that it is slightly greater than the last one, because the ball is accelerating.
f Plot this speed on your graph at the point where time equals $\frac{1}{30}$ second as this is the speed of the ball $\frac{1}{30}$ second later.
g Carry on doing this for the rest of the images of the ball on the photograph.
h What sort of graph do you get? What does it tell you about the way the ball falls?
i Work out the acceleration of the ball.

If you did all the work on Worksheet **P5C**, you may realize that the fact that the acceleration of the ball is constant means that a constant and unchanging force is acting on the ball as it falls.

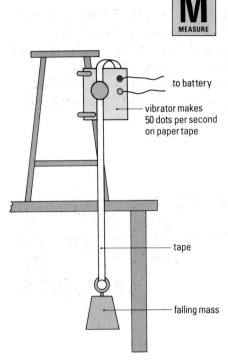

Figure 7.12
Using a ticker-tape vibrator to investigate the motion of a falling object.

Making your own record of a falling object

You may see a stroboscopic photograph taken in the laboratory, but there is an easier way of making your own record of a falling object. Instead of photographing it, we attach a strip of paper to it. As the mass falls it drags the paper underneath a vibrating strip of metal (figure 7.12).

The vibrator makes a dot on the paper strip 50 times a second. So the dots on the paper strip will be spaced apart in just the same way as the pictures of the ball on the multiflash photograph. You can try this experiment for yourself using Worksheet **P7A**.

P7.3   Air resistance

You may wonder whether the experiment you did using a strip of paper tape is quite fair. Surely the paper tape will drag back on the falling mass and try to slow it up? Gravity is not then the only force on the falling mass.

You would be quite right to be concerned about this. But the mass you were told to use was carefully chosen so that the friction of the paper tape was a much smaller force than the pull of the Earth's gravity.

Now look at the multiflash photograph in figure 7.13. The photograph shows a model parachutist falling. If you measure the distance between each image you will find it does not change.

7a If the space between one image and the next on the photograph is always the same, what can you say about the speed of the parachutist's fall?
b (Do this part if you have already done question **6**.)
Plot a graph of the distance the parachutist falls against time. What sort of graph do you get? Does this also show that the parachutist falls with constant speed?
c Think back to the work you did in Chapter **P5**. What can you say about the force on something that moves at an unchanging speed? Are the forces balanced or unbalanced?

Figure 7.13
A multiflash photograph of an object falling at a steady speed.

We saw in Chapter **P5** that something that moves with a steady speed has either no force acting on it, or the forces are balanced.

If the forces on the parachutist are balanced then there has to be another force on him which just balances the pull of gravity. This force is referred to as *air resistance* (figure 7.14).

If you have tried some of the questions in Chapter **P8**, on why cars have a top speed, you will know that the size of air resistance increases with speed. When things fall they gain speed. If they are falling through air, the air resistance gets greater and greater. Eventually the force of air resistance is as big as the pull of gravity and the falling object does not increase its speed any more – it just carries on falling at that steady speed.

We did not have to worry about air resistance in the multiflash photograph of the falling ball because a small smooth steel ball was used to do the experiment. The ball did not gain much speed in the experiment. So the air resistance was much smaller than the pull of gravity and we could ignore it.

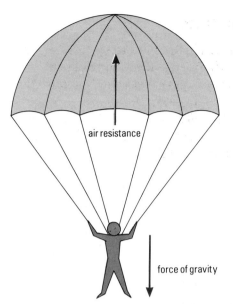

Figure 7.14
The forces acting on a parachutist falling
to the ground.

Figure 7.16
What may happen if you fall without a
parachute!

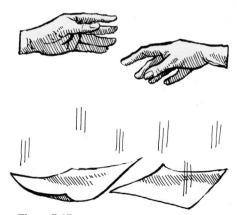

Figure 7.17
Letting two sheets of paper fall through
the air.

How do sky-divers land safely?

Figure 7.15 shows a picture of some sky-divers in "free-fall". They do not use
parachutes until they are within a thousand metres or so of the ground.

Parachutes slow the fall of the sky-divers and they land safely. You have all
probably seen cartoons like the one in figure 7.16 where someone has
supposedly fallen from a great height without a parachute and left a hole in
the ground. In cartoons they often seem to climb out of the hole – but not so
in real life.

Figure 7.15
Sky-divers in "free-fall".

Speed is not the only thing to affect air resistance. Try the following
experiment.

1 Take two identical sheets of paper. Hold them both out horizontally
and then let them go (figure 7.17).
2 Do this several times. Do both sheets reach the ground together?
3 Now screw one of the sheets up into a ball. Drop the paper ball
alongside the other sheet of paper. Which reaches the ground first?

As the two pieces of paper were identical, the pull of the Earth on each of
them was the same. But suppose air resistance balanced out the pull of the
Earth on the spread-out sheet when it had gained only a small speed. Once the
forces on the paper are balanced, the paper sheet will stop accelerating. The
paper sheet will continue to fall, but at this small, steady speed.

At this same, small speed, air resistance on the ball of paper is smaller than
that on the spread-out sheet. The pull of the Earth on the paper ball is still
greater than the air resistance on it. So the paper ball will continue to gain
speed. In the small distance to the ground, it is probably still speeding up as it
hits the ground. Now try this experiment.

1 Take another two identical sheets of paper. Hold one horizontally as
before and the other vertically. (It is important when doing this
experiment to make sure the vertical sheet really is vertical when you let it
go. Hold it loosely and do not bend over the edge you are holding.)
2 Let them both go. Repeat your experiment several times. Which piece
of paper reaches the ground first? Explain your observations.

If the screwed-up ball of paper is dropped from a greater height, it too reaches a steady speed as soon as air resistance balances the pull of gravity. But by then it will be moving much faster than the spread-out sheet of paper.

Sky-divers in free-fall also reach a steady speed when they fall. Air resistance balances the pull of gravity when they have reached a speed of about 50 m/s. That is a speed of over 100 miles per hour. It takes 20 seconds to fall 1000 metres at this speed. Then their parachutes open. At this speed of fall, the air resistance on the opened parachute is far greater than the pull of gravity.

8a If air resistance (which acts upwards) is greater than the pull of gravity downwards, what happens to the falling sky-divers?
b What happens then to the size of the air resistance?
c When the air resistance has become equal again to the pull of gravity, what happens to the sky-divers?

Eventually the sky-divers land safely with their parachutes at a speed of no more than 9 m/s.

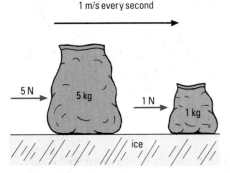

Figure 7.18
Both bags of potatoes will accelerate at 1 m/s every second on a frictionless surface.

Figure 7.19
Large mass means large weight!

P7.4   Mass and weight

A shopping bag full of the week's groceries weighs more than one containing just a few things for the next meal. When we describe something as being heavy, we mean we have to use a great deal of muscular force to lift it. Its heaviness is due to gravity – the pull of the Earth. The force we have to overcome to lift something is called its *weight*.

All objects have weight – whether we can lift them or not! A lorry is heavier than a motor car, although we do not have the strength to lift either. In Chapter **P**5 we explored briefly another property of objects that we called their *mass*. We said that a lorry had a greater mass than a car because it was harder to get it moving. Another name for mass is *inertia*. It is the quantity that determines how much force we shall have to use to give an object a particular acceleration. We measure mass in kilograms (kg).

A force of one newton gives a mass of one kilogram an acceleration of one metre per second, every second.

Suppose we have two bags of potatoes, one with a mass of 5 kg and the other with a mass of 1 kg. The 5-kg bag will need a force five times greater than the 1-kg bag if the two are to be given the same acceleration (figure 7.18). But we know from experience that the bigger the mass of something, the greater is its weight. This is so well known that we usually **weigh** things in order to find their **mass**.

Another thing we can say about the two bags of potatoes is that the 5-kg bag contains five times as much "potato" as the 1-kg bag. If the 1-kg bag will do for two meals, then the 5-kg bag will do for ten. Isaac Newton used this fact when he described mass as the "quantity of matter" in a body.

People usually talk about mass and weight as though they are the same thing. They say, "Did you see that massive man? I wonder how much he weighs?"

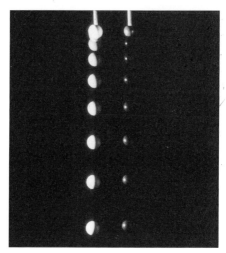

Figure 7.20
A multiflash photograph of two balls of different mass falling side by side.

They say this because they know that the bigger the pull of the Earth's gravity on the man, the bigger will be his mass (that is, how much there is of him!). Jockeys and boxers both have "weigh-ins" before a race or a contest. In both cases, however, the thing which is being measured is their mass. This is the thing which affects the speed of the horse or the power of the boxer.

Because mass and weight are so closely linked it does not usually matter if we use the words in a mixed-up way. But occasionally it does matter, and if you are not clear about the difference between the two words, then you can become very confused. **Mass** is what determines the acceleration of an object under an unbalanced force; **weight** is a force due to the action of gravity.

Do heavy objects fall faster than light ones?

We know that the weight of something with a large mass is greater than the weight of a small mass. So the Earth's gravity pulls down on the larger mass with a greater force than it pulls on the smaller one. Does this mean that it will fall faster?

Try an experiment for yourself. Take a large stone and a small one and drop them side by side. Which reaches the floor first? Were the results what you expected?

There is a story about Galileo investigating falling objects. He was supposed to have dropped a small iron ball and a large cannon ball from the top of the famous Leaning Tower of Pisa, in Italy. The crowd who were gathered at the bottom of the tower were supposed to be amazed that the two objects reached the ground at practically the same time.

9 Why do you think the crowd were amazed? What do you think they expected to happen?

Figure 7.20 shows you another multiflash photograph. This is a photograph of two balls of different mass, falling to the ground.

10a What can you say about the acceleration of the two objects?
b Polished steel balls are often used in experiments such as this. Why?

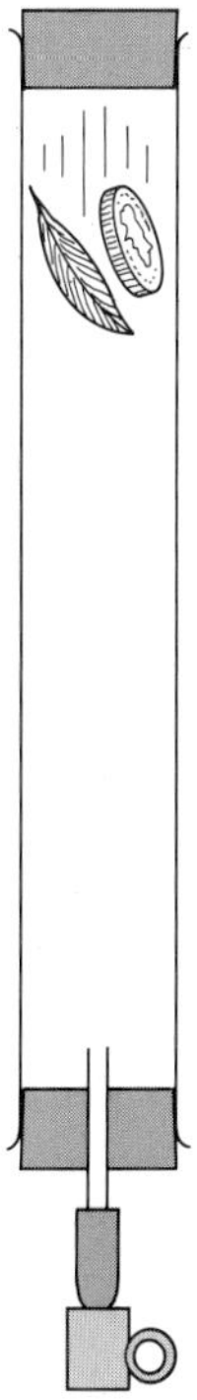

Of course our everyday experience is that different things fall at quite different rates. We saw, in the last section, that air resistance was the reason for this.

Isaac Newton is said to have been the first scientist to show that everything falls with the same acceleration, if air resistance is removed. To do this he is said to have put a guinea (a gold coin) and a feather in a tube and to have pumped out all the air.

If you try dropping a coin and a feather together in air, you will certainly find that the coin reaches the ground far sooner than the feather. But if the two start to fall together in a tube with **no** air inside, then they do indeed reach the bottom of the tube together. You may see such an experiment demonstrated.

the coin and the feather fall together down the tube

all the air has been pumped out of the tube

Figure 7.21
The guinea and feather experiment. This experiment, reputed to have first been suggested by Isaac Newton, shows that a coin and a feather will fall with the same acceleration in a vacuum.

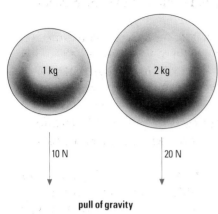

pull of gravity

Figure 7.22
The larger mass is pulled downwards with twice the force acting on the smaller one. As the larger one has twice the mass, it falls with the same acceleration as the smaller one.

Why are such experiments important?

It may seem strange to you that scientists should take such trouble over these experiments. The people who watched Galileo's experiment must have expected the heavier mass to reach the ground first. That experiment, and all others since, show that if gravity is the only force to act then **everything**, no matter what its mass, falls with the same acceleration.

In Chapter **P5**, we looked at the effect on the acceleration of a sledge when two girls rode on it rather than one. We saw that mass affected acceleration. Suppose that Galileo had dropped two objects, one with twice the mass of the other. We have already said that the object with the larger mass will have twice the pull of gravity acting on it. The heavier object will fall at the same rate as the lighter one. This is because the greater force has an equally greater mass to accelerate. Differences in the mass of objects are exactly compensated for by an increase in the pull of gravity.

Experiments show that the force of gravity on the Earth's surface is very nearly 10 N/kg. This means that every kilogram of mass is attracted towards the Earth with a force of 10 newtons.

11 Work out the force that the Earth exerts on the following masses.
a 10 kg
b 30 kg
c 100 kg
d 150 kg.

12 The Moon has a gravitational force field as well, but it is much weaker than the Earth's. On the Moon's surface the force of gravity is approximately 1.6 N/kg. How large are the forces that the Moon exerts on each of the masses in question **11**?

The next section goes a bit further into how we can send rockets into space so that they do not fall back. It is not necessary to work through this section in order to understand the rest of the work of this course, and you could omit it if you wish.

P7.5   Why what goes up does *not* always come down!

Javelin throwers can probably throw something a greater distance than anyone else. To throw a javelin a great distance, the thrower has to launch it with as much speed as possible. The faster it is thrown, the further it travels. It is the pull of gravity which eventually brings the javelin back to Earth.

Large guns on battleships can fire shells distances of many miles. The shells travel so far that the ship which launched them cannot be seen from the point where the shell lands. The curvature of the Earth hides the ship from view (figure 7.24).

Even so, gravity eventually pulls the shell back to Earth. But what if a "super gun" was invented which could fire shells any distance you liked?

This was an idea that fascinated Isaac Newton. In one of his books he drew a diagram to show a "super gun" on the top of a high mountain. He asked where shells (or cannon balls in his day!) would land if they were fired with

Figure 7.23
To throw the javelin a great distance it has to be launched at a great speed.

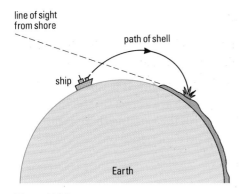

Figure 7.24
Ships can fire shells with such velocity that they land below the horizon.

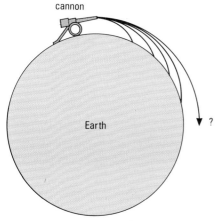

Figure 7.25
Isaac Newton suggested that if a cannon ball could be fired with enough speed it could travel all the way round the Earth without ever coming down.

ever-increasing speeds. Figure 7.25 is a diagram similar to the one Newton himself drew.

Gravity pulls the cannon ball back to the Earth, once it has been fired. But the Earth is curved and the surface "falls away" from the cannon ball. Newton pointed out that if the cannon ball was fired fast enough it might fall towards the Earth no faster than the Earth's surface was curving away underneath the cannon ball.

What would happen then? It seems that the cannon ball would "go into orbit". It would never come back to the Earth's surface, but carry on going round it.

Gravity is still acting on the cannon ball, but instead of bringing it back to the Earth, it is keeping it in orbit above the Earth's surface. Newton had invented the world's first satellite launcher. He could even work out how fast the cannon ball would have to travel to go into orbit round the Earth. The speed necessary is about 8000 m/s. (This speed is referred to on page 109 of Chapter **P6**, where we look at the fuel required to put satellites into orbit.) It was not until the late 1950s that it was possible to give an object this speed.

This is how artificial satellites are launched by rockets. The rockets start off slowly, carrying with them the huge mass of fuel necessary to achieve this great speed. As the fuel is used up and the mass drops, the rockets travel faster and faster. At the same time their direction of travel is changed until they are travelling parallel with the Earth's surface.

Then, about 100 km above the Earth's surface and about 4 minutes after "blast off", the final piece of the rocket reaches the speed of 8000 m/s needed to keep the satellite in orbit. The satellite is released and orbits the Earth.

"Weightlessness"

When astronauts are orbiting the Earth they are said to be "weightless". You may have seen films made inside satellites showing the astronauts (and any loose objects) floating around inside the satellite (figure 7.26).

Figure 7.26
Astronauts in orbit round the Earth. Gravity still pulls them towards the Earth, but because of their speed round the Earth, they never get any closer to it. There is no force on them counterbalancing gravity (as there would be if they were on the surface of the Earth), so they feel as though they are "weightless".

Of course the astronauts are not really weightless – the Earth still pulls on them. As a result, the astronauts and all the objects inside the satellite are "falling" round the Earth along with the satellite itself.

You saw in Chapter **P1** that anything at rest on the Earth's surface has a force acting on it that counterbalances the object's weight. It is this counterbalancing force that we experience when we are at rest on the Earth's surface. Since the astronauts are falling freely with the satellite there is no counterbalancing force on them and they have no experience of their own weight.

Communications satellites

Satellites carry their own small motors so that "ground control" can make small adjustments to their orbit. Communications satellites have to be pushed even further from the Earth, using their own motors. Finally, 42 300 km out from the centre of the Earth, they are travelling at the right speed to stay over the same point of the Earth's surface, spinning in space. They can then be used to "bounce" radio and TV waves around the world. This is how an event such as the soccer World Cup can be held in Italy and the matches seen "live" everywhere on the Earth's surface.

Figure 7.27
Modern communications satellites are launched from rockets at such a speed that they continuously orbit the Earth.

13 Satellites in orbit close to the Earth's surface do eventually come out of orbit and burn-up in the Earth's atmosphere. Suggest a reason why such satellites do not stay up indefinitely.

Summary

Imagine a friend has just read this chapter. Your friend has found each of the words listed below in the chapter and asks you what they mean.

Write one or two sentences giving your own explanation of each of them. Remember your friend has read the chapter, so he or she will not be helped if all you do is repeat what is in it!

Here are the words:

predictability	**force field**
multiflash photography	**air resistance**
weight	**communications satellites**

Topic **P**3   **Energy**

What this topic is about

The idea of energy is helpful to us in explaining and understanding many things in the world around us. We are having to learn to put limited energy resources to good use and to get energy to the places where it is needed – to industry and transport; to homes and hospitals; in fact to almost everywhere. Energy is studied as a part of physics, but it is not just about the things with which physics is concerned. You will almost certainly have used the idea of energy in science before. Energy plays a part in growing, moving and feeding – in every living process. It plays a part in every sort of chemical change. It is involved in the Earth's continual process of change. It is an idea that is useful everywhere in science. Before starting work on this topic it will help you to read and think about the things you ought already to understand about energy.

What you should already know about energy

Energy makes things happen. Having a lot of energy is a bit like having money – it can get things done. But just **having** money does not make things happen. It is when you hand it over to someone else that something useful happens. Energy is like this. If a mass is to be lifted or a lamp lit, energy has to be transferred. Energy is transferred when plants grow and when chemical reactions take place.

There are many ways that energy can go from one thing to another. The Sun transfers energy to growing plants through light radiation (see Biology, Chapter **B**3). An engine can transfer energy to a flywheel through a shaft. These are both ways in which energy can be transferred.

All kinds of different things have energy they can give away to something else. You can usually tell when energy is being transferred because you can see something happening. You can often **guess** that energy may be transferred before this actually happens. This is because you learn from experience what to expect.

Sometimes, when energy is transferred, a force acts which moves something. Lifting a shopping bag up on to a table needs energy to be transferred in this way. This gives us one way of measuring the energy transferred. In force-moving jobs we say that:

energy transferred = force × distance moved in the direction the force acts

This quantity is called *work*. The word "work" has this special meaning in science. It always means that a force is moving something. We do not always mean this when we use the word "work" in everyday speech. The unit in which work or energy is measured is the newton-metre. This unit is given the special name *joule* (symbol, J).

We believe that energy never vanishes. Again this is like money. When you buy something, the money you pay goes into someone else's pocket. If you tried to keep track of the original money you paid, you would probably find that it got broken down into smaller and smaller amounts. Energy is the same. Whenever it is transferred, some of it always gets spread out to the surroundings.

Once energy has become spread out in this way, we cannot make use of it again.

What you should already know about transferring energy from hot to cold

Hot objects, like a central heating radiator, warm up their surroundings. They can do this in three ways. The first is called *conduction*. Energy flows along a hot poker to your hand by conduction (figure 1).

The second method is called *convection*. Convection can take place in gases or liquids. Milk in a saucepan close to the flame on a gas stove gets hot. In getting hot, it expands and becomes less dense. As a result it rises away from the hot bottom of the pan and colder liquid takes its place (figure 2). In this way the energy of the hot milk at the bottom of the pan is distributed throughout the liquid.

The third method is called *radiation*. All hot objects can radiate energy in the form of a wave, but it is not until they are very hot that they transfer much energy to their surroundings in this way (figure 3). Black objects are better radiators than shiny ones, which is why tea pots which we wish to keep warm are often made of shiny metal.

Figure 1

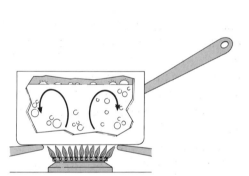

Figure 2

Figure 3

Figure 4

Some revision questions

1 Suppose a lamp is switched on for an hour and then switched off. It looks as though the energy transferred to the lamp is lost. Since the energy has not vanished, what else happened to it? Can the energy be used again?

2 A crane is lifting a heavy load of machinery when the cable breaks and the load falls to the ground. Has the energy already given to the load been lost? What has happened to it? Can the energy be re-used to repair the damage?

3 You lift a heavy case weighing 300 N from the floor on to your bed, 60 cm above the floor. What is the **least** energy you would have to transfer to the case? Why might you have to transfer more energy than this?

4a Which picture in figure 4 shows the football with the most kinetic energy?
b In which picture is the energy shared out amongst the nearby particles?
c In which picture is there most energy stored chemically?

Chapter P8

Machines and engines
An investigation into power and efficiency

Look at the pictures of the athlete and the car (figure 8.1). The car is not an ordinary one and the athlete has run faster over some distances than many other athletes. What sort of words would you use to describe them and compare them with an ordinary car and an ordinary person? One of the words you might use would be "powerful". What do we mean when we say the car has a powerful engine or the athlete has a powerful physique?

Figure 8.1
An athlete and a racing car. You might use the word "powerful" when referring to either.

Different people do not always mean the same thing when they use the word "powerful", but in science "power" has only one meaning. Power means **how quickly** energy can be transferred. That is certainly one of the meanings we give to "powerful" when we talk of the racing car or the athlete. To move the car or to run we have to burn fuel (petrol or food). When the fuel burns, energy is transferred to the movement of the car or the runner. Both the car and the runner can transfer energy **more quickly** than most other cars and athletes.

To see the importance of this idea, we will apply it to the design of a small domestic lift.

Designing a stair-lift

A stair-lift provides a way elderly or disabled people can go up and down stairs. It is driven by an electric motor. The electric motor has to raise both

Figure 8.2
A small lift that can be used alongside an ordinary staircase to help disabled people.

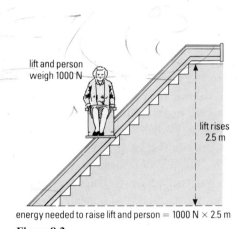

lift and person weigh 1000 N

lift rises 2.5 m

energy needed to raise lift and person = 1000 N × 2.5 m

Figure 8.3
Energy transferred in raising a lift 2.5 m.

the lift and one person up from one floor to the next. In a typical house there are 14 steps from downstairs to upstairs and each step is 18 cm high. This makes the first floor approximately 2.5 m above the ground floor. We will suppose that the person and the lift together weigh 1000 N. To work out the energy needed to lift the person upstairs, we multiply the force required by the distance moved in the direction the force acts (figure 8.3).

energy transferred = 1000 N × 2.5 m
= 2500 J

(Remember that a force of 1 newton moved through a distance of 1 metre transfers 1 joule of energy.)

The motor not only has to suppply at least this amount of energy, it also has to supply it in a time most people would expect to take to get upstairs. Most people would take about 10 s to climb a normal flight of stairs. We can now work out the *power* of the motor – that is, **how quickly** it has to transfer the energy.

power = 2500 J in 10 s
= 250 J/s

We say "J/s" as "joules per second". The symbol "/" always means "per" in physics. Another way of thinking of "per" is to say "every". So 250 J/s is said "250 joules per second" and means "250 joules every second". This is the **rate** of energy transfer with time by the motor, called the motor's output *power*.

You have probably met the word "rate" already in biology (in your Biology book, section **B**3.6). If you have already read Chapter **P**4, you will also have seen the word "rate" used there as well. "Rate" is a word we use when we want to describe how one thing changes with another. You meet it elsewhere in this book in things like *speed* (the rate of change of distance with time) and *electric current* (the rate of transfer of charge with time). The symbol "/", meaning "per", is always found when we talk of *rates of change*. This is because we work out rates of change by dividing one thing by another, and "/" is a sign for division. You can see this in the way we work out power.

$$\text{power} = \frac{\text{energy transferred}}{\text{time taken to transfer the energy}}$$

The unit of J/s is given the name *watt* (symbol, W). So the output power of this motor is at least 250 W.

Some experiments on human power

*Worksheet **P**8A gives you a number of activities to do which will help you to become familiar with the idea of power. The questions below may also help.*

1 In the stair-lift calculation the set of stairs had 14 steps, each of height 18 cm. Check that this gives a vertical distance between the two floors of 2.5 m.

2 Suppose that a stair-lift weighing 400 N has to lift a man weighing 800 N up a vertical height of 2.5 m in 12 s.
a Calculate the energy transferred to the lift and the man in raising them up the stairs.
b What is the minimum output power of the motor?
c Why would the output power have to be a little greater than this in practice?

3 A box is dragged 5 m across some ground in 6 s. A force of 30 N is needed to drag the box.
a What energy has to be supplied by the person dragging the box?
b How much power does the person need?
c What happens to the energy transferred?

Force and power

The word "power" is often used so loosely in everyday speech that it is not at all clear what it means. It often seems to mean "strength" or "force", rather than how quickly energy is transferred. To see why this is, think again about the stair-lift. Suppose a new motor is installed with an output power of 500 W. How much energy will this new motor transfer in 10 s? The answer is 500 W × 10 s = 5000 J.

Suppose the lift, this time carrying a **different** load, is still raised 2.5 m in this time. If the new motor exerts a force, F, the work done by the motor is:

$$\text{force} \times \text{distance moved by force} = \text{energy transferred}$$

$$F \times 2.5\,\text{m} = 5000\,\text{J}$$

$$\text{So, } F = \frac{5000\,\text{J}}{2.5\,\text{m}}$$

$$= 2000\,\text{N}$$

So the new motor, which is twice as powerful as the old, is capable of exerting twice the force and so raising twice the load in the same time (figure 8.4).

This is why "power" often seems to have a double meaning. Mechanically, larger power usually means a bigger force as well, but this will only work with mechanical things. It is no good thinking of "power" as "force" when comparing, say, a domestic light bulb which has a power of 100 W with a TV floodlight which may have a power of 2000 W. The TV floodlight is twenty times more powerful than the domestic light bulb because it transfers energy from the electrical supply to light twenty times more quickly. To speak of "force" in this case has no meaning. So scientists restrict the word "power" to mean "how quickly energy can be transferred" and **nothing** else.

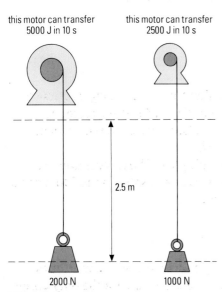

this motor can transfer
5000 J in 10 s

this motor can transfer
2500 J in 10 s

2.5 m

2000 N   1000 N

Figure 8.4
Comparing two motors of different power.

P8.2   Machines

Whenever anything useful happens, energy is transferred. Every job has an energy *cost*. We can easily work out the energy cost of simple jobs. Suppose I want to raise the front wheels of a car 20 cm off the ground and that this needs a force of 2500 N. How much energy must be transferred to the car?

$$\text{energy transferred} = \text{force} \times \text{distance moved}$$
$$= 2500\,\text{N} \times 0.2\,\text{m}$$
$$= 500\,\text{J}$$

(Notice the change from cm to m in this calculation.)
We cannot hope to lift the car without "paying" 500 J to do the job.

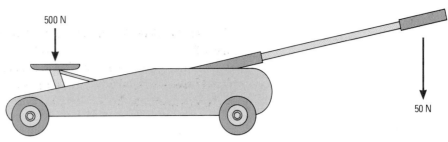

Figure 8.5
A car-jack is a machine used when changing a wheel on a car.

However, it is most unlikely that we can lift the front of the car on our own. To help, we use a car-jack (figure 8.5).

A car-jack is a machine that helps us to transfer energy. The car-jack lets us raise the front of the car by applying a much smaller force, say 50 N. But if we do this we must still find the energy cost of 500 J. How can this be done? The only way is to move the smaller force through a much larger distance, d.

energy transferred = force × distance through which force moves
So, 500 N m = 50 N × d (Remember, 1 J = 1 N m)

$$d = \frac{500 \, \text{N m}}{50 \, \text{N}}$$

$$= 10 \, \text{m}$$

So we pay the energy cost by applying a smaller force over a larger distance. A machine such as this one is called a *force multiplier*. Most machines are force multipliers, but a few (such as the muscle-bone machine you meet in Biology Chapter **B**10) are *distance multipliers*.

The robot arm in figure 8.6 is a distance multiplier. The force is applied only a small distance from the arm's pivot. This enables the "hand" to move a much larger distance than the force is moved.

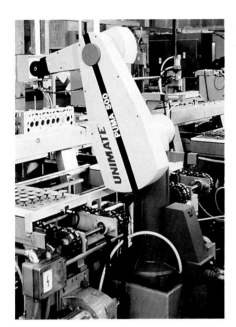

Figure 8.6
Robot arms such as the one shown here are used increasingly in industry to perform complex tasks.

Machines and engines

Machines which are force multipliers make life easier for us. All machines have an input force and an output force. But machines are not the only things that can make life easier. Often we use devices which can transfer energy from fuels or electricity and so produce a force to move something. A petrol engine and an electric motor are examples of such devices. Things which transfer energy in this way to do useful jobs are called *engines*. The human body is an engine transferring energy from food. The great advantage other engines have over the human body is that they can transfer energy much more quickly than we can. In other words, they have much greater power. This is so important

Figure 8.7
A variety of different machines.

mincer

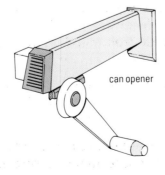
can opener

bicycle

that we are prepared to pay a very high energy cost for the advantages they bring us. At the end of the worksheet on the experiments on human power (Worksheet **P**8A) you will find a way of measuring your own maximum power and comparing this with the output of a light bulb. How did you do? Probably not much better than a 100 W lamp!

P8.3   Energy cost

In the previous section we saw that the energy cost of raising the front wheels of the car by 0.2 m is 500 J. A force of 50 N needs to be moved 10 m to pay this energy cost. But is this all we have to pay in practice? If you try raising the front wheels with the sort of car-jack supplied with a car, you will find that an effort of much more than 50 N has to be moved through a distance of 10 m to lift 2500 N through 0.2 m. Let us suppose that one particular car-jack required an effort of 120 N to be moved through 10 m to lift the 2500 N weight 0.2 m.

the energy transferred to the car in lifting it $= 2500 \text{ N} \times 0.2 \text{ m}$
$= 500 \text{ J (as before)}$
the energy put **into** the machine $= 120 \text{ N} \times 10 \text{ m}$
$= 1200 \text{ J}$

More energy is put into the machine than the amount transferred to the car. What has happened to the extra 700 J of energy that has been paid out? Whenever energy is transferred things tend to get warm, whether you want them to or not. Some things, like electric motors, can get warm due to the electric current passing through them. Machines often get warm due to friction between the moving parts. Energy is needed to warm things up. We cannot avoid some of the energy being transferred in this way. For the car-jack quite a lot of the input energy is used, via friction, in simply warming up the car-jack and its surroundings.

We do not want to waste energy and engineers go to a great deal of trouble to cut down on the waste of energy in machines. To judge how good a machine is at **not** wasting energy, we use the term *efficiency*.

Efficiency

What do we mean when we describe processes as efficient? You may be told that you are not doing a job in a particularly efficient way. The government often tells people in industry that they should try to be as efficient as possible. Makers of a vacuum cleaner may say that the machine is a more efficient way of cleaning a room than doing it by hand.

All these statements have one thing in common. Doing something efficiently is doing it with the least trouble or perhaps at the least cost. One way of being efficient is to do a job with the **least** expenditure of energy. All jobs have a **minimum**, or smallest, energy cost. This energy cost is the energy which **has** to be transferred to bring about the change. But with all machines we have to pay more than this minimum cost in order to get the job done.

You will find this same idea of energy cost comes into considering chemical manufacturing processes, for example the Haber process described in Chapter C16.

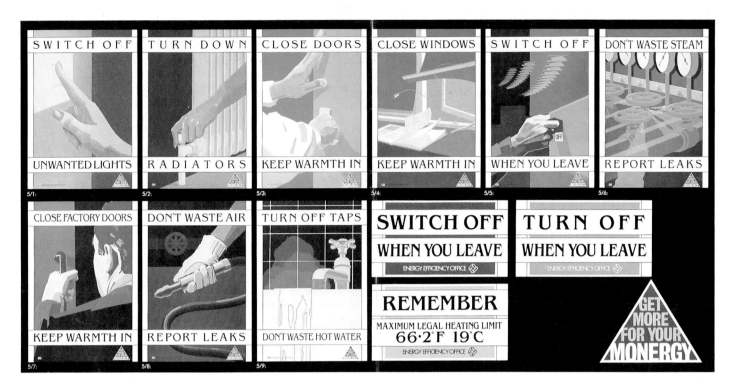

Figure 8.8
Posters designed to encourage the saving of energy. Notice the large number of ways in which energy can be wasted.

In the case of the car-jack considered earlier, the minimum energy cost of raising the car was 500 J. This was the energy transferred to the car in lifting it. But in that particular example the actual energy cost was 1200 J because of the energy also transferred in warming the car-jack and its surroundings.

The efficiency of the car-jack (and any other machine) is defined as:

$$\frac{\text{useful output energy}}{\text{total input energy}}$$

(This ratio is usually multiplied by 100 to give the efficiency as a percentage.)
In this case,

$$\text{efficiency} = \frac{500\,\text{J}}{1200\,\text{J}}$$

$$= 0.42$$

In other words, the car-jack was 42 per cent efficient as a machine.

Power and efficiency

Another way of working out the efficiency of a machine or engine is to compare its *output power* with its *input power*. Suppose that a particular electric motor had an output power of 1500 W and an input power of 2000 W. This means that in one second, the motor would transfer 1500 J of useful energy to something else. During the same time, 2000 J would be transferred to the motor.

$$\text{So the motor's efficiency} = \frac{\text{useful output energy}}{\text{total input energy}}$$

$$= \frac{1500}{2000}$$

$$= 0.75$$

This is exactly the same thing as saying

$$\text{efficiency} = \frac{\text{useful output power}}{\text{total input power}}$$

4 The stair-lift described in section P8.1 transferred 2500 J to the lift and its passenger in getting her upstairs. During the same time 3125 J of energy were transferred from the electrical supply to the motor.
a Calculate the efficiency of the stair-lift motor.
b What is the motor's input power?

5 Asha runs 200 m up a hill of gradient 1 in 4 in 40 s. (A gradient of 1 in 4 means that the hill rises 1 m vertically for every 4 m along the slope.) Asha's weight is 400 N.
a What vertical height does Asha climb?
b How much energy does she transfer in raising herself up the hill?
c What is the output power of her "human engine"?

*You can learn more about the "human engine" in Chapter **B9** of your Biology book.*

6 Efficiency can be worked out in two ways:

i $\dfrac{\text{energy usefully transferred}}{\text{total energy transferred}}$

ii $\dfrac{\text{useful output power}}{\text{total input power}}$

Explain as carefully as you can why these two expressions amount to the same thing.

An investigation into the performance of a simple machine

It is almost certain that one of the first machines used by man was a ramp. It is, for example, highly probable that ramps were used to haul stones into place when the pyramids in Egypt were built (figure 8.9). Although the ramp can be very useful as a force multiplier, it is also often very inefficient. Worksheet **P8B** outlines an investigation you can undertake into the efficiency of a ramp as a machine.

P8.4   The efficiency of engines

Inefficient machines waste energy, but careful measurements show that this wasted energy does not vanish. Most of it seems to warm up the surroundings. If this wastage is reduced, say by oiling parts of the machine, we find that not only does the machine become more efficient but also the parts of the machine no longer warm up so much.

Some of this wasted energy may even warm up the load it is intended to move – as when a heavy load slides up a rough plank. This is why the definition of efficiency says "energy **usefully** transferred".

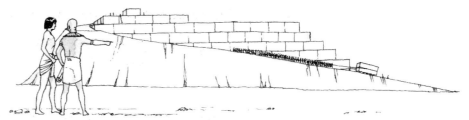

Figure 8.9
Ramps were almost certainly used in the building of the pyramids in Egypt.

"Heat engines"

Engines transfer energy from fuels to do useful jobs, and, just as with machines, there is some wastage. In machines, energy is wasted in doing work against friction. This leads to a warming up of the machine and its surroundings. Machines are built to reduce this energy wastage as much as possible. However, many engines **depend** upon a rise in temperature in order to work.

Figure 8.10
Three different engines.

> **7** Look at the pictures of engines in figure 8.10.
> **a** Find out which of them depend in some way upon a rise in temperature.
> **b** How does a rise in temperature enable them to work?

In a steam turbine, for example, the energy of the fuel is used to turn water into high-temperature steam (figure 8.11, on the next page). In topic **P**1, you saw that a rise in the temperature of a gas can result in a rise in its pressure. It is this rise in pressure that provides the moving force which is the engine's output. In this way energy is transferred from the fuel to do something useful – for example, pump water from a well or turn an electrical generator.

Apart from the useful work steam turbine engines do, large amounts of energy are also transferred to the surroundings from the hot gases. This means that the efficiency of such engines is low. Unfortunately, there is nothing anyone can do about engines of this sort losing energy to their surroundings. At the end of this section you will find a simple explanation of how such "heat engines" work.

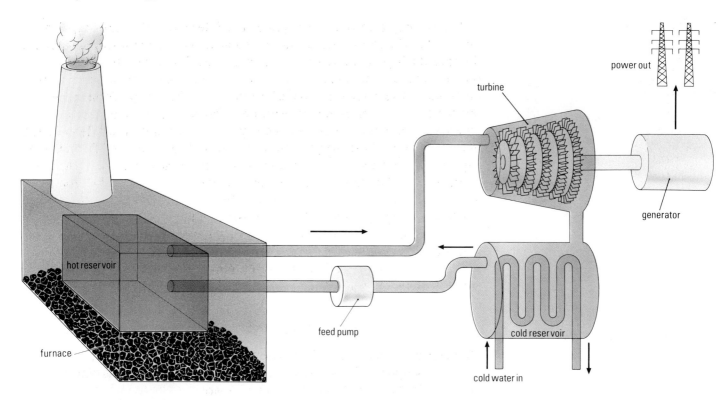

Figure 8.11
A cut-away view of the inside of a steam turbine. Steam turbines are used in power stations to drive the generators.

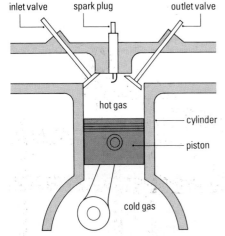

Figure 8.12
One cylinder of an internal combustion engine. This is the engine that is used to drive cars and motorcycles and a wide variety of other machines.

Using electric motors

Electric motors do not depend on "getting hot" in order to work. You will learn how they transfer energy from electricity in Chapter **P**18. Because electric motors transfer less energy to their surroundings, they have a much higher efficiency than other types of engine. However, the energy is first transferred to the electricity in power stations. In most power stations, the energy is transferred from fuels by burning them. The energy from the burning fuel is used to raise the pressure of steam to drive turbines. The turbines in turn drive generators which transfer the energy to the electricity. So even when we use electric motors, we usually depend somewhere along the "energy chain" on engines which burn fuel.

*You can find out more about generators and power stations in Chapters **P**11 and **P**12.*

Engines which burn fuel in order to make use of its energy have a low efficiency. But there is a limited amount of fuel available in the world. Because of this, a great deal of research is going on to try to improve the efficiency with which the energy of fuels is utilized.

*You will learn how fuels are able to transfer energy in Chapter **C**13 of your Chemistry book. We shall look at more about the world's available energy resources in Chapter **P**12.*
    *The last section shows why it is that engines which depend on a rise in temperature have an **unavoidably** low efficiency. It is not essential to understand this in order to understand the rest of the topic on energy.*

"Heat engines" again

Engines that work by making gases hot are usually referred to as "heat engines". This section considers why such engines always "lose" some energy to their surroundings and warm them up.

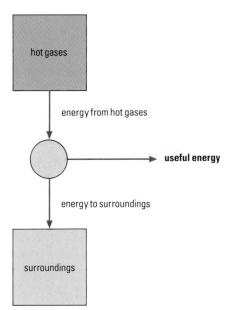

Figure 8.13
A diagram to show the transfer of energy in a "heat" engine.

As an example, look at the diagram of an internal combustion engine in figure 8.12. The gases in the cylinder are able to push the piston down because they are at a higher pressure than the air outside. The gases gain this high pressure because they are made hotter by the burning petrol. So the pressure difference between the top and the bottom of the piston **depends upon** the temperature difference – no temperature difference means no pressure difference and so no energy from the engine. But a temperature difference will mean that some of the energy of the hot gases will be transferred through the engine to the outside world. This energy is simply wasted in warming up the world around the engine! The diagram in figure 8.13 illustrates the process of getting useful energy from all "heat" engines.

Although energy is always lost to the surroundings in such engines, the efficiency of the engine depends on how big the temperature difference is. The bigger the temperature difference, the higher the efficiency. Engineers use this fact in trying to improve the efficiency of things as widely different as motor car engines and power stations.

8 Find out how a hydraulic car-jack works.

9 The pulley block in figure 8.14 can be used for raising loads. Suppose that a container weighing 500 N is lifted up a distance of 2 m. The force used to raise the container is 125 N and 10 m of rope have to be hauled in.
a How much energy is transferred to the load?
b How much work is done in hauling on the rope to raise the load?
c What is the efficiency of the pulley system?
d Is this machine a force- or a distance-multiplier?
e What happens to the energy not usefully transferred to the load? (Try to think of two **different** things that have happened to it.)
f In what ways could you improve the efficiency of this machine?

10 Joe is using a rope to pull a bag of cement up a ramp (figure 8.15). The bag weighs 500 N and slides 5 m along the ramp in being lifted onto a platform 2 m above the ground.
a What is the minimum energy cost of getting the bag of cement onto the platform?
b If no energy is transferred to the surroundings, how much energy will have to be used by Joe in pulling on the rope?
c With how much force does Joe have to pull on the rope?

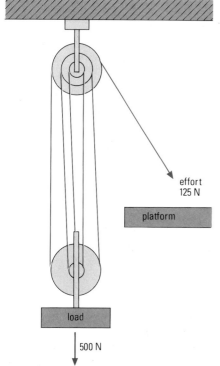

Figure 8.14

Figure 8.15
Pulling a bag of cement up a ramp.

10 (continued) Unfortunately the rope snaps as one bag of cement is being pulled up the ramp and it slides down again to the bottom. Pete suggests that a rougher plank should be used so that friction can stop this happening another time. Joe complains that this will mean that he will have to pull harder to get the sacks up the ramp. Pete agrees and suggests they use a longer ramp.

d Explain why Joe will in fact have to pull harder if a rougher plank is used. What happens to the extra energy he transfers?

e Explain how Pete's idea of using a longer plank will help reduce the effort required to lift the bags.

11 The engine in a motor car is often described as an *internal combustion* engine and as a *four-stroke* engine. Its output power is often given in *horse-power*. Find out and explain the meaning of each of the phrases in italics.

Summary

The following passage summarizes the main ideas in this chapter. Copy out the passage, filling in the blanks with either a word or phrase from the list at the beginning of the passage. (There is only one word or phrase to each blank; the words are not listed in the order you will need to use them, and you may use any word more than once.)

force	distance	watt	zero
energy	time	newton	transferring
work	fuel	joule	warming up the surroundings
power	efficiency	measuring	raising the load
greater than	less than		

Work, measured by multiplying the _____ acting by the distance it moves, is one way of measuring _____ transfer. The unit in which it is measured is the _____.

_____ is a measure of how quickly energy can be transferred. It is calculated by dividing the energy transferred by the _____ taken to transfer the energy. The unit in which power is measured is the _____. Power is often confused with _____ which is measured in newtons. However, the two quantities are not the same.

A machine is a mechanism for _____ energy. It differs from an engine, which is a device for transferring energy from _____. All processes that involve transferring energy have an _____ cost. In all practical machines, the energy cost is always _____ the energy value of their output.

The fraction obtained by dividing the useful output energy by the total input energy is called the _____ of the machine or engine. The _____ is always _____ 100 per cent because some of the energy is always used in _____.

This last section uses the ideas of power and efficiency to explore a new problem. "Why do cars have a top speed?" Some parts are quite straightforward, but other parts are difficult. If you leave out this section entirely, you will not miss anything essential to the rest of the course.

On the other hand you will come across air resistance here and that is an idea taken up again in Chapter P7. So you may find it helpful to read some of it.

P8.5   Why do cars have a top speed?

A great deal of damage can be done to the engine of a family car if it is
"revved up" too hard. However, car engines are rarely damaged in this way
as the top speed of a car is well below that which would cause damage to the
engine.

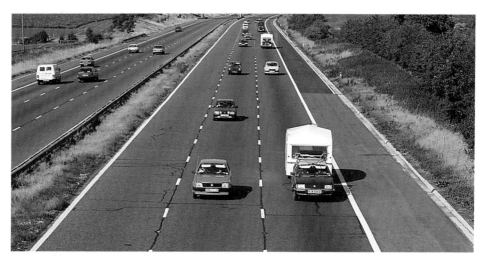

Figure 8.16
Cars travelling at high speed along a motorway.

Power and friction

What then are the limitations on the speed of a car? To answer this question
we must first look at where the output energy of a car engine goes to. Some of
it may be used to speed up the car, but a great deal of it goes into raising the
temperature of the surroundings via friction: friction against the air and in
the moving parts of the car.

Once the car is travelling at a steady speed, **none** of the engine's output
energy goes into the kinetic (or "motion") energy of the car. All of it goes into
warming up the surroundings as the car overcomes friction. If the engine is
turned off, the car comes rapidly to rest. The force of the friction brings the
car to rest and the car's kinetic energy is transferred to warming up the air
around it.

How much power is used in working against friction? To answer this, let us
suppose that a car travelling at a steady speed of 20 m/s has to overcome a
total frictional force of 300 N (figure 8.17).

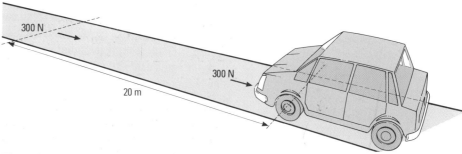

300 N

300 N

20 m

Figure 8.17
A 300-newton frictional force opposing the motion of a car.

In one second the car would move 20 m against this force. So the car engine has had to do work equal to

$$\text{force} \times \text{distance moved} = 300\,\text{N} \times 20\,\text{m}$$
$$= 6000\,\text{J}$$

It does this amount of work against friction every second. So the power expended by the engine against friction is 6000 W (or 6 kW). If, instead of taking particular numbers, F is used for force and v is used for speed, we can work out a formula for this use of power.

$$\text{work done against friction every second} = F \times v$$
$$\text{so, power} = Fv$$

This is a very useful result which you will be able to use in the rest of this section.

Friction and speed

The force of friction that a car has to overcome is not constant, but increases as the speed of the car increases. Experiments show that, to a good approximation, friction is proportional to (speed)^2 at normal driving speeds. Here is a table of the frictional forces for a typical car at different speeds (figure 8.18).

Frictional force, F, in newtons	Speed, v, in metres/second	Power ($= Fv$), in watts
0	0	
19	5	
74	10	
167	15	
296	20	
463	25	
666	30	
907	35	
1184	40	

Figure 8.18
The way the frictional force on a typical car varies with its speed.

12a Copy out figure 8.18 and complete the last column using your calculator. This last column gives the power the engine has to develop just to overcome friction and keep the car running steadily at each speed.
b Plot a graph of the engine power required to overcome friction against speed.
c Suppose that the car engine of a small car has an output power of 37 kW (1 kW = 1000 W). This power has to be used both to speed up the car and to work against friction. What is the **most** power that this engine can use against friction?
d If this car is using all this power working against friction will it be travelling at a steady speed or not?
e How fast will the car be travelling if it is using all its 37 kW working against friction? (Use your graph.)
f Explain why this must be the highest speed at which the car can travel.

Speed, in m/s	Power, in kW
7.0	6.9
10.5	10.2
14.0	14.3
17.5	18.6
21.0	23.0
24.5	27.5
28.0	32.1
31.5	35.2
35.0	36.7
38.5	36.7

Figure 8.19
The variation of output power of a small car engine with the road speed of the car.

Real engines

Real engines do not in fact give a constant power output. The power output varies with the speed of the engine. The table on the left (figure 8.19) shows the way the power output of a typical small car engine varies with the road speed of the car.

13a To find out the car's top speed, plot these engine-power values on to the friction power graph. Where the two graphs cross will be the top speed of the car.
b Explain why this gives the value of the car's top speed. (You may find it helpful to discuss this with someone else.)

If you have drawn the second graph as a smooth curve, you should find that the engine has a maximum power output of about 37 kW and that the line crosses the friction power graph very close to this maximum. This should mean that this **real** car has the same maximum speed as the one you worked on earlier. Most cars have "power curves" (as they are called) like this one. They all reach maximum power at just about the speed at which all their power is working against friction. You might like to consider the advantages of this.

Figure 8.20
A moped. Mopeds are designed to have a top speed of about 30 miles/hour.

Mopeds

The engine "capacity" of a car engine is very roughly proportional to its maximum power. The engine capacity is the total volume of its cylinders. So a 4-cylinder, 1000 cm³ engine has four cylinders each of 250 cm³ in volume. The small car engine described earlier, with a maximum power of 37 kW, might have an engine capacity of 1000 cm³.

14 Suppose you had to design an engine for a moped. It is to be designed to have a top speed of 30 miles per hour (that is, 13.5 m/s).
a Using your friction power graph, work out the engine capacity of the engine needed in the moped.
b Find out the engine capacity of a typical moped and check whether it is close to the size you have calculated.

Chapter P9

Keeping yourself warm
Heating: a way of transferring energy

As you work your way through this chapter you will be asked to undertake an investigation into heating your home. You should carry out the investigation in two stages. In the first stage you will investigate how much energy you are using to heat your home. Then you will learn about ways in which the loss of energy to the outside can be slowed down.

In the second stage of the investigation you will investigate how some of these ideas could be applied to your own home.

As an alternative, the project could be applied to your school and then your science group could make its recommendations to the Head. Of course you will have to support them with evidence!

Figure 9.1

P9.1 What should I wear today?

Have you ever asked yourself the question above? Maybe you have to consider fashion when you answer it. Sometimes you might think about comfort. In some places, people's lives could depend on what they are wearing. Suppose you had to take a baby outdoors in winter or that you were going to climb a high mountain in Scotland in cold, dry, windy weather. What sorts of material would be best for the clothes you choose? Some manufacturers might claim that the material they use is the best available for the purpose. How could you test their claim? Could you devise a test at home or in the school laboratory? Worksheet **P9A** gives you some help to make such an investigation.

P9.2 Keeping your home warm

Our clothes and our houses should keep us warm in winter. You probably found a way of checking how well different materials behaved in keeping us warm in the previous investigation (Worksheet **P9A**). You can now start to investigate your home.

Whichever way you keep your home warm, you need energy. It may be transferred from fuels like gas, coal, oil, wood or paraffin. You will find out how to measure the energy they store when you study fuels in chemistry.

*Section **C13.2** in the Chemistry book shows you how fuel costs can be compared. Using Worksheet **C13D** you will be able to measure the energy that can be transferred from burning a fuel.*

Many homes are warmed using electricity. The energy transferred to your

Figure 9.2
Drawings like this are designed to encourage people to "save energy" in homes and offices.

home by the electricity comes from a distant power station. You will learn more about this in Chapter **P**11.

All homes "leak" energy, so if a comfortable temperature is to be maintained energy has to be continually supplied to replace that which has leaked away. The ideas you will find in this chapter may help you reduce the transfer of energy from your home. If less energy leaves your home, then less will have to be replaced. This can save quite a lot of money over a period of time.

Now is the time to start your home heating project. After giving you some help with starting it, the main work of the chapter carries on with "Reducing energy transfers to the outside world".

Home heating investigation – part 1

Before you can test any recommendations you have to make, you need to find out how quickly you are replacing the energy in your home now.

To do this you need to keep a check on your electricity and gas meters and measure how much coal, oil, wood or paraffin you are using. Worksheet **P9B** will help you to read your meters.

Over a period of two weeks (or longer) follow these three instructions.

1 Read your electricity and gas meters **at the same time** every day. Write the readings down. Keep a record of how many buckets of coal or how many logs you burn. Check how much oil or paraffin has been used each day.

Of course you will not need to do all of these, just keep counting how much fuel and electricity you use each day.

2 At the same time, keep a diary about daily changes which you think might have caused you to use more or less energy. For example, everybody might decide to take two baths on one particular day; or it might be colder than usual outside; or it might be very windy; or you might have visitors staying; or anything else you think might alter your fuel consumption.

Figure 9.3
Reading an electricity meter.

Figure 9.4

Figure 9.5

3 Draw some bar charts to show your fuel consumption for each day during your investigation. If your meter reading at the start is 66 125 and at the same time on the next day it is 66 137, your consumption for that day is
66 137 − 66 125 = 12 units.

Draw a bar chart for each fuel you use. Now compare the bar charts with the entries in your diary. Can you suggest reasons for any changes in consumption? Keep these results as you will need them for part 2 of this investigation.

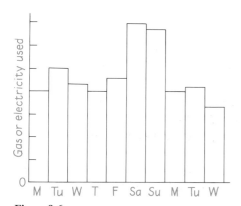

Figure 9.6
This is the sort of chart you should be able to produce for each fuel that you measure.

Reducing energy transfers to the outside world

The hot water cylinder

Find out where hot water is stored in your home. It is usually kept in a cylinder until you want to use it. The cylinder should be lagged with a special jacket which is **at least** 5 cm thick. If it is not the hot water will quickly lose energy to its surroundings. Then you will have to use **more** energy to replace the energy lost.

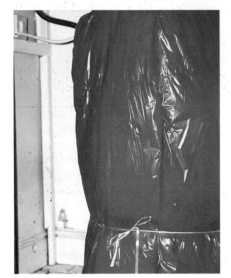

Figure 9.7
A well-lagged hot water cylinder.

Loft insulation

If you live in a flat, this may not apply to you. But if your home has a roof, it is possible that energy is being used to heat cold air in a badly-insulated loft. When air in your home is heated, the hot air rises. This is because it expands and becomes less dense than the cool air. The cool air sinks and pushes the warm air so that it floats up to the ceiling. This is known as *convection*.

If the air on the other side of the ceiling is colder, then energy will be transferred from the hot air to the cold. To do this it has to pass through the ceiling. The energy is transferred through the ceiling by *conduction*. As the hot air transfers its energy to the ceiling, it cools and then slowly sinks. Some of the energy will be transferred from the ceiling to the cold air in the loft. Eventually it leaves your home through the roof.

Figure 9.8
Energy can escape from the roof of a house.

Figure 9.10
Two forms of loft insulation. Both forms trap air amongst the fibres or particles to help in the insulation.

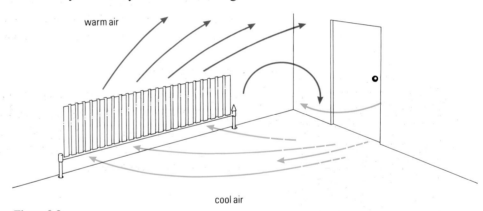

warm air

cool air

Figure 9.9
Convection currents in a room.

We cannot prevent the transfer of energy from something hot to something cold. But some materials, called *insulators*, transfer energy slowly. To slow the transfer down as much as possible, insulating materials are laid on the floor of the loft.

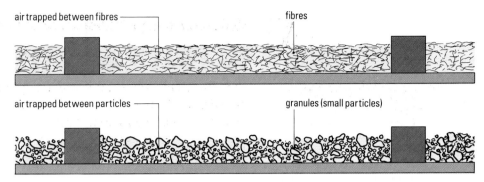

Figure 9.11
These diagrams show how the structure of two common forms of loft insulation can trap air.

Insulating materials used in lofts are poor conductors. This does **not** mean they cannot transfer energy. It means they do so very slowly. They act like this because they trap thousands of tiny pockets of air in between their fibres.

> **1** Sally says many insulating materials trap air between layers or in little pockets. This proves air is a bad conductor. Do you agree? How could you test Sally's suggestion?

The air in between the fibres of the loft insulation is warmed but cannot rise because it is trapped. So the rate at which energy is passing through your ceiling is slowed down. If your loft is well insulated, only a small amount of energy from inside your home will be used to warm the cold air in the loft.

Draught proofing

Hold your hand close to the edges of a door or near a window frame. You might feel a draught of air blowing into your home. What you may not realize at once is that **warm** air is being pushed out of your home by the **cold** air coming in. This means that your heaters have to work harder to keep the rooms in your home warm.

> **2** What do we mean when we say ''your heaters have to work harder''?

Draught proofing is not expensive, but it can save a lot of money. But be careful when you draught proof. You need some ventilation in your home, especially if you have solid fuel, oil, gas, paraffin or bottled-gas heaters.

Answer question 3 when you have studied the burning of fuels in Chapter C13 in your Chemistry book.

> **3** Why is it essential to have some ventilation when burning fuels in your home?

Figure 9.12
Draughts around a door. A great deal of energy can escape from a room in this way.

Wall insulation

This works in a similar way to loft insulation. However, this is not something you can usually put in yourself.

brick wall   brick wall
    air gap

Figure 9.13 (above left)
The construction of a cavity wall.

Figure 9.14 (above centre)
Cavity wall insulation. The foam replaces
the air between the inner and outer bricks.

Figure 9.15 (above right)
Insulating a solid wall.

Figure 9.16a
Double glazing installed in a library.

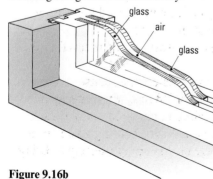

glass
air
glass

Figure 9.16b
The two sheets of glass trap air between
them to form an insulating layer.

Cavity walls

Many homes in Britain have been built using cavity walls. This means that the building has two walls with a gap in between. Until recently the gap was left filled with air. If the gap is filled with an insulating material, it will help reduce the rate at which energy is transferred through the walls. Figure 9.14 shows insulating material being inserted into a cavity wall.

4 Earlier in this chapter it was suggested that air itself might be a poor conductor. If that is so, why does replacing it by an insulating material reduce the energy transfer through cavity walls?

Solid walls

If your home does not have a cavity to fill, you can still insulate your walls. In this case you need to line the walls with insulating material and then fix plaster or wooden boarding over the lining.

5 Why do you need to fix boards over the insulating lining on a solid wall?

Double glazing

By now you should be able to explain how double glazing can help keep your home warm. It does this by reducing the rate of transfer of energy from the warm air inside to the cold air outside the window.

Reducing energy loss from homes saves money. But installing double glazing can be costly. You may find that it would take several years before the money saved by installing double glazing balances the cost of having it installed. You might be able to reduce energy transfers through windows, at night, by having heavier, lined curtains, which would be much cheaper.

The main theme of this chapter continues with section P9.3. The second stage of your home heating project comes next.

Home heating investigation – part 2

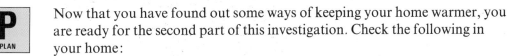

Now that you have found out some ways of keeping your home warmer, you are ready for the second part of this investigation. Check the following in your home:

- How thick is the jacket on your hot water cylinder? (It should be at least 5 cm thick.)
- How thick is your loft insulation? (It should be at least 10 cm.)
- Are there any draughts around doors, window frames or skirting boards?
- Are the walls insulated?
- Are the windows double glazed?

Prepare a report about how energy is leaving your home. Recommend different ways of reducing this loss. Try to make at least one recommendation that will not cost much to put into practice. (The best ones will cost nothing!)

Perhaps you will find that your home is already well insulated and draught proofed. If so, you can study carefully when electricity, gas, oil, etc. are being used and suggest ways of using them more effectively. This is harder, and the energy you "save" may be less.

P9.3   Measuring energy transfers

In this chapter we have looked at ways of reducing unnecessary energy transfer from your home. In the case of double glazing you have already seen that there is a cost attached to this. To judge the value of improvements in home insulation you have to be able to compare the cost of the energy saved with the cost of the improvement. To do this, you need to be able to find out how much energy is actually transferred when something gets hotter or colder.

Look at figures 9.17 and 9.18. How much energy would be transferred from the hot water tank if it cooled by 10 °C? How much energy would have to be transferred to the baby's milk to get it to the right temperature? You should have some ideas about answering these questions when you have finished this chapter.

In Chapter **P8**, when energy was transferred there was always a force (which you could measure) moving some object. You measured the energy transferred by multiplying that force by the distance it moved.
Force × distance moved is called *work*. The energy transferred is equal to the work done.

In this chapter we are concerned with energy transfers that cause temperatures to change. You have seen in Chapter **P8** that when energy is transferred, some of it almost always brings about a change in temperature. Usually, this is a waste. But when we are concerned with heating water for a bath, or boiling some water to make tea, we are using energy usefully to bring about a change in temperature.

In Chapter **P10** you will see that energy transferred as work can sometimes all be used simply to change the temperature of an object. But when we raise

Figure 9.17
An unlagged hot water cylinder.

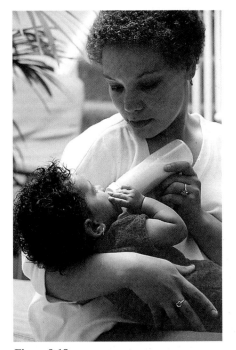

Figure 9.18
A baby drinking from a bottle.

the temperature of our homes we do it by first raising the temperature of something else (a fire, or radiators). Then we let it transfer energy to the surroundings. When this happens, there is no force we can measure. This seems to be a different way of transferring energy from working. We call it *heating*.

Unlike work, we have no direct way of measuring the energy transferred in heating. But what we can do is to measure its effect on the object to which the energy is transferred.

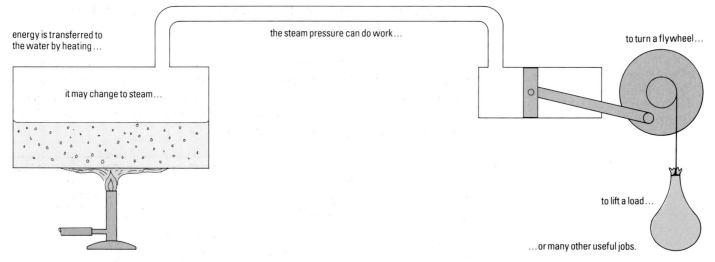

Figure 9.19
Some of the consequences of heating water.

What is the effect of heating some water? It will certainly get **hotter**. It may change to **steam**. The steam pressure may be used to do **work** and drive a steam engine.

But what if the water did **not** change to steam and did **not** do any work as a result? The only result of heating the water will be to raise its temperature. We can use this change in temperature to measure the energy transferred.

We have already said that having energy is like having money. It is only useful when it is transferred. The next few questions are about **cash** transfers. They should help you to understand how energy is transferred to different materials.

Simon works on the vegetable counter in a large market. Each vegetable is priced in £ per kg. To purchase some vegetables, a customer has to transfer some money to Simon. Simon can work out how much money has to be transferred (the price) if he has a table like the one in figure 9.21.

Figure 9.20
Selling fruit and vegetables from a stall.

Vegetable	Price in £ per kg
aubergine	2.18
broccoli	1.76
cabbage	0.64
carrot	0.42
cauliflower	0.52
leek	1.43
mooli	1.94
mushroom	3.10
onion	0.64
potato	0.33
yam	1.74

Figure 9.21
A comparison of the prices of some vegetables in 1992.

6 Draw a bar chart comparing the prices of different vegetables.

7 Imagine you had to do Simon's job. How much money will be transferred to buy each of the following?
a 5 kg potatoes **b** 2 kg carrots
c 1 kg onions **d** 500 g mushrooms.

8 These prices were correct in 1992. Go to your local greengrocer or supermarket and find out the present prices. If they have changed, make another bar chart to compare the prices. Can you draw any conclusions about the changes in price since 1992?

Energy transfers which cause a change in temperature can be worked out in a similar way. David is a scientist who needs to calculate how much energy transfer causes certain temperature changes. He uses a table of energy values (figure 9.23). This table shows how much energy has to be transferred so that the temperature of 1 kg of each substance changes by 1°C.

Figure 9.22
A young scientist at work. Scientific work often requires looking up data.

Substance	Energy in joules per kg for 1°C change in temperature
air	990
aluminium	900
concrete	3400
copper	390
cotton	1400
glass	670
iron	450
polystyrene	1300
water	4200

Figure 9.23
The specific heating capacities of some materials.

9 Draw a bar chart comparing the energy transfers in figure 9.23.
10 Which substance needs the most energy to warm it up?
11 Which substance is the easiest to warm up?

Imagine you had to do David's job. Use the table to answer the following questions.

12 A tea urn holds 7 kg of water. When it is empty the tea urn, which is made of aluminium, has a mass of 2 kg.
a How much energy would be needed to change the temperature of the empty tea urn by 1°C?
b How much energy would be needed to change the temperature of the tea urn by 1°C if it was full of water?

13 How much energy would be needed to change the temperature of a 1-kg glass container by 5°C?

14 How much energy would be needed to raise the temperature of a 3-kg block of concrete by 20°C?

15 Water is always used to fill bottles for warming beds. A hot concrete brick wrapped in a cloth can also be used. Why are these two materials the best for warming something up?

16 In terms of energy transfer, how does a **rise** in temperature differ from a **fall** in temperature?

Specific heating capacity

A table of energy values like the one in figure 9.23 is useful if you want to work out energy transfers in your home. For example, you could use it to work out how much energy is needed to warm up the hot water cylinder illustrated in figure 9.17.

Each value in this table is called the *specific heating capacity* of the material. Some people call it the "specific thermal capacity". Other terms used are "specific heat capacity" or just "specific heat". Sometimes it is even abbreviated to s.h.c. They all mean the same thing.

Energy transfer by heating

How did you set about answering question **12**? You were only told the energy needed to raise the temperature of 1 kg of aluminium by 1°C. Did you assume that the energy needed to raise the temperature of 2 kg is twice this?

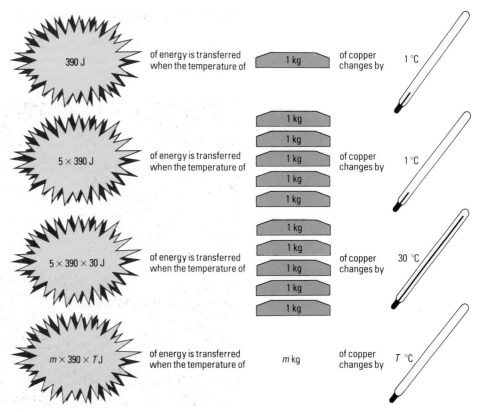

Figure 9.24
The effect of transferring different quantities of energy to various masses of copper.

How did you answer question **13**? Again you were only told the energy needed to raise the temperature of 1 kg of glass by 1 °C. Did you assume the energy needed to raise the temperature of 1 kg of glass by 5 °C was five times this?

Both of these assumptions would have been sensible. We can combine them together to give a "formula" for finding the energy transferred when mass m of specific heating capacity c changes its temperature by an amount T. The relationship is:

$$\text{energy transferred} = m \times c \times T$$

Figure 9.24 summarizes this equation for you as a sequence of diagrams. However, we ought not to rely on guess work however reasonable it may seem. Worksheet **P9C** gives you some details of an investigation you can carry out to test the truth of this formula, using water. In order to test it, you will need to have some way of transferring constant amounts of energy to the water. There are several ways this could be done, but the simplest way is to use an electric immersion heater. Connected to a 12-volt supply, you can assume that it will always transfer the same amount of energy in (say) one minute, whenever it is switched on. Alternatively, you can connect the immersion heater to the electricity supply via a *joulemeter*. A joulemeter records the energy transferred from the electricity supply to the heater. The electricity meter described in Worksheet **P9B** makes a similar record.

*It is not essential to do Worksheet **P9C**. If you like you can simply take the result "on trust", relying on other people's experiments to test its truth. This is acceptable – no scientist can test everything for him or herself. We often have to rely on the results of other people's work in this way – but we have to be prepared to look at their experiments critically.*

Measuring specific heating capacities

The price of vegetables changes. When carrots are plentiful they are cheap. Year after year prices continue to rise because it costs more to produce food and move it to the shops. (This is something we refer to as "price inflation".)

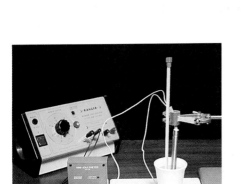

Figure 9.25
A simple joulemeter in use measuring the energy being transferred electrically to a small heater.

Figure 9.26
Prices of fruit and vegetables on a greengrocer's stall.

So the amount of money transferred for the same quantity of vegetables keeps changing.

Energy transfers are **not** like this. The energy transfer which causes a certain temperature rise or fall in a particular quantity of some material will not change. There is no inflation for energy exchanges! This means that the specific heating capacity of a substance is fixed.

You can find the amount of energy transferred when the temperature of 1 kg of a substance changes by 1 °C from tables in a data book. Nevertheless, someone had to measure these specific heating capacities at some time. You will find out how this can be done in Chapter **P**10.

17 Plan a short investigation to find out whether it is cheaper to take a bath or have a shower. Say what measurements you would make and how you would combine them to arrive at an answer.

This completes the work in this chapter. If you have time, however, you may like to make an investigation into the efficiency of an electric kettle. You will find some help in doing this in Worksheet P9D.

Summary

Try to write down an explanation of each of the following words. If you cannot do so, look back through this chapter to find out again what they mean.

> **conduction**
> **convection**
> **work**
> **heating**
> **specific heating capacity**

Chapter P10 Ideas in physics

Energy and change in temperature

P10.1 Scientific theories

Many people think that science deals only with facts. Scientists themselves are often pictured as people who are extremely clever and who know lots of things that mystify everyone else.

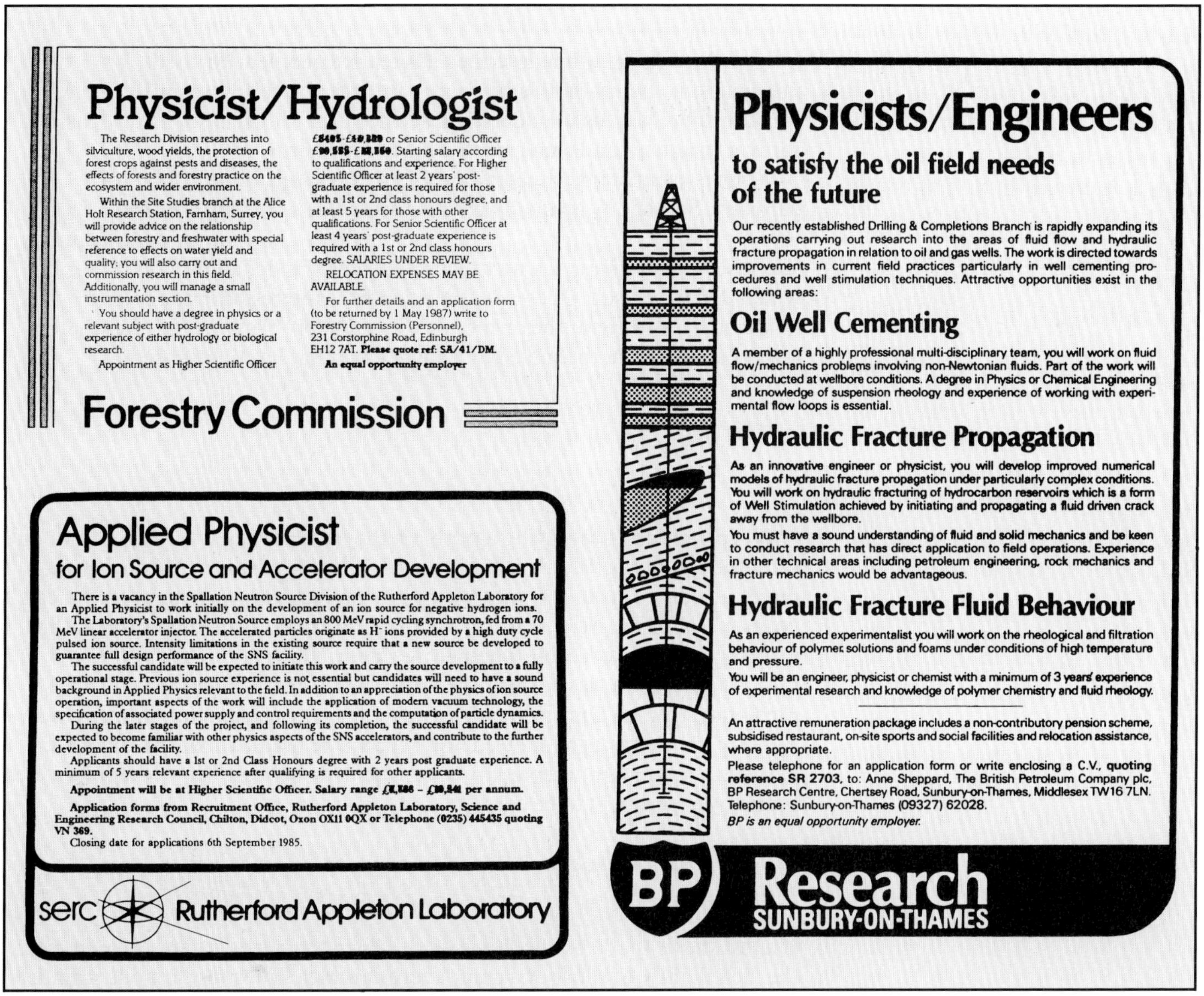

Figure 10.1
Some job advertisements for scientists.

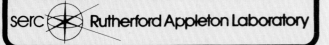

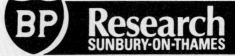

Figure 10.2
Working in an industrial laboratory.

Scientists are not often described as creative people with vivid imaginations. Let us think a bit more carefully about how scientists work because it will help us to understand science itself. It will also make it easier for you to understand some more ideas about energy.

When a scientist investigates a problem, it is rarely done just out of curiosity. Somebody is usually paying the scientist to carry out that investigation. For example, a firm which manufactures motor oil will employ scientists to investigate the way their oil behaves under all the conditions in which it may be used. Of course, the scientist is interested in the problem and in learning more about the science of which the problem is a part but there is always a problem to be solved or a suggestion that has to be tested.

1 Who do you think decides what problems a scientist will try to solve?

When scientists are solving a problem they usually begin with an idea about what the solution is. You probably have lots of ideas passing through your mind each day. If you deal with your ideas in a certain way, then you can call yourself a scientist. Scientists test their ideas by making predictions and then working out ways of seeing whether they are right or not. If the test shows that the prediction was correct, then the scientist may go on to make more predictions. When Dmitri Mendeléev explained his idea about the Periodic Table of the elements he showed how it could be used to make predictions. His idea was quickly accepted by other scientists because his predictions were found by experiment to be correct.

You can find out more about Mendeléev and his work in Chapters C17 and C18 of your Chemistry book.

If a test shows that a prediction is wrong, then the scientist can either change the idea slightly or think of a completely new idea. The most famous scientists

Figure 10.3
Leonardo da Vinci (1452–1519), a famous scientist, engineer and artist.

are often remembered because they were the first people to think of certain very useful ideas, to test them and then show that they work. To do this, they must have had lots of imagination. Michael Faraday and his ideas about electricity are a good example. You will hear more about his ideas in Chapter **P**18. The world's most famous scientists were just as creative as the most famous artists or musicians.

Not all scientific discoveries are made as the direct result of trying to solve a problem. Many important discoveries have been made by accident, when scientists were studying something else. You can read in Chapter **C**12 of Perkin's chance discovery of the dye called mauveine. Henri Becquerel's discovery of radioactivity mentioned in Chapter **P**3 also came about by chance. Although they were lucky the scientists were all following a definite plan of investigation when the chance discovery was made.

The ideas which scientists create may later be changed by other scientists, and then their ideas are changed by others, and so on. A good example of this is the way our ideas about atoms have changed since the days of John Dalton. Dalton thought of atoms as solid spheres. Later on J. J. Thomson put forward the idea that they were like plum puddings, with things called electrons as the "currants". Today, we picture atoms as having a tiny nucleus surrounded by a cloud of electrons. Even so, Dalton's picture of an atom is still helpful in understanding formulae and equations in chemistry. But if we want to understand radioactivity, a more up-to-date picture of atoms is needed.

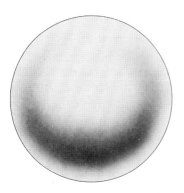

Dalton's atom

Figure 10.4
Models of an atom. The pictures scientists have used to describe atoms have changed a great deal during the past hundred years.

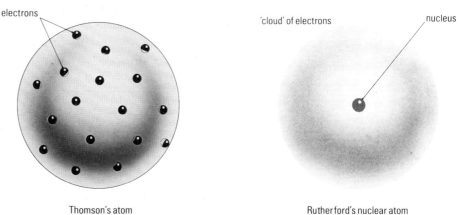

Thomson's atom   Rutherford's nuclear atom

*You will learn more about this picture of an atom in Chapter **P**3 and in Chapter **C**18 of your Chemistry text. Chapter **C**1 tells you more about the work of John Dalton.*

So you see science deals with **ideas** as well as facts. Any scientist, or indeed a person who is not a scientist, can suggest ideas which may solve problems or suggest explanations of things they see. If such an idea proves successful in solving the problem **and** can be used successfully to make other predictions, then the idea is usually called a *theory*. What you should realize is that scientific theories are made by people; they are **not** facts. A theory in science is useful until it fails to predict something found to happen, or predicts something found to be incorrect. Even then the theory may still be useful in a limited way, but usually scientists go on to try to think of a better one.

2 In the introduction, you looked at the way scientists do experiments. In this chapter we are talking about another scientific activity – "making a theory". Write a few lines to explain to a friend the difference between a theory and an experiment.

*In this chapter we are going to look at the way scientists have tried to make theories to explain what happens to a body when it gets hot. The next two sections give you two paths to follow. Section **P10.2** describes two alternative theories and then asks you to decide for yourself which theory is the most useful. Section **P10.3** explains the theory which we use today. You should choose one path or the other.*

P10.2   The "caloric" theory versus the "kinetic" theory

There is more than one way to make something hot!

3 Suppose you are given an iron nail. Write down as many ways as you can think of to make it warmer.

Some of the ways you have suggested probably involved putting the nail in contact with something that was already hot. This is the usual way of making things hotter. If we want to boil a saucepan of milk we put the saucepan in contact with a hot electric ring or a gas flame, or we can put it on a wood fire. This is such a common way of making things hotter that it leads to the first of our theories, called the *caloric theory*.

The caloric theory

When a saucepan of milk gets hot by being placed on a fire it seems as though something is going from the hot fire to the cooler saucepan to make the saucepan hotter. We could imagine that everything contains some sort of "fluid" which flows from things that are hot to things that are cold. The temperature of an object could depend on how much of this "heating fluid" it contains. ("Fluid" is the name we give to any substance that flows easily – like a liquid or a gas.) When this explanation of heating was first suggested, the "heating fluid" was given a special name – it was called *caloric*.

When something is heated, more caloric passes into it. When something cools down, caloric flows out of it. Caloric flows from one thing to another

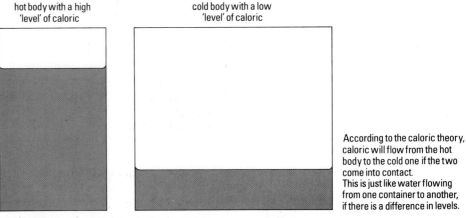

hot body with a high 'level' of caloric

cold body with a low 'level' of caloric

According to the caloric theory, caloric will flow from the hot body to the cold one if the two come into contact.
This is just like water flowing from one container to another, if there is a difference in levels.

Figure 10.5
The flow of caloric from a hot body to a colder one.

when there is a difference in temperature between them (in the same way as water will flow from one container to another if there is a difference in water levels). So two identical objects at the same temperature contain equal amounts of caloric.

This is our first explanation (or theory) about heating. Here is another one.

Energy and rise in temperature

When you suggested ways of warming an iron nail, you probably included ways like rubbing it or hammering it. Rubbing or hammering a piece of metal both involve moving a force through a distance. When this is done, energy is transferred. You have also seen that everything is made from small particles that we call atoms, molecules and ions.

The difference between atoms, molecules and ions has been described to you in Chapter **C5**. But as far as this chapter is concerned, the difference is unimportant. The important thing is that they are all particles which are difficult to break down into anything smaller if no **chemical change** takes place.

These two ideas – that everything is made from "particles" and that energy often seems to be transferred when temperatures change – lead to the second theory about heating. This theory is called the *kinetic theory*.

The kinetic theory

This theory says that everything consists of particles (atoms and molecules) that are always moving. The kinetic theory of heating suggests that when an object is heated, energy is transferred to its particles. The temperature of a body depends on how fast its particles are moving. The particles in a hot object move faster than the particles in the same object when it is colder. When the particles of bodies at different temperatures meet they tend to share out their kinetic energy.

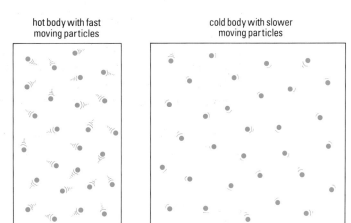

hot body with fast moving particles

cold body with slower moving particles

According to the kinetic theory, energy will be transferred from the faster moving particles to the slower ones if the two bodies come into contact. This will result in the hotter body cooling down and the colder one warming up.

Figure 10.6
How the kinetic theory explains differences in temperature between bodies.

Testing the two theories

You can now test out these theories in some experiments, all of which involve raising the temperature of an object. The experiments are illustrated in figure 10.7 on the next page.

Figure 10.7
Illustrations of four different ways of
changing the temperature of a body.

Experiment 1
A lit bunsen burner is
placed under a beaker
containing 250 cm³ of cold
water and a thermometer

Experiment 2
250 cm³ of boiling water is poured into a large beaker
containing 250 cm³ of cold water and a thermometer

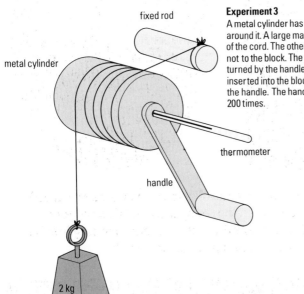

Experiment 3
A metal cylinder has a belt or cord wound
around it. A large mass is tied on to one end
of the cord. The other end is tied to a bar,
not to the block. The metal block can be
turned by the handle. A thermometer is
inserted into the block through the centre of
the handle. The handle is turned rapidly
200 times.

fixed rod

metal cylinder

thermometer

handle

2 kg

Experiment 4
500 g of lead shot are taken from a plastic cup
containing a thermometer and put in a cardboard
tube. The tube is sealed at both ends and then turned
upside-down 50 times. The lead shot is quickly
poured back into the plastic cup.

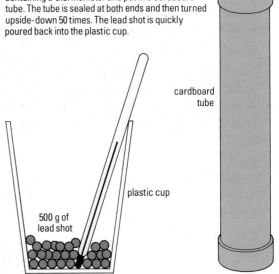

cardboard
tube

plastic cup

500 g of
lead shot

What you have to do is to use both the theories to **predict** what will happen
to the temperatures in each case. You will probably be able to **guess** what will
happen, but that is not important. What you have to do is to think out what
the **theories** would say will happen. That may be something quite different
from what you **believe** will happen.

After this you may either see these experiments as demonstrations or be
able to try them for yourself. In each case, you should write down what
actually happened. When you have done that, work out for each experiment
the theory that was the most useful in predicting the outcome.

*You will probably find it best to work in small groups and to discuss amongst yourselves both the
predictions' and the theories' successes and failures. Another method would be for half your class
to use only the caloric theory and the other half to use only the kinetic theory. Then you can have a
debate to see which theory is best able to predict the outcomes of these experiments.*

4 Which do you think is the more useful theory? Why do you come to this conclusion?

The two theories in history

You may have wondered why these two theories were chosen for you to test. The reason is that both have been important at one time or another in the history of science. While we favour the kinetic theory today, the caloric theory has also proved very useful.

The caloric theory was a theory made popular by the work of Joseph Black in the middle of the eighteenth century, but many other scientists, such as Lavoisier and Laplace, also contributed to it. It was very useful to scientists in understanding the heat engines you met in Chapter **P8**.

Figure 10.8
Three scientists who contributed to the development of the caloric theory of heating.
a (left) Joseph Black (1728–1799).
b (centre) Pierre Laplace (1749–1827).
c (right) Antoine Lavoisier (1743–1794).

However, for thousands of years people all over the world have realized that force and motion can produce a rise in temperature. We have good evidence to show that people in ancient times started their cooking fires by such methods as striking flints and rubbing dry sticks together.

Figure 10.9
Starting a fire using friction.

5 How do we produce fires now? Is there any similarity between ancient and modern methods?

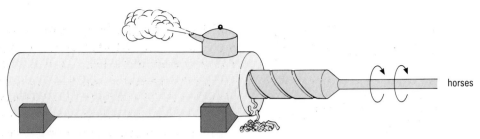

Figure 10.10
A diagram of Count Rumford's experiment. The results from this experiment showed the need for a new theory of heating.

Greeks such as Plato and Aristotle were able to explain the relationship between fire and motion in terms of their own theories about the four "elements" – earth, water, air and fire. By the early nineteenth century, ideas about energy were beginning to appear. Count Rumford carried out some famous experiments boring the muzzles of cannon which got hotter and hotter as the boring went on.

6 Why do your hands feel warmer when you rub them together?

By the middle of the nineteenth century, scientists such as John Dalton were providing convincing evidence that all matter was made up from atoms and molecules. Many other scientists were involved in the development both of the idea that energy transfer might be a part of "getting hotter" and of the idea that all matter is made from particles. These two ideas together gave rise to the second of our theories – the *kinetic theory* – the theory we favour today.

*If you have chosen to follow section **P10.2**, rather than section **P10.3**, you should now go on to read section **P10.4**.*

P10.3   A kinetic theory of heating

The connection between temperature and energy puzzled scientists for many years. Today we use the kinetic theory to explain how these two are linked. The kinetic theory is described in Chapter **P2**. This theory assumes that everything is made from particles in a state of continual movement. In your work in chemistry, these "particles" are described as atoms, molecules or ions. It is often important in chemistry to say which is which. The difference between them is described in Chapters **C1**, **C5** and **C18**. Here we are only interested in the fact that matter is made of tiny pieces of matter that are not easily broken down into anything smaller. It does not concern us whether they are atoms, small groups of atoms (called molecules) or ions (which are electrically-charged atoms and molecules) – so we shall simply call them "particles".

Figure 10.11
Dalton's theory of atoms and Rumford's experiments that linked energy to temperature were combined to produce the kinetic theory.
a (top) John Dalton (1766–1844).
b (bottom) Count Rumford (1753–1814).

7 Draw three diagrams which show the differences between the particles in solids, liquids and gases.

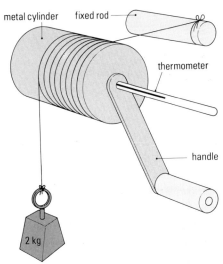

metal cylinder   fixed rod

thermometer

handle

2 kg

Figure 10.12
An experiment that enables energy
transfer to be linked to temperature rise.

If the particles in a body are moving, they have kinetic energy. When
energy is transferred **into** a body it may give the particles more kinetic energy.
They move or vibrate faster, and at the same time the temperature rises. So
you see the speed with which the particles move is linked to the temperature
of the object. The faster the particles move, the higher the temperature. When
the particles slow down, the temperature falls.

Friction is something you experience every day. It is essential for us just to
walk or run. At the same time, it can be a nuisance. Friction transfers energy
to the molecules of objects when we would prefer to have that energy
somewhere else. For example, when you oil the wheel bearings on a bicycle
you are trying to reduce friction.

You will probably see a demonstration of the experiment illustrated in
figure 10.12. In the experiment we use friction between the cord and the
cylinder. When the handle is turned, the metal block rubs against the cord.
This transfers energy to the atoms inside the metal drum and makes them
vibrate faster. If the atoms move faster, what, according to our theory, should
happen to the temperature of the metal block?

8 Make your prediction and write it down. Now try it out. Record the temperature,
turn the handle 200 times and record the temperature again. Was your prediction
correct?

If the prediction you make using the theory proves correct, then the theory
is useful. Figure 10.13 illustrates another experiment you can do. In this
experiment, 500 g of lead shot is put into a plastic cup and the temperature of
the lead measured with a thermometer. The lead shot is then put into a
cardboard tube which is then sealed at both ends. The tube is tipped upside
down 50 times.

9 Predict what will happen to the lead shot.

The lead shot is poured back into the plastic cup and its temperature is read
again.

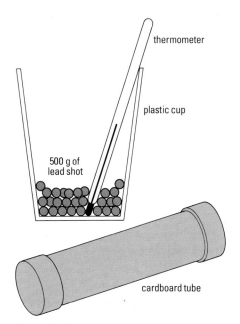

thermometer

plastic cup

500 g of
lead shot

cardboard tube

Figure 10.13
By tipping the lead shot down the tube
several times, energy is transferred to the
lead and its temperature rises.

10a Did your prediction prove to be correct?
b Why is a plastic cup used to hold the lead shot rather than a glass beaker? (Apart
from fear of breaking the glass!)

11 Predict what would happen in the first experiment if the handle were turned 400
times rather than 200 times.
If you can, test out your prediction.

12 The measured effects are rather small in the second experiment.
a Predict the effect of turning the tube upside down 100 times rather than 50.
b Predict the effect of using 1000 g of lead rather than 500 g.

In each case, try to check your prediction. In particular, how does the kinetic theory
explain the result found in part **b**?

P10.4   Energy and temperature

So far you have seen how the kinetic theory of heating is useful because it helps us with our predictions. We have great faith in these ideas, even though we cannot see the "particles" on which the theory is based!

The reason why the kinetic theory was accepted in place of the caloric theory was because it could explain the link between temperature rise and energy transfer. Although everyone agrees today that a rise in temperature depends on the transfer of energy, it was very difficult in the nineteenth century to test the theory by experiment. A scientist called Edward Mayer was sure there was a connection between temperature and energy, but he was unable to convince his fellow scientists by argument alone.

At about the same time, a Manchester brewer and amateur scientist, James Joule, was also convinced of the link between energy and temperature. Joule spent 40 years designing and building pieces of apparatus to show this. A picture of one of his experiments is shown in figure 10.15a. In that experiment, he churned up water with some paddles. As a result the water got warmer. He measured carefully the energy he transferred to the water when churning it up. He also measured how much the temperature of the water rose as a result. His experiment showed that he had to transfer 4200 joules of energy to raise the temperature of 1 kilogram of the water by 1 °C.

Figure 10.14
J. P. Joule (1818–1889). It was Joule's experiments that finally convinced everyone that change in temperature of a body was a result of transferring energy to it.

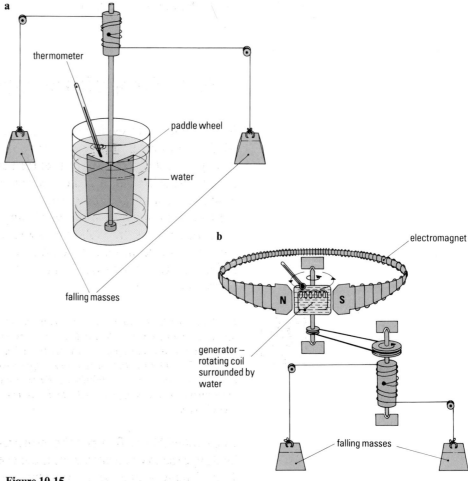

Figure 10.15
Two of James Joule's most famous experiments.

But the importance of Joule's work lies in the way he made similar measurements in many different experiments. He always found that 4200 joules of energy had to be transferred to raise the temperature of 1 kilogram of water by 1 °C. There is a story that he was so enthusiastic about these experiments that he even measured the water temperature at the top and bottom of a waterfall while on his honeymoon in Switzerland!

13 Explain why James Joule expected to find a difference between the temperatures of the water at the top and the bottom of a waterfall.

Because Joule was an "amateur" scientist, his experiments were not taken seriously by other, full-time, scientists. However, despite the fact that the Royal Society refused to publish one of his papers, he continued with his hobby. Eventually, 30 years after his first published experiments, he was presented with the Copley Medal by the Royal Society, the highest honour it awards. One year later, in 1871, Mayer received the same honour. Perhaps if Mayer had been able to devise a method of testing his theory, we would now measure energy in mayers instead of joules!

Section P10.5 describes some experiments you can do to measure the temperature rise produced when a measured amount of energy is transferred to some metals. It is not essential to work through this slightly more difficult section in order to understand the rest of the chapter. You could omit it and go on to section P10.6.

P10.5 Comparing energy transfers

In experiment 3 in section **P10.2** you transferred energy to a metal block using friction. As a result, the temperature of the block increased. The caloric theory cannot account for this temperature rise. According to the caloric theory, the caloric fluid in the block would have to increase. But there is nowhere it could have come from.

Instead, we say that the *internal energy* of an object is increased when its temperature rises. In a solid the increase in internal energy means that the particles vibrate more. In a liquid or a gas, the increase in internal energy means that the particles move faster. In both cases the kinetic energy of the particles increases.

Worksheet P10A describes an experiment you can do to measure the rise in the internal energy of the metal block used in section P10.2. The worksheet gives you two ways in which this can be done, but you will not be able to attempt the second way until you have worked through Chapters P16 and P17. This would be a very good experiment to return to after you have understood the work in those two chapters. Worksheet P10A gives you only a little help in designing your experiment – if you can, you should do this yourself. If you run into difficulties, you can ask for a "help" sheet.

In Chapter **P9** you first met the term *specific heating capacity*. The specific heating capacity of a substance is the energy which must be transferred to 1 kg of the substance to raise its temperature by 1 °C. The specific heating capacities of several substances (such as concrete and water) were given to you as numbers with the promise that you would be shown where they came from later on.

The experiment you have done using Worksheet **P**10A showed you how to find the change in the internal energy of a metal cylinder. We can use measurements such as these to find the specific heating capacity of substances. An example may make this clear.

Suppose that in a carefully-performed experiment it was found that an aluminium cylinder of mass 1 kg rose in temperature by 2.0 °C when it was rotated 360 times against a 20 N frictional force. The circumference of the cylinder was 0.25 m so it moved a distance of 0.25 m against the frictional force for every rotation. (The "circumference" of a cylinder is the distance all the way round the curved edge.)

We can now calculate the energy transferred to the block, and thus its increase in internal energy:

the distance moved against frictional force $= 360 \text{ turns} \times 0.25 \text{ m per turn}$
$= 90 \text{ m}$
so the work done against the frictional force $= 20 \text{ N} \times 90 \text{ m}$
$= 1800 \text{ J}$

The energy was transferred to the aluminium block and as a result its temperature rose by 2 °C. So 1800 J of energy raised the temperature of 1 kg of aluminium by 2 °C.

To raise the temperature of 1 kg of aluminium by 1 °C would thus require:

$$\frac{1800 \text{ J}}{2} = 900 \text{ J}$$

Remember that the specific heating capacity of aluminium is the energy that has to be transferred to raise the temperature of 1 kg of aluminium by 1 °C. So these measurements show that the specific heating capacity of aluminium is 900 J/kg per °C rise in temperature.

14 As you have just seen, the specific heating capacity of aluminium is 900 J per kg for each °C change in temperature.
a Using the rise in temperature you measured in the experiment in Worksheet **P**10A, calculate the increase in the internal energy of the block from your knowledge of its specific heating capacity.
b You will probably find that you needed to transfer more than this amount of energy when you did work against friction. Explain why this is so. Your suggestions are very important, so take care to give full explanations.

Energy can be transferred to the internal energy of a body by working or by heating. The transfer of a fixed amount of energy by **either** method will increase the internal energy by the same amount. It is because of this, we can measure the specific heating capacity in a direct way by doing a known amount of work to increase the internal energy of a body and measuring the resulting rise in temperature of the body.

Of course we must make sure that all the energy transferred as work goes into raising the temperature of the body, and none goes elsewhere. The experiment described in Worksheet **P**10B uses the equipment used in experiment 4 in section **P**10.2 to do just that. If you have time, you may like to measure the specific heating capacity of lead in this way.

Figure 10.16
Exchanging money for goods or services.
It is only when money changes hands that
it becomes useful.

P10.6 The conservation of energy

We have already said that energy is like having money (on page 130). Just keeping it is not very useful. Money is only useful when it is exchanged for services or goods.

Energy is only useful when it is transferred. You can probably think of many examples where energy is transferred. Here are four important points to remember about energy:

- when things happen, energy is usually transferred
- change in temperature involves energy transfer
- in any change in which energy is transferred, the total amount of energy stays the same
- many changes involve energy being transferred to the surroundings, but the temperature rise which results is often so small that the energy appears to have vanished.

When energy is transferred, we can always count up where all the energy goes. A scientist who is interested in energy is a bit like an "energy accountant". An accountant balances the income and expenditure before and after financial deals. A scientist balances the energy before and after energy transfers. The scientist has to make sure that all the energy is accounted for. It is assumed energy cannot disappear or be created out of nothing. This is known as the "conservation of energy".

Figure 10.17
An accountant is a person who keeps track of money and balances income against expenditure.

*The last part of this section of work describes some experiments which will help you with the idea of energy conservation. The "energy circus" uses experiments with which you may feel yourself quite familiar. If this is the case, try the energy investigation described in Worksheet **P**10C.*

A "circus" of energy transfers

The diagrams in figure 10.18 (on the next page) illustrate a range of energy transfers that you may have seen before. What you have to do in this case is to think about energy conservation during each transfer.

For each example illustrated write down:

1 What useful job is being done.
2 Where the energy is transferred from.
3 Where the energy is transferred to.

Instruction 3 is the part you should think about most carefully. During transfer, energy often gets distributed in lots of small amounts as well as one big quantity. You have got to include all these small amounts as well. You do not have to count how much is transferred, just say where it comes **from** and all the places it goes **to**.

Figure 10.18
A range of different energy transfers.

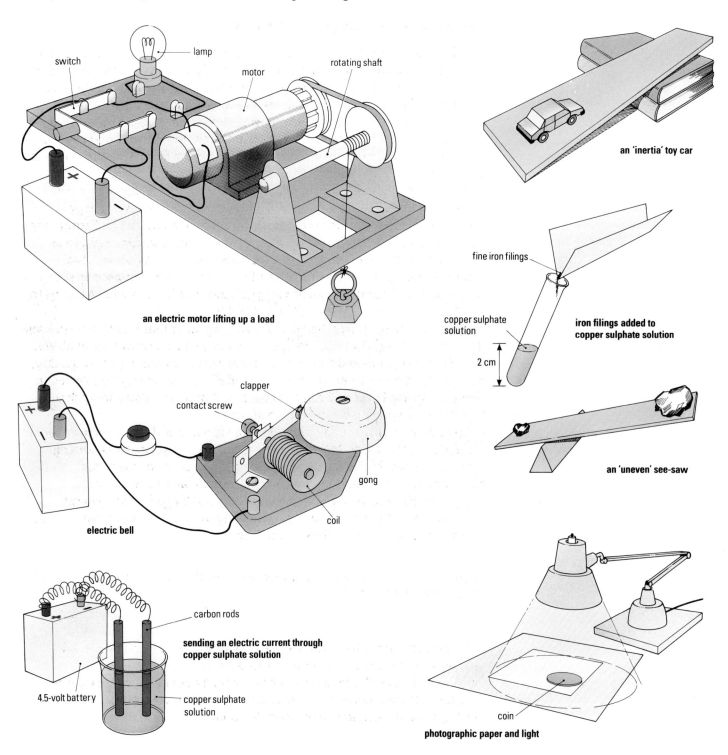

switch — lamp — motor — rotating shaft

an electric motor lifting up a load

clapper — contact screw — gong — coil

electric bell

carbon rods

sending an electric current through copper sulphate solution

4.5-volt battery — copper sulphate solution

an 'inertia' toy car

fine iron filings — copper sulphate solution — 2 cm

iron filings added to copper sulphate solution

an 'uneven' see-saw

coin

photographic paper and light

The range of energy transfers in figure 10.18 may be set out for you to try, in which case a worksheet will be provided to help you. If you have seen them before, you may need only to do one or two to make sure you can handle the idea of "energy conservation".

An investigation into energy conservation

If you are very familiar with the experiments illustrated in figure 10.18 you can try instead an investigation into energy conservation. The details of the investigation are given in Worksheet **P**10C.

Energy cost and energy conservation

Any job that brings about change costs energy. Moving from place to place, manufacturing goods, building houses, hospitals or roads are just some of the things that cost energy. In Chapter **P**8 the energy costs of several jobs were calculated. The energy cost of a job is the energy that has to be transferred to do it. In Chapter **P**12, you will see the range of energy resources that we draw on in order to be able to do all these useful things. But as you will see in that chapter, there is a concern that many of the energy resources we use at present are "running out". It is important to find new energy resources.

Experiments have been done however that show that energy is not lost when it is transferred. So why should there be this concern over energy resources? Can't we use the same energy over and over again? Unfortunately we can't do this. Although energy is never lost, it becomes less useful to us when it is transferred. The study of machines in Chapter **P**8 shows that whenever energy is transferred, some of it always goes to warming up the surroundings. Sometimes, when energy is transferred, this is what happens to all of it.

It is when energy is transferred to the surroundings that it cannot be re-used. This chapter has shown what happens to energy when it warms up an object. The particles (atoms and molecules) take up energy by moving more quickly, but they then move about in every direction and all the energy transferred to them is dispersed over millions and millions of particles. This energy cannot be harnessed again to do a useful job of work.

Spreading things around always decreases their usefulness. You meet the same idea in chemistry. Many valuable metals (like copper) are becoming scarce, not because the metals are disappearing, but because they are becoming spread around so that it becomes impossible to re-use them.

Chapter **P**12 shows not only where we may be able to find new energy resources, but also how we can "save" energy by not allowing so much of it to become spread around in the surroundings.

You can find out more about recycling materials in Chapter C6 "Glasses and ceramics" (section C6.6) in your Chemistry book.

15a Describe three different jobs that require energy to be transferred and in which all the energy transferred ends up in the surroundings.
b For one of these jobs, suggest a way that some of the energy transferred could be "saved". (You can save energy either by transferring less in the first place, or by finding a way to re-use some of the energy transferred.)

P10.7   Changes: from liquid to gas and solid to liquid

By now you should be quite a good "energy accountant". You should also realize that useful jobs involve energy transfers. Boiling water for a hot drink is a useful job. Suppose you fill a kettle with tap water which is at 15°C. You light the gas and put the kettle on the flame. Can you explain the energy transfer? Energy is transferred from the hot flame to the base of the kettle and the water. The internal energy of the kettle and the water is increased because the atoms and molecules from which they are made move faster.

Figure 10.19

16 Read the following account about cooking potatoes. Discuss it for a few minutes in small groups and prepare a short paragraph which gives your explanation.

"Sylvia and Howard were camping. They were boiling potatoes on two small stoves. When the water in both pans was boiling, Sylvia turned her stove down low so that the water just kept boiling. Howard left his stove burning with a full flame because he said it would cook the potatoes faster. Sylvia said it would make no difference."

Who do you think was right? Give an explanation for your answer.

You know that if you leave a kettle on the gas flame the water gains more and more internal energy. This means the molecules move faster and faster. As a result the temperature rises higher and higher.

Eventually the water boils. As you saw in Chapter **P2** the temperature does **not** rise any more (as long as the pressure remains the same). Energy is still being transferred to the boiling water, but the temperature remains the same (about 100°C). According to our theory this means the molecules do not move any faster. But if molecules do not gain any more kinetic energy, what happens to the energy which is still being transferred from the flame?

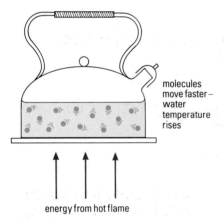

molecules move faster – water temperature rises

energy from hot flame

Figure 10.20
A kettle of water being heated on a stove.

17a How do you know the kinetic energy of the molecules is not increasing?
 b Suggest where the energy from the flame is being transferred to now.

Developing the idea of internal energy

The internal energy of a substance is not just the total kinetic energy of the particles from which it is made. So far, we understand that transferring energy to these particles makes them move faster and consequently raises the temperature. Now we are going to suggest that transferring energy to these particles can also make them move further apart.

Of course the suggestion we have just made is not just a wild guess. It is based upon our understanding of the differences between solids, liquids and gases dealt with in Chapter **P2**. There are forces holding molecules together in solids and liquids. To separate the molecules from each other requires a force which moves them apart. This means energy has to be transferred.

18 Where has the energy been transferred to?

19 How can you tell when molecules in a liquid or a gas are moving faster?

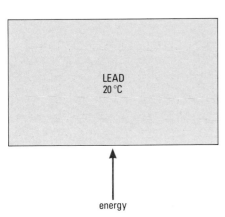

Figure 10.21
Heating a block of lead.

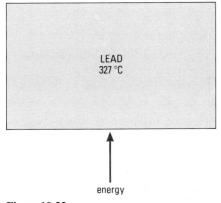

Figure 10.22
The block of lead has reached its melting point. What happens to it now if you continue heating?

Figure 10.23
Albert Einstein (1879–1955), one of the most famous scientists of the twentieth century.

*You will learn in the Chemistry book (Chapter **C7**, section **C7.2**) that the forces **between** the molecules which make up liquids and gases are much smaller than the forces which hold the atoms together in the molecule. Very, very high temperatures have to be reached before there is enough energy to break up the molecules themselves.*

Investigating melting solids

The "extra" energy gained by the molecules in a boiling liquid is used to change the liquid into a gas, without raising the temperature. In the case of boiling water you can see the water forming bubbles of steam. Once this happens, supplying more energy simply gives more molecules enough internal energy to evaporate into vapour bubbles. Therefore the temperature stays constant at the "boiling-point".

Can you make a similar connection with the particles which make up a solid? Suppose you had a block of lead at room temperature (say 20 °C) and you heat it.

20 What happens to the atoms of lead as the block is heated (figure 10.21)?

Eventually the lead will reach its melting point of 327 °C.

21a What happens to the atoms if you continue heating the lead (figure 10.22)?
b What happens to the temperature of the lead?

This extra energy is transferred to the lead atoms when the lead melts. This energy does not make the atoms move faster.

New theories for old?

In this chapter you have used scientific theories to make predictions. Science only makes progress when scientists can make predictions from their theories. Making predictions from theories can be the hard part of science – and particularly of physics. This is where mathematics often has to be used. But you do not need to be able to understand mathematics to understand theories. You have made predictions without using mathematics. Using mathematics, however, has made the kinetic theory and the law of conservation of energy very powerful indeed.

Early in the twentieth century, Albert Einstein extended our ideas about energy even further. According to Einstein, stored energy increases the mass of a body. The increase in the mass of a body brought about by the stored energy is given by the famous equation

$$E = mc^2$$

In this equation, E is the energy in joules, m is the equivalent mass in kilograms and c is the speed of light in metres per second. As an example of how this works out, when a kilogram of uranium splits up in a nuclear reactor, one gram vanishes and as much energy is released as a large power station produces in 24 hours.

*You can find out more about nuclear reactors in Chapter **P12**.*

Summary

The sentences below summarize some of the most important ideas of this chapter. However, if you read them, they do not make sense in the order they have been written. Write out the sentences in an order that you think makes sense.

- These molecules are continuously moving.
- If enough energy is transferred to the water it may boil.
- All of his experiments showed that 4200 joules of energy must be transferred to raise the temperature of 1 kilogram of water by 1 °C.
- When water boils, energy is transferred in moving the molecules further apart.
- The kinetic theory explains the results of his experiments by picturing the water as made up of many small molecules.
- James Joule did many experiments in which he transferred energy to water and measured its rise in temperature.
- When the molecules move faster we describe the water as "getting hotter".
- When energy is transferred to the water the molecules move faster.

In this chapter you have learned of the difference between **facts** and **theories**. Some of the sentences in the passage you have just written out are facts and some are theories. (Remember that theories are descriptions of the way we **think** things are. They are made to explain what we **see**.)

Which of the sentences in the passage are **facts** and which are a part of **theories**?

Chapter **P**11

Energy where it is needed
Energy transmission

P11.1 **Energy on the move**

Backpacking, or hiking, is a popular activity. There is a sense of independence involved in packing into a rucksack everything you need to survive for a few days, and walking through a part of Britain. You could visit the north-west Highlands in Scotland or the Lake District in England or Snowdonia in Wales. But you would not stay in a hotel or an organized camp site. Backpackers prefer to use footpaths and find places to camp where there are very few other people. They enjoy "getting away from it all".

1 What do you think "getting away from it all" means?

2 Suppose you were planning a three-day backpacking trip across a part of the countryside. You do not expect to visit any villages or farms on the way. Make a list of all the essential things you need to take.

3 How many different energy supplies did you include in your list in question **2**? What were they?

Figure 11.1
Getting away from it all!

Figure 11.2 (below left)
The remains of huts in Cumbria that were once used to store peat.

Figure 11.3 (below right)
Delivering coal on a winter morning.

We would find it impossible to live without one source of energy – our food. But we would also find life difficult without other sources of energy which we use to give us light and keep us warm. Materials which are used to provide us with energy, such as wood, coal, gas, oil and also uranium, are all called *fuels*.

*You will learn more about fuels in your Chemistry book, Chapter **C13**.*

Many years ago peat was an important fuel. It was cut and dried before being stored in huts like those shown in figure 11.2.

In Britain coal has been used for many years because of the rich deposits underground. Coal is still delivered to homes for burning. We could think of coal as energy being delivered by the sackful.

Early in the nineteenth century a method was found of heating coal to a very high temperature to produce a gas which could be burned. This gas is a mixture of compounds such as methane and carbon monoxide, and is called *coal gas* (or sometimes, *town gas*). This discovery led to "gas works" (as they were called) being built in every major town and city. The gas was stored in huge gasholders like the ones shown in figure 11.4. From there it was delivered to local homes along pipes. For the first time many people had energy available "on tap". This was a tremendous convenience as cookers and heaters could be lit much more easily than solid fuel fires. It was also a much more efficient use of the energy stored in coal.

You can learn about the properties of gases like methane in your work in chemistry.

During the 1970s "town gas" supplies in Britain were replaced by "natural" gas which is piped from under the North Sea. The cost of laying miles of pipes right across Britain, carrying gas to people's homes, is very high. So many small communities are not connected to a gas pipeline.

However, this is not too great an inconvenience because nearly every home in Britain is connected to the electricity supply.

It is easier to join your home to a power station with electricity cables than it is to join your home to the North Sea gas fields by pipes. If you are lucky, you may enjoy the benefits of both. But nearly all people can now obtain as much energy as they need, at home and at work, whenever they want it, simply by the flick of a switch.

*In this chapter you are going to look at the way energy is transferred to your home by electricity. In doing so we will be bringing together ideas about energy and electromagnetism which are in Chapters **P8** to **P10** and Chapter **P18**.*

*If you finished the last part of Chapter **P18** (about generators) then you can leave out the next section and go on to section **P11.3**. If you have not studied generators yet, then work through section **P11.2** and then go on to section **P11.4**.*

Figure 11.4
A gasholder. "Town gas" produced from coal was once stored in giant gasholders from where it was piped to houses. These same pipes now carry natural gas.

Figure 11.5 (below left)
Electricity pylons. The construction of pylons varies with the voltage of the electricity supply they carry. This is a 400 kV transmission line. Try to find out which type of pylons carry which voltage.

Figure 11.6 (below right)
Underground cables carrying electric current. Cables such as these are used in some areas of outstanding natural beauty, but they are much more expensive to lay and maintain than pylons.

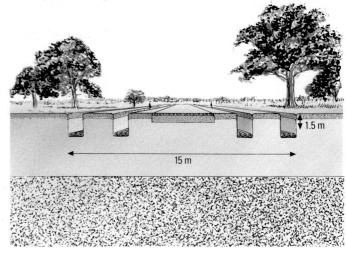

P11.2   Generators

OBSERVE

Whenever you bring two magnets together, you can feel what we call a *magnetic force*.

Chapter **P**18 shows how the same force is responsible for moving a wire which carries an electric current in another magnetic field. By clever design, this force can be used to operate an electric motor. To do this, you have to:

- Pass an **electric current** through a coil of wire, which can turn on an axle. (The axle is a rod on which the coil is fixed.)
- Provide another magnetic field which surrounds the coil of wire.

Figure 11.7
Feeling a magnetic force.

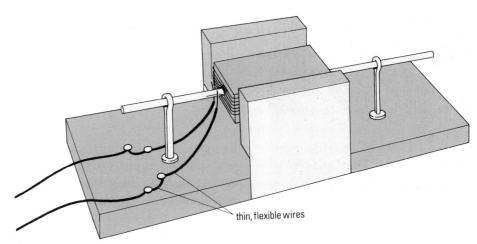

thin, flexible wires

Figure 11.8
A model electric motor that you can build for yourself.

Of course, to make the coil and axle spin round and round continuously you have to connect it to the power supply with a sliding switch that we call a *commutator*. This is described in Chapter **P**18 in section **P**18.4.

INTERPRET

So two things are needed to make a motor work – an electric current and a magnetic field. We could summarize this in the following way:

Now, if we re-arrange this statement as follows what would you expect to be produced?

4 Suppose you are given a sensitive ammeter and an electric motor. Think of a way of finding out what motion + magnetic field will produce. You could either use a model motor such as the one in Chapter **P**18 or a real electric motor.

You may have guessed that an electric current will flow in the circuit, but remember that the purpose of question **4** is to work out a way to test your prediction.

This short investigation should help you to understand how electricity is produced by generators. This statement summarizes how generators work:

Devices which can produce an electric current by moving wires through a magnetic field are called *electricity generators*. They are also known as *dynamos* and as *alternators*. The term "electricity generator" is not a good one. "Generate" means "make", but "electricity generators" do not **make** anything; they **transfer** energy (usually from fuels) to electric charge. Figure 11.9 shows a bicycle dynamo which may be like one you might have on your own bicycle. It is a small electricity generator.

Figure 11.9
A close-up view of a bicycle dynamo.

5a Where does a bicycle dynamo get its energy from?
b Where does it transfer its energy to?
c What would you expect to happen to a light powered by a cycle dynamo as the bicycle slows down and eventually stops?

Figure 11.10 shows a large generator in use in a power station. The generator produces a current by turning a magnet (called the *rotor*) whilst

Figure 11.10
A power station generator. (The word "generator" is misleading as neither electricity nor energy is generated. Instead the "generators" transfer energy from fuels to electric charge.)

electricity is produced inside a coil (called a *stator*) which remains still. In a power station the rotor is an electromagnet.

The current produced by a cycle dynamo and a power station generator is different from that produced by a battery. It is called alternating current. You will learn more about this in section **P**11.4.

---

6 Why is an electromagnet used in a power station generator and a permanent magnet in a bicycle dynamo?

The generator in figure 11.10 has a power of 1771 MW. In Chapter **P**12 we will consider the different energy sources used to turn generators in different types of power station. Whatever the energy source, all power stations use generators to transfer energy to electric charges.

P11.3 Using energy resources in the best way

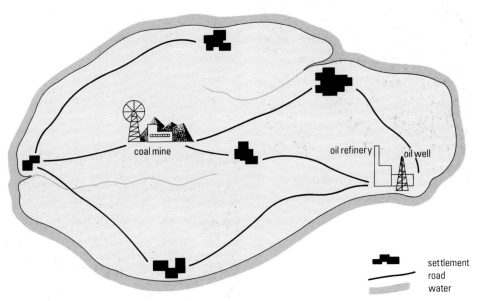

coal mine

oil refinery · oil well

settlement
road
water

Figure 11.11
A map of the imaginary island of Pylos.

Figure 11.11 is a map of an imaginary island called **Pylos**. The island is (very) roughly circular and has a radius of 30 miles. Pylos has a coal mine with plenty of reserves and its own oil well and refinery. The government of Pylos has decided to use these energy resources to supply every home on the island with electricity. The government has put forward two different ways of doing this.

Scheme 1

Deliver coal from the coal mine to each individual home. Install a miniature power station in each home which will drive a small generator and provide enough electricity for the home.

Figure 11.12
Scheme 1.

Scheme 2

Deliver coal from the coal mine to a large power station. Drive a large generator and connect it to every home by cables to provide each one with electricity.

Figure 11.13
Scheme 2.

The local population is divided over the two schemes. Opponents to scheme 1 say that too much energy will be "wasted" by delivering the coal to each home. Opponents to scheme 2 say there will be just as much "wasted" energy needed to send electricity along the many kilometres of cable between the power station and each home.

7 Both schemes will indeed "waste" energy! But what would you do to try to find out which scheme was likely to waste more energy?

8 Apart from wasting energy, both schemes will have other advantages and disadvantages. Make a list of as many advantages and disadvantages of each scheme as you can.
  You can think about the effect on the environment, the number of jobs involved, the relative costs and convenience. It will help if you discuss your ideas with other people.

P11.4   Transmitting electricity

One of the reasons why electricity is so important in our lives is because it is easy to deliver. All we need is a length of cable.
  Energy is transferred along a wire by electric charges. These charges transfer energy from a large generator in a power station to your home, or anywhere else it may be needed. Some of the cables which are used to transfer this energy may be many kilometres long. A picture of some of them was shown in figure 11.5. With other cables, you can in turn transport that energy to the blades of your lawn mower and cut the grass, or to any other electrical appliances in your home.

Figure 11.14 (above left)
A modern 3890 MW coal-fired power station at Selby, North Yorkshire.

Figure 11.15 (above right)
An electric lawn mower. This one is connected to the "mains" supply. How else could a mower be driven electrically?

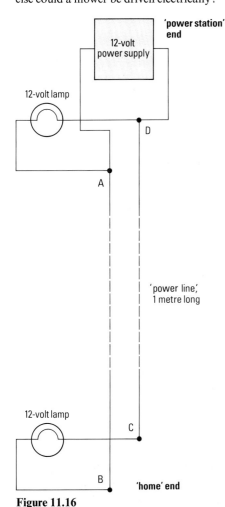

Figure 11.16
A model power transmission line. The wires are made of high resistance wire so that they can imitate the behaviour of real lines (which are of course very much longer).

Power lines

Transmitting energy from place to place using electricity may seem very simple, but it does have problems of its own. Figure 11.16 shows a model power transmission line. In real life, thick aluminium and copper wires are used to connect power stations to the places where the energy is needed. These are many kilometres in length and so have quite a large electrical resistance. The wires used to represent the power line in the model are only about 1 m long. So to make them behave like real power lines, a thinner wire is used. This way they will have a resistance more like that of true power lines.

You should see this next experiment demonstrated or be able to try it for yourself. Either way you should be able to discuss what you see with other people.

12-volt lamps have been connected at each end of the transmission line. A 12-volt power pack represents the generator in the power station. Switch on the power supply and make a note of the brightness of the lamps.

9a Which of the two lamps is brighter?
b How could you find out whether or not it is just a difference between the lamps which causes the difference in brightness?

If you have worked through and understood the sections on voltage in Chapter P17, you can carry on with this section and measure some voltages. This may help you to see why one lamp is brighter than the other.

Connect one voltmeter across A and D and a second across B and C. Compare the brightness of the lamps and the readings on the voltmeters. Remember from Chapter P17 that a voltmeter measures how much energy per coulomb is transferred between two points in a circuit. So, if the voltmeter across A and D reads 12 V, it means that 12 joules of energy are transferred for every coulomb of charge flowing round the circuit between A and D. (Remember, 1 volt = 1 joule per coulomb.)

Sam made the following observations when she saw the experiment. The lamp at the "power station" end was very bright, but the one at the "home" end was hardly glowing at all. The voltmeter joined across A and D read 12 V and the voltmeter joined across B and C read 2 V.

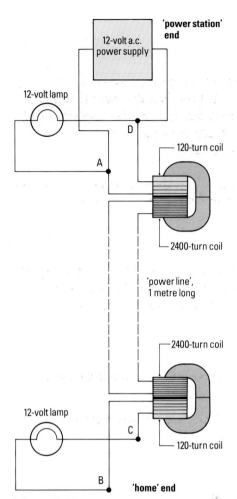

Figure 11.17
Model transmission line with transformers at each end.

Figure 11.18
A transformer of the sort that can be used in the model transmission line shown in figure 11.17.

10a How much energy is transferred per coulomb of charge flowing between B and C?
b If 12 joules are transferred per coulomb of charge flowing between A and D, how much energy per coulomb is "wasted" along the power line?

11 How could Sam have checked that the answer to question **10**b was correct? Look at your own observations and predict how much energy is transferred per coulomb of charge as it flows down your power line. If possible, check your answer with some measurements.

This experiment shows that there is a problem in using cables to convey electricity. If your home or a factory is a long way from the power station, you would find that very little power is available at the cable's end using the arrangement shown in figure 11.16. It seems that energy is being "lost" on its way to the home or factory. The next experiment shows how this problem can be overcome.

Figure 11.17 shows a different arrangement for a model power line. In this new arrangement, the same power line and the same lamps are used, but at each end of the power line there is a pair of coils. Each pair of coils is wrapped around an iron core (figure 11.18). One coil of the pair has 120 turns of wire. The other coil has 2400 turns. Each pair of coils, with their iron core, is called a *transformer*.

To see what effect the transformers have, the power supply is switched on. (You should not do this yourself as dangerously high voltages are involved, as you will see.)

Once again, compare the brightness of the lamps. What difference do you see compared with the previous power line arrangement in figure 11.16? Using transformers with the model power line you can see that less energy is "wasted" in moving the charges along the power lines. Since the same power lines were used, it seems that the difference is caused by the transformers.

If we measure the voltage across AD in figure 11.17, we again find it to be 12 V. But this time the voltage across BC is also 12 V. This is why the lamp at the "home" end is now fully lit. But if you look at the voltage across the 2400-turn coils on the transformers you will find that it is about 240 V! (This is why the experiment is dangerous to do yourself.)

So the transformers are changing the voltage. They take 12-volt electricity and turn it into 240-volt electricity to transmit it along the power line. Then at the other end, the transformer turns the electricity back to a safe 12 volts. As a result of this, far less energy is "lost" during transmission.

Why can high-voltage electricity be transmitted more efficiently than low-voltage electricity? How do transformers work? These are two questions that we will try to answer. But before doing that, there is one more thing to notice about this experiment. The "power station" is producing *alternating current*.

Alternating current is an electric current that surges back and forth in wires, like the tide at sea. The current produced by an electric cell or battery is different from this. That current flows steadily in one direction, like the flow of water along an inland river, and is called a *direct current*.

Electricity generators can produce alternating current more easily than direct current. The way they do this is described in Chapter **P**18. If you have not previously looked at this, it would be a good idea to do so now.

Transformers will not "work" if direct current is used. The reason for this will become clear in the next section.

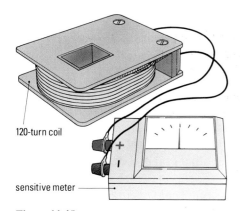

Figure 11.19
A coil connected to a sensitive meter.

P11.5 Transformers

You have already seen how an electric current can be produced in a generator. Producing an electric current in this way is called *electromagnetic induction*. Electric currents produced by electromagnetic induction are called *induced* currents. The next series of experiments show you how electromagnetic induction is used in transformers.

You will probably see these experiments done as a series of demonstrations. If you worked through the last part of Chapter P18, you may be able to omit some of these experiments now.

Moving a magnet through a coil

Figure 11.19 shows a 120-turn coil connected to a sensitive meter. If a magnet is moved in and out of the coil, you will find that a current flows when the magnet is moving. No current flows if neither the coil nor the magnet is moving.

12 What difference is there in the movement of the meter needle when the magnet goes in compared with when it comes out?

13 Is there any difference if the magnet is moved into the coil slowly or quickly? If so, what is it?

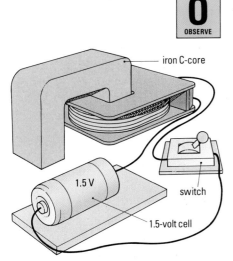

Figure 11.20
An electromagnet. Large electromagnets, carried by cranes, are often used in scrap yards. What does this tell you about much of the metal in scrap yards?

Switching an electromagnet on and off

You may already have investigated the behaviour of an electromagnet (Worksheet **P**18C). The electromagnet is made from an iron C-core and a 120-turn coil, as shown in figure 11.20. It is connected, via a switch, to a 1.5-volt cell.

14 Using iron nails, how would you show that both ends of the C-core are magnetized?

15 Would both ends be magnetized in the same way? If not, what would be the difference?

Using an electromagnet to induce an electric current

The diagram in figure 11.21 shows a circuit attached to the electromagnet of the last experiment. This second circuit consists of a 120-turn coil connected to a sensitive meter. The coil is around another iron C-core placed firmly in contact with the electromagnet.

16 How would you show that an electric current is only induced when the magnetic field changes?

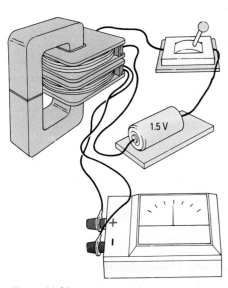

Figure 11.21
Using an electromagnet to induce an electric current in another coil of wire.

A model transformer

A
APPLY

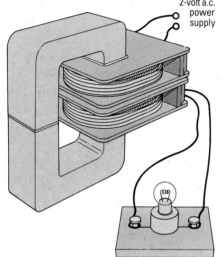

2-volt a.c.
power
supply

Figure 11.22 shows the two coils and C-cores used in the last experiment. One coil is now joined to a 2.5-volt light bulb. The other coil is connected to a 2-volt a.c. supply.

The alternating current from the supply is continually changing. This means that the magnetic field passing through the C-cores also changes continually. As long as the magnetic field changes, an electric current will be induced in the coil joined to the lamp. This is shown by the bulb lighting up.

Figure 11.22
A model transformer, such as you might use in a laboratory, connected to a light bulb.

Energy transfers in transformers

You should have noticed that the two coils in a transformer are separate. They are both wound on to the same iron core, but the wires do not meet.

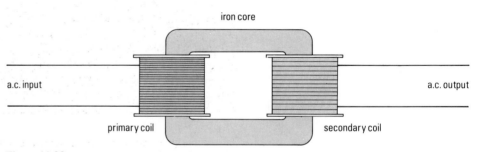

iron core

a.c. input

a.c. output

primary coil

secondary coil

Figure 11.23
Model transformer showing that the two coils are separate.

One coil, called the *primary* coil, is connected to an a.c. supply. The other coil, called the *secondary coil* is connected to the load. ("Load" is the name given to whatever the energy is to be transferred to, such as a light bulb or a motor.)

When in use, an electric current is passed through the primary coil. The current in the primary coil magnetizes the iron core. The magnetic field in the iron core also goes through the secondary coil. When the magnetic field changes in the secondary coil, an electric current is induced. As a.c. is used as the input, the magnetic field changes continuously and the secondary coil provides a continuous a.c. output. The transformer thus transfers energy from its input to the load.

Transformers are normally very efficient. Over 90 per cent of the input energy is transferred to the load. The 10 per cent of the energy which is "wasted" must of course be accounted for. Here are two ways energy is wasted in transformers:

1 The changing magnetic field induces electric currents in the iron core itself. These are called *eddy currents*. They cause the temperature of the iron core to rise and energy is transferred to the surroundings. A thick iron core has a low resistance so large eddy currents would flow. They are kept as small as possible by using an iron core made from a stack of thin slices. Each slice has a high resistance, and is insulated from its neighbours with varnish.

2 The induced currents also produce a rise in the temperature of the wire of the coils. This energy is also wasted. This cannot be avoided, but it can be reduced by making the coils from a good conductor. Copper is usually used.

In a large transformer, such as that in figure 11.24, the input power could be 500 MW. Even if this transformer was 95 per cent efficient there will still be a power "loss" of 25 MW. Most of this "wasted" energy goes into heating the transformer. If it is not transferred somewhere else parts of the transformer would eventually get so hot they would melt. A liquid is circulated around the transformer through the pipes. You can see some of these pipes in figure 11.24. The circulating liquid is heated and transfers the energy away from the transformer to the air outside.

Figure 11.24
Although transformers are very efficient, large ones still transfer a great deal of energy to their surroundings. This energy has to be taken away by a cooling liquid.

19 There is a transformer in your television set. Explain why it does not need to have a liquid circulating through it to prevent it from overheating.

Changing voltages

Remember why transformers were used for the power line. They are used because the output voltage is different from the input voltage. It may be increased or reduced. This is so useful we can accept the small "loss" of energy which is involved. After you have completed the experiments on Worksheet **P11A**, you will realize that the change in the voltage may be summarized as follows:

$$\frac{\text{input voltage}}{\text{output voltage}} = \frac{\text{number of turns on primary}}{\text{number of turns on secondary}}$$

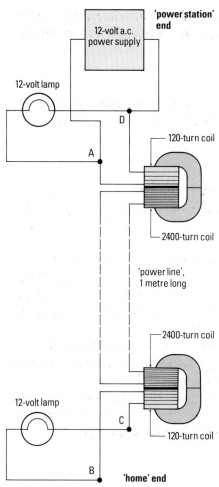

Figure 11.25
This diagram is a repeat of that shown in figure 11.17. It shows the model power line with transformers.

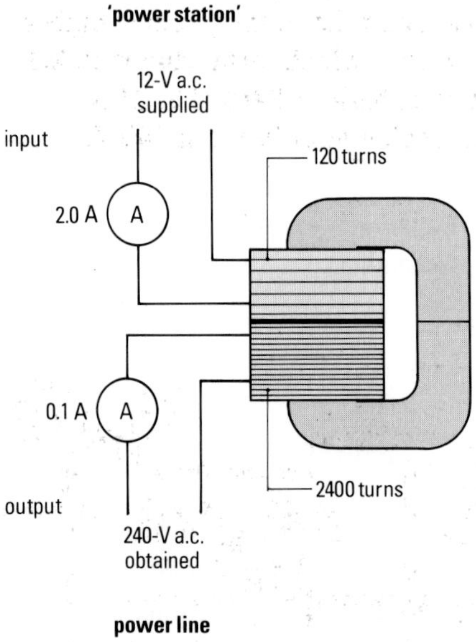

*The final part of this section returns to the power line again and looks in a little more detail at how transformers can improve its efficiency. To understand this section you have to have understood all the work of Chapter **P17**. This section is not essential to the rest of the course, and your teacher will advise you whether to read it or not.*

The power line again

Figure 11.25 is a repeat of figure 11.17. It is drawn again here to save you turning back several pages.

Let us think about the transformer at the power station end. The power pack supplies electricity to the 120-turn coil at 12 V. This means each coulomb of charge transfers 12 J of energy. When you measured the voltage across the 240-turn coil you probably found that it was about 240 V. This means each coulomb of charge transfers 240 J of energy.

Now we have to think carefully. Remember from Chapter **P10** that energy cannot be created, it can only be transferred from one thing to another. Each coulomb of charge flowing into the 120-turn coil transfers 12 J of energy. Each coulomb of charge flowing out of the 2400-turn coil can now transfer 240 J of energy. This is only possible if less charge flows out of the 2400-turn coil per second, compared with the amount which flows into the 120-turn coil per second. In other words, the electric current is less.

Here are some measurements to illustrate what is happening. Look at figure 11.26 which shows the transformer connected to the "power station" end of the power line.

1   At the 120-turn coil

The input voltage is 12 V. This means each coulomb transfers 12 joules of energy. The input current is 2 A. This means 2 coulombs per second flow through the 120-turn coil. So in one second the energy transferred is:

12 joules/coulomb × 2 coulombs/second = 24 joules/second
= 24 W

2   At the 2400-turn coil

The output voltage is 240 V. This means each coulomb transfers 240 joules of energy. The output current is 0.1 A. This means 0.1 coulombs per second flow through the 2400-turn coil. So in one second the energy transferred is:

240 joules/coulomb × 0.1 coulombs/second = 24 joules/second
= 24 W

All a transformer does is to change the way that energy is transferred. For this transformer, the input current is 2 A, but only 12 J of energy is transferred by each coulomb of charge flowing through the primary coil. On the other hand, the output current is only 0.1 A, but each coulomb of charge flowing through the output circuit now transfers 240 J.

$$\frac{\text{current in the output circuit}}{\text{current in the input circuit}} = \frac{0.1}{2} = \frac{1}{20}$$

$$\frac{\text{energy per coulomb in output circuit}}{\text{energy per coulomb in input circuit}} = \frac{240}{12} = \frac{20}{1}$$

What is "lost on the roundabouts is gained on the swings"!

Figure 11.26
A model transformer at the "power station" end of a transmission line. Which is higher – the output or the input voltage?

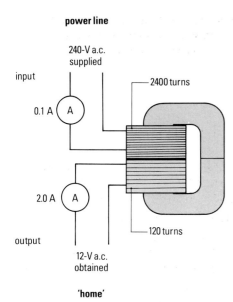

power line

240-V a.c.
supplied

input

0.1 A

2400 turns

2.0 A

output

120 turns

12-V a.c.
obtained

'home'

Figure 11.27
A transformer placed between the end of the transmission line and the place where the energy will be used. Is the output voltage of this transformer higher or lower than the input voltage?

Ideally the power output of a transformer is **always** the same as the power input, as it is in this example. In reality the power output of a transformer is less than the power input.

> **20a** What do the words ''ideally'' and ''in reality'' mean in the paragraph above?
> **b** Why do you think the power output of real transformers is less than the power input?

In the example, 24 joules per second were transferred from the power station to the transformer by a current of 2 A. The same number of joules per second were transferred from the transformer down the power line using a current of only 0.1 A.

Energy has to be used to transfer the charges down the power line. This energy is wasted warming up the power lines and their surroundings. But the smaller the current along the power line, the smaller this energy wastage will be. So it is more efficient to transmit power electrically at the highest possible voltage, and therefore at the lowest possible current.

At the "home" end, reasons of safety mean that the electricity must be reduced in voltage. In the model power line, this means using a transformer to reduce the voltage from 240 V back to 12 V (figure 11.27).

To do this, the ends of the power line are connected to the 2400-turn coil of a second transformer. The lamp is connected to a 120-turn coil. A voltmeter across the output of the transformer shows that the voltage is again 12 V.

The National Grid

Figure 11.28
The National Grid is a network of cables that connects up all the power stations in Britain and distributes their output to the homes, factories and other places that need it.

While it would be much safer to use electricity at 12 volts in the home, there would be too much energy wastage in the house wiring. In Britain electricity is used at 240 volts in the home. Great care has to be taken in using electricity at this voltage, but energy losses in the house wiring system are small.

When it comes to transmitting electricity around the country, much higher voltages can be used. Electricity is carried on wires which form what is called the "National Grid". The voltage used can be as high as 400 000 V. This voltage is reduced in several stages before it reaches your home at 240 V.

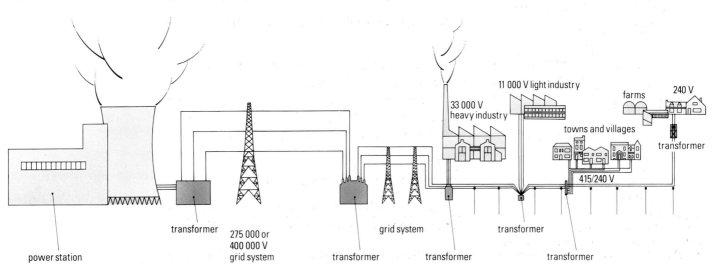

power station

transformer

275 000 or
400 000 V
grid system

transformer

grid system

transformer

33 000 V
heavy industry

11 000 V light industry

transformer

towns and villages

415/240 V

transformer

farms

240 V

transformer

21 In the diagram of the grid system (figure 11.28) how many times is the voltage changed by transformers between the generator in the power station and a home in the town?

Figure 11.29
A very large commercial transformer. You can judge its size by the man nearby.

Transformers come in many sizes. The two extremes are shown in figures 11.29 and 11.30. They work only with a.c. current. This is the reason why electricity from the mains in all our homes is a.c. It would not be possible to raise the voltage for transmission and lower it again using transformers and d.c.

Real transmission lines have low resistances. Although it might be many kilometres between a village and a power station, the total resistance of the cable may be only 20 Ω.

At a certain time, the total energy demand made by the village is 480 kW. The voltage of the transmission line is 400 kV which is reduced to 240 V by a series of transformers.

Figure 11.30
A miniature transformer. Transformers such as these are used in many electronic devices.

22a What current must flow in the transmission line to transfer 480 kW?
b What voltage would be needed to send this current along the transmission line which has a resistance of 20Ω?
c What is the power loss in the line?

Suppose that transformers were not available.

d What current would be needed to supply 480 kW of power at 240 V?

e (*Hard!*) Explain why the 20 Ω transmission line would not be able to transfer 480 kW of power at 240 V.

P11.6   Other methods of energy transmission

We have dealt with electricity as the principal method of energy transmission in this chapter. We also mentioned the delivery of gas and solid fuels. Although these are the most common ways of moving energy today, there are other systems that have been used in the past and are still in use today.

Belts

Before the spread of electric power, factories were powered by steam. One engine would be used to provide the energy for many machines. Often this was done by using the steam engine to turn a rod to which a number of pulley wheels were fixed.

These wheels were connected to the machines by **belts**. Belts could only run at right angles to the driving rods. This meant that the machines had to be carefully laid out on the factory floor. Figure 11.31 shows a picture of a factory using belts to transfer power to its machines. Belt drives are still in use today, but usually only on a small scale.

Figure 11.31
Belt-driven factory machines. It was not long ago that all factories distributed energy in this way. Find out what sort of engine was used to drive the belt shafts.

Hydraulic systems

You may know that the footbrake of a car is connected to the brakes on the wheels by pipes which contain a liquid called *brake fluid*. The use of liquids to transmit forces is a part of what is called *hydraulic engineering*.

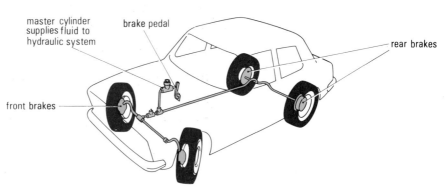

master cylinder supplies fluid to hydraulic system

brake pedal

rear brakes

front brakes

Figure 11.32
A car-braking system. The force exerted on the brake pedal is distributed to the brake pads by a liquid in pipes.

Figure 11.33
Mechanical diggers make considerable use of hydraulics to transfer energy where it is needed.

This system of transmitting moving forces, and thus energy, is also used in many cars to operate the *clutch*. This is the part of the car that connects the engine to the car's gear box. Whenever the "gears" are changed it is necessary to stop the engine driving them for a moment. This is done by pressing on the clutch pedal.

Transmitting energy using hydraulics is also used a great deal in mechanical diggers and big earth movers such as those used in motorway construction.

Towards the end of the nineteenth century a network of pipes was laid down in central London so that hydraulic power could be conveyed from place to place. The use of electricity has made this network out-of-date. The original passageways of this hydraulic system are now being used for a telecommunications system.

What will the future hold in store?

Yet other means of energy transmission are being considered today. Worksheet **P11B** contains an article on the use of hydrogen as a "fuel for the future". You may like to read this and answer some of the questions on the worksheet.

Summary

You will have met each of the following words in this chapter. Write a short explanation of each of them.

fuels	**alternating current**
transformers	**power lines**
generators	**hydraulic power**

Chapter **P**12

Waste not, want not?
Energy resources

In this topic we have tried to build up an understanding of energy. It is not something which we can see or touch, but we can see its effect when it is transferred. You have learned how to measure energy in different ways – but again, only when it is transferred.

This idea of energy only being useful during transfer is an important one. We will return to this idea again in this chapter.

P12.1 Human resources

Your personal energy supply comes from the food you eat. In Biology (Chapter **B**9) you have seen that your body is like an engine. It requires food as fuel and it needs oxygen. The food and the oxygen react together inside your body to transfer energy from the food. Your muscles will transfer the energy elsewhere when you do some work.

Figure 12.1 (above left)
Cereal crops.

Figure 12.2 (above right)
Pigs are raised to supply us with food.

Some of our food is grown as plants such as vegetables, cereals and fruit. These plants use energy from the Sun to grow by using the process called *photosynthesis* which you have studied in Biology, Chapter **B**3.

Animals also provide us with food. But such animals eat plants. So all of the energy we obtain from food comes originally from plants, which in turn get their energy from the Sun.

Figure 12.3 (above left)
All the food we eat gets its energy directly
or indirectly from the Sun.

Figure 12.4 (above right)
Many jobs use a lot of energy in a day.

Figure 12.5
Even school pupils use a lot of energy each
day which comes from the food they eat.

Each person is an individual with energy requirements that differ from
everyone else's. But on average, an adult such as those in figure 12.3 requires
about 13 MJ of energy from food each day. People with very strenuous jobs,
involving digging for example, may require 20 MJ daily; whilst a school pupil
might rquire only 10 MJ per day. (1 MJ stands for "1 megajoule" – in other
words 1 000 000 joules.)

The table in figure 12.6 shows the energy **per second** required by many
ordinary activities. These energy requirements are met by transferring energy
from the food we eat.

ACTIVITY	Rate of energy demand, in watts	ACTIVITY	Rate of energy demand, in watts
sleeping	70	ironing	285
reading	85	washing clothes	320
eating	100	swimming	340
standing	160	chopping wood	340
playing the piano	180	walking upstairs	350
preparing a meal	230	farm work	500
walking	250	playing hockey	600

Figure 12.6
The energy needed for a variety of activities.

1 Estimate how much energy you require during a 24-hour period using the table in
figure 12.6.

You may need to make a guess at the energy requirement of any activity not on the
chart. You can do this by comparing the activity with something similar that is on the
chart.

When you have found your total energy, draw up a chart to show how this amount
of energy is shared between the different activities.

Figure 12.7
All these activities need energy to carry them out.

Human efficiency

In Chapter **P**8 we introduced the idea of **energy cost**. Every activity has an energy cost which we can measure. If you run up a flight of stairs, the energy cost is equal to the work you do in lifting your weight up the stairs (figure 12.8).

We also saw in Chapter **P**8 that when we use machines or engines, the energy price we pay is higher than the cost of the activity. This is because all machines and engines waste energy.

> **2** How is energy wasted in a machine or engine when it is used to do a job?

weighing scales

W

energy cost in climbing stairs = work done = Wh

height climbed h

Figure 12.8
How to work out the energy cost involved in climbing some stairs.

We can work out the energy price paid by measuring the energy we put into a machine or engine in order to do the job.

The human body is an engine. Whenever we perform an activity (like running upstairs) we can measure its energy cost. To run up the stairs we use energy from a small amount of food. This is the energy price we pay. (See Chapters **B**6 and **B**9 in the Biology book.)

The efficiency of the human "engine" in performing an activity is

$$\frac{\text{energy usefully transferred to the activity}}{\text{total energy transferred from food in doing the activity}}$$

Another way of stating this is to say that the efficiency is:

$$\frac{\text{energy cost of doing activity}}{\text{energy price paid}}$$

Worked out in this way the efficiency of the human body is about 25 per cent. This is a figure very close to that for other engines which use fuel to do useful jobs.

> **3a** Using the table in figure 12.6, estimate the energy requirement of a farm worker for an 8-hour working day.
> **b** Now, assuming that the human body is only 25 per cent efficient in transferring this energy to a useful output, work out how much useful energy a farm worker transfers in a working day.

Your answer to the second part of question **3** should have been 3.6 MJ.

Of course people are not paid to transfer energy. Farm work like any other job demands skill – it is this that the farmer pays for. But suppose you lived in a community in which the only available source of energy was that which people could provide themselves. You could not expect any one person to provide much more energy in a day than farm work demands. If you look again at the table in figure 12.6, you will see that this is an activity requiring more energy than most. So we might guess that 3.6 MJ is about as much energy as one person could provide.

In Britain energy is needed to run factories, heat homes, and move goods and people around the country. You can probably think of many more day-to-day activities that need energy.

To do all these things, we transfer most of the energy we need from *fuels*. Often this energy comes to us via electricity. In 1991 a householder paid approximately 7p for transferring energy at a rate of 1 kW for one hour.

1 kW is a rate of transfer of energy of 1000 joules per second. 1 hour is a period of time equal to 3600 seconds. So if we transfer 1 kW of power for one hour, we are transferring:

1000 joules/second $\times$ 3600 seconds = 3 600 000 joules of energy.

That is just 3.6 MJ – the same energy as a human could transfer in a day.

This means that in Britain in 1991 it cost approximately 7p, in money, for the supply of the same amount of energy by electricity as a human could supply in a working day.

> **4a** Would you expect a payment of 7p for 8 hours' work?
> **b** What does this suggest about the cost of humans as an energy resource compared with electricity?

This section has shown how much we depend on energy resources. If we were only able to rely on food as our energy source and humans for transferring energy, then our way of life would have to change dramatically. Fuels have provided us with cheap energy resources. So we have developed a life style that is very dependent on using energy.

At present we are able to supply our demands, but some of the energy resources which we are using are limited. Eventually they will run out. We must either find other energy resources or learn how to use our present energy resources more efficiently. This means using less energy and wasting less energy. The ideas discussed in Chapter **P9** suggested simple ways in which you, as an individual, might be able to use energy more efficiently.

Energy consumption around the world

We can estimate how much energy is used per person in a country by dividing the total energy requirement of a nation by its population. A person in Western Europe uses between 10 and 20 times as much energy as a person living in some countries in Africa. A person in the United States uses between 2 and 3 times as much energy as a European.

5 In a discussion, someone suggests that these figures show that people in some countries in Africa are much more energy-efficient than the rest of the world. Do you think this is the correct conclusion to draw from these figures? Explain your answer.

P12.2   Energy from fuels

About 99 per cent of the energy available for use on Earth comes, directly or indirectly, from the Sun. The other 1 per cent comes from naturally-occurring radioactive materials, the hot core of the Earth and the movement of the oceans. Photosynthesis transfers energy from the Sun to the plants and trees (see Biology, Chapter **B**3). These are the sources of many fuels such as wood, peat, coal, oil and gas.

In Chemistry, Chapters **C**2 and **C**13, you see how crude oil can be refined to produce a variety of fuels for different purposes. We call fuels such as coal, oil and gas that come from once-living organisms "*fossil fuels*". The store of energy in all fossil fuels was transferred to them long ago from the Sun.

To show you how quickly we use up fuel, think about heating your home using firewood. Suppose a tree is allowed to grow for 30 years and then is chopped down to produce firewood. This firewood will give you enough energy to heat your home for about 30 days.

Once we have used the Earth's present store of fossil fuels, they cannot be replaced quickly enough to satisfy our future energy needs. Scientists in some countries have been developing alternative fuels which transfer energy from the Sun much more rapidly.

Read the account on the next page of how some scientists have been investigating the use of sugar as a fuel.

Figure 12.9
The Sun: the ultimate source of most of our energy.

Sugar: fuel for the future

(This is an adapted and shortened version of an article by Peter de Groot published in *The Observer* on 9 February 1986.)

In Western Europe there is less public concern than there was a few years ago over the possibility of an "energy crisis". This is because in Europe there has been an increase in oil stocks and a fall in its price. But many other countries in the world are suffering from rapidly rising prices and the cost of oil, which they have to import, has risen dramatically. As a result these countries are putting a great deal of effort into finding alternative energy sources.

One of the countries that has been most successful in finding an alternative to oil is Brazil. There are ten million motor vehicles in Brazil. Two million of these are now powered entirely from ethanol. The remainder run on a mixture of ethanol and petrol. The ethanol is made by fermenting juice obtained from sugar cane, in the same way that wine can be made by fermenting the juice from grapes. The ethanol is then separated from the remainder of the juice and purified. Last year, Brazil produced 10 700 million litres of ethanol in this way, for use as a fuel.

All plants trap energy from the Sun by the process of photosynthesis. A family of tropical grasses, which include sugar cane, can do this far more efficiently than many other plants. Until recently, sugar was in great demand all over the world as a "sweetener". Varieties of sugar cane have been specially bred for years to produce large quantities of sugar. Then, a few years ago, the need for sugar from sugar cane dropped. This was partly due to the discovery of artificial sweeteners and partly due to the amount of sugar being produced from sugar-beet. Brazil found itself with far too much sugar, and set about converting it into ethanol. In the early 1970s there was a huge increase in the price of oil and it became important for Brazil to find a replacement for it. Since then, other countries such as Zimbabwe have also started producing ethanol from sugar and mixing it with petrol as a motor fuel.

But this is not the only way that sugar cane can be used as a source of energy. When sugar is extracted from the sugar cane, a material is left that once went to waste. It has been found that this "waste" (called *bagasse*) can be burned to release even more of the energy originally trapped by the sugar cane. Bagasse has about 70 per cent of the energy value of wood when used as fuel. Many sugar factories throughout the world now get all the energy they need from burning sugar cane bagasse. In some countries, these sugar factories are even able to produce electricity for their National grid, as well.

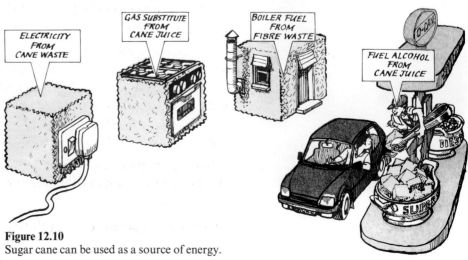

Figure 12.10
Sugar cane can be used as a source of energy.

Research groups, working in countries where sugar cane grows well, have found out that it is as worthwhile to grow this plant for its bagasse as to grow it for the sugar. Some new varieties grow to over 3.6 m high and produce well over 300 tonnes of sugar cane plant per hectare. (One hectare is an area of land equal to 10 000 m².) By growing these new varieties (called "energy cane"), it is possible to capture three times more energy from the Sun than before. And that is true for each hectare of land planted with sugar cane.

There are more ways of using bagasse than simply burning it. A gas which is a mixture of hydrogen and carbon monoxide can be made from it, just as it can from the fossil fuels. This gas is similar to natural gas. Just as a chemical industry has been built up on natural gas, so could a similar industry be built up on the gas from what was once sugar cane "waste". Bagasse can also be used to make paper and card, and construction materials such as hardboard.

Ethanol, also, has other uses. It is possible to produce ethene from it. Ethene is the starting point of a wide variety of plastics. It can also be used to produce paints, solvents and artificial rubber. Again a new chemical industry could be created.

The world demand for sugar may be dying, but the future of the sugar cane plant seems to be assured.

6a What is meant by "bagasse"?

b Which plants transfer the Sun's energy by photosynthesis most efficiently?

c What is the sugar converted to and how is the conversion made?

d Where do the sugar factories obtain their energy from?

e "Energy cane" yields less sugar than traditional sugar cane and yet an "energy cane" crop produces three times as much energy as a traditional sugar cane crop. Explain how this is possible.

f Explain why the author predicts that "energy cane" could be important to the world's chemical industry.

---

*You can find out more about chemicals from plants in Chapter **C3** of your Chemistry book.*

P12.3   Nuclear energy

In Chapter **P3** you studied radioactivity. It may be useful to remind you of some of the important ideas which we use to explain radioactivity:

- An atom of a radioactive material has an unstable nucleus.
- The nuclei of all atoms are built up from protons and neutrons.
- When a radioactive nucleus "decays" the structure of the nucleus changes.
- Energy may be transferred from the nucleus in two ways:
  1 as kinetic energy of the particles which make up alpha and beta radiation
  2 as radiation carried away by gamma radiation.

In Chapter **P3** you looked at the ways in which radioactivity is helpful. It also explained why it might be dangerous to living things.

---

7 What are the dangers of radioactivity to humans?

Figure 12.11
A nuclear power station at Calder Hall. This 200 MW nuclear power station, opened in 1956, was the first to produce electricity commercially.

Energy from the nucleus

The power station in figure 12.11 transfers energy which is released from the nuclei of atoms. The energy is used to heat water to form high pressure steam. The rest of the power station is exactly like a coal-fired power station: the steam drives a turbine that in turn drives a generator that transfers the energy to electricity.

The use of "nuclear energy" to produce electricity is an important social issue which you may already have definite opinions about. Nuclear reactors are used in nuclear power stations to release energy in a controlled way. The same processes take place in nuclear weapons, but in these, vast amounts of energy are released very quickly indeed. Nuclear power and nuclear weapons both raise issues which are the concern and responsibility of everyone. In order to share in that responsibility you should first understand the scientific principles involved.

Nuclear fission

Nuclear fission is a process in which a nucleus splits into fragments, releasing energy as it does so. In this process, energy is transferred from the original nucleus to the kinetic energy of the fragments. Nuclear fission is a process that occurs naturally in a few elements of large atomic mass and very unstable nuclei. One of these is a rare form of uranium called uranium–235. (The number "235" is the number of protons and neutrons that make up the nucleus, as shown in Chapter **C**18 of your Chemistry book.)

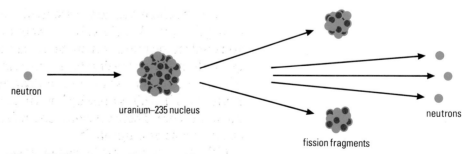

Figure 12.12
The fissioning of a uranium nucleus. "Fissioning" means "splitting". We use the same sort of word for a split in the Earth's surface. Find out what that word is.

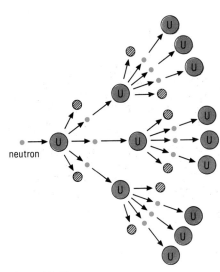

Figure 12.13
A diagram showing how a chain reaction is set up.

When such a nucleus breaks up, it releases a few neutrons as well. If one of these neutrons happens to collide with another uranium–235 nucleus, this too immediately splits up (figure 12.12). Every fission produces two or three neutrons. If all of these collide with and break up other nuclei, you can see from the diagram that it is not very long before millions and millions of uranium nuclei will have broken up. This is called a *chain reaction* (figure 12.13).

In a chain reaction huge amounts of energy are released from the unstable nuclei in a very short space of time. This energy transfer results in a very big rise in the temperature of the uranium and its surroundings.

A nuclear reactor

The purpose of a nuclear reactor is to set up and then control a chain reaction so that the energy is released at the rate it is needed. A chain reaction will only occur if the neutrons released by the process bring about further nuclear fission.

In many reactors in use today, it is necessary to **slow down** the neutrons, produced by fission, to make sure this happens. This "slowing down" is brought about by embedding the uranium "fuel" in a material called a *moderator*. Graphite or a special form of water (called "heavy water") are usually used as moderators. The moderator with the uranium embedded in it is called the *reactor core*.

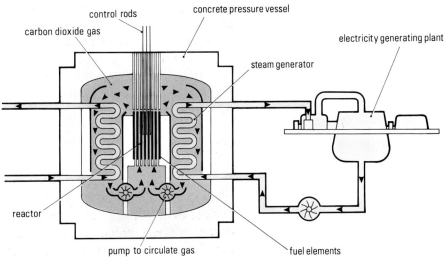

Figure 12.14
A nuclear reactor. There is one, and often two, at the heart of all nuclear power stations.

Once the chain reaction has started, there has to be some way of controlling how quickly it takes place. If you want to control how quickly a fire burns, you control the rate at which the air can get to it. The more slowly the air can get to the fire, the slower it burns. In a similar way, to control the rate at which the uranium fissions in a nuclear reactor you have to control the flow of neutrons in it. This is done by lowering or raising rods of *boron steel* into or out of the core. These are called *control rods*. Boron steel harmlessly absorbs any neutrons passing into it.

If the control rods are lowered right into the reactor core, all neutrons will be absorbed and the nuclear reaction stops. As the rods are lifted out, more neutrons become available for fission. When the rods have been pulled out to a certain point, a sufficient number of neutrons are free to keep the nuclear reaction going. Raising the rods still further will increase the rate of fission and so increase the rate at which energy is released.

The first nuclear reactor was operated in 1942. The man mainly responsible for its development was Enrico Fermi.

Enrico Fermi

Figure 12.15
Enrico Fermi (1901–1954), the scientist who first set up a nuclear reactor.

Enrico Fermi was an Italian physicist born in Rome in 1901. Enrico and his elder brother, Giulio, were both interested in mechanical things, and Enrico developed many skills assembling electric motors and drawing aeroplane designs. These skills were important in later life when he used them to put his own ideas into practice. When Enrico was 14, his brother died and Enrico threw himself into studying the technical and scientific books which they had both found so absorbing.

Enrico had no difficulty at school and he extended his knowledge by buying many second-hand books. A colleague of his father encouraged him and supplied him with more books. Eventually he won a scholarship to the University of Pisa, the city of Galileo, in 1918. In 1922 he received his doctorate. Five years later he was made Professor of physics at the University of Rome.

During the next few years Fermi became known throughout the world as a brilliant physicist, and he was awarded the Nobel prize for physics in 1938. He and his family travelled to Sweden for the award of this prize. They then left for the United States of America, so escaping from the Fascist rule of Mussolini in Italy.

In 1942, he led the team of scientists which built the world's first nuclear reactor at the University of Chicago in the United States. This first reactor was built in a squash court. It was successfully operated for the first time on 2nd December 1942.

Figure 12.16
Fermi's first nuclear reactor. It was built in a squash court.

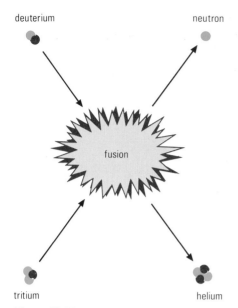

Figure 12.17
Nuclear fusion. Energy is released by making two nuclei of "heavy" hydrogen combine to form a nucleus of helium.

Nuclear fusion

The principle of nuclear fusion is just the opposite to nuclear fission. During nuclear fission, energy is released when a large nucleus is split into fragments. Nuclear fusion releases energy when small nuclei are joined together to produce a larger nucleus. A simplified diagram is shown in figure 12.17 of the way two small nuclei join up to produce the very stable helium nucleus and so release energy.

The great difficulty in producing fusion is making the two small nuclei move fast enough to overcome their natural repulsion and so join together. One way of doing this is to heat deuterium and tritium (two rare forms of hydrogen) to a temperature of about 100 **million** °C. At this temperature the atoms of the gas are ionized and form what is called a *plasma*. The problem is then to build a container which will hold the plasma and let it reach such a high temperature. The plasma has to be held out of contact with its container if it is to be heated up to such temperatures.

8a Why do the nuclei of deuterium and tritium naturally repel each other?
b How does heating up the gas enable the nuclei to collide?
c Why is it not possible to heat up the plasma if it is in contact with the container? (You may find the Data section in your Chemistry book helpful in answering this question.)

Although fusion reactions are the natural source of the energy of the Sun and stars, no one has yet managed to achieve all the conditions required for a fusion reactor, although very high temperatures (up to 200 million °C) have been achieved. Figure 12.18 is a photograph of a piece of equipment being used to try to produce controlled nuclear fusion. The plasma inside it is kept away from the walls of the container by using a strong magnetic field.

9 How is it possible to use magnetic fields to hold the plasma away from the walls of the container?

Figure 12.18
a (left) The JET experimental toroid fusion chamber at Culham in Oxfordshire. It is used for research into nuclear fusion.
b (right) Inside the chamber in which fusion reactions take place.

The advantage of nuclear fusion

Although a fusion reactor has not yet been developed, if it is eventually successful, a fusion reactor will have two main advantages over a fission reactor.

● It will run on deuterium which is a form of hydrogen readily available in water.
● It will produce far fewer radioactive "by-products" than a fission reactor does.

Figure 12.19
A traditional windmill. In the UK they were used to grind corn, but elsewhere they were (and still are) used to pump water.

Figure 12.20
A modern windmill used to transfer energy from the wind to electricity. This one is on Orkney.

P12.4   Alternative energy resources

So far we have considered two main sources of energy. Fossil fuels are studied in Chapter **C13** of your Chemistry book. In this chapter we have looked at how the energy stored in the nuclei of atoms can be used. But there are limited reserves of both traditional fossil fuels and of uranium on Earth.

It is clear that the supply of fossil fuels will eventually run out. Added to this is the fact that these energy resources are not equally distributed among the different nations in the world. We could thus face the prospect of rival nations competing for energy resources which are themselves getting smaller and smaller.

Nuclear energy using fission is itself only a temporary solution, since uranium, like fossil fuels, will eventually be used up. However, some people are concerned about even a temporary use of nuclear fission. Worksheet **P12A** looks at the way we use nuclear energy and asks you to think about some of the issues for yourself.

There is no one answer to what many people refer to as the "energy crisis", so it is worth looking at some of the other energy resources that may be available to us.

An energy resource which is neither a fossil fuel nor a nuclear fuel is called an *alternative* energy source. Many alternative energy resources have been suggested. Research has shown that some of these suggestions could be turned into useful energy resources. But apart from nuclear fusion, no single alternative source to those now in use is likely to supply the huge energy demand of the world. Yet combinations of various sources may provide a significant amount of energy which would go some way to easing any world shortage of energy.

We will look at each of these alternatives in turn. Then you can think when and where each might prove useful.

The wind

Huge quantities of kinetic energy, transferred to the air molecules of our atmosphere, have been a useful source of energy in Britain since the Middle Ages. Windmills have "sails" which the wind moves as it passes. Provided the sails are big enough, a large amount of energy can be transferred from the wind. In the first windmills this energy was used to grind grain or move water. Today we could use it to drive a small generator and produce "free" electricity.

10 Obviously windmills or wind turbines would have to be situated in windy places. Suggest some possible places for them.

What do you think might be the effect on the environment of a lot of windmills?

The sea

The oceans around the world are continually moving. Tides are produced by the gravitational pull of the Moon and, to some extent, the Sun. This tends to cause the water on the Earth's surface to "heap up". These heaps of water move round the Earth as it spins. The change in water level that the tides produce can be used as an energy resource.

As well as this tidal movement, the winds blowing across the surface of the oceans produce waves. Each of these water movements can be used as an energy resource and we will look at them separately.

Figure 12.21
Waves crashing against the sea-front. Huge amounts of energy are transferred in this way – often destructively.

Wave power

Professor Salter of Edinburgh University has developed a very efficient floating device called a "duck" which rocks in the sea. Energy from waves is transferred to electricity generators by the rocking movement of these "ducks". Around the north-western isles of Scotland, there is believed to be enough "wave power" to provide half of the total output of all the power stations in Britain using about 1000 km of floating "ducks".

11a Find out how the rocking motion of a Salter "duck" can be used to drive an electric generator.
b What problems do you think engineers might have to overcome in putting such a device to practical use?

Figure 12.22
These devices are known as "Salter's ducks" after their inventor Professor Stephen Salter. They are designed to harness wave energy from the sea and drive electrical generators.

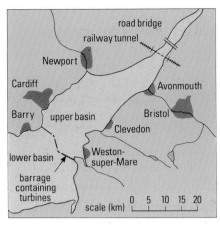

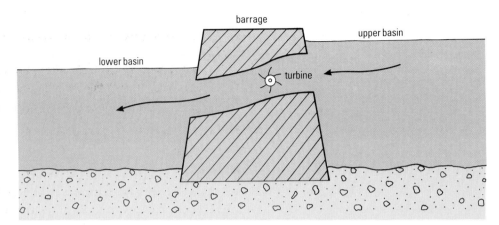

Figure 12.23 (above left)
A plan showing the way the tides in the Severn Estuary could be harnessed to provide energy to generate electricity.

Figure 12.24 (above right)
This diagram shows the way water would flow between an upper and a lower basin in the Severn Estuary.

Tidal power

Look at the picture in figure 12.23. This shows plans to transfer energy from the tides in the Severn estuary. As the tide rises, water is allowed to enter the **upper** basin. Once high tide has passed, the water in the upper basin is made to flow back to the **lower** basin through the turbines in the barrage (figure 12.24). The turbines turn generators which transfer the energy to electricity.

When low tide is passed, the process is repeated, with water flowing into the upper basin again.

12 It has been estimated that the Severn tidal barrier could provide 10 per cent of the energy requirements for Britain. What problems can you think of which would have to be considered in building such a "tidal power station"?

Hydroelectric power

In hydroelectric power stations water falls down pipes from high level mountain lakes or from reservoirs. The moving water transfers its energy to the electricity via the generators many metres below the lake. In countries like Canada, huge amounts of water are held as snow or in glaciers at a high level. Enough hydroelectric power can be generated to meet Canada's needs. But in Britain the mountains are much lower and only the rain cycle can be relied on to restore the water to the high reservoirs. So hydroelectric power makes only a small contribution to total energy resources in Britain.

However, hydroelectric power is put to another use in Britain. Power stations of the sort shown in figure 12.25 are used to store energy at times of low demand by using energy from the National Grid to pump water from the lower lakes up to the high reservoirs.

Then, at times of high demand, the water is allowed to run down again, driving generators as it falls.

Figure 12.25
A pumped storage power station in Scotland. You can see the upper reservoir in the mountains and the power station below. Find out where in Britain there is another pumped storage power station.

13 Power stations like those shown in figure 12.25 are called "pumped storage stations".
a Explain whether or not such stations actually increase the nation's energy resources.

13b When are there likely to be times of low demand and times of high demand for energy?
c Why would it not be better to build enough power stations to meet the highest energy demand, rather than build pumped storage stations?

Solar energy

It has been estimated that about 99 per cent of the total energy resources on the Earth come from the Sun. We have seen earlier (section **P**12.2) how all our fossil fuels rely on the Sun to provide their store of energy. The Sun also provides energy for the rain cycle, some of which we use in hydroelectric power schemes. It is energy from the Sun which causes winds in our atmosphere. Energy from the winds can be used by windmills, and helps create waves at sea. You might ask "Where does the Sun's energy come from?" We have already answered that. It is being released by nuclear fusion. So in reality there is very little non-nuclear energy used on Earth!

The amount of energy falling on the Earth's surface from the Sun varies from time to time and from place to place. At night, there will be no energy from the Sun, while during the day there will be a great deal. In some parts of the Earth, the Sun will be directly overhead, while in others the Sun's rays come in at an angle.

14 Which parts of the Earth's surface will receive more than the average amount of energy from the Sun, and which will receive less? Give reasons for your answer.

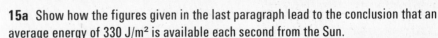

Figure 12.26
A satellite photograph of the Earth.

On average, the half of the Earth bathed in sunlight receives about 700 joules of energy on each square metre of its surface, every second. 30 per cent (nearly one-third) of this is reflected back into space, and a further 23 per cent (about one-quarter) is used in evaporating water from the oceans, etc. But this still leaves an average of 330 joules per second on each square metre of the Earth's sunlit surface. This all "adds up" to quite a lot of energy, and only a very small part of this is being taken up by plants.

15a Show how the figures given in the last paragraph lead to the conclusion that an average energy of 330 J/m² is available each second from the Sun.
b What is the minimum area of the Earth's surface that would have to be used to capture as much energy per second as is generated by a 1000 MW power station?
c Where on the Earth's surface would you think about building a power station that obtained its energy directly from the Sun?

Solar cells are devices that make use of sunlight by transferring its energy directly to electricity (figure 12.27). *Solar panels* use the Sun's energy to heat water directly from sunlight (figure 12.28). However, there is an *energy cost* in making such devices. Solar cells at present cost a great deal to make in terms of other energy resources. They are therefore mainly used for small scale applications – for example, in providing energy for space craft to collect data.

Figure 12.27 (above left)
Solar cells transfer energy directly from the Sun to electricity.

Figure 12.28 (above right)
Solar panels can be used to heat water using energy from the Sun. This house is in an experimental village in North Wales where all energy needed is derived from "renewable" sources such as the Sun, wind, and moving water.

Figure 12.29 (below left)
A geyser (hot water fountain) in Iceland.

Figure 12.30 (below right)
A volcanic eruption. Huge amounts of energy are released in volcanic eruptions, but no one has yet managed to harness that energy.

16 Another name for alternative energy sources is *renewable energy*. Explain why the term renewable energy is a good one for alternative energy sources.

Energy from the Earth

Volcanoes and earthquakes make us aware of the huge quantities of energy which are held below the Earth's surface. Beneath the crust that we live on, the Earth is very hot. In Iceland, New Zealand, and some other places, water seeps through the hot rocks and can be drawn from springs where it has been heated for no cost. In this way, Reykjavik, the capital city of Iceland, has its pavements heated by hot water pipes to melt ice in winter. Iceland is also Europe's largest producer of bananas. They are grown in hothouses heated by hot water pipes.

P12.5   "Waste not, want not"

The search for energy resources continues. Choices will have to be made as fossil fuels gradually run out. In your lifetime there will probably be considerable changes in energy supply. Before we complete our study of energy, it is worth thinking about how efficiently we are using energy.

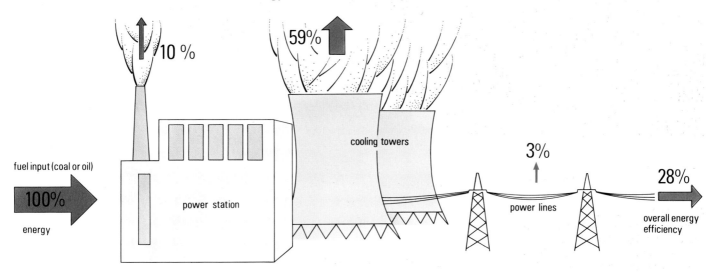

Figure 12.31
Our normal method of distributing energy wastes a great deal of it.

When coal and oil are plentiful it may not be very important that we are only usefully transferring 28 per cent of the energy in a conventional power station. (The remaining 72 per cent is "lost" to the surroundings.)

It has been estimated that about 47 per cent of the useful energy transferred in the United Kingdom is for water or room heating. If you look at figure 12.31, you will see that power stations waste a lot of energy in heating their surroundings. We could save a great deal of energy if some of this "wasted" energy from power stations could be used to heat our homes and factories as well as the water we use.

17 "Making use of the energy presently wasted in power stations could reduce the quantity of fuel Britain uses in a year."
   Write a paragraph in your own words explaining why this is so.

18 Why is it important that we try to improve the efficiency with which we use the energy available from fuels?

One way of reducing the energy wastage at power stations is to use some of the "wasted" energy to provide heating locally. This is common in towns in northern Europe, and "community heating" schemes of this type are being developed in Nottingham and Sheffield.

19 If homes were to be heated using the hot water that comes out of the turbines, the hot water could not be piped over long distances.
a Explain why the distance would have to be short.
b Write down one advantage and one disadvantage of this scheme to the community.

Another idea being tried out is to build small "power stations" (called *mini chips*) to provide energy for a local community. There is much less energy wastage using such power stations because they provide hot water as well as electricity to the surrounding houses. In this way they make use of some of the 72 per cent of the energy wasted in normal large power stations.

The word mini chip comes from "**mini** **c**ombined **h**eat and **i**n-house **p**ower". A diagram showing the construction of a mini chip is shown in figure 12.32. The way one of them might be connected up to a group of houses in a housing estate is shown in figure 12.33. Such schemes could serve up to 50 homes.

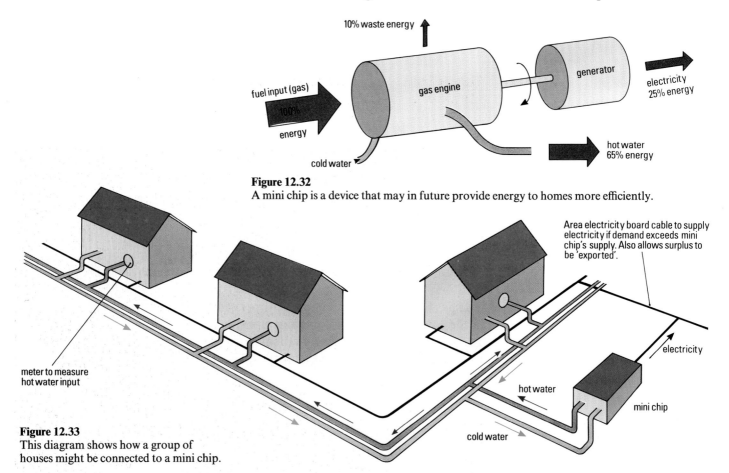

Figure 12.32
A mini chip is a device that may in future provide energy to homes more efficiently.

Figure 12.33
This diagram shows how a group of houses might be connected to a mini chip.

Hotels, hospitals and some industries could reduce their energy costs by installing their own mini chips. The hot water would be piped straight into the central heating system. In winter it would provide 95 per cent of the total heating need. A central heating boiler would "top up" the heating system when necessary.

A combination of greater efficiency and more ways of making use of the Sun's energy on Earth may eventually solve the "energy crisis".

Conclusion

To conclude this chapter, you should study Worksheet **P**12B. This worksheet asks you to plan for the energy needs of a scientific party on an isolated Pacific island called Ashton Island. There are no fossil fuels available on this island – you will have to use other resources. You could work on this individually, but it might be better if you worked in small teams and "pooled" your ideas.

Topic **P**4 **Waves**

What this topic is about

The idea of energy has been used in almost every chapter of this book. It is the transfer of energy that "gets things done".

But so far we have been interested in what happens as **a result of** energy being transferred. Think about some of the topics we have looked at already. Liquids can be changed to gases by transferring energy to them from a flame. Electric motors can lift a load by transferring energy to them from an electricity supply. Rockets can be launched into space by transferring energy to them from the fuel.

You have seen in your work in biology that "light means life". The energy transferred to living things comes to us from the Sun. It is this energy transfer that plants use to grow and provide food for animals. But the energy from the Sun has travelled a very great distance to reach the Earth. How can energy be transferred over such large distances? This topic investigates one important way that energy can be transferred over large distances. It is a way of transferring energy that we refer to as *waves*. It is in fact the way energy from the Sun reaches this planet.

You can find out more about the way energy from the Sun is used by plants in Chapter B3 of your Biology book.

Figure 1
Light transfers energy from the Sun to growing plants.

You may have learned something about waves already. They are important in understanding **sound** as well as understanding **light**. Because of this, we shall start this topic by recalling ideas about light and sound that you have already met. To make this more interesting, we shall look at two topics where understanding the behaviour of light and sound is important.

The first topic is *fibre optics*. You may have heard of cable television. Pictures for cable television are sent to your home along cables, rather than through the air. These cables are not like electricity supply cables, which are made from copper and carry electric charges. Instead they are made from glass and carry light beams.

The second topic is *noise*. After this we shall make an investigation into waves and then see how waves can explain the behaviour of light and sound. In doing this, you will meet a whole family of waves called the *electromagnetic spectrum*.

What you should already know about light and sound

*This is a **very brief** summary of work that you probably have already covered in science. If any of the ideas are unfamiliar, your teacher will be able to give you more help with them. These notes are here only to remind you – not to explain to you.*

Light

Light can travel in straight lines through air, water, glass or anything that is transparent. It can travel just as well through empty space.

If light from a lamp passes through a pinhole in a box, it makes a picture of the lamp on the back of the box (figure 2). Such a box is called a *pinhole camera*. The picture is built up because light from each point on the lamp makes one small point of light on the back of the box.

Figure 2 (below left)
A picture of the lamp is formed by light from each point on the lamp making a single spot on the back of the camera.

Figure 3 (below right)
A lens can form a brighter and sharper picture, which we call an *image*. The lens bends all the light falling on it from one point on the lamp so that it passes through another point where the image is formed.

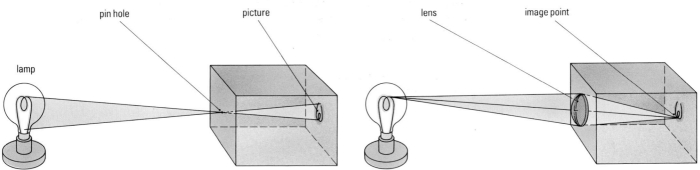

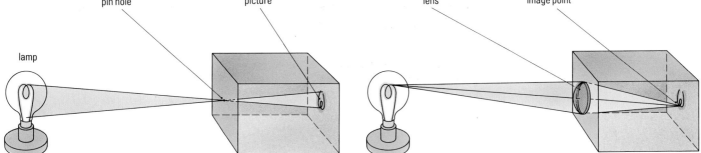

A *lens* can also do this. Light from one point on the lamp in figure 3 falls on the lens. The lens bends all that light so that it passes through another point, which is called the *image point*. The lens makes an image point of every other point on the lamp by bending the light from it in a similar way. So the lens builds up an image of the lamp. Your *eye*, a *camera*, and a *slide projector* all work in this way.

A lens works by changing the direction of travel of light falling on it. Whenever light reaches the surface of another transparent substance (like glass) at an angle other than $90°$, its direction of travel changes in this way. This is known as *refraction* (figure 4).

Light is *reflected* by any object in its path (even transparent ones). Usually the light is reflected in all directions (figure 5). We see the world around us because our eyes pick up the light reflected by objects. If the surface of an object is highly polished (such as glass, the surface of a liquid or a metal) then the light is reflected in one direction. This is called *regular reflection* (figure 6).

Figure 4 (below left)
The light ray in the diagram makes an angle *I* with the perpendicular to the glass surface. When the ray passes through the glass, the angle between the ray and the perpendicular is **less** than *I*.

Figure 5 (below centre)
When a ray of light falls on a piece of white card, it is reflected in all directions.

Figure 6 (below right)
When a ray of light falls on a mirror all the light is reflected in just one direction.

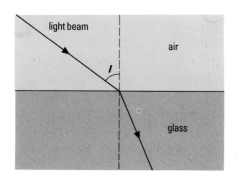

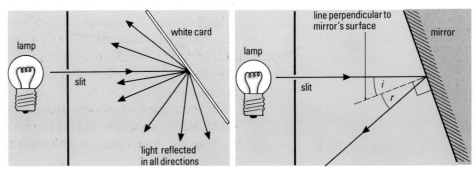

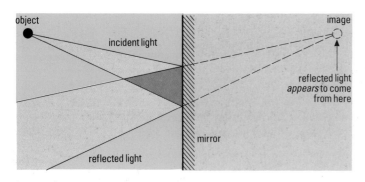

Figure 7
When light from an object is reflected by a mirror it forms an image. The image is at the point the reflected light appears to come from.

Figure 8
Not all light falling on a glass surface passes into the glass; some of it is reflected.

Images can be formed by regularly reflected light. This is how we can see ourselves in a mirror (figure 7).

When light meets the surface of something like glass or water, some of the light passes into it and some is reflected (figure 8).

Sound

Sounds can vary greatly in intensity from very loud to very soft. Sounds also often have a quality that we call pitch. We talk of a musical note being of high pitch or low pitch. Sound with no distinguishable pitch is called noise.

Things which emit sound are always found to be *vibrating*. As you saw in Chapter **P4**, a vibration is a regular to-and-fro motion. You may know already that the number of vibrations made every second is called the *frequency*. The higher the frequency of vibration, the higher the pitch of the sound.

Sound will travel through any substance (solid, liquid, or gas), but it will not travel through empty space. The speed of sound is different in different materials. For example, it travels much more quickly through a metal than through air.

Figure 9
All of the pictures involve sound. In which of them would you describe the sound as "noise"?

Some revision questions for you to try

1a What advantages does a lens camera have over a pinhole camera?
b Does the pinhole camera have any advantages over "lens" cameras?

2a One of the rays in figure 10 is bending as it would through water, glass or plastic. Which one is it?
b You could write down a "rule" for a ray of light passing from air to water (or glass) to help you remember which way a ray bends. Invent a rule that says whether rays bend to become "more slanting" or "less slanting".

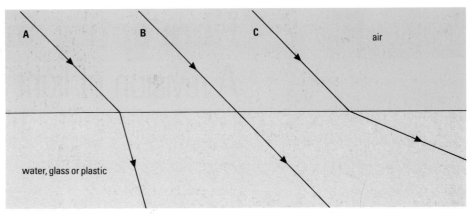

Figure 10

You have probably realized that the meaning of the words "more slanting" and "less slanting" are not at all clear. To overcome this difficulty, we usually refer to the amount light bends, or is reflected, in another way. Look again at figure 4. The dotted line, drawn in where the light beam crosses the glass surface, is at right angles to the surface. This direction is usually referred to as "the perpendicular".

When we want to refer to the direction in which light is travelling, or in which it bends at a surface, we usually link it to the "perpendicular" to the surface at that point.

3 Now write down the rule you stated in question **2b** using instead the words "towards the perpendicular" and "away from the perpendicular".

4 "This table doesn't bend when I sit on it", says your friend in the lab. You say, "Yes it does. The bending is too small to see, but it happens all the same." Explain how you could show your friend that the table bends, using a small mirror and a lamp arranged to give a narrow beam. (There is a white ceiling over the table that may help.) Draw a rough diagram showing where you would put the mirror relative to the table legs and the position of your friend on the table.

5 Two people decide to find out how far away a building is by shouting and listening for the echo. Sound travels at about 340 m/s in still air and they judge the echo takes 0.5 s to get back to them. How far away is the building?

6a If you watch a football match from behind one goal you will often see the goalkeeper at the other end kick the ball before you hear the sound. Explain why this is.
b If you are standing in the same place with your back to a strong wind, why is there an even greater delay between seeing the ball kicked at the far end and hearing the kick?

7 Explain why it is that **low-pitched** musical instruments are generally bigger than **high-pitched** ones.

P13.1   Fibre optics

Light signals

"A sudden idea occurred to me, and I took the candle from the window-sill, where the butler had placed it.

'He must have been holding it as a signal,' said I. 'Let us see if there is an answer.'

I held it as he had done, and stared out into the darkness of the night. Vaguely I could discern the black bank of trees and the lighter expanse of the moor, for the moon was behind the clouds. And then I gave a cry of exultation, for a tiny pinpoint of yellow light had suddenly transfixed the dark veil, and glowed steadily in the centre of the black square framed by the window.

'There it is!' I cried."

This extract has been taken from *The Hound of the Baskervilles* by Sir Arthur Conan Doyle. This is not the only story in which his hero, Sherlock Holmes, is involved in night-time adventures in which people use light to signal to each other. Since Conan Doyle's earliest mystery stories, night-time signalling has been a feature of almost all adventure stories.

Using lights to signal messages came into use long before the crime novel. Navies have used lights for signalling at sea for centuries. One of Britain's first early warning systems – designed to alert the nation of a threatened Spanish invasion – depended on a series of "beacons" (brushwood bonfires) each to be lit on successive hill tops across the country (figure 13.1).

Figure 13.1
Lighting beacons was one of the earliest means of sending messages quickly over a long distance.

> **1** Estimate how long it would take for the people of Newcastle to be aware that the Spanish Armada was approaching the south coast of Britain following the first sighting of the ships.
>   To make this estimate, you will have to:
>   i Estimate how close the beacons must be to each other to ensure they can be seen.
>   ii Estimate how long it would take for each brushwood bonfire to give a sufficient blaze to be seen after being lit.
>   iii Estimate (or find out) how far it is from Newcastle to the south coast.

There are many problems, however, in using light for more than simple, short-distance communication. In the first place, some sort of **code** has to be used. The light itself will be either **on** or **off**. A series of flashes has somehow to be turned into a message by the person receiving it. The code could be very simple, for example: "Three flashes means I've dumped the 'goods' on the sea shore!"

Making a code to carry information is not really very difficult (you will find something about how it is done in Chapter **P21**). Communicating the information **fast enough** and **far enough** is much more of a problem. If these two problems can be overcome, light offers many advantages – it travels quickly and it is not easily disrupted (as electrical signals can be). Another advantage that is less easy to understand is that by using light a great deal of information can be "packed" into a very small space. This is something we shall return to in Chapter **P21**.

If you want to use light to send a message as quickly as possible you need to turn a light on and off quickly. Recent inventions and discoveries have meant that this can now be done **electrically**. You have already used light sensitive devices which can be used to control timers in Chapter **P4**. Energy can be transferred from electricity to light and back again by such devices. They allow small light sources to flash at a rate of more than a million times per second. You will learn more about them in Chapter **P20**.

In this chapter we shall look at the problem of getting the light to travel far enough.

> **2** What problems would you expect in trying to send signals over a long distance?

The problems involved in sending light signals over long distances explain why the Armada beacons were built on hill tops and why signalling at night has so often been confined to ships at sea. However, in recent years these problems have been overcome.

"Light pipes"

"Light pipes", or *optical fibres* to give them their correct name, are a means of transmitting light over long distances. The cables do not have to be straight. You may see a demonstration in which a pulse of light runs down such a cable while it is still wound on a drum.

The diagram in figure 13.2 shows the construction of an optical fibre. The first experiment on Worksheet **P13A** shows you how to investigate the transmission of light by an optical fibre.

The first requirement of the fibre is that it must let light through as easily as possible. For long distance travel a type of very pure sodium borosilicate glass is used. This is so transparent that a 20-km length is as transparent as a window pane. For short distances, something less transparent (and cheaper) can be used. The optical fibre you use in the laboratory is made from a plastic polymer.

*You can find out more about glass in Chapter **C6** of your Chemistry book. The term "polymer" is explained in Chapter **C8**.*

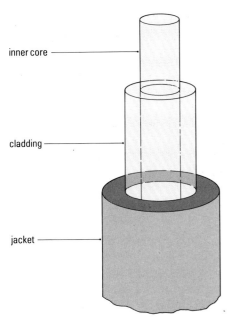

Figure 13.2
An optical fibre consists of a transparent core of glass or plastic surrounded by a cylinder of another transparent material. The optical fibre is covered by a plastic jacket through which light cannot pass.

inner core

cladding

jacket

How do optical fibres work?

When light hits the boundary between one transparent substance and another, two things happen. Some of the light is *reflected* though most of it passes into the other substance. However, unless the light beam happens to be travelling at right angles to the surface, the direction in which it travels is changed. This change of direction is called *refraction*.

The direction of travel of the light is always given as the *angle* the light beam makes with the *perpendicular* to the surface of the medium. (This use of the word "perpendicular" is explained on page 213.) The angle the approaching light beam makes with the perpendicular to the surface is called the *angle of incidence*. After changing direction, the angle the light beam makes with the perpendicular is called the *angle of refraction* (figure 13.3).

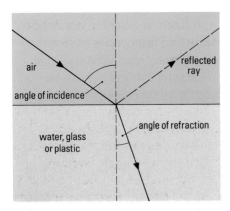

Figure 13.3
When light passes from air into a transparent material, the refracted ray makes a smaller angle with the perpendicular to the surface than the incident ray does.

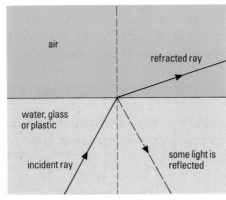

Figure 13.4
When light passes from a transparent material into air, the refracted ray makes a larger angle with the perpendicular to the surface than the incident ray.

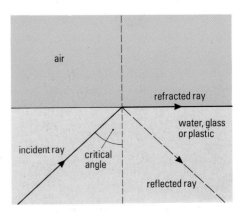

Figure 13.5
If the angle of refraction in the air is 90°, the angle of incidence is called the *critical angle*.

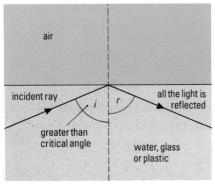

Figure 13.6
For angles of incidence greater than the critical angle, all the light is reflected; none is refracted into the air.

If you have done the experiments in Worksheet **P**13A you will have seen that light, when it passes **from** a plastic or glass medium **to** air, bends **away** from a line perpendicular to the surface of the medium (figure 13.4). The angle of refraction is **greater** than the angle of incidence. So you will have seen that if the angle of **incidence** is increased from 0°, there comes a point when the angle of refraction is 90°. The angle of incidence at which this happens is called the critical angle (figure 13.5). If the angle of incidence is greater than the critical angle, the light can no longer be refracted out of the glass or plastic. Instead all the light is internally reflected (figure 13.6). As before, the angle of reflection is equal to the angle of incidence.

Now look at light entering the piece of plastic at A in figure 13.7. It is first bent towards the perpendicular as it enters the end of the plastic from the air. It then travels along AB and meets the long edge at angle ABX, which in this case happens to be greater than the critical angle for light travelling from the plastic to air. Because the light cannot be **refracted** into the air, all of it is **reflected** along the direction BC. But because the angle of reflection is equal to the angle of incidence, the light meets the other long edge of the strip at the angle BCY, which is just the same as angle ABX. So again it cannot leave the strip and it is **reflected** along the direction CD to meet the other edge. Eventually the light reaches the far end of the strip and passes out into the air.

Optical fibres are able to pass a light signal down their length by a similar process. You may have seen decorative optical fibres open to the air which have light "piped" through them. The optical fibres used for communication

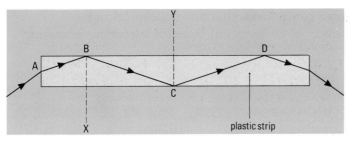

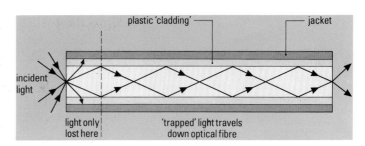

Figure 13.7 (above left)
This diagram shows the way light will pass along a plastic strip. The angle ABX is greater than the critical angle.

Figure 13.8 (above right)
A section through an optical fibre showing how light can pass along it.

Figure 13.9
A copper cable carrying telephone messages compared with an optical fibre that can carry the same number of messages, shown to the same scale.

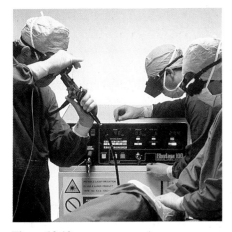

Figure 13.10
Using an optical fibre for medical examination. The instrument is called an endoscope.

are not open to the air in this way. Often many fibres will be bunched together in a single cable. To make sure they work as intended, each fibre is coated with a second layer of transparent plastic which behaves in the same way as an outer layer of air would. Once the light has been "trapped" by the fibre, it is reflected along its length until it reaches the far end. None gets out through the sides (figure 13.8).

Because the fibre is quite narrow (the one you have used has a diameter of 1 mm) quite sharp bends can be made in it without affecting the internal reflection of the light.

Optical fibres and telecommunications

The telephone was invented by Alexander Graham Bell and first shown publicly by him in 1876. It represented a great advance in communications and is described in Chapter **P21**. It led to the laying down of thousands of kilometres of copper cable all over the world to carry telephone messages. But the use of the telephone network, not only for carrying conversations but also for communication between computers, has led to severe problems, three of which are given below:

- To cope fully with today's demands would mean large quantities of very expensive copper cable, occupying a great deal of space.
- The electrical signals can easily be upset by electric currents in nearby wires.
- The electrical signals get weaker and need amplifying about every 2 km.

Optical fibres can help overcome these difficulties. You can see a comparison between cables used to transmit telephone calls in figure 13.9. The information to be transmitted is first turned into a *digital code* (see Chapter **P21**) which is in turn changed to light pulses. The light pulses are transmitted down an optical cable. Four of the advantages of optical cables are:

- Many more messages can be combined to travel down one optical fibre than can be sent, electrically, down one wire.
- The cables are much lighter and smaller than electrical cables designed to carry the same amount of information.
- The signals can travel tens of kilometres without the need for amplification.
- The signals are not upset by other signals on nearby wires.

Optical fibres have uses other than in telecommunications. They have been used to provide novel forms of decoration. They are also used in medicine (figure 13.10) to "pipe" down light and "pipe" up images from inside patients' bodies along optical fibres which can be passed along natural pathways in the body. In fact, optical fibres can be passed down channels as small as arteries.

Using the information from this chapter and any other you may read, try

Figure 13.11
When sounds can become disagreeable!
Many essential jobs have loud noises
associated with them. How is this man
protected against the bad effects of loud
noise?

Worksheet **P13B** which is concerned with some of the social and
technological consequences of using optical fibres for telecommunications.

P13.2   Noise

What is noise?

Most people would use the word "noise" to describe any sound they find
disagreeable (figure 13.11). (Have you ever been told to "Switch off that
dreadful noise!!" when you are listening to your favourite music?)

The degree to which sound can be disturbing or unpleasant depends on
many factors. Mostly it depends on its intensity – something described as
loudness. But *pitch* can also be important – very high-pitched and very low-
pitched sounds can be unpleasant. A quiet sound in the dead of night can be
disturbing when it might go unnoticed in the day.

An enquiry into noise

The increasing amount of disturbing sound in our environment has led many
people to talk of "noise pollution". Worksheet **P13C** is about an
investigation into noise. It should take you about a week to complete. You
should work together with three or four others to complete the enquiry on:
"How noisy is your school?"

Summary

The following passage summarizes the main ideas in this chapter. Copy out
the passage, filling in the blanks with either a word or phrase from the list at
the beginning of the passage. (There is only one word or phrase to each
blank; the words are not listed in the order you will need to use them, and you
may use any word more than once.)

colour	**copper wires**	**energy**	**hearing**
loudness	**optical fibres**	**pitch**	**reflected**
refracted	**scattered**	**sight**	**speed**

Both light and sound are important means of communication, related to
the senses of _____ and _____. In this chapter we have considered
two technologically and socially important aspects of light and sound.

The first dealt with the way our understanding of the behaviour of light has
led to a new means of communication using light pulses down _____.
This process depends on the ability of light to be internally _____ in
transparent materials and thus to travel considerable distances with little loss
in _____.

The second aspect considered was the social nuisance presented by the
wrong sound in the wrong place. Sounds can be irritating due both to
_____ and _____. Society at large is becoming increasingly aware of
the bad effects noise can have on people and some steps are being taken to
limit its impact.

Chapter P14   Making waves
Energy transfer without matter transfer

Figure 14.1
People on the edge of waves at the seaside.

Look at the picture in figure 14.1.

Is this the sort of picture you have in your mind when anyone mentions the word "waves"? Many people in Britain would agree that it is. But some countries, such as Zambia in Africa, have no "shore line". (This means that the sea does not reach any of its borders.) Many children grow up without seeing the sea at all.

1 Write a short letter to an imaginary Zambian friend describing the sea waves which continually break along the shores of Britain.

Figure 14.2
The rubber ball bobs up and down and surges backwards and forwards as the wave passes it.

This chapter is about waves of all sorts and how they behave. The trouble with using sea waves as an example is that they are slightly different from all other waves. One of the things you would probably mention to your imaginary friend is the way the water surges forward and back as the wave breaks. If you stand in the sea it is easy to see and feel the up and down motion of the water. Watch a wave crest coming in from the distance (easy to do when the weather is a bit "rough"); you can see the water rising as the crest passes and then falling down behind it. Does this bit of the wave carry the water forward until it reaches the shore? Watch a piece of seaweed or a rubber ball move as the wave crest passes. It bobs up and down and surges forward and back – but it does not move far from its original spot. The wave crest soon leaves it far behind.

All waves have this up-and-down motion. Sea waves have a backwards-and-forwards motion as well, so the wave **rolls** forward. (Have you heard the phrase "Atlantic rollers"? This is a good description of the motion of sea waves.) In this respect sea waves are unlike most other waves which only make an up-and-down motion as they pass along.

You can see some much more typical wave motion if you put some water in a bath. When the water is quite still, just touch the surface at one end. Ripples (as we often call the waves that run over the surface of water) spread along the water surface. If you put a few bits of paper on the surface you can watch what happens to them as the ripples pass by. The important thing to notice is that the scraps of paper just bob up and down. The ripples run for long distances across the water surface, transferring energy from point to point, but they do not carry the water with them.

2 Imagine after reading this that someone says to you, "I can't see any good reason for saying the waves are transferring energy". How might you persuade that person that energy is in fact being transferred?

P14.2   Waves on a spring

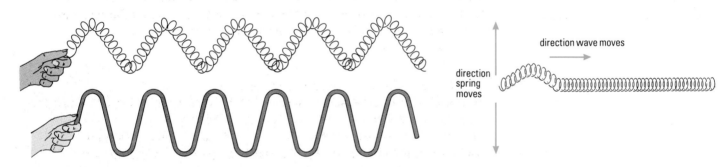

Figure 14.3 (above left)
Making waves on a long spring and on rubber tubing.

Figure 14.4 (above right)
A transverse wave on a spring.

You will see in Chapter **P**15 that waves are a part of many everyday things, such as light and sound. But we do not notice anything "bobbing" up and down in these waves. Waves on water give us our most obvious everyday experience of waves because we can see the change in the water as the wave passes by. An even better way to see the way a wave moves is to send one along a heavy rope or a long coiled spring.

Worksheet **P**14A describes some investigations you can make into wave motion using one of these long springs. You may see these demonstrated, or you may be able to try them out for yourself. All of them can be tried at home with a long piece of rope or even a hose-pipe.

If you move the end of a spring from side-to-side, a wave travels along the spring at right-angles to the side-to-side motion. This sort of wave is called a *transverse wave* (see Worksheet **P**14A and figure 14.4).

When a transverse wave passes along a spring, the side-to-side motion of one coil is passed on to the next.

There is another way that a wave can travel along a spring and that is when each coil of the spring moves back and forth in the **same** direction as the wave travels. This sort of wave is called a *longitudinal wave* (see Worksheet **P**14A and figure 14.5).

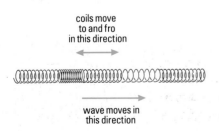

Figure 14.5
A longitudinal wave on a spring.

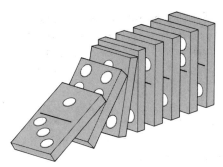

Figure 14.6
A line of dominoes falling over. Each domino pushes over the next one as it falls.

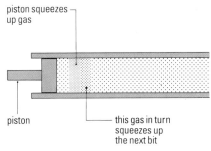

piston squeezes up gas

piston

this gas in turn squeezes up the next bit

Figure 14.7
How a wave can travel through a column of air.

With a longitudinal wave the motion of each coil pushes and pulls its next door neighbour, which in turn pushes and pulls the next one, and so on. All wave motion is like a "chain reaction" – the movement of one piece of the spring is passed on to the next. A good example of a "chain reaction" can be produced by placing a line of dominoes on edge next to each other and then pushing over the first one. As it falls it knocks over the next, and then the next, and so on (figure 14.6).

A "falling-over wave" passes down the line. No one domino moves very far, but the "falling-over" motion (and the energy which goes with it) passes all the way down the line. How far it travels depends only on the length of the chain of dominoes. Of course once all the dominoes have fallen over no more energy can be passed along them.

But what if there were some force that brought them all upright again? Well, then energy could be continually transferred down the line. This is what must happen in anything that can carry a wave – if one bit is displaced, internal forces push it back again. In Chapter **P**1 we looked at the behaviour of solids and we saw that all solid materials can do just that. Whenever something pushes against the atoms, the atoms move together a bit and push back. So all solids can transfer energy as a wave.

What about gases? Robert Boyle's experiments (see Chapter **P**2) showed that gases push back if they are compressed, just as some springs do. He called this "the spring of air". If we have some gas in a long tube and try to squeeze up the gas at one end with a piston, the extra pressure will push forward the next bit of gas and so on through the gas (figure 14.7). If we pull the piston the other way, we **reduce** the pressure slightly and the gas "next door" will move to fill the space, and so on down the column.

3a What sort of wave can be passed through a gas?
b Describe the sort of movement at the end of a spring or a column of gas that can produce a wave.
c Is there any evidence you can think of that might suggest that sound is a wave motion in air? If it was, what sort of wave motion would you expect it to be?

A wave "pulse"

When we experiment with waves it is often helpful to make the wave from a single to-and-fro motion. This sends a "hump" along a rope or spring (figure 14.8). Such a short wave is called a *pulse*. You use the same word when you feel the flow of blood in your arteries. Each surge of blood is produced by one squeeze of your heart – a single to-and-fro motion.

*You can find out more about the way your blood flows through your body in Chapter **B**8 of your Biology book.*

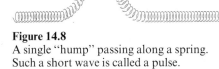

Figure 14.8
A single "hump" passing along a spring. Such a short wave is called a pulse.

---

4 A small toy boat is floating quite still in the middle of a pond.
a How could you make a pulse (a single wave hump in the water) go across the pond?
b What will happen to the little boat as the pulse passes it?
c Suppose you send a whole lot of little pulses one after each other. What will happen to the boat?

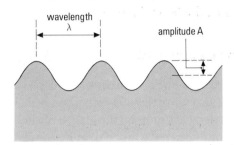

Figure 14.9
The pattern formed by a transverse wave passing over the surface of water or along a spring.

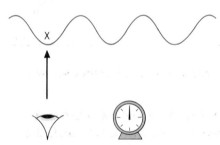

Figure 14.10
Measuring the frequency of a wave.

P14.3   Measurements of waves

A wave is a moving pattern which transfers energy without transferring matter. In a transverse wave, it is produced by a sequence of up-and-down movements. When such a wave passes over the surface of water, it produces the humps and dips that we commonly picture when anyone mentions the word "wave". Figure 14.9 shows a "snap shot" of the wave pattern that you might take with a camera. Each complete up-and-down movement of whatever is producing the wave gives one complete bit of the pattern – one hump and one dip, or, as it is frequently called, one "crest" and one "trough". The pattern repeats and we call the repeat-distance the *wavelength* (figure 14.9).

We shall use the symbol λ to represent the wavelength of a wave. λ is the Greek letter "l" and is pronounced "lambda".

There are three other important wave measurements.

- The *amplitude* is the maximum distance up or down (or out or in) from the calm position. It is the distance marked A in figure 14.9.
- The *wave speed* is the speed at which the pattern travels along, so it is the speed a crest or trough moves. We shall use the symbol c to represent wave speed.
- The last measurement is the *frequency* (symbol, f). Imagine you are watching a wave pass the point X in figure 14.10. You could count the number of crests that passed X every second. This number would give you what we call the wave frequency – it is the number of crests to pass a particular point every second. Of course, you could equally well count the number of troughs – the answer would be the same.

Every time the vibrating source of a wave makes one complete up-and-down (or to-and-fro) motion (called one *cycle*) it makes one complete wave pattern. So every time the source completes one cycle, one crest and one trough move past point X in figure 14.10. This means that the frequency of a wave is also the number of cycles made by the wave **source** every second.

Units for frequency

Although any unit of time can be used to measure frequency, it is usual to count the number of crests or troughs passing a point in **each** second. When frequency is measured in this way, it is said to be measured in *hertz* (symbol, Hz). 1 hertz is a frequency of one crest or trough per second passing a particular point. It is also equal to 1 cycle of the wave source vibration per second. For this reason, you may still sometimes see frequency measured in "cycles per second".

You will have found in experiment 3 of Worksheet **P14A** that the wave speed is unaffected by the length or height of a wave pulse (a single crest). If you make a wave of high frequency on a water surface you will find that the waves are short in length; if you make a wave of low frequency on the same water surface, you will find the waves are long (try it for yourself). There is an important relationship linking wave speed, wavelength and frequency. It is:

wave speed $=$ frequency $\times$ wavelength

Some people like to remember this as the "formula" $c = f\lambda$.

The "wave formula"

Look at the sprinter in figure 14.11. Suppose he covers 2 m every stride and makes 5 strides per second. How far does the athlete run in one second? . . . Yes, 10 metres.

his speed = [5 strides per second] × [2 metres per stride]
= 10 metres per second

In other words,

his speed = number of strides per second × length of each stride

Suppose he takes f strides per minute, each of length λ, in metres. Then he travels a distance $f\lambda$ metres in a minute

or, $c = f\lambda$.

5 strides per second

sprinter covers 10 m each second

2 m

Figure 14.11
The passage of a wave across the surface of water can be likened to a sprinter travelling over the ground.

Now think of waves. When a train of waves has travelled one wavelength along, its appearance is unchanged. One wavelength is like one stride. If the vibrating source of the waves turns out f whole wavelengths per second, the wave speed is given by

wave speed = [number of wavelengths turned out per second]
× [wavelength]

wave speed = [frequency] × [wavelength]

or, $c = f\lambda$

5 A wave passing along a spring was found to have a wavelength of 80 cm and a frequency of 5 Hz.
a Calculate the speed of the wave along the spring.
b What would be the new wavelength of the wave if the frequency was changed to 10 Hz?

6 Some ripples on the surface of a pond have a wavelength of 5 cm and travel across the pond at 20 cm per second. What is the frequency of the waves?

7 The radio waves which carry Radio 4 on the long-wave band are generated at a frequency of 200 000 Hz and travel at a speed of 300 000 km per second. What is the wavelength of such waves?

Figure 14.12
Water waves spreading out.

P14.4   Waves on the surface of water

Look at the waves on the surface of a pool of water (figure 14.12). A small object dropped onto the surface sends out ripples that travel in every direction until they meet something. What happens to them then? You can find out using a specially constructed tank. The tank is called a *ripple tank* because the experiments are performed using ripples on the surface of water (figure 14.13). The light from the lamp above the tank passes through the water and casts "shadows" of the waves on the paper beneath. In this way you can see the waves and watch their behaviour.

You may see these experiments demonstrated, or you may be able to work in groups and do the experiments yourself. Worksheet **P14B** will help you.

Some questions about waves in a ripple tank

The next set of questions is concerned with things you should have seen or done using a ripple tank.

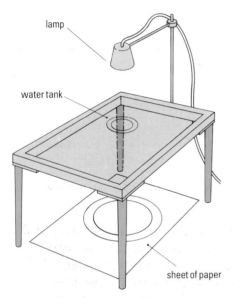

Figure 14.13
A ripple tank used for experiments with waves.

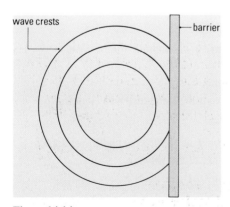

Figure 14.14
Circular waves reaching a barrier. What happens next?

8 You have a ripple tank with water already in it.
a What do you see when you touch the surface of the water with one finger?
b What do you see when you let a drop of water fall into the tank?
c You have a roller in the water in your ripple tank. What do you see happening if you give the roller a small push and then stop?
d Describe or draw sketches of anything else you noticed about your ripples.

9 When a round pulse reaches a straight barrier it does not stop and disappear; the barrier bounces it back. We say the barrier *reflects* the wave.
a Copy the diagram (figure 14.14) and sketch in the reflected part of the ripple.
b Explain how you were able to draw the reflected part of the wave correctly.

10 The roller in figure 14.15 has made a single straight pulse. The pulse goes across the ripple tank to a straight barrier. The arrows show the way the pulse is going.
a How can you use a roller to make a straight pulse?
b Draw sketches to show the pulse:
  i just before it meets the wall
  ii just after it has met the wall.
Put arrows on both sketches to show the direction in which the pulse is moving.

11a By doing an experiment with a ripple tank how would you show that two waves pass through each other **without changing**?
b What happens to ripples when they arrive at the sloping "beach" at the edge of a ripple tank?

12a What happens when two glass marbles are rolled in opposite directions along a groove in a plank so that they meet head-on?
b In what way is this different from what happens when two **waves** meet head-on?

Questions **11** and **12** make a very important distinction between energy transferred with waves and energy transferred with particles. For waves the energy always "gets through"; with particles it may not.

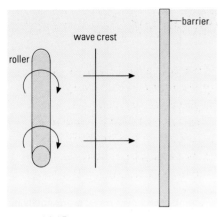

Figure 14.15
Making straight waves with a roller in a ripple tank.

13 You have seen what happens when ripples meet a barrier.
a What happens if there is a small gap in the barrier to let some of the ripples through?
b Figure 14.16 (one-third actual size) shows two barriers, A and B, in a ripple tank. In each case, a series of straight ripples arrives head-on at the barrier in the manner shown. A shows a barrier with a single small gap. B shows a barrier with a gap 6 cm wide. Copy the diagram of barrier A **three times** the size shown. Draw the incoming ripples and show the shape of a ripple that has travelled 3 cm beyond the barrier. Do the same for barrier B.

These pictures are a 'snap shot' of the waves as they come up to the barriers.

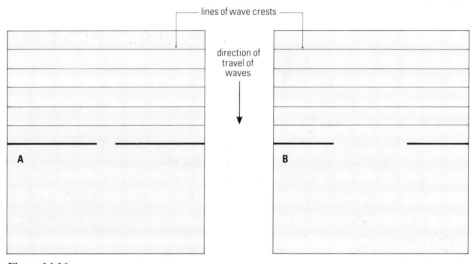

Figure 14.16
Straight waves approaching gaps in a barrier. What happens to the waves when they pass through the gap?

The wave behaviour you have described in answering question **13** is called *diffraction*. This is another behaviour of waves that makes the transfer of energy by waves different from the transfer of energy by, say, a stream of particles. To see what this means, imagine we have a stream of particles produced from an aerosol paint spray. Suppose this spray is directed at a sheet of cardboard with a small hole in it (figure 14.17). The paint spray coming through the hole would not spread out in the way a wave does when passing through a small gap.

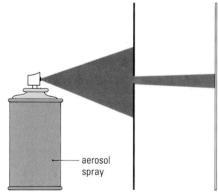

Figure 14.17
Directing an aerosol spray at a piece of card with a hole in it. What will be the pattern of the spray that emerges from the hole?

14 Figure 14.18 (on the next page) shows a "snapshot" of a set of ripples in a tank. The ripples come from a vibrating bar that produces continuous waves, and they are travelling from the righthand side of the diagram. A flat glass plate has been placed over part of the bottom of the tank, making the water shallower in this region. The ripples are parallel to the edge of this plate.
a Where is the edge of the plate situated? (Is it between ripples 2 and 3, or 8 and 9, or somewhere else?)
b Is the plate on the right side or the left side of the diagram?
c What is the wavelength of the waves on the right of the edge?
d What is the wavelength of the waves on the left of the edge?

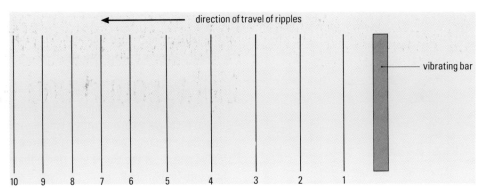

Figure 14.18
Straight waves crossing over a shallow region in a ripple tank. The waves travel more slowly in the shallower water.

The effect of a change of speed on the wave frequency

When water ripples cross the edge of a glass plate into a shallower region, they slow down. Experiments you have done or seen in a ripple tank have shown that the waves also change in wavelength – the wavelength is shorter in the shallower region. What happens to the **frequency** of the waves? The next question gives an argument for supposing that the frequency of the waves **does not change at all**. You have to supply some missing words or phrases in the argument.

15 Copy out and complete the paragraph below. It shows that the frequency of water waves will not change even if their speed does.
  ''When the waves in the deeper water reach the edge of the glass plate, they will cause the water at that edge to move up and down. This moving water will in turn force water on the other (shallower) side of the edge to _____ as well. Every time the water on the deep side of the edge makes one complete up and down motion, the water on the _____ side of the edge will also make one complete _____. This means that the water on the deep side of the edge makes as many up and down motions each second as does the water on the _____. Consequently the frequency of the waves in the _____ water is the same as the _____ of the waves in the shallow water.''

16 (This question refers to the diagram and data in question **14**.) The speed of the ripples on the right of the diagram (figure 14.18) was measured as 21 cm per second. If the frequency of the waves is unchanged as they cross from the deep to the shallow region, what is the speed of the ripples on the left?

Summary

Imagine that one of your friends has missed the lessons on waves. Describe the following to your friend in one or two sentences.
a How an up-and-down motion can pass along a spring as a wave.
b How waves behave when they are reflected by a barrier.
c How waves behave when they pass through a small gap.

Making use of waves
Light, sound and earthquakes

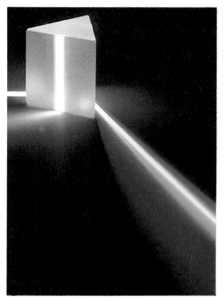

Figure 15.1
Making a spectrum with white light.

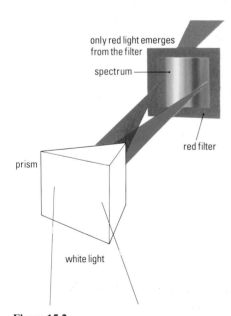

only red light emerges
from the filter

spectrum

red filter

prism

white light

Figure 15.2
The effect of placing a red filter across the
spectrum of colours produced from white
light.

P15.1   Colour

We live in a coloured world, but the light from the Sun which bathes it has no
colour – we call it daylight, or white light. Under daylight conditions, colours
are at their most vivid. Artificial light is often a poor substitute for daylight,
although our brain is so good at deceiving us that we often think of artificial
light as "white" as well. However, an experienced shop assistant knows better
and will often suggest that an attractive dress is taken to a window to "see it
properly". Many large stores go to some trouble to make sure that their
artificial light is as close to natural daylight as possible.

When white light is passed through a *prism* (a triangular piece of glass) the
light that emerges is spread out into a whole range of colours spreading from
red, through orange, yellow, green, blue and violet. We call this a *spectrum*
(figure 15.1). Worksheet **P**15A shows you how to set up such an experiment
and asks you to try to solve the problem first put by Isaac Newton, "Are the
colours of the spectrum a part of white light, or are they made by the prism?"

*Worksheets **P**15B, **P**15C, and **P**15D give details of some investigations you can make into colour
and how we see it. The rest of the section summarizes some of the things you will find out if you do
these investigations and then asks some questions for you to answer. If you intend doing these
investigations, do them first, then read this summary and try the questions.*

*These worksheets could take you some time. If you want to complete all the work in section
P15.4, you may have to spend less time on this work on colour. Your teacher will advise you which
you should do.*

Why things appear in colour

Why does a piece of transparent blue glass or plastic look blue when you hold
it up to the light? Your experiments should have shown that a piece of blue
glass or plastic absorbs all the colours in white light except blue. The blue
light passes through to your eyes. Transparent objects will always appear
coloured if they absorb some of the colours in white light and pass on the rest.
Pieces of coloured glass or plastic which are used in stage lighting or
photography to produce colour effects are called *filters*. (You use the same
word when you speak of *filtering* a liquid. In both situations you are removing
something.)

We do not look at many things by the light that passes through them. We
see most things by the light that they *scatter*. (Scattered light means light that
bounces off an object in all directions.) Objects may not scatter all the light
that falls on them. They may absorb some colours, just like the blue glass.

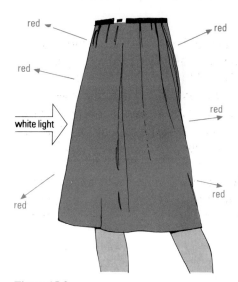

Figure 15.3
Seeing colours by reflected light. The red skirt absorbs all the colours in white light **except** red.

A red dress looks red because the dyes in it are absorbing the blue and green part of the spectrum. The rest of the spectrum – the red light – is scattered and picked up by our eyes.

Very early on in your work in biology (Chapter **B**3) you investigated the important link between light and life. Energy is transferred from light to the food store in plants by a process called *photosynthesis* (figure 15.4).

The substance that brings about this energy transfer is called chlorophyll. Chlorophyll is green in colour. Chlorophyll appears green because it absorbs, and makes use of, only the red and blue parts of the spectrum. Only the green part is left, so chlorophyll appears green to our eyes.

*You will have learnt more about photosynthesis in Chapter **B**3 of your Biology book.*

Colour vision

In another experiment you will have passed red light through a prism. If you do this you find that the prism will not split up the light into any more colours. The same is true if you use green light and blue light.

But if an ordinary yellow filter is placed in a beam of white light, which then passes through a prism, the "yellow" light is found to contain red and green light as well as yellow.

Colour mixing experiments (figure 15.5) show that if red light and green light are mixed, we see the colour "yellow".

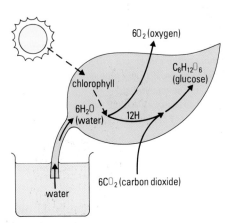

Figure 15.4
Plants use the red and blue parts of white light in photosynthesis. That is why leaves appear green. Green is the colour left after red and blue have been absorbed from white light.

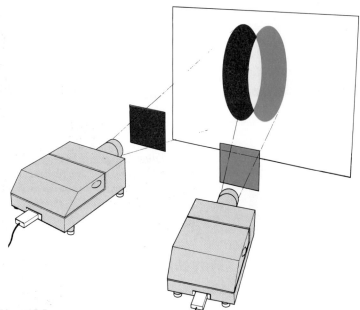

Figure 15.5
A mixture of red and green light appears as yellow light to the eye.

Not all light that looks yellow contains red light and green light combined. Light from table salt heated in a Bunsen flame is not split up into red and green by a prism (figure 15.6). We call such light "pure yellow light". All the colours of the spectrum are pure colours.

1 What test could you do to find out whether a particular filter produced a pure colour or not?

Examining the colours produced by placing chemicals in a flame is an important way of identifying certain elements.

We cannot rely on our **colour vision** to tell us whether a particular colour is pure or not. Pure yellow light appears to our eyes as yellow. But our eyes also give the impression of the colour "yellow" if red light and green light are mixed. Many yellow things in the world around us do not reflect pure yellow light only, but a range of colours in the red/yellow/green part of the spectrum.

Similar experiments show that a mixture of blue and green light produces a bluish-green colour called *cyan*; while red and blue produce a colour called *magenta*. The colours red, green and blue cannot be made by mixing other coloured lights. However, every other colour can be produced by mixing red, green and blue lights either in pairs or all together. For this reason, **red**, **green**, and **blue** are called *primary colours*. The colours produced by mixing any **two** of these are called *secondary colours*.

Figure 15.6
Sodium chloride in a flame gives out **pure** yellow light. This light is not a mixture of red and green.

> **2** Make a list of the three primary colours and the three secondary colours. Write down how each of the secondary colours can be produced from the primary colours.

If lights of the three primary colours are mixed and care is taken to see that they are all of the same intensity, then white light is produced (figure 15.7).

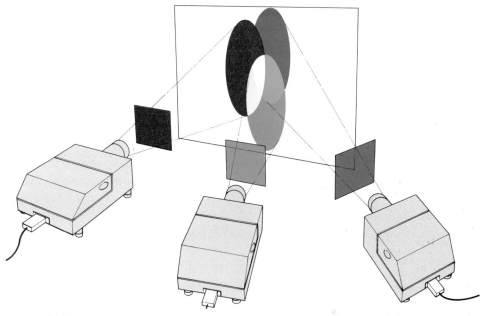

Figure 15.7
Mixing red, green and blue light of equal intensities will produce white light.

In everyday life we see coloured things by white light. As you saw on page 228, objects appear coloured because they **absorb** some of the colours from white light. Thus an object will appear to be green if it absorbs red and blue from the white light falling on it. An ordinary yellow object will appear "yellow" because it absorbs the blue from the white light falling on it, leaving red and green to be scattered to your eyes. (Of course it could also look "yellow" by absorbing all the colours of the spectrum except "pure" yellow. In practice this turns out to be so rare that we can ignore it.)

magenta light is a mixture of red and blue light

in white light, this duster looks
yellow – this is because it
absorbs blue light, scattering
away red and green

Figure 15.8
Magenta light is a mixture of red and blue.
Suppose such light falls on a duster that
appears as yellow in white light. What
colour will the duster appear to be in
magenta light?

Worksheet **P**15D asks you to look at objects of various natural colours under **coloured** light. By remembering the colours a particular object absorbs and reflects, you should be able to predict its appearance in coloured light. For example a yellow object absorbs blue and reflects red and green. So:

- in **blue** light, a yellow object will appear **black**;
- in **green** light, a yellow object will appear **green**;
- in **magenta** light (red + blue) a yellow object will appear **red** (as it absorbs blue and scatters red, see figure 15.8).

3 Suppose you have four patches of coloured cloth:
patch R is pure red　　　　patch G is pure green
patch M is magenta　　　　patch W is white
These are the colours the patches will appear if you look at them in white light. Assuming you are in a pitch dark room, write down the colour each patch would appear under the following lights:
a pure red light
b pure green light
c pure yellow light
d ordinary (mixed) yellow light.

4 White light can be made from red, green and blue light. White light can also be produced by combining each primary colour in turn with **one** other secondary colour.
a Write down the secondary colour that combines with red to produce white light.
b Repeat this for green and blue light.

The primary colour and the corresponding secondary colour that together produce white light, are called *complementary* colours.

Colours by addition and subtraction

Your experiments have shown that the full range of colours that our eyes can see can be produced by using only red, green and blue light, and mixing them as required. This is how **colour television** works. You will learn something of how electrons can be used to produce pictures in Chapter **P**19. On the screen itself, the colour picture is made up of a *mosaic* of red, green and blue dots (figure 15.9). You can actually see these if you look closely at the screen. From a distance, a cluster of red and green dots close together will give the same impression as red and green light mixed – in other words, yellow.

Colour photography uses a different principle. Starting with white light, it produces its colours by *subtraction*. You may have tried an experiment in Worksheet **P**15D in which you looked at white light shining through combinations of filters of *secondary colours*. Secondary colour filters will not only produce their own colours, but, in combination, all the other colours as well. For example, if white light shines through a **magenta** and a **cyan** filter, the colour blue is produced (figure 15.10). Colour photographs and colour transparencies consist of three layers of transparent material, one with a magenta image, one with a yellow image and one with a cyan image. By varying the intensity of the dyes at different places on the photograph, a full colour range can be produced. Varying the dye intensity is something that is done during the process of producing the image called *development*.

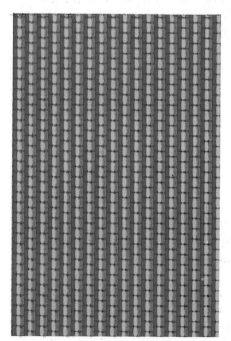

Figure 15.9
The colour picture on a television screen is built up from red, green and blue dots.

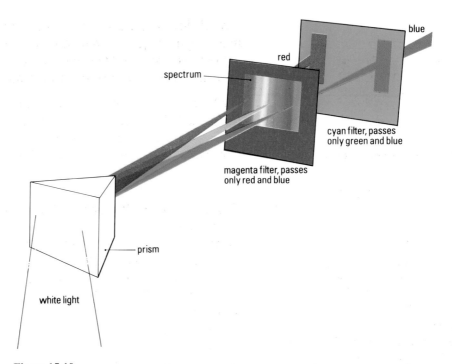

Figure 15.10
A magenta filter passes only the red and blue parts of the spectrum. When magenta-coloured light falls on a cyan (blue–green) filter, only the blue light is passed.

You cannot expect to understand all about colour photography from this brief account. However, if the topic interests you, you will find that there are many books about it. There is probably one in your library. It is something that you can do practically as well. Your school may well have a photographic club.

> **5** Why can't primary colour dyes be used to produce colour photographs? (To answer this, ask yourself what happens if two primary colour filters are placed together in a beam of white light.)

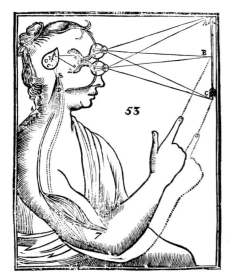

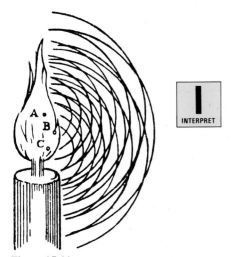

Figure 15.11
a (top) Descartes thought of light as a stream of particles.
b (bottom) Christian Huygens believed it to be a longitudinal wave.

P15.2 More about light

The nature of light has puzzled scientists since the time they first began to explore the world through experiments and to make theories about the way the world works. Isaac Newton and the French philosopher/scientist René Descartes both believed that light travelled as a stream of particles, although they were unable to explain what the particles were. During the same period of history, a Dutch scientist, Christian Huygens, believed that the energy associated with light travelled as a longitudinal wave – but he was unable to say what the wave was.

It was not until the middle of the nineteenth century that scientists became convinced that light did indeed travel as a wave, and that it travelled not as a longitudinal wave, but as a transverse wave. We shall not follow all the details that eventually convinced them of the truth of this. Neither shall we bother about what sort of wave it might be. Instead all we need ask here is if light is a wave, does it behave in the way we expect waves to behave?

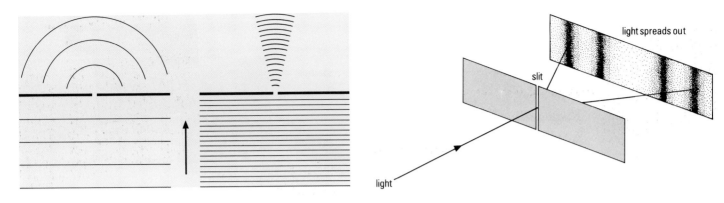

Figure 15.12 (above left)
The different amount of diffraction of long and short wavelength waves passing through the same aperture.

Figure 15.13 (above right)
The diffraction of light when it passes through a narrow slit.

Diffraction

Do you remember what happens to a wave when it passes through a narrow gap? In the experiments with a ripple tank in Chapter **P**14 you found that the wave spreads out after passing through a gap. The smaller the gap (compared with the wavelength) the more the wave spreads out. The diagram in figure 15.12 shows the difference between waves of long wavelength and short wavelength passing through a narrow gap.

If you make a thin scratch on a piece of blackened glass and look at some light through it, you will see that light behaves in the same way.

If you have a slit of variable width you can see for yourself how the band of light broadens as the gap gets **narrower**. If you look very carefully you will notice something else as well – there are some colours in the band. The outermost colours are red. You may also be able to see that the inner ones are blue.

6 Let us suppose that light **is** a wave, as this experiment seems to suggest. It seems that red light spreads out more than blue light. This could be due to red light having a different wavelength from blue light. Explain whether red light or blue light would have the longer wavelength. (Think about the ripple tank experiments.)

You may see a demonstration of the equipment shown in figure 15.14b. A *diffraction grating* is a piece of glass with a large number of closely spaced lines scratched on it. Light can pass between the lines, so the glass behaves as though it were made like the drawing in figure 15.14a. If the diffraction grating is put in a beam of white light, it will split up the light into its many colours according to their wavelength.

7a Which colour is diffracted the most by a diffraction grating? Which colour is diffracted the least?
b Compare this with a prism. Is the colour that is diffracted the most by a diffraction grating the same one as is bent the most by a prism?

The wave theory of light (or as it is often called the wave *model* of light, because it is something we **picture** rather than **describe**) has at least given us a good explanation of colour. Ordinary daylight consists of waves of various wavelengths. The different pure colours represent the separate wavelengths which go to make up natural daylight.

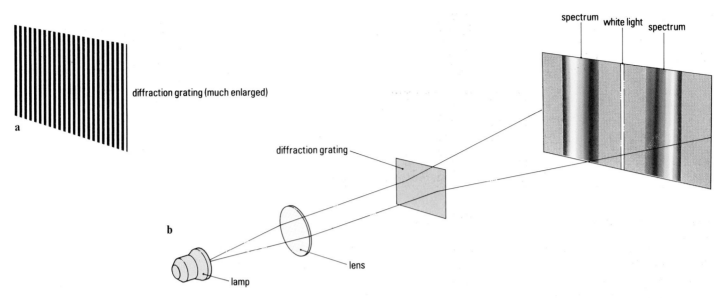

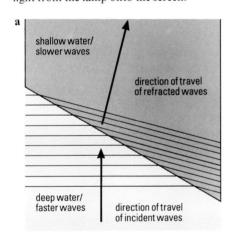

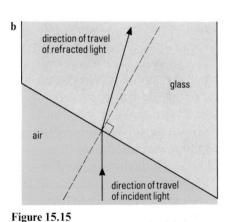

Figure 15.14
a A diffraction grating consists of a piece of glass or plastic covered in closely spaced parallel lines.
b When white light passes through a diffraction grating, it is spread out into a spectrum. The lens is used to focus the light from the lamp onto the screen.

Figure 15.15
a The refraction of water waves when they pass from deep water to shallow water.
b Refraction of light waves.

*It is not essential to work through the last part of this section in order to understand the work of the rest of this chapter. If you have chosen to spend more time on colour, you may want to omit this next part and go on with section **P15.3**. Your teacher will advise you.*

The speed of light

There is one other piece of evidence that we can show that supports the wave theory. In Worksheet **P14B** you experimented with waves that travelled from a deep region of the ripple tank to a shallow region. When waves travelled from the deep region to the shallow region, they slowed down. If the edge of this shallow region is not parallel to the line of the ripples, the wave changes direction (figure 15.15a). Notice that the new line of the ripples makes an even greater angle with the edge than before. The direction in which the ripples travel has changed in just the same way that the direction in which light travels changes when it passes from air to glass (figure 15.15b).

8 If light is a wave, explain whether this change of direction means that light travels slower in glass than in air, or quicker.

Many experiments have been done to measure the speed of light in air or through empty space. The answer is always the same – just about 300 000 km per second.

9 The Sun is 150 million km from the Earth. How long does it take light to travel from the Sun to the Earth?

10 The stars are so far away that it is common to measure their distance in light-years, that is, the distance light will travel in one year! The nearest star is 4 light-years away. How far is this in kilometres? (To answer this question, you will need to know that there are 32 million seconds in a year. To make the calculation a little easier, you can assume that there are approximately 30 million seconds in a year. Scientists often use approximate figures in this way when they want to get a general idea of the size of things.)

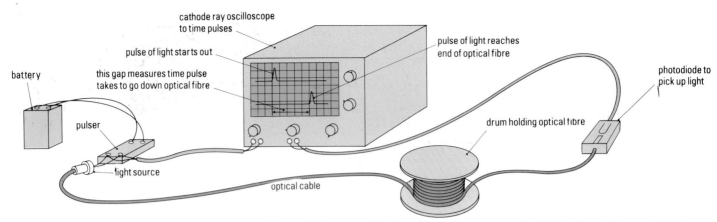

Figure 15.16
An experiment to measure the speed of
light along an optical fibre.

It is possible to send light pulses down an optical fibre (see Chapter **P**13) and measure the time it takes for the pulse to do the journey using a cathode ray oscilloscope. You may see such an experiment demonstrated to you (figure 15.16). Such measurements show that the speed of light down an optical fibre is only about 200 000 km per second.

This is much slower than the speed of light in air or empty space. This is what we would expect if light travels as a wave.

Prisms and the spectrum of white light

Prisms cause light to change direction. The amount of "light bending" that occurs depends on the difference between the speed of light in air and the speed in glass. Because the speed of red light is not reduced by glass as much as the speed of blue light, it "bends" less. This is why the prism spreads out white light into a spectrum of waves of different wavelength.

Figure 15.17
Using a light-sensitive cell and a light
beam to measure the speed of a trolley.

P15.3   The electromagnetic spectrum

Ultra-violet and infra-red waves

The eye is not the only thing to respond to light. You may already have done some experiments in which you measured the time taken by a trolley to cross a light beam. The light fell on something sensitive to light called a *photodetector* (figure 15.17).

A similar light detector is used in the experiment illustrated in figure 15.18. When light falls on the detector, the meter reading changes. You may see such a detector set up so that a spectrum from white light falls on it. The detector registers light from the red end to the blue end of the spectrum. But the surprise is that it **also** registers **something** just outside the visible spectrum!

Does this mean that there are waves just like light (which we can see) but of longer and shorter wavelengths (which we cannot see)? Experiments like these suggest that there are. The waves associated with daylight extend in wavelength to both shorter wavelengths and longer wavelengths than visible light. Because violet light has the shortest wavelength of visible light, the invisible waves in daylight of even shorter wavelengths are called *ultra-violet* (meaning "beyond violet"). Similarly the invisible waves of even longer wavelength than red light are called *infra-red* (meaning "below red").

Light does seem to behave in the same way as a wave. So by now you

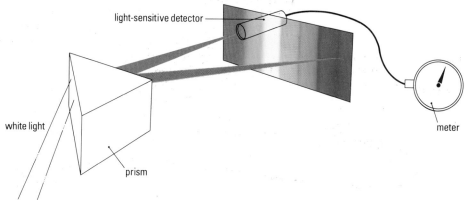

Figure 15.18
Detecting infra-red light using a light-sensitive detector.

should be asking, "If light is a wave, what is its wavelength?" Measurements (which are too difficult for our work here) show that the wavelength of light is very small – in fact very small indeed. 2000 complete wave patterns of green light would only occupy one millimetre in length. It is because of this short wavelength that we are not usually aware that light is a wave. In order to deal with such small numbers we use a special unit called the *nanometre* (abbreviated to nm). There are 1000 million nanometres to the metre.

11a How many nanometres are there in a millimetre?
b If 2000 complete green light wave patterns occupy one millimetre, what is the wavelength of green light in nanometres?

Visible light waves cover a range of wavelengths from about 650 nm (red) to 400 nm (violet). Infra-red waves have wavelengths longer than about 700 nm, while ultra-violet waves have wavelengths shorter than 400 nm.

Waves of even longer and shorter wavelengths

Ultra-violet, visible light and infra-red waves have one property in common – they all travel at the same high speed of 300 000 km per second in air or empty space. We also know of waves of even longer and shorter wavelengths which belong to the same family.

Shorter wavelengths than ultra-violet waves are *X-rays*. These have a wavelength of around 0.1 nm. You meet them in Chapter C5 of your Chemistry book which describes the way Lawrence Bragg and his father used them to unravel the structure of matter. You saw in an earlier experiment the way light behaves when it passes through a diffraction grating. The regular spacing of atoms and molecules in matter forms a similar "diffraction grating" for X-rays. The pattern of X-rays produced when they pass through matter tells its own story of the way the atoms are arranged.

X-rays can also be used to take photographs of the insides of our bodies (figure 15.19). You can see several examples of such photographs in your Biology book.

Gamma rays (which you studied in connection with radioactivity) are from the same family of waves as X-rays, but they have a wavelength so short that 100 000 complete wave patterns would fit into a nanometre. *Infra-red waves* occupy a wide range of wavelengths – anything from 700 nm to 100 000 nm (100 000 nm is the same as 0.1 mm).

Figure 15.19
An X-ray machine in use in a hospital. The woman is about to drink some barium sulphate, which will show up white on X-ray photographs of her stomach.

Figure 15.20
A radar installation, in use for tracking aircraft. This radar is in use at an RAF flight control centre in Britain.

Figure 15.21
The television transmitting aerial at Crystal Palace. This aerial sends out both television and VHF local radio programmes.

Waves travelling at the same speed as light but of even longer wavelength than infra-red waves are known collectively as *radio waves*. The shortest of these, with wavelengths ranging from 0.1 mm to a few centimetres, are called *microwaves*. These are used for radar (figure 15.20) and microwave cooking. We shall return to microwaves in the next section.

After this, with wavelengths up to 1 m, are the waves used for television transmission. These are often referred to as UHF waves ("UHF" stands for Ultra High Frequency). Waves used for sound-only radio have even longer wavelengths (up to 10 km). They are referred to as *VHF, short wave, medium wave* and *long wave*, depending on their particular wavelength.

"VHF" stands for Very High Frequency. They are the shortest wavelength radio waves in use for sound only. They are used for high-quality broadcasts, many of which are now in stereo (figure 15.21).

This whole family of waves is called the *electromagnetic spectrum*. It is common to illustrate this family on a diagram displaying the whole range of radiations from the very long wavelength to the very short. Worksheet **P15E** shows you how to construct such a diagram and asks you to find out some more about the importance to us of the members of this family of waves.

The next section, about transferring energy from waves, is rather harder than the previous work. It could be omitted without harming your understanding of the rest of the chapter.
*Your teacher will advise you whether to leave it out and go on to section **P15.5**.*

P15.4   Transferring energy using waves

The importance to us of light and similar waves is the way in which they can transfer energy. In this section we will explore how waves can transfer energy. First, you should try the experiment illustrated in figure 15.22. The trolley is held in the middle of the runway by a pair of springs. Attached to the trolley is one end of a long spring or piece of rubber tubing. Your task is to make the trolley move to and fro by waggling the far end of the rubber tubing!

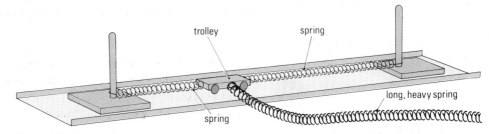

Figure 15.22
Forcing a trolley-and-springs oscillator into oscillation by sending waves down a long, heavy spring.

As you waggle the end of the tubing to and fro, a wave will travel down the tubing to the trolley. This wave transfers energy from you to the trolley.

12a What happens to the trolley if you waggle the end of the tubing very quickly?
b What happens to the trolley if you waggle the end of the tubing very slowly?
c Can you find a particular "waggling rate" that will make the trolley move backwards and forwards?

Oscillations

Now take the rubber tubing off the trolley and pull the trolley back against one of its springs. When the trolley is released it will move backwards and forwards on its own for a little, pushed and pulled by its springs. This sort of motion is called a *vibration*, or *oscillation*. Many things around us vibrate if given a small push. Look at the diagrams in figure 15.23. All of these things show a backwards and forwards motion if given a push. You saw, in Chapter P4, how the oscillations of a pendulum are used in a clock.

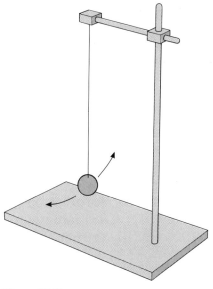

Figure 15.23
All of the things in this diagram will oscillate to and fro if given a small push.

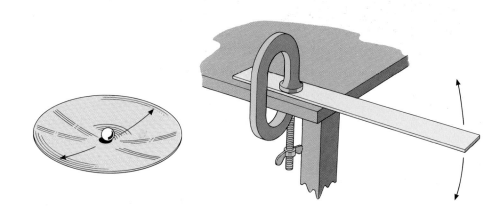

> **13** Find five examples from the world around you of things which will oscillate, or vibrate, in this way.

Things which naturally vibrate are called *oscillators*. The trolley attached to its springs is an oscillator. You should measure the frequency at which the trolley naturally oscillates. When you have done this, you should measure the frequency with which you have to waggle the end of the rubber tubing to make the trolley move backwards and forwards.

> **14a** What is the simple relationship between the frequency with which the trolley oscillates on its own and the "waggling frequency" of the tubing that makes the trolley move?
> **b** Can you give an explanation for this?

It is only when the wave motion keeps time with the trolley's natural oscillating frequency that energy can be transferred from the wave to the trolley. We will now look at some examples of this behaviour in electromagnetic waves.

Figure 15.24a
Toasters depend on the emission of infra-red radiation in order to toast bread.

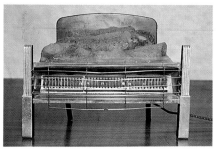

Figure 15.24b
Many electric fires also depend on the emission of infra-red radiation to warm their surroundings.

Toasters, grills and electric fires

Many things that use electricity for heating depend upon infra-red radiation (figure 15.24). Atoms are bound to each other by strong forces in solids. If an atom is displaced, these forces will try to pull it back in the same way that the springs on the trolley pulled the trolley back.

Figure 15.25
Microwave cookers are a recent energy-efficient invention for cooking food.

In hot solids, the atoms oscillate vigorously and emit electromagnetic waves, many of which are in the infra-red wave band. This is how hot things like the wire in a toaster transfer energy by *radiation*.

We have seen how waves can transfer energy to other oscillators. When infra-red waves fall on something else (like the bread in the toaster) they will make its atoms vibrate more. This is because the waves have the same frequency as some of the atoms in the bread. If the atoms are forced to vibrate they will take up energy from the wave. This extra energy shows itself as a rise in the temperature of the bread. So energy has been transferred from the electricity supply to the bread in making the toast.

Microwave cookers

Cooking by infra-red radiation is not very efficient, as the energy is transferred to everything with which it comes in contact – not just the food. Microwave cookers (figure 15.25) are a much more energy-efficient way of cooking food. They deliver their energy to just where it is needed.

All food contains large quantities of water. You will have seen a diagram of a water molecule in your work in Chemistry (Chapter **C**1). Two hydrogen atoms are attached to an oxygen atom (figure 15.26). Such a molecule can vibrate and rotate in many complicated ways, all of which have their own natural frequency. If electromagnetic waves with one of these frequencies fall on the water molecules, energy will be transferred from the waves to the water, just as it was transferred from the rubber tubing to the trolley. The food therefore gets hot and cooks. No energy is transferred by the waves to the dish or the oven. Consequently this way of cooking food is very efficient.

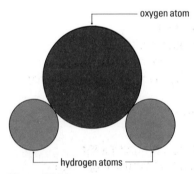

Figure 15.26
A diagram of a water molecule.

Radio and television

Television and radio reception both depend on the ability of electromagnetic waves to transfer energy. If electric charges are given a "push" (perhaps by connecting a battery for a moment to the special circuit shown in figure 15.27) they will oscillate backwards and forwards in the circuit with a particular frequency. Electromagnetic waves of the same frequency can also make this happen, but it doesn't work with waves of a different frequency. The electromagnetic waves are picked up by an aerial which passes them on to the special circuit. The charges in the circuit only respond to one particular wave frequency, so the circuit can pick out one station from another.

Figure 15.27
a An electric circuit that can oscillate.
b To receive a particular television programme, similar circuits oscillate in time with the waves carrying the programme.

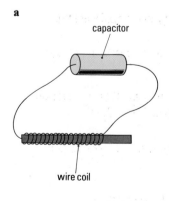

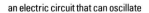
an electric circuit that can oscillate

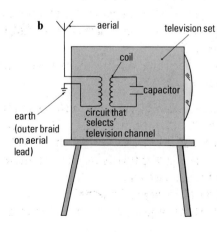

Question 15 is long and quite difficult. It draws on work from other parts of the course as well.

15 A particular microwave cooker carries the following information on a data plate on the back of the cooker:

Output power: 650 W
Input power: 1.35 kW
Volts: 230 V
Current: 5.9 A
Frequency: 2450 MHz

500 g of water were put into a plastic measuring jug and heated at full power in the microwave oven. The jug was removed from the oven every 15 s, the water was stirred and the temperature taken. This was repeated for 2 minutes. The following readings for the temperature were recorded.

Time in seconds	0	15	30	45	60	75	90	105	120
Temperature in °C	10	13	17	21	24	27	30	34	37

a Plot a graph of the temperature readings against the time at which they were taken.
b Why was the water stirred before each reading was taken?
c Write down the temperature the water would have reached after 100 s.
d By how much has the temperature of the water risen since the start?
e If the water continued to heat up at this rate, how long would it have taken for it to reach 70 °C from the time it was first put in the oven?
f Why is your answer to **c** more reliable than your answer to **e**? (If you are not sure about this look up Chapter **P2**, page 41.)
g The specific heating capacity of water is 4200 J per kg per °C. Using the temperature rise you have worked out in part **c**, find out how much energy has been transferred to the water in 100 s. (If you cannot remember how to do this, look at Chapter **P9** and use the formula: energy transferred = mass × specific heating capacity × temperature rise.)
h The plate on the back of the cooker says that its output power is 650 W. How much energy does the cooker transfer from the electricity supply in 100 s?
i Does this figure agree with the result you have just found in part **g**? If not, say which is the greater figure and try to give an explanation for the difference.
j The input power is given as 1.35 kW. Does this agree with the current and voltage figures also given on the cooker's data plate?
k Why is the input power greater than the output power quoted on the data plate?
l What is the efficiency of the cooker
   i using the figures on the cooker's data plate, and
   ii using the data plate input figures and the output energy calculated from the experiment?
m What experiments would you do to check the results obtained experimentally for the output power of the cooker?

16 An electric kettle of input power 2000 W was also used to heat 500 g of water for 100 s. During this time the temperature of the water rose from 9 °C to 83 °C.
a How much energy was transferred to the water?
b How much energy was transferred from the electrical supply to the heater in the kettle in these 100 seconds?
c What is the efficiency of the kettle?
d Do you think it is a good idea to use a microwave cooker to heat water?

17 This question refers to the information given on the data plate on the back of the cooker referred to in question **15**.

a The speed of microwaves in air is 300 000 km per second. What is this speed in metres per second?

b What is the wavelength of the radiation? (Use the wave equation $c = f\lambda$.)

P15.5   Other waves around us

All the waves we have looked at so far in this chapter have been a part of the electromagnetic spectrum. As you have seen, this "family" of waves is of great importance in many different ways. However, they are not the only waves to affect our everyday lives. In this last section we shall look very briefly at some of the others.

Sound

The work you have already done on sound has probably shown you that sound is also a wave. Figure 15.28 shows an experiment which demonstrates that a loudspeaker vibrates when it emits a sound. The loudspeaker is connected to an instrument called a *signal generator*. All this does is to make the loudspeaker cone oscillate backwards and forwards. The frequency of the oscillations can be changed. If the frequency is increased, the loudspeaker cone can be seen vibrating more quickly, and at the same time the *pitch* of the note it emits also rises. Similarly, if the frequency is decreased, the loudspeaker cone vibrates more slowly, and the pitch of the note falls. So it seems that pitch depends on the *frequency* of the sound waves.

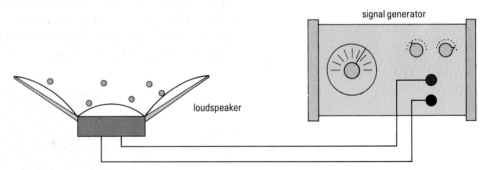

Figure 15.28
An experiment to show that a loudspeaker emitting a sound is also vibrating.

*You will make a fuller investigation into the relationship between hearing and frequency in your work in Chapter **B**11 of your Biology book.*

It is easier to understand how sound waves move through the air than how light waves do it with light. The push and pull of the loudspeaker in figure 15.29a causes the air in front of it to move backwards and forwards in the same way that a longitudinal wave can be sent down a long spring (figure 15.29b).

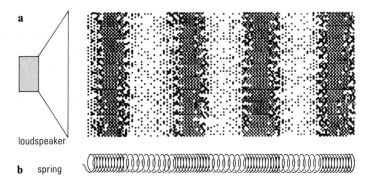

a

loudspeaker

b spring

Figure 15.29
a A vibrating loudspeaker cone pushes and pulls the air in front of it, sending out a sound wave.
b The sound wave is a longitudinal wave like this wave on a spring.

18 If you have not already measured the speed of sound, try to think of a way of doing it. Sound travels at about 340 metres per second. When you have thought of a way, try it out.

19 Musical sounds have a frequency range from about 30 Hz to about 10 000 Hz. The speed of sound is 340 metres per second.
a Using the wave equation $c = f\lambda$, work out the wavelength of the sound corresponding to these two frequencies.
b People will often pay a lot of money to get loudspeakers with what is called "a good bass response". However, experts say that loudspeakers able to give notes down to 30 Hz will be quite ineffective in a small room. Can you suggest any reason for this?

Earthquakes

Earthquakes are produced by the movement of rocks deep down below the Earth's surface. The energy associated with this movement is transferred to places on the Earth's surface by waves, often causing a great deal of damage (figure 15.30). Understanding earthquake waves is important and a lot of scientific effort is being given to it. Worksheet **P15F** gives you some

Figure 15.30
Earthquake energy is transmitted as a wave. The energy in the wave can do a great deal of damage as shown in this photograph taken after an earthquake in Columbia.

information about earthquakes and their effects and then asks some questions. To answer these you will have to use some of the knowledge you have gained about waves in the last two chapters.

Summary

Light and sound both behave in the same way as waves. Knowing how waves behave helps us to understand light and sound, and also helps us to make use of them.

Here are three lists. The first is a list of things you already know about waves. The second is a list of things you know about light, and the third list is about sound. Because all three are waves, they all behave in a similar way and an item in one list can be matched to a similar item in the others. What you have to do is to match them up! For example one answer would be: "W6 goes with L3 and S1 because they are all about the speed of the waves".

Now try to match up the rest.

Waves

W1   Waves are produced by a source which oscillates.
W2   Waves can differ from each other in frequency and wavelength.
W3   Waves may change direction if they cross a boundary where their speed alters.
W4   Waves bounce off flat surfaces.
W5   Waves spread out if they pass through a narrow gap.
W6   Waves travel at a steady speed over water of constant depth.
W7   The energy from waves is easily taken up by an object which has the same natural frequency as the wave.

Light

L1   Light is reflected by a mirror.
L2   A source of light looks wider when seen through a narrow slit.
L3   Light travels from the Sun to the Earth at 300 000 km/s.
L4   Radio waves, which are like light, are produced by electrical circuits in which the charges are oscillating.
L5   Light may change direction when it passes from air into glass.
L6   White light is made up of a range of different colours.
L7   Microwaves, which are like light, can heat up food because their energy is easily absorbed by water.

Sound

S1   Sound travels through air at 340 m/s.
S2   Sounds can vary in pitch.
S3   An ear can distinguish sounds of different pitch.
S4   Sounds easily spread round any objects in their path.
S5   A tuning fork can be felt to be vibrating when it emits a sound.
S6   Loud sounds produce echoes.
S7   Sound can change direction if it goes into a balloon filled with a dense gas like carbon dioxide.

Topic P5 Electricity

What this topic is about

It hardly needs saying that electricity is one of the parts of physics that has most influence on our lives. If you are uncertain about that, try question **1** in Chapter **P**16. These next six chapters explore some of the basic principles upon which our use of electricity is founded. Chapter **P**16 and Chapter **P**17 are about the flow of electric charge in a circuit and the transfer of energy.

Chapter **P**18 shows how energy can be transferred from fuels to electricity and how it can then be used to do useful force-moving jobs in industry, transport and the home.

Chapters **P**19 to **P**21 are concerned with another very important use of electricity which is generally called "electronics". Here we shall look at three topics – making pictures (Chapter **P**19), controlling things (Chapter **P**20) and communication (Chapter **P**21). Do not expect to become an "electronics wizard" after reading these chapters! In this course we can do no more than see how the basic behaviour of electricity enables us to do these things. If you are interested in **how**, then you should at some time take up or read a course in electronics.

Understanding electrical ideas is best achieved by having a lot of practical experience with electricity. Often this means going over the same work several times. So instead of starting off this topic with a revision of what you should already know, we shall start straight away with Chapter **P**16, the first section of which outlines some very basic ideas in electricity with some questions to answer. If you find the questions quite straightforward, go on to the next section. If you feel uncertain about some of the answers to the questions, you should try Worksheet **P**16A which gives you some practice at these basic ideas using circuits you build yourself.

Using electricity
Electric currents and ammeters

P16.1   Using electricity

Figure 16.1 shows a picture of a London tube station. This is part of a railway system known today as the London Underground Railway. Not all of it is in fact underground! When the first part of it was constructed, steam trains were the only sort of rail transport. The underground system we have today was not built until electric trains had been invented. Today, the output of two power stations is needed just to run the London underground system.

Figure 16.1
Passengers boarding a "tube" train on the London Underground.

1a Why was the underground railway system not developed in London until electric trains became available?
b What disadvantages are there in using electricity to provide the energy to run the system?

Many people think of electricity as dangerous. One of the disadvantages you may have thought of in answering question **1** is that people have been killed by falling on "electric rails". But electricity is not always so dangerous. Look at figure 16.2. Why do the birds sitting on the power lines not get electrocuted?
You also use electricity to power a torch or a personal radio. This electricity is not dangerous.

Figure 16.2
Birds sitting on an uninsulated power line.
Why don't the birds get electrocuted?

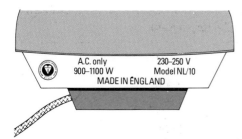

Figure 16.3
A diagram of a manufacturer's label on an electric iron.

Figure 16.4
a The label on the end of a 100-watt light bulb.
b The label on the neck of a torch bulb.

Electricity at home

The picture in figure 16.3 shows a maker's label on an electric iron. If you look at anything electrical at home you will almost certainly find a similar label. To use electrical appliances properly, it is helpful to know what these labels mean. First the label tells us that the iron is for "A.C. only". "A.C." stands for "alternating current". This is the sort we get from the "mains" supply and you can learn more about it in Chapter **P**18.

Then the label goes on to say "230–250 V" and "900–1100 W". You may not understand what "230–250 V" means. But you should by now realize the meaning of "900–1100 W". It tells us the **power** of the iron.

Power is investigated in Chapter **P**8 where the idea is used in connection with machines and engines. Power is the rate at which energy is transferred by a machine or engine. The label tells us that this particular electric iron will transfer energy from electricity at a rate of between 900 and 1100 joules every second.

2a Why is the iron stated to have a range of power outputs, rather than just one?
b What is the significance of the symbol on the left of the label (often called the "kite mark")?

Figure 16.4a shows the label on the end of a light bulb (lamp). It is marked "240 V 100 W". Because it is marked "240 V" it is suitable for connection to our "mains" supply. But its power output is quite different from the electric iron. The light bulb (lamp) transfers only 100 joules every second.

Figure 16.4b shows a picture of a torch bulb. On the neck of the bulb is written "3.5 V 0.3 A". This apparently tells us nothing about power at all! But you know that the torch bulb gives a much weaker light than the mains lamp. And you may also realize that the figure "3.5 V" has something to do with it being run from a battery rather than the mains.

How can two different electrical gadgets, like the mains lamp and iron, transfer **different** amounts of energy every second when connected to the **same** supply? What is the difference between "240 V" and "3.5 V"? It is the purpose of these next two chapters to find out.

The table in figure 16.5 shows a range of electrical "gadgets" we use and the typical voltage and power at which they operate.

3 Add three more electrically-powered devices to the table in figure 16.5 and write down their operating voltage and power.

4 The following questions refer to the table in figure 16.5.
a Why is a range of power outputs written alongside the electric cooker?
b To what do "Input power" and "Output power" for the portable radio refer? Why is the output power so much smaller than the input power?
c Jane decides to work out the energy used by a refrigerator in one hour. To do this she writes: "Energy used = 120 W × 3600 s = 432 000 J". Karen says she thinks it most unlikely the refrigerator will use this much energy in an hour.
  i Why does Jane multiply the power by 3600 to get the energy?
  ii Why does Karen think the refrigerator is most unlikely to use this much energy in an hour?

Device	Voltage, in volts	Power, in watts	
table lamp	240		60
refrigerator	240		120
fan heater	240		2 000
hair drier	240		1 200
hair styling brush	240		20
toaster	240		1 000
washing machine	240	motor	500
		heater	2 650
tumble drier	240	motor	200
		heater	2 200
food mixer	240		450
microwave oven	240		1 600
electric cooker	240	to	1 000 11 000
portable radio	6	Input	10
		Output	2
electric drill	240		450
portable TV set	240		30
portable tape recorder	6		4
calculator	3		0.00043

Figure 16.5
Ratings for some domestic electrical appliances.

P16.2   Simple circuits

5 Look at the circuits drawn in figure 16.6. In which circuits will the bulb light when the switch is pressed? (You can assume that the battery is a new one and that the bulb is not broken and it is the correct one for the battery.)

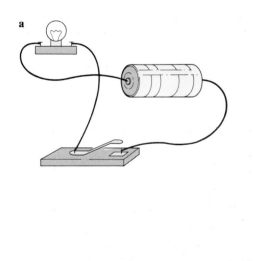

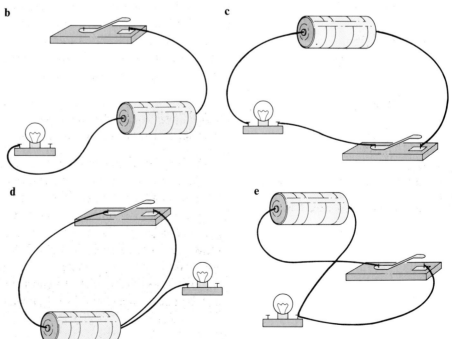

Figure 16.6
A number of electric circuits. In which will the light bulb light up when the switch is closed?

To work, an electric circuit always has to form a complete loop from one terminal of the power supply to the other. The material which completes the loop can be a metal wire, an element like carbon, or certain solutions of chemicals. All of these materials are called *electrical conductors* – or "*conductors*" for short. Some materials cannot be used to complete an electrical circuit. These are called *electrical insulators*.

Electric circuits often contain more than light bulbs, batteries and switches. They may also contain resistors, motors and many other things that make use of electricity. Often we need to refer to the things in a circuit without referring to a particular item, such as a light bulb. So we use the word *component*. A circuit component is any item which forms a part of a circuit – it could be a lamp, a resistor, a motor – or something else.

To make the drawing of electric circuits simpler, special symbols are used to represent the components you use in them (figure 16.7), and all wires are drawn in straight lines. Such drawings are called *circuit diagrams*.

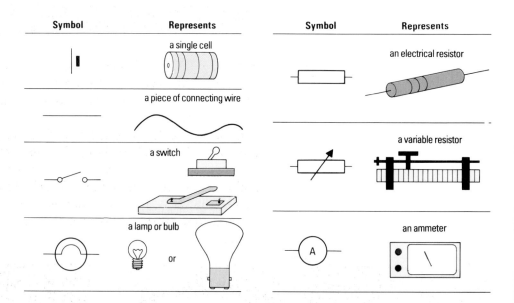

Figure 16.7
The electrical symbols used for some common electrical components.

6 Look at the photograph in figure 16.8. Draw a circuit diagram to show how the various items have been connected together.

Figure 16.8
An electrical circuit in which several items have been connected together.

You can now do Worksheet P16A which will give some practice in wiring up circuits and drawing circuit diagrams.

7a Take a torch to pieces and draw a diagram of the electric circuit formed by the battery and the light bulb. Mark on your diagram the parts of the torch that form some of the circuit connecting the battery and light bulb.
b Suppose someone gave you a similar torch that was not working. Describe what you would do to find out why it was not working.

Question 7 also forms a part of Worksheet P16B. This worksheet gives you some more things to do that are related to "electricity in the home". It is not essential to do this worksheet, but you may choose to do it instead of some of the more difficult sections in this chapter.

P16.3   Electric currents

The photographs in figure 16.9 show two circuits. The first has a 1000-watt electric fire connected to an ammeter and the 240-volt mains supply. The second has a 100-watt lamp connected to an identical ammeter and the 240-volt mains supply.

In the rest of this chapter and in Chapter **P17** we shall frequently need to refer to "light bulbs" or "lamps". Manufacturers usually use the term "light bulb" to refer to the low-voltage bulbs in cars and torches, while they refer to mains "light bulbs" as "lamps"! We shall stick to the term "lamp" in future to mean all such devices whether they are for mains voltage or for low voltage. Remember, in this book "lamp" and "light bulb" refer to the same thing.

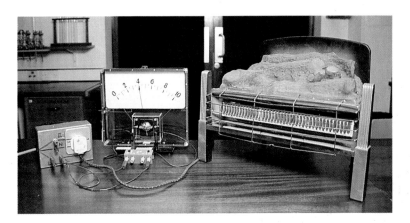

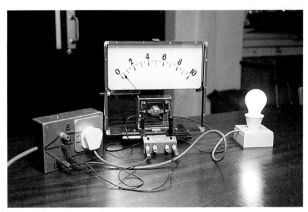

Figure 16.9
A 1000-watt electric fire and a 100-watt light bulb, each connected to the mains supply through an ammeter. The full-scale reading of the ammeter is 10 A.

8a Draw circuit diagrams of the two circuits.
b Write down the reading of each ammeter.

The electric fire transfers 1000 J of energy every second from the 240-volt mains supply. The lamp transfers 100 J of energy every second from the 240-volt mains supply. In each second the fire transfers ten times more energy than the lamp.

Did you notice that the ammeter connected to the fire gives a reading ten times bigger than the reading of the ammeter connected to the lamp? The ammeter reading is directly proportional to the rate of energy transfer from the 240-volt mains supply.

What happens in an electric circuit?

To try to understand these observations we need to think about what is happening in an electric circuit when energy is being transferred from an electricity supply.

The last section reminded you that a complete circuit extends from one terminal of the supply back to the other. It must be complete if energy is to be transferred. Any break in the circuit will stop the transfer of energy. This is how a switch works – it puts a break in the circuit.

From earlier work in electricity you probably know that "electricity" flows round a circuit when it is complete. It is this "electricity" (or *electric charge* to give it its correct name) which transfers energy from the power supply to the electric fire or lamp in the circuit.

The more electric charge there is flowing round a circuit per second from a particular power supply, the more quickly the energy will be transferred.

What do ammeters measure?

The amount of electric charge flowing round a circuit every second is called the *electric current*. The electric current is read on an *ammeter*.

We can now understand why the ammeters shown in figure 16.9 gave the readings they did. Both the fire and the lamp were connected to the same supply. The fire transferred energy from the supply ten times more quickly than the lamp did. To do this, the electric current through the fire had to be ten times larger than the electric current through the lamp.

Electric current is measured in amperes (symbol, A). The current through the electric fire in figure 16.9 is 4 A, while the current through the lamp is 0.4 A. In circuits in which very small currents flow, their size is often given in milliamperes (symbol, mA). There are 1000 mA in 1 A.

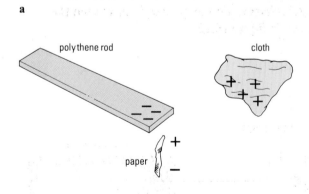

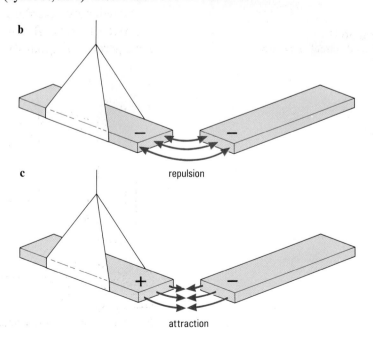

Figure 16.10
a An electrically-charged polythene rod will attract small pieces of paper.
b Two charged polythene rods repel each other.
c A charged polythene rod will attract a charged rod made from cellulose acetate.

9a What is the current through the lamp in mA?
b What is a current of 20 mA in amperes?

This picture of electric charge flowing round a circuit transferring energy as it goes is not an easy one to understand. This is because we are unable to see the electric charge. The next section (section P16.4) looks in more detail at electric charge.

If you are prepared to take section P16.3 "on trust", you could omit this section and go on to section P16.5 which looks a little more closely at what we mean by "electric current". Your teacher will advise you whether to read section P16.4.

P16.4 Electric charge

When a polythene rod is rubbed with a cloth, the rod is able to attract small pieces of paper to itself (figure 16.10a). If the rod is brought close to another polythene rod that has also been rubbed on a cloth, the two rods repel each other (figure 16.10b).

The polythene rods are said to be *electrically charged*. Other types of plastic, such as cellulose acetate, behave in the same way. However, when pieces of charged cellulose acetate are brought close to pieces of charged polythene, they **attract** each other (figure 16.10c). To distinguish between the two sorts of electric charging, we say one is *positively charged* (the cellulose acetate) and the other *negatively charged* (the polythene).

The Van de Graaff generator shown in figure 16.11 can produce electric charge by friction, just like rubbing the polythene rod with a cloth. A charged Van de Graaff generator can produce large sparks and can also light fluorescent lamps if they are held near to it. In the process the Van de Graaff generator becomes discharged.

We can also produce sparks and light lamps using ordinary electric power supplies like dry batteries or the 240 V mains. So it seems that electric power supplies as well as rubbed plastic rods produce electric charge.

We will now describe a very important experiment to show that what ammeters read is a **flow of electric charge**. You may already have seen the arrangement of apparatus shown in figure 16.12.

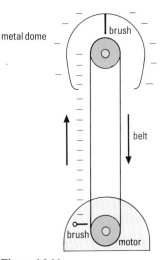

Figure 16.11
A Van de Graaff generator.

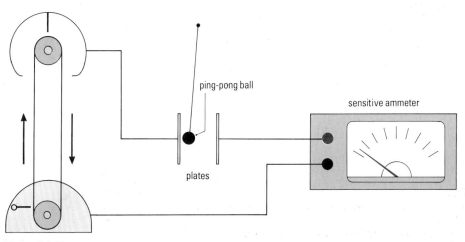

Figure 16.12
A Van de Graaff generator connected to an ammeter and a pair of metal plates.

When the Van de Graaff generator is working, you will notice the following things can happen.

1 The ping-pong ball, coated with a conducting material, oscillates back and forth between the two plates, and at the same time . . .
2 The ammeter shows a deflection.
3 If the ping-pong ball is prevented from moving, the ammeter reading returns to zero.

The moving ping-pong ball passes electric charge between the two plates and the charge then travels round the circuit. We call this movement of electric charges a **flow** of electric charge.

The electric charge passes on through the ammeter and the ammeter registers the flow of electric charge. The ammeter's deflection seems to be caused by electric charge flowing through it. If the ping-pong ball stops moving, the ammeter reading falls to zero, as electric charge has stopped flowing through it.

The metal plates can be pushed closer together. Because the ping-pong ball hasn't so far to travel, it rattles back and forth more quickly, transferring more charge every second. The ammeter reading increases. On the other hand, if the plates are moved further apart, the reading on the ammeter goes down.

The Van de Graaff machine can be replaced by an electricity power supply. Again the ping-pong ball rattles back and forth. And again, the ammeter shows a reading when the ball is moving. So here too electric charge is travelling round the circuit.

10 (*Hard!*) You have already seen that we call the charge acquired by rubbed polythene "negative". The terminals of electric cells and batteries are also labelled "positive" (coloured red) and "negative" (coloured black). How could you show that the charge on rubbed polythene and the charge associated with the black terminal of a battery or power pack are both negative?

Figure 16.13 (below left)

Figure 16.14 (below right)
A coulombmeter. These instruments will measure electrical charge.

When we draw a battery symbol in a circuit, the longer line always represents the positive (red) terminal. In a circuit, we think of electric charge flowing from the positive terminal of the battery and back to the battery (figure 16.13).

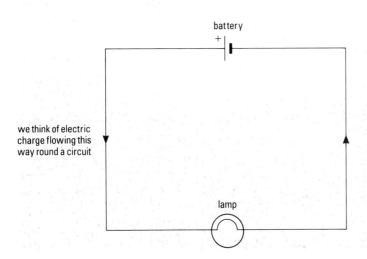

Measuring electric charge

A quantity of electric charge is measured in coulombs (symbol, C). Figure 16.14 shows an instrument called a *coulombmeter*. It can be used to measure the charge acquired by a polythene rod when it is rubbed by a cloth, or to measure the charge collected on a metal plate from an electric power supply.

You may see a coulombmeter demonstrated. If you do, you will find that the charges on a rubbed polythene rod are quite tiny when compared with one coulomb. It would take the charge on about 10 000 000 such rods to make up a total charge equal to one coulomb.

You will learn in Chapter **P19** *what carries electric charge round a circuit. Electrically charged atoms and groups of atoms are of great importance in chemistry. You can learn more about them in section* **C18.3** *of your Chemistry book.*

P16.5   Electric current again

The flow of electric charge round a circuit is called an *electric current*. What is meant by the word "current"?

Notices on some beaches tell you that it is unsafe to swim because of dangerous currents. When the word "current" is used in this sense it refers to a flow of water. The currents are dangerous both because of their size and because of their direction.

But what do we mean by the **size** of the current? Used in this way we are referring to how fast the water is flowing. We might say that the water current in a Welsh mountain stream is much greater than in the slower-moving Thames (figure 16.15), meaning that the water in the stream is moving faster. But suppose we stood by the bank of each and measured the **amount** of water passing a particular point in an hour. We would certainly find that the amount of water flowing down the Thames each hour was much greater than that flowing down the Welsh stream, even though the Thames moves much more slowly.

Figure 16.15
a (left) A fast-moving stream.
b (right) The slower-moving River Thames.

In physics, the word *current* always means the amount of substance flowing past a point per second. When we want to refer to how quickly things are travelling we use the words *speed* or *velocity*.

Here is a question to help you see how we would describe the size of a current of water.

---

11 A 9-litre bucket took 27 seconds to fill from a tap.
a What was the rate of flow (or current) of water from the tap in litres per second?
b How many seconds would it take to fill a 250-litre water tank from the same tap?

The rate of flow of the water in question **11** is measured as the amount of water leaving the tap each second. Similarly, an electric current is measured as the amount of electric charge passing a point in the circuit each second.

The amount of water in question **11** is measured in litres, just as the amount of electric charge is measured in coulombs. We measure the size of an electric current in *coulombs per second*. You may not have heard of the "coulomb per second" as a unit. But you have already met the *ampere*. This is simply the name for a coulomb per second. One ampere is the same as one coulomb per second.

In the circuit shown in figure 16.16, 2 coulombs of electric charge pass through the lamp in 5 seconds. The electric current through the lamp is the number of coulombs of electric charge passing through the lamp each second.

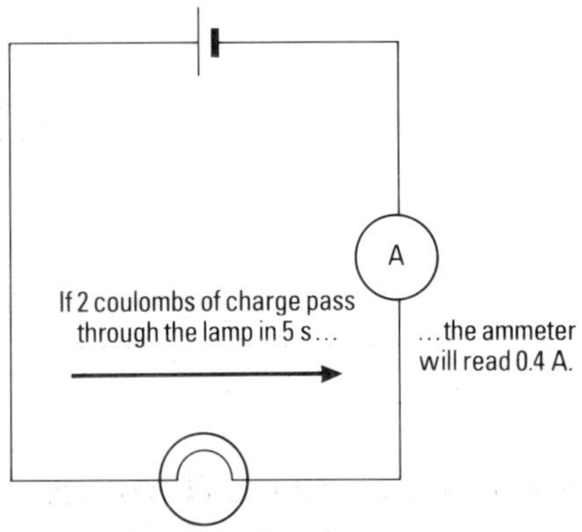

$$\text{So, electric current} = \frac{2\ \text{coulombs}}{5\ \text{seconds}}$$

$$= 0.4\ \text{coulombs/second}$$
$$= 0.4\ \text{amperes}$$

The electric current at any point in a circuit is always equal to an amount of charge passing that point divided by the time it takes to pass.

$$\text{current} = \frac{\text{charge passing}}{\text{time taken}}$$

This result can be used in a number of ways, as shown in the next questions.

If 2 coulombs of charge pass through the lamp in 5 s...

...the ammeter will read 0.4 A.

Figure 16.16
A circuit containing a cell, an ammeter and a light bulb.

---

12 What is the electric current passing through an electric motor if 10 C of charge pass through it in 5 seconds?

13 A current of 12 A is measured flowing through the heating element of an electric kettle. If it is switched on for 600 s (that is, 10 minutes), how many coulombs of electric charge will pass through the heating element?

14 How long will it take one coulomb of charge to pass a particular point in a circuit carrying a current of 0.02 A?

Measuring electric current

It is not easy to measure the amount of charge passing a point in an electric circuit. Fortunately, we have a ready-made instrument for measuring electric current. It is the *ammeter*. If we want to know the charge passing through a point in a circuit for a certain period of time, we have only to measure the electric current at that point and multiply this by the time.

By now you may feel you know enough about ammeters in order to be able to use them in a circuit. The next section makes a deduction about how electric currents ought to behave in an electric circuit and then uses ammeters to see if they give the readings we would expect.

*It is not essential to work through this simply in order to understand the rest of the work on electricity. You could omit it and go on to section **P16.6**. Your teacher will advise you whether to do this.*

Do ammeters read what we would expect them to?

Look at the picture of the road in figure 16.17a. If there are no side roads, no car parks, and no factories along the road and the cars travel along it at a steady speed without any of them stopping, we would expect the number of cars passing the shop every minute to be the same as the number of cars passing the trees. Electric currents behave in the same way. Figure 16.17b shows a simple electric circuit with no "side turnings". Ammeters have been placed at several points round the circuit.

Figure 16.17
a A road along which non-stop traffic flows.
b A "series" circuit containing four ammeters, two light bulbs and two cells.

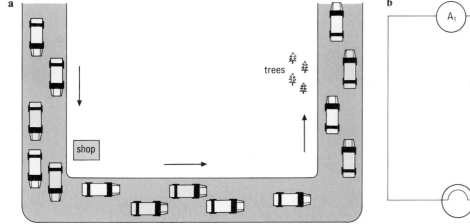

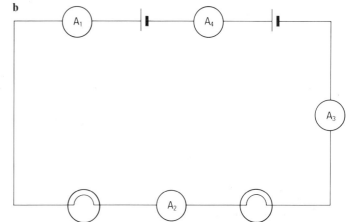

Experiments show that all the ammeters give the **same** reading. This is just what we would expect if the ammeters are reading the size of the electric current at each point. Electric charge is not "used up" in the circuit; it just passes round it.

Figure 16.18a shows a branching circuit. The electric current passes down two branches at X and rejoins at Y. Think of this circuit as a one-way road

Figure 16.18
a A branching electric circuit.
b A branching road. The road divides at X and then rejoins at Y.

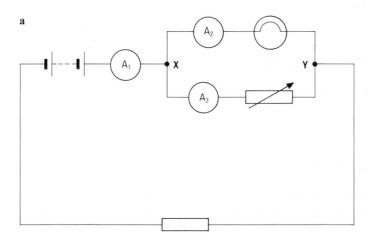

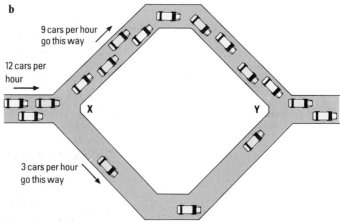

9 cars per hour go this way

12 cars per hour

3 cars per hour go this way

which forks at X into two roads which join together again at Y (figure 16.18b). Suppose there are 12 cars an hour reaching junction X. If 3 of those 12 cars go along the bottom road every hour, how many go along the top? The answer must be 9, since we cannot "lose" any of the cars, nor can they pile up at the junction. So 3 cars per hour travel down one road and 9 cars per hour down the other. There is a simple rule to describe this. The number of cars coming **into** the junction every hour **equals** the number of cars passing out along the top branch each hour **plus** the number of cars passing along the bottom branch each hour.

Electric currents behave in the same way. Ammeter A_1 in figure 16.18a measures the current (electric charge per second) along the "main road" of the circuit. The current branches at X. A_2 reads the current along one branch while A_3 reads the current along the other branch. So we should expect that

$$A_1 = A_2 + A_3$$

You may see an experiment that confirms that this is so.

Worksheet **P16C** gives a series of experiments which will help you understand these ideas. You may see these experiments as demonstrations, or you may be able to try them for yourself.

15 Figure 16.19 shows a circuit containing resistors, lamps and ammeters. What reading would you expect to find on each of the ammeters A_1, A_2 and A_3?

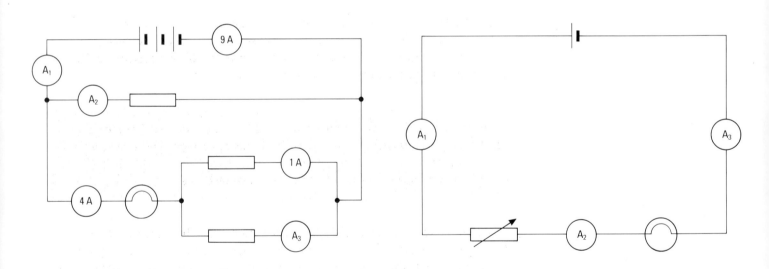

Figure 16.19 (above left)
A complex circuit of resistors, ammeters, cells and a light bulb.

Figure 16.20 (above right)
A circuit containing a cell and a light bulb, with a variable resistor to act as a "dimmer".

16 Figure 16.20 shows a circuit containing a variable resistor and a lamp. The resistor acts as a "dimmer" for the lamp. Jane decides to do an experiment to see what happens to the current in the circuit when the variable resistor changes. She puts ammeters in the circuit at three places, as shown in the diagram.
a When the circuit is first switched on A_1 is found to read 2 A. What will be the readings on A_2 and A_3?
b Jane now increases the resistance of the variable resistor and finds that the current measured by A_2 is 1A. What will happen to the lamp? What will be the reading on A_1? What will be the reading on A_3?

P16.6   Transferring energy using electricity

By now you should have a picture in your mind of what is happening in an electric circuit when you transfer energy from the electricity supply to something else. The "electricity supply" may be a battery or it may be the "mains". It could even be the dynamo on your bicycle or the alternator inside a car. All of these use the electric charges in the circuit to transfer energy to whatever is connected to the supply. It might be an electric fire, a hair drier, or even an electric locomotive.

Figure 16.21 (below left)
A water circuit containing a pump, a tap and a water wheel connected together with water-filled pipes.

Figure 16.22 (below right)
An electric circuit containing battery, switch and motor.

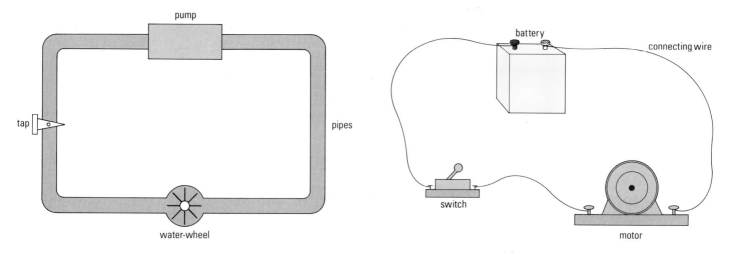

Figure 16.21 shows a diagram of a "water circuit". In many ways it behaves like an electric circuit. The energy supply is a pump. Water-filled tubes connect the pump to a water-wheel. Compare this with figure 16.22 which shows a battery connected to an electric motor.

17a Which part of the water circuit corresponds to the switch in the electric circuit?
b What in the electric circuit corresponds to the pump and to the water-wheel in the water circuit?
c What in the water circuit corresponds to the connecting wires?

When the tap is opened, the water-wheel immediately starts to rotate. Energy is transferred from the pump to the wheel by the water in the pipe. You will see that the pipes are full of water before the tap is switched on. The water-wheel starts turning as soon as the tap is switched on. It does not have to "wait" until water from the pump reaches it.

It is the same in an electric circuit. As soon as the switch is closed, energy is transferred from the battery to the motor by the charges which are already in the wire. In both cases, the bigger the current, the more quickly energy is transferred from the supply.

Transferring energy to the surroundings

When an electric current passes through the "heating element" of an electric fire, the electric charges transfer energy to the wire. This raises the temperature of the wire.

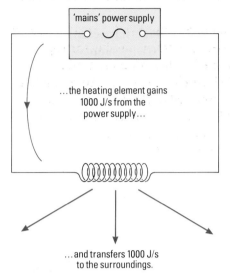

Once a 1000-watt heater has reached a steady temperature...

'mains' power supply

...the heating element gains 1000 J/s from the power supply...

...and transfers 1000 J/s to the surroundings.

Figure 16.23
Transferring energy from the mains supply to the surroundings via an electric current.

Figure 16.24
A mains fuse of the sort that is used in house wiring circuits.

Figure 16.25
A square pin (13-amp) socket and plug.

What stops the wires in the heating element getting hotter and hotter? In Chapter **P9**, we saw that a hot object will transfer energy to its surroundings. The bigger the temperature difference between the hot object and its surroundings, the more quickly it will transfer energy to them.

As the heating element gets hotter, it transfers energy to the surroundings more quickly. Eventually it is transferring its energy to the surroundings as quickly as the electric charges are transferring energy to the heating element. What will happen then? When the heating element loses energy as quickly as it gains it, its temperature will stop rising (figure 16.23).

> **18a** Look back at Chapter **P2** and describe another situation where a quantity stops changing because something is being lost as quickly as it is being gained.
> **b** Chapter **P9** describes some of the things that control how quickly energy is transferred from something that is hotter than its surroundings. Make a list of some of the other factors (apart from temperature difference) that might control how quickly the heating element of a fire transfers energy to its surroundings.

Many things you use in the home depend on wires getting hot when an electric current is passed through them. Electric toasters, hair driers and styling brushes all have wires that do this.

Fuses

Wires getting hot can also be a danger. You have seen that if the current through a wire is increased, the wire gets hotter. If this wire is insulated and hidden under the floorboards of a house, it may not be able to lose energy to the surroundings very quickly. The wiring in a house is quite thick. When normal currents (up to 30 A) pass along these wires, little energy is transferred to them each second. The wires can easily transfer this energy to the surroundings without getting noticeably warm. But if there is a fault (so that the two wires leading from a wall socket or a lamp fitting touched, for example) then there could be a very high current indeed along the wires. They might no longer be able to get rid of all the energy being transferred to them. The wires will get hotter and hotter and could eventually start a fire.

To prevent this happening, the electrical wiring in houses is protected by *fuses*. A fuse contains a wire so thin that if the current gets too large, the energy transferred to it causes it to melt and so break the circuit.

The mains wiring in modern houses is designed to carry a current of up to 30A. Figure 16.24 shows the sort of fuse used to protect these circuits. They are placed in a fuse box close to where the electricity supply enters the house.

Mains current

The maximum safe current to be drawn from sockets in the home is 13 A. For this reason such sockets, with their square holes, are referred to as "thirteen-amp sockets" (figure 16.25). This misleads some people into thinking that **anything** connected to them draws a current of 13 A. This is not true. The safe maximum current flowing through a particular device may be much less than 13 A. For this reason, plugs using such sockets should carry a fuse which will "blow" when the safe limit **of the device to which the plug is attached** is exceeded. Figure 16.26 shows a range of plug fuses which are now available.

Figure 16.26
A range of fuses that are available for fitting into 13-amp, square pin plugs.

P16.7   Using electricity safely

At the beginning of this chapter we saw that one of the disadvantages of using electricity is that it can be dangerous. An electric current passing through your body can be fatal if it exceeds quite a small value (a very few milli-amperes). The energy carried by "mains" electricity is sufficient to pass a fatal current through a person touching wires connected to the 240 V mains supply.

In fact, a person only has to touch the "live" wire to receive an "electric shock". The reason for this is that the ground we stand on also forms a connection back to the electricity supply (figure 16.27).

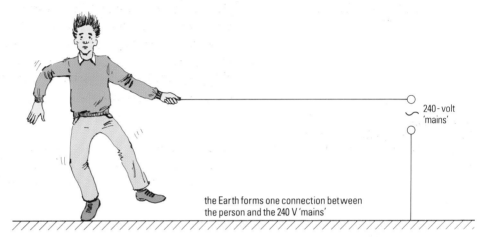

the Earth forms one connection between the person and the 240 V 'mains'

240-volt 'mains'

Figure 16.27
Getting a shock from a "live" wire!

The wire from the supply that is also connected to the ground is called the "neutral" wire. The other one is called the "live" wire. Of course most people are not stupid enough to touch the live wire from the supply deliberately. But if the live wire to an appliance becomes loose or broken it could touch metal parts (figure 16.28) and so come into contact with someone using it.

To protect people from such an accident, a third wire (called the "earth" wire) is connected to any metal parts someone could touch. The other end of this wire is *earthed* (connected to the ground). This gives a very easy path along which the electric current can flow, should a live wire touch these metal parts. The current flows through the earth wire to earth, rather than through the person to earth.

In circuit diagrams we often want to show that the earth around us is being used as an electrical connection between two things (as it is in figure 16.27). It would be difficult always to draw in the surface of the earth, so we use a special symbol to show when a connection is being made to "earth". The symbol is shown in figure 16.29.

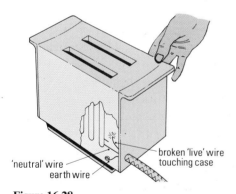

'neutral' wire
earth wire
broken 'live' wire touching case

Figure 16.28
The function of the earth wire. If the live wire touches the metal case of the toaster, the current flows to earth through the earth wire, rather than through someone touching the case.

Figure 16.29
The symbol used for a connection to earth.

19 The birds sitting on the power line in figure 16.2 are not electrocuted. Why is this?

20 Another way in which some electrical devices are protected now is by "double insulation".
a Find out what is meant by "double insulation".
b Why do doubly-insulated devices not need an earth wire?

Figure 16.30
A residual current circuit breaker (often referred to as an RCCB). This one is plugged into an ordinary socket to protect against accidents such as cutting through the mains cable.

21 Make a list of five different electrical devices used in your home. For each one, say how it is protected if something should go wrong.

22 Some houses now have a device fitted to the mains wiring to protect people from electric shock. It is an earth leakage circuit breaker (sometimes called a "residual current circuit breaker" or RCCB). Many people refer to it as a "trip switch" (figure 16.30).
a Find out how such a device works.
b Why is such a device said to give much better safety protection than either earth wires or fuses?

Summary

Write down the names of each of the components 1 to 5 in the circuit diagram in figure 16.31.

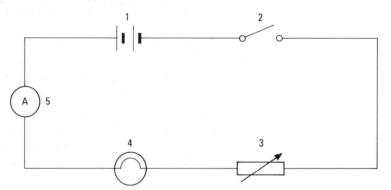

Figure 16.31
A circuit containing several different electrical components.

Here are the beginnings of six sentences, labelled **A** to **F**. Below these you will find the ends of six sentences labelled **1** to **6**. Match up each of **A** to **F** with its correct ending.

A The electric current through a lamp is . . .
B One ampere is the same as . . .
C Electric charge is . . .
D When a battery lights a lamp, the battery, lamp and wires form . . .
E Fuses prevent . . .
F Earth wires help to prevent . . .

1 . . . a wire over-heating.
2 . . . measured in coulombs.
3 . . . a complete circuit.
4 . . . an electric shock.
5 . . . measured in amperes.
6 . . . one coulomb per second.

Energy and electricity
Voltage and electrical resistance

This chapter is about using electricity to transfer energy. The energy comes from a battery or power station. How the energy is transferred inside the battery or power station is not in this chapter. You can find out about how energy is transferred to electricity in a battery in Chapters C14 and C18 in your Chemistry book. Chapters P11 and P18 show how power stations can transfer energy from fuels to electricity.

P17.1 Putting electricity to use

As we have seen in the topic on energy, useful jobs involve transferring energy. Electricity is useful because we can use it to transfer energy. Electric charges can move energy from one place to another along cables. We depend more and more on electricity for the transfer of energy from remote power stations along a "grid" of power (or transmission) lines to the places where we need it. (You can learn more about how this is done in Chapter **P11**.) Electricity is also transferred along cables to provide the energy for part of the railway system. A great deal of money is being spent to "electrify" British Rail in this way.

Scientists have learned of the importance of electricity in other areas of science. In the atmosphere, electricity shows itself with spectacular results in thunderstorms. Air currents in clouds act like a giant Van de Graaff generator, transferring charge up through the cloud. Eventually the charge has so much energy that it can overcome the insulating properties of air. The charge then travels to a nearby cloud, or to the Earth, as a lightning flash (figure 17.1).

You may not have seen the spectacular Aurora Borealis (or Northern Lights as it is often called). But if you lived further north than the British Isles you would be familiar with the appearance of these sheets of light in the night sky (figure 17.2, overleaf). These are another natural electrical effect, produced this time by high-energy, electrically charged particles from the Sun.

As you saw in the last chapter (section **P16.4**), positive and negative charges are attracted to each other. It is this force of attraction between charged particles that binds atoms together into molecules and giant structures.

The telephone, radio and television all depend on electric currents to send messages, in the form of words and pictures, from place to place. We can create electric waves that can carry these messages through the air and even through space. These waves are called *electromagnetic waves*. Electromagnetic waves are studied in Chapter **P15**. Communication by electricity is investigated in Chapter **P20**.

Figure 17.1
A lightning flash.

Figure 17.2
The Aurora Borealis (Northern Lights).

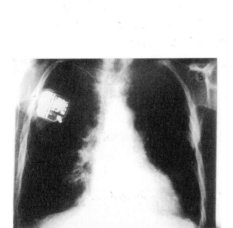

Figure 17.3
An X-ray photograph showing a heart
pace-maker in place.

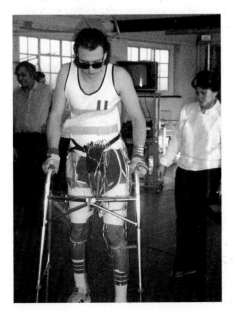

Figure 17.4
An electrical device is helping this
physically-handicapped person to walk.

The use of electricity to carry messages existed long before the invention of any of these modern forms of communication. Nerve fibres and nerve cells, which form a communication network in animals, use electricity. Our understanding of this is being put to increasing use. The heart pace-maker is one example (figure 17.3). This electrical device gives small electric shocks to the heart to keep it beating steadily. There are even more remarkable electrical devices that are enabling otherwise paralysed people to walk. They do this by delivering small electrical impulses to important nerve centres (figure 17.4).

We have already seen that the energy carried by electricity can itself be a danger. Dry batteries are safe enough, but great care has to be exercised over the use of the "mains" as death from electric shock is unfortunately still common.

In what way is the electricity from a dry cell different from the "mains"? Why are electric shocks dangerous and yet small "electric shocks" to nerve cells are proving a life-saving development? To answer these questions we have to look more closely at the energy carried by electric charges and learn what a volt is.

1a The present-day "main line" electrification of British Rail uses overhead power cables to carry the electric current to the engines. When the Southern region of British Rail was electrified many years ago, "electrified" rails were used for this purpose. What are the advantages of using overhead power cables?
b What is another name for "electrically-charged atoms"?
c Describe another area of science (not mentioned in this section) where ideas about electricity have been used.
d Name another use to which electricity has been put in hospitals (apart from providing lighting and heating).

P17.2   Energy in electric circuits

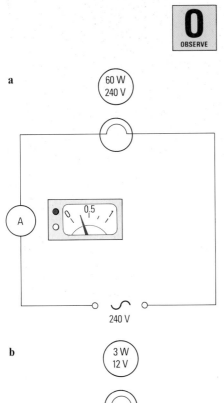

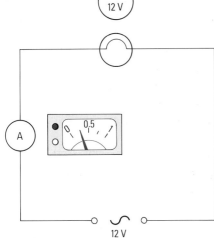

Figure 17.5
An experiment to show the difference between electricity from a 12-volt supply and the electricity from the 240-volt mains.

You may see a demonstration of the experiment illustrated in figure 17.5. This experiment shows the difference between the electricity from a 12-volt transformer and the electricity from the 240-volt "mains". In both circuits the electric current is the same and identical ammeters can be used to measure them. Yet one lamp is far brighter than the other.

In an experiment using the circuits shown in figure 17.5, the current recorded by each ammeter was 0.25 A. The mains lamp was marked "60 W 240 V" while the other lamp was marked "3 W 12 V".

You will remember from earlier work that one watt is a rate of energy transfer of one joule per second. The mains lamp transfers 60 joules every second from its electricity supply to the lamp. The 12-volt lamp transfers 3 joules every second from its electricity supply to the lamp.

The electric current through each lamp is 0.25 A. In the last chapter we saw that one ampere is the name for a rate of flow of electric charge of one coulomb per second. How long would it take for one coulomb of charge to pass through each lamp? The answer is 4 seconds, because

0.25 coulombs/second × 4 seconds = 1 coulomb

We can now work out how much energy is transferred from the electricity supply to each lamp in 4 seconds.

For the 60-watt lamp, energy transferred from its supply in 4 seconds
= 60 joules/second × 4 seconds
= 240 joules.

For the 3-watt lamp, energy transferred from its supply in 4 seconds
= 3 joules/second × 4 seconds
= 12 joules.

Do these figures look familiar? The "60 W 240 V" lamp transfers 240 joules of energy from the supply for every coulomb of charge that passes through the lamp. The "3 W 12 V" lamp transfers 12 joules of energy from the supply for every coulomb of charge that passes through the lamp. We get the same pattern of results in every electrical circuit:

The energy transferred from the electricity supply by one coulomb of electric charge is the same as the "voltage" of the supply.

This is what the word "voltage" means. When we talk of the voltage of the "mains supply" as 240 V, we mean that every coulomb of electric charge passing round a circuit from the supply will transfer 240 joules of energy.

A brief summary

The voltage of an electricity supply tells us how much energy the supply transfers per coulomb of electric charge. The higher the voltage, the bigger the energy transferred per coulomb of electric charge.

You may feel you now know enough about "voltage". Certainly this is enough for you to be able to understand the work on resistance in the last part of this chapter. You could go on now to the work called "Measuring voltage" on page 267.

The remainder of this section gives you some problems to try for yourself and takes the ideas about voltage a bit further. Your teacher will advise you whether to continue with this section.

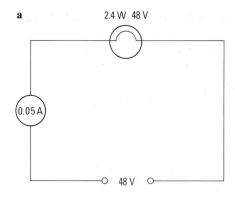

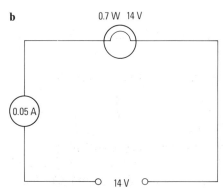

Figure 17.6
A similar experiment using lamps of
different voltages.

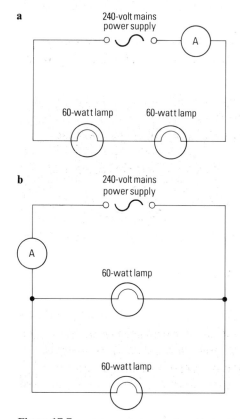

Figure 17.7
a Lamps wired in series.
b The same lamps wired in parallel.

2 (Use the method just described to answer this question.) Electronic components catalogues list a wide variety of lamps (manufacturers usually refer to low-voltage lamps as filament bulbs). These run off a wide variety of voltages. Two particular lamps listed in their catalogues are a 2.4 W, 48 V bulb and a 0.7 W, 14 V bulb.

In an experiment (figure 17.6) the 2.4 W, 48 V lamp was connected in series with an ammeter and a 48-volt supply. The current recorded by the ammeter was 0.05 A. In the second circuit the 0.7 W, 14 V lamp was connected to a 14-volt supply. The current through it was also 0.05 A.

a How many coulombs of electric charge pass through each lamp every second?
b How long would it take 1 coulomb of electric charge to pass through each lamp?
c How much energy is transferred from the supply each second by the 2.4-watt lamp and by the 0.7-watt lamp?
d How much energy was transferred to each lamp during the time it took 1 coulomb of charge to pass through the lamp?

The longer any lamp is switched on, the more coulombs of charge pass through the lamp and the more energy the lamp transfers from the electricity supply.

The next question refers to the circuits shown in figure 17.5 and asks about the energy transferred from the electricity supply to the 60 W, 240 V mains lamp and the 3 W, 12 V lamp.

3a How long would the 60-watt mains lamp in figure 17.5 have to be switched on for it to transfer 3600 J of energy from the electricity supply?
b How much energy would be transferred by the 3-watt lamp in this time?
c How many coulombs will have passed through each lamp in this time?

Lamps in series and in parallel

The 240-volt mains supply will fully light the 60-watt lamp. But a house needs the same supply to light more than just one such lamp! How can this be done? Two possible circuits for lighting two lamps are shown in figures 17.7a and 17.7b. You may see in a demonstration that only the circuit in figure 17.7b lights both lamps fully. In the circuit in figure 17.7a the lamps are in *series*, while in figure 17.7b they are in *parallel*.

With only **one** 60-watt lamp connected to the supply, the current was earlier found to be 0.25 A (figure 17.5a). In another experiment:

- with **two** 60-watt lamps in **series**, the current was measured to be 0.15 A.
- with **two** 60-watt lamps in **parallel**, the current was measured to be 0.5 A.

How many coulombs of charge passed through the two lamps in series each second? The answer is 0.15 C, because a current of 0.15 A means a rate of flow of charge of 0.15 coulombs per second.

If each coulomb of charge transfers 240 joules of energy, the energy transferred by 0.15 C

= 0.15 coulombs × 240 joules/coulomb
= 36 joules

This energy is shared between two lamps, so each only gets 18 J of energy every second, which is far less than the 60 joules per second they need for full brightness.

We can do the same calculation for the lamps in parallel. How many coulombs of charge pass through the two lamps each second? The answer this time is 0.5 C, because the current from the supply is 0.5 A.

If each coulomb of charge transfers 240 joules of energy, the energy transferred by 0.5 C

$$= 0.5 \text{ coulombs} \times 240 \text{ joules/coulomb}$$
$$= 120 \text{ joules}.$$

This energy is also shared between two lamps, each getting 60 J of energy every second. This is just the right amount for full brightness.

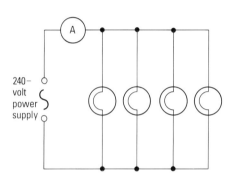

Figure 17.8
Four 60-watt mains lamps wired in parallel.

4 What happens to the current provided by the supply if first three and then four similar lamps are connected in parallel (figure 17.8)?

5 Suppose four 60-watt lamps are connected in parallel across the 240-volt mains (figure 17.8).
a What will be the current through each lamp?
b What will be the total current provided by the supply?
c Suppose the lamps are left on for 40 s. How many coulombs pass through **each** lamp? How many coulombs pass from the supply?
d How much energy is transferred **by all four lamps** from the mains supply in 40 s?

6 Houses are wired so that all their sockets and all their lamps are in parallel. Sockets are usually connected together in what is called a **ring main**. Find out and then draw how a ring main is wired up.

Here is a question that "works backwards". Knowing the supply voltage for a lamp and the current through it, you have to work out the lamp's power.

7 A 3-volt dry battery is used to light a lamp (torch bulb).
a How much energy, in joules, does the battery supply to each coulomb of electric charge?
b If the current passing through the lamp is 0.4 A, how many coulombs pass through the lamp in 10 s?
c How much energy is transferred to the lamp in this time?
d What is the power of the lamp?

Finally a harder question that goes "back to basics".

8 In all the work of this section we have accepted the markings on the lamps as correctly stating their power. Design a "heating" experiment to test whether a lamp marked "12 V, 24 W" really does transfer energy at a rate of 24 joules per second.

This next section could be omitted without harming your understanding of the rest of this chapter. Your teacher will advise you whether to work through it, or go on to the work called "Measuring voltage" on page 267.

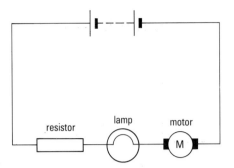

Figure 17.9
An electric circuit containing a battery, resistor, lamp and motor.

Potential difference

So far the term "voltage" has meant only the energy transferred from the electricity supply by one coulomb of charge passing round the circuit. But it can mean more than that.

In the simple circuit of a lamp and a power supply (figure 17.5), all the energy the charge gained from the supply was delivered to the lamp. But what if there are other components (in series) in the circuit as well? Figure 17.9 is an example, with a resistor and an electric motor, as well as a lamp.

The charge has now to share out the energy it received from the supply amongst each of the components through which it passes. This is rather like a rock falling down the side of a hill. First, it has energy transferred to it by being lifted up to the top of the hill. Then it tumbles down the hill transferring its energy as it goes – flattening a plant here, dislodging some stones there and so on. In some ways, electrical charge going round a circuit is like a rock tumbling down a hill.

In a way, a battery is like a moving ramp, such as the machines used to raise coal or gravel to the top of a tower for sorting. It raises electric charges uphill to a higher level of electrical energy. Then, as the electric charge travels round the rest of the circuit it is "running downhill" (figure 17.10). As it does so it transfers energy to lamps and resistors in the circuit.

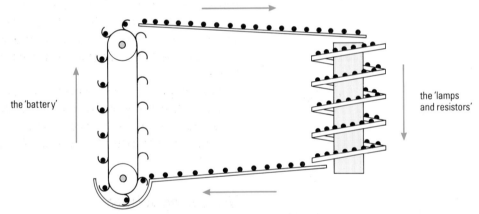

Figure 17.10
The balls run down the helter-skelter and are then lifted back up to the top by the conveyor belt.

If the charge goes through a motor a force is generated which can raise a load, and so the charge will transfer some of its energy. Then, as the electric charge reaches the battery again more energy is transferred to it.

We can draw a "hill" diagram which shows how the battery pushes the electric charge up to a high level of energy. It then spends that energy as it runs down various "hills" to the bottom on its way round the circuit (figure 17.11).

The charges do not carry energy units like eggs in a shopping basket. They are being pushed round the circuit by electric forces generated by the battery – the same forces that caused two charged polythene rods to repel each other. These forces drive the charges round the circuit, so that they deliver energy which comes ultimately from the battery.

The energy transferred to each component in the circuit by each coulomb of charge that passes through it is called the *potential difference* across the component (often abbreviated to "p.d."). Sometimes this is called the voltage across the component, but p.d. is better. The p.d. between two points is the

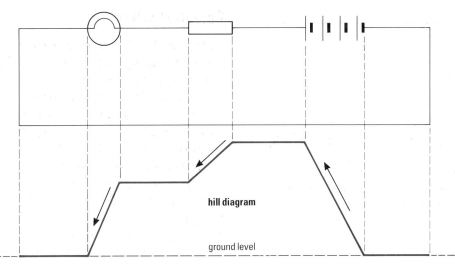

Figure 17.11
A battery gives electric charges energy which they transfer "running down" through the other circuit components.

energy transfer (in joules) which would occur if one coulomb of charge moved between the points. This is true whether we refer to the energy transferred when charge moves all the way round the circuit, or if we mean the energy transferred when the charge passes through just one or two components.

You may remember that in Chapter **P**16 we stressed that the electric current is the same all the way round a series circuit. Charge does not get "used up". All the charge leaving one terminal of the supply comes back to the other.

This chapter has shown that it is energy that gets "used up", or transferred, when electric charge passes round a circuit – the current stays the same. It is the same when we "use" electricity at home or in industry. We do not really pay for the "electricity" – it is free! What we pay for is the energy we transfer from it.

Measuring voltage

Worksheet **P**17A takes you through some experiments you can try which will help you understand "voltage" better. You may prefer to do these experiments before reading the next section.

The instrument used to measure voltages in a circuit is called a voltmeter. Figure 17.12 shows a diagram of a simple circuit with a voltmeter and an ammeter correctly connected. The ammeter is reading the current in the circuit, while the voltmeter is reading the potential difference **across** one of the lamps. Voltmeters are alway connected **across** the component. They sample the difference in the energy of the charge on either side of the component.

It is always safest and easiest to connect voltmeters if you first connect up the whole circuit without the voltmeter and then add the voltmeter across the part of the circuit you are investigating.

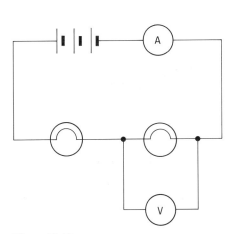

Figure 17.12
A simple circuit of a battery, two lamps, an ammeter and a voltmeter.

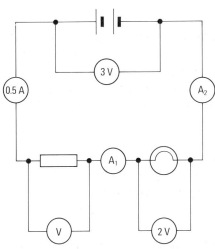

Figure 17.13
This circuit is no more complex than that in figure 17.12, but it contains more ammeters and voltmeters.

9 The circuit in figure 17.13 has a number of voltmeters and ammeters in it. All except three are marked with their readings. Write down the reading you would expect to find on the unmarked voltmeter (V) and the unmarked ammeters (A$_1$ and A$_2$). Give a reason for each answer.

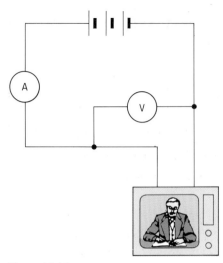

Figure 17.14
Reading the voltage across and the current through a portable television set.

P17.3   Voltmeters, ammeters and power

Here is one simple example to show the way that measurements of voltage and current in a circuit can produce values for the electrical power involved.

Figure 17.14 shows a portable television set connected to a battery. An ammeter has been connected into the circuit and a voltmeter placed across the television set's battery connections.

The ammeter records that 2 A of current are passing through the television and the voltmeter reads 12 volts. We want to find out the **power** taken by the set. To do this you will find it helpful to "unroll" each of the statements about current and voltage – this is, say exactly what each tells you, like this:

"The current is 2 amperes: this means that 2 coulombs of charge pass through the television set in each second."

"The p.d. is 12 volts: this means that 12 joules of energy are transferred to the television set per coulomb of charge passing through it."

Now these **two** statements can be put together. Every second 2 coulombs of charge pass through the television set; 12 joules of energy are transferred to the set for each coulomb of charge flowing through it.

This means that in every second, $2 \times 12 = 24$ joules of energy are transferred to the set. The energy transferred per second is what we call the **power**.

$$
\begin{aligned}
\text{power} &= \text{2 coulombs per second} \times \text{12 joules per coulomb} \\
&= \text{24 joules per second} \\
&= \text{24 watts}
\end{aligned}
$$

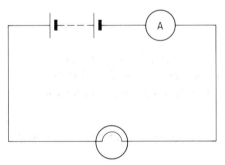

Figure 17.15
A simple circuit of battery, lamp and ammeter.

10a Copy the circuit in figure 17.15 and add a voltmeter to read the voltage across the lamp.
b The voltmeter across the lamp reads 6 V. How many joules of energy have been transferred to it by the time one coulomb of charge has passed through it?
c The ammeter reads 2 A. How many coulombs pass through the lamp each second?
d So how many joules of energy are transferred in the lamp in 1 second?

*You can now either try Worksheet **P**17B, which gives you some easy experiments on the measurement of power in circuits, or you can go straight to Worksheet **P**17C. This is an investigation into the efficiency of an electric motor. It uses the relationship between voltage, current and power to measure the input power to the motor.*

11 This question refers to the circuit shown in figure 17.16. The voltmeter reads 2 V and the ammeter reads 0.5 A.
a How many joules of energy have been transferred to the lamp by the time one coulomb of charge has passed through it?
b How many coulombs go through the lamp each second?
c How many joules per second are delivered to the lamp?
d What is the power of the lamp in watts?
The rheostat (variable resistor) is adjusted to make the current greater. Suppose the voltmeter now reads 3 V, and the ammeter reads 0.8 A.

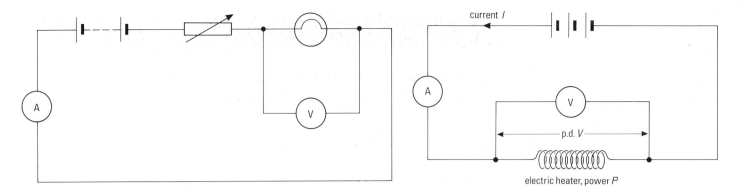

Figure 17.16 (above left)
A lamp in series with a variable resistor.

Figure 17.17 (above right)
An electric heater in a circuit. What determines the size of the electric current flowing through it?

11e How many joules are delivered to the lamp now in one second?
f How will the appearance of the lamp differ?
g What is the new power of the lamp?
h There is a quick way of working out the power from the voltage and the current. What is it?

The rate at which energy is transferred by the electric heater in figure 17.17 is calculated by multiplying the number of coulombs passing through the lamp each second by the number of joules of energy transferred by each coulomb:

$$\frac{\text{joule}}{\text{second}} = \frac{\text{coulomb}}{\text{second}} \times \frac{\text{joule}}{\text{coulomb}}$$

The number of coulombs of charge passing through the lamp per second is the current in amperes. The number of joules of energy transferred to the lamp per coulomb passing through it is the potential difference across the lamp. So:

power (in watts) = current (in amperes) × p.d. across component (in volts)

12 In Chapter **P16**, figure 16.5 there is a table of the voltages and powers of some devices that "use electricity".
a Use the table and the equation power = current × voltage to work out the current drawn by the table lamp, the fan heater and the hair drier.
b What is the "current rating" of the fuse you should put in the plug connected to each of them? (Remember fuses are only available in certain current ratings – see page 259.)
c What is the maximum power that can be drawn from a 13-ampere mains socket?
d What is the power generated by each of the following:
   i a 12-volt car battery giving a current of 300 A (roughly the current needed to start a car on a cold morning!)
   ii a power station generator feeding a current of 1000 A into the "National Grid" at 132 000 V?

13 A 6-volt bicycle dynamo has to light two 6-volt lamps fully. Both draw a current of 0.4 A when fully lit.
a Draw a circuit diagram to show how the lamps should be connected to the dynamo.
b What is the power being generated by the dynamo when the two lamps are fully lit?

P17.4   Electrical resistance

Look again at the circuit in figure 17.17. The battery provides the energy which is transferred to the heater. It also provides the force which drives the charges round the circuit.

The size of the current depends on the size of the battery's voltage. But the circuit itself also affects the size of the current. A different heater may allow a larger or a smaller current to pass, even though the battery is the same.

We think of the wires and the heater in the circuit in figure 17.17 as resisting the flow of the charges. Pipes carrying water resist the flow of water through them. Long pipes give more friction than short pipes; narrow pipes give more friction than wide pipes. It is very much the same with electrical conductors. We say that they have a *resistance* to an electric current. Worksheet **P**17D gives you some experiments to do which will allow you to investigate some of the things that affect the size of an electric current in a circuit.

*You should try to do the experiments in Worksheet **P**17D before reading the next section. The section summarizes some of the things you ought to have found out by experiment.*

Figure 17.18 shows a circuit in which the number of cells can be varied. The ammeter records the current passing round the circuit. The more cells that are used, the bigger the current that flows in the circuit. In this particular circuit one of the things that controls the size of the current is the voltage of the battery – the greater the voltage, the greater the current in the circuit.

It is important to remember that it is the **voltage** that controls the size of the current – **not** the other way round.

Voltage is not the only factor controlling the size of the current in a circuit. The current also depends on the wires and components through which it passes. The circuit drawn in figure 17.19 allows thin pieces of a wire of various lengths (but of the same material and diameter) to be placed in a circuit. Experiment shows that the longer the wire, the smaller will be the current that flows in the circuit. The wire provides a resistance to the flow of electric charge through it – a sort of electrical "friction".

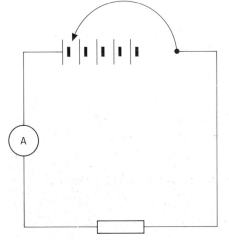

Figure 17.18
Varying the number of cells that drive a current through a fixed resistor.

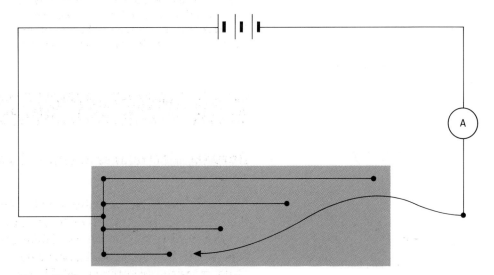

Figure 17.19
Investigating the effect on the current in a circuit of changing the length of a piece of resistance wire.

Measuring electrical resistance

If the variable resistor in figure 17.20 is altered so that it has an increased resistance, the current in the circuit falls – the greater the resistance, the smaller the current.

We need some way of expressing this fact numerically so that one resistance can be compared with another. If we divide the potential difference across the resistor by the value of the current flowing through it we get a number which does get bigger as the current gets smaller. We call this number the *electrical resistance* of the resistor.

The value of the resistance (R) of any component in a circuit is equal to:

$$\frac{\text{potential difference } (V) \text{ across the component, in volts}}{\text{current } (I) \text{ through the component, in amperes}}$$

In symbols this is:

$$R = \frac{V}{I}$$

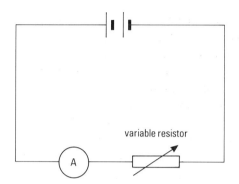

Figure 17.20
A circuit to investigate how a variable resistor affects the current flowing in a circuit.

The unit of electrical resistance is the *ohm* (symbol, Ω).

A piece of wire, a component or even a whole circuit is said to have a resistance of 1 ohm if it requires a potential difference of 1 volt across it to drive a current of 1 ampere through it.

14a How many amperes does 1 volt drive through a resistance of 1 ohm?
b How many amperes will 6 volts drive through a resistance of 1 ohm?
c How many amperes will 6 volts drive through a resistance of 2 ohms?

15 The mains voltage connected to an electric heater is 240 volts. The heater takes 4 amperes. What is its resistance?

16 Work out the resistance of the table lamp, fan heater and hair drier referred to in question **12**.

---

*The next section looks at whether the resistance of components ever changes. It is not essential to work through this section in order to understand the rest of the chapter. You could omit this and instead do Worksheet **P17F** which gives you some practical experience in measuring resistance. Your teacher will advise you which you should do.*

P17.5   Changing electrical resistance

Does the electrical resistance of a component always remain the same?

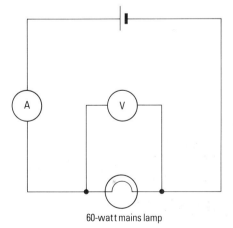

Figure 17.21
Measuring the resistance of a 60-watt mains lamp.

Obviously the electrical resistance of different components is not the same. Wires of different lengths and different thicknesses will have different resistances. Similar-sized wires of different materials will also have different resistances. But what about a particular component – a particular lamp, say? Does its resistance ever change? The circuit in figure 17.21 can be used to measure the resistance of a mains lamp.

This circuit is perfectly safe because low voltages are being used. The lamp

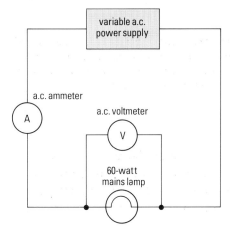

Figure 17.22
Measuring the resistance of a 60-watt
mains lamp at various voltages.

Current, in amperes	Voltage, in volts
0.25	240
0.21	155
0.17	98
0.13	59
0.09	17

Figure 17.23a
Measurements obtained using the circuit in
figure 7.22.

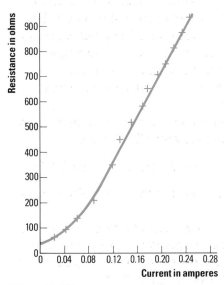

Figure 17.23b
A graph of the variation of the resistance
of a 60-watt mains lamp with the current
passing through it.

does not light up, but we can use the measurements to work out the expected rate at which energy should be transferred in the lamp each second when connected to the 240-volt mains supply.

In one particular experiment, the current through the lamp was measured to be 60 mA and the p.d. across it 7.2 V. The resistance, R, is given by:

$$R = \frac{7.2\,\text{V}}{0.06\,\text{A}}$$

$$= 120\,\Omega$$

The lamp is designed to be used with a 240-volt mains supply. From the result above we could make a prediction of the current, I, that the 240-volt mains supply should drive through the lamp.

$$120\,\Omega = \frac{240\,\text{V}}{I}$$

$$I = \frac{240\,\text{V}}{120\,\Omega}$$

$$= 2\,\text{A}$$

We can now work out the expected power, P, of the lamp.

$$P = 2\,\text{A} \times 240\,\text{V}$$
$$= 2\,\text{C/s} \times 240\,\text{J/C}$$
$$= 480\,\text{J/s}$$
$$= 480\,\text{W}$$

This high value immediately suggests that something has gone wrong! Inspection of the lamp shows that it is marked "60 W".

The resistance of a lamp

Figure 17.22 shows a circuit that can be used to measure the resistance of a 60-watt lamp at various voltages up to its running voltage. You can do a similar experiment using a 12 V, 24 W lamp (Worksheet **P**17E).

17 Work out the resistance of the lamp to the flow of current for each of the voltages in the table in figure 17.23a.

Figure 17.23b shows the graph obtained by plotting the resistance of the 60-watt lamp against the current through it. You will see that the resistance is not constant, but increases with the current through it.

18 Work out the power of the lamp at 240 V using these new figures. Does it agree now with that marked on the lamp?

A further exploration of resistance

As the current through a lamp increases, its resistance increases. But the lamp also gets brighter. To do this, the filament in the lamp must be getting hotter.

This suggests that hot wires may have more resistance to the flow of an electric current than cold ones do.

When we carried out the experiment with the lamp, we also had to change the voltage across the lamp and the current through it. It may be that resistance depends on voltage and current as well. The experiment on Worksheet **P**17G looks at this.

*You should now try Worksheet **P**17G. In this experiment you measure the current passing through a wire at various potential differences (voltages) across it, but none are so high that the wire's temperature rises much above that of its surroundings. Do this experiment before reading the next section as it discusses some of the things you may have found in the experiment.*

Ohm's Law

In Worksheet **P**17E you measured the current through the resistor at each of several different voltages. You then divided each voltage by the current. You probably found that the result of this division produced a number that was almost constant. You probably guessed that it **ought** to be constant if it were not for experimental error.

In Chapter **P**4 we saw that if ten people timed the swing of a pendulum they were likely to get different answers, even though the pendulums were identical. We said this was due to *experimental error*. People make different decisions about the start and end of a pendulum's swing. They may also use different clocks.

The same sort of differences come about when other measurements are made. When measuring currents and voltages, different people use different meters, and make different judgements about where the needle is on the scale.

A better way to test whether voltage/current is constant is to plot a graph of voltage against current. If $\dfrac{\text{voltage}}{\text{current}}$ is constant, then the graph should be a straight line passing through the origin, the point (0,0). Voltage and current are said to be *directly proportional* to each other. We discussed proportionality in Chapter **P**1 (page 18).

When you plot such a graph you may find that the points do not quite lie on a straight line. If you draw the straight line that seems best to match the points (called the *best straight line*), you find some points lie on one side of the line and some on the other (figure 17.24). If this happens at random then we believe this is due to experimental error. On the other hand, if the points of the graph seem to be a **smooth curve** then we need to think more carefully about either our experiment or our theory!

The other advantage of drawing a graph is that we can measure the slope of the best straight line and from this get an average result for the ratio $\left(\dfrac{\text{voltage}}{\text{current}}\right)$. There is more about using the slope of graphs in Chapter **P**4. In this case, you probably found that your readings of current and voltage made a good straight-line graph.

If the glass envelope of a 12 V, 24 W lamp is carefully removed, the filament can be immersed in water to keep it a constant temperature. A graph of the current passing through the filament plotted against the voltage across it, gives a similar straight-line graph to that shown in figure 17.24.

We can summarize the results of these experiments by saying that the current through a wire is directly proportional to the p.d. across it, if the temperature of the wire remains constant. This is known as *Ohm's Law*.

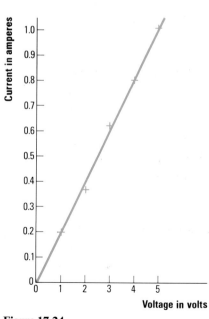

Figure 17.24
Drawing a "best" straight line through points on a graph.

19a What current does a 6-volt battery supply when joined to a 2-ohm resistor?
b Use Ohm's Law to predict what current would flow through the same resistor if it was connected to
　i　a 2-volt supply
　ii　a 240-volt supply.
c If these connections were tried in practice (which they should **not** be) would you expect to find the predicted currents in each case? Give a reason for your answer.

Georg Ohm

Figure 17.25
Georg Ohm (1787–1854)

In the 1820s, Georg Ohm (figure 17.25), a German schoolmaster, set out to find a relationship between the current through a wire and the voltage (or p.d.) between its ends. He already had an idea of a wire having *resistance*, much as a pipe has resistance to the flow of water.

He was the son of a mechanic, so he knew how to make metal wires of different sizes for his experiments. (At that time, wires were not available in shops as they are in today's age of electricity.)

Ohm tried different lengths, different thicknesses, different metals, and even different temperatures. His instruments, and even his voltage supply, were very primitive; but Ohm established a "law" that said $\dfrac{\text{voltage}}{\text{current}}$ is constant for a wire. That constant value was the wire's resistance – the idea he had dreamed of. And he found rules for the way resistance depends on the length and thickness of the sample.

Ohm hoped for rewards of fame and promotion for his discovery, but the authorities took little notice of his work. It was only when his discoveries became known and appreciated outside Germany that he was made a professor – to his great happiness.

Ohm's Law is a very useful link between current and voltage. It has helped in the design of telegraph lines, motors, power lines – in fact, the whole development of electrical equipment through the last century and on into this century.

Nowadays, electrical components for which the current is not proportional to voltage are also very important. The current through many of the components found in radios, television sets, computers and calculators do not fit into this simple pattern.

P17.6　The design of a hair-drier

In the last two chapters we have considered two important ideas to do with electricity (the sort of ideas that were referred to as "connecting ideas" in the introduction). These two ideas are those of *current* and *voltage*. They turn up time and time again in physics.

We have linked current and voltage together with two other ideas – *power* and *resistance*. We have tried to think about all these ideas as they relate to the electrical things we use day-to-day. So we will finish this chapter by looking at something with which you are all probably familiar – an electric hair-drier.

Figure 17.26
A modern hair-drier (**a**, left), contrasted with one made twenty-five years ago (**b**, right).

Hair-driers (the sort used in the home) have undergone a revolution in design. It is now possible to buy a compact hair-drier with a power rating of 1600 watts (figure 17.26a). In 1965, a "best buy" was twice the size and had a power rating of only about 350 W (figure 17.26b).

20a Calculate the current drawn from a 240-volt supply by each of the hair-driers.
b Assuming that all the energy drawn from the supply goes into the heating element, calculate the resistance of the wire used in each hair-drier.
c What is the energy from the supply used for apart from heating?

The purpose of a hair-drier is to dry hair as quickly as possible. But the air it blows out must not be too hot, or it will be dangerous and your hair could be damaged. So the main problem for the designers is to get as much energy per second transferred to the air as possible, without allowing either the air or the drier to become too hot. To do this the air has to be driven across the heating element by a motor-driven fan.

There is no difficulty in making a heating element of the right resistance. The more powerful the drier, the lower the resistance of the wire in the heating element and the thicker it can be. The problem lies in making small motors which can move the air at a fast enough rate. This will keep the temperature of the heating element, and the air it heats, down to a safe level. The recent improvement in the power of hair-driers is entirely due to the availability of small, yet powerful, electric motors.

21 In the future, yet more powerful and even smaller electric motors may become available. Do you think that hair-driers will become even more powerful? Can you see any disadvantage in this?

22 It is very dangerous to block the air inlets and outlets of a hair-drier. Explain why this is so.

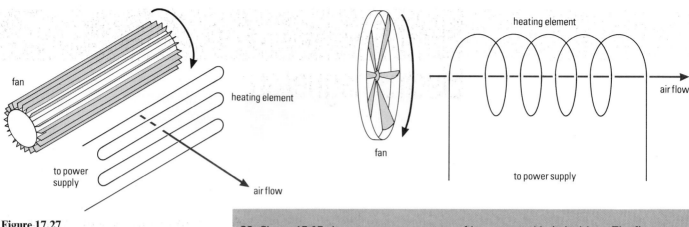

Figure 17.27
Two arrangements of heating wires that
have been used in hair driers.

23 Figure 17.27 shows two arrangements of heaters used in hair-driers. The first
shows a flexible coil of wire arranged perpendicular to the air flow. In the second the
air is blown down the axis of the coil. What do you think are the advantages and
disadvantages of each arrangement?

Summary

The following passage summarizes the main ideas in this chapter. Copy out
the passage, filling in the blanks with either a word or phrase from the list at
the beginning of the passage. (There is only one word or phrase to each
blank; the words are not listed in the order you will need to use them, and you
may use any word more than once.)

Boyle	**amperes**	**charge**	**decrease**
Faraday	**coulombs**	**current**	**equal to**
Newton	**joules**	**energy**	**greater than**
Ohm	**volts**	**power**	**increase**
work	**watts**	**resistance**	**less than**
temperature	**stay the same**	**proportional to**	**second**

Power is the rate of transfer of _____. It is measured in _____. The
p.d., in volts, across a component in a circuit is the number of _____ of
energy transferred by each coulomb of electric _____ that passes through
it. The electric current passing through a component in a circuit is the number
of _____ of electric charge passing through the component every second.
If you multiply p.d. by current, this gives the number of _____ of energy
transferred to the component every _____.

Dividing the p.d. in volts across a component by the _____ measured
in amperes gives the value of the _____ of the component.

The resistance of a component is not necessarily constant. It can be affected
by a number of factors. However, a metal at constant _____ has a
constant resistance. This means that the _____ passing through it is
directly _____ the p.d. across it. This is called _____'s Law. Raising
the temperature of a wire will cause its resistance to _____.

When energy is transferred via electrical charge to most electrical
components, they get hot. Their temperature stops rising once the rate at
which they are gaining energy from the charge is _____ the rate at which
they are losing it to the surroundings.

Making use of electricity
Electromagnetism

*This chapter is mainly about electric motors. There are many investigations to do. As you carry these out you will learn a lot about magnetism and electricity. The last sections (**P**18.6 and **P**18.7) are about dynamos. If you feel you need to work slowly through the first three sections, you could omit the work on dynamos for now. It is important to understand clearly how motors work before trying to understand dynamos as they are more difficult to understand. Your teacher will advise you on what you should do.*

*You will find a simpler treatment of dynamos and generators in Chapter **P**11.*

P18.1   Electric motors

Look again at the table in figure 16.5. How many of the things listed in this table use electric motors? You will probably find that more than half of them contain an electric motor. Electric motors are also used a great deal in the world outside your home, though, apart from railways, they are still little used for transport.

1 List as many uses as you can where electric motors are used for getting things from place to place.

Worksheet **P**18A is about electric vehicles. It compares them with petrol driven vehicles and asks you some questions about their advantages and disadvantages.

P18.2 Forces from electric currents

The electric motor in figure 18.1 is lifting a heavy load. It is transferring energy from the electric supply to the load by doing work. The force which lifts the load is provided by the electric current which flows through the motor. How is an electric motor able to do this? To find out, you should first try the experiments in Worksheet **P**18B.

The space around a magnet where its effects can be felt is called a *magnetic field*. You have already come across the idea of a force field in section **P**7.1.

The experiment illustrated in figure 18.2 (on the next page) shows that a force can act on a wire carrying an electric current when the wire is in a

Figure 18.1
An electric fork-lift truck in operation.

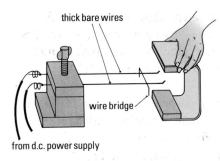

Figure 18.2
A movable wire bridge carrying a current through a magnetic field.

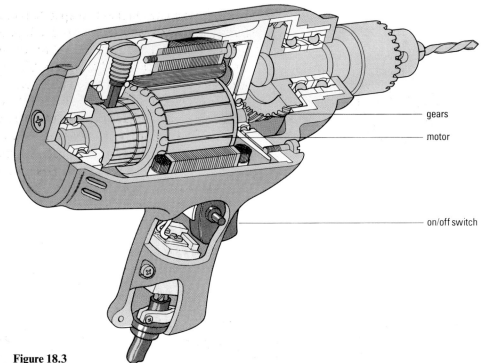

Figure 18.3
A sectional drawing of a portable electric drill, showing the electric motor inside.

gears

motor

on/off switch

magnetic field. This is the force that moves the free wire. (The "free" wire is the wire bridge which rests on top of the pair of wires from the power pack.) To move the wire, you will have found that the magnetic field has to be in a particular direction. This is how electric motors work! A coil of wire is placed in a magnetic field. When an electric current flows through the coil a force makes it rotate and the motor can do work.

Figure 18.3 shows a picture of the electric motor in a small electric drill. The drawing shows that the design of an electric motor is quite complicated. How does the electric current get in and out of the coil without twisting the wires up when it spins? What provides the magnetic field? How should the coil and magnetic field be arranged to get the biggest force? To answer these questions we need to recall some ideas about magnets.

The next section recalls some of the ideas about magnets and magnetic fields that you have probably met earlier in your work in science. If you feel confident about these ideas, you can go on to section P18.4, which investigates how to build a model electric motor.

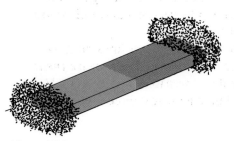

Figure 18.4
A bar magnet that has been dipped in iron filings.

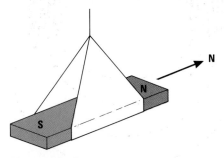

Figure 18.5
A freely-suspended bar magnet will swing so that one end points approximately towards the Earth's North pole.

P18.3   Magnets

Magnets are pieces of material, normally with iron in them, which have been specially treated. They attract other pieces of iron brought close to them with what we call a *magnetic force*. This force is so common that we use the word "magnetism" to mean "attraction" in everyday speech. We speak of someone having a "magnetic" personality – meaning that he or she has an immediate impact on anyone nearby.

If a bar magnet is dipped into iron filings, the filings cluster round the ends where the magnetic force seems to be concentrated (figure 18.4). These regions are called *magnetic poles*.

Figure 18.6
A magnetic compass.

Suppose a bar magnet is suspended on a thread as shown in figure 18.5. Such a magnet always hangs so that it points approximately north-south. The magnetic pole at the north end of the magnet is called the *north-seeking pole*. This is usually shortened to *N-pole*. Similarly the other pole is called the *south-seeking pole* – shortened to *S-pole*.

A small magnet, mounted on a pivot, is used in a magnetic *compass* (figure 18.6). The magnet itself is called the *compass needle*. Together with a map, it is very useful for finding your way about unfamiliar countryside. A small version of this compass can be used for tracing out magnetic field patterns.

When one magnet is brought close to another magnet it is found that an N-pole will attract an S-pole, but **repels** a similar N-pole. A similar rule is found to be true for S-poles (figure 18.7).

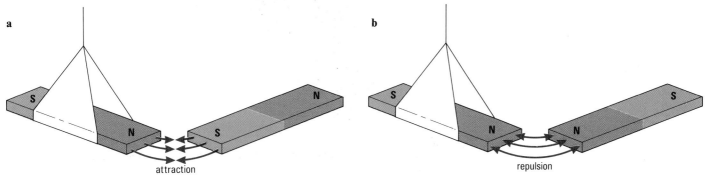

Figure 18.7
a The opposite poles of two bar magnets attract each other.
b Similar poles repel each other.

We have already seen in the previous section that the space around a magnet where its influence can be felt is called the magnet's *magnetic field*. The drawing in figure 18.8 shows several small compasses placed in a magnetic field. Each is pointing in a different direction. The direction of the compass needle is the direction of the magnetic field at the point where the compass needle is. We mark this direction with an arrow pointing from the S-pole of the compass to the N-pole. The arrows always point in the direction the magnetic field pulls on the N-pole of the compass.

The compass needles in figure 18.9a trace out continuous lines running from the N-pole to the S-pole of the magnet. These lines are called *magnetic field lines*. We mark the direction of the field on these lines with arrows. Many such lines can together show the pattern of magnetic field directions in a magnetic field (figure 18.9b).

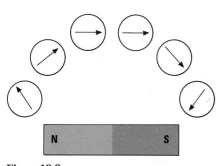

Figure 18.8
Several small compasses placed in the magnetic field of a bar magnet.

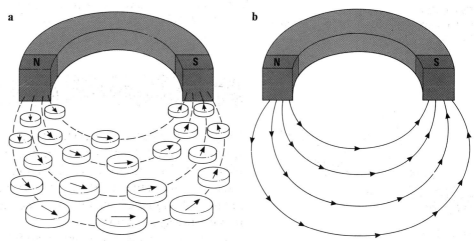

Figure 18.9
a Mapping out a magnetic field line using small plotting compasses.
b A magnetic field pattern.

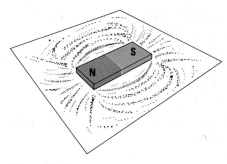

Figure 18.10
Mapping out a magnetic field pattern
using iron filings.

Michael Faraday was the first scientist to "map out" magnetic fields in this way. He imagined a "field line", which extended from the N-pole of one magnet to the S-pole of another, as a piece of stretched elastic pulling the magnets together. But you must always remember that this is only a "thinking aid" – magnetic field lines are no more than maps, showing the direction of the field at various points.

An easier way to make magnetic field patterns is to use iron filings. Each small filing is magnetized by the magnetic field and acts like a mini compass, pointing in the direction of the magnetic field at that point. Filings scattered over all the field quickly map out the field for you (figure 18.10).

Magnets which are very short compared with their width are sometimes useful for experiments (figure 18.11a). Such magnets are often called *slab* magnets. Two such magnets can be mounted on a piece of C-shaped iron. You have used a pair of magnets like this already when you investigated the way a magnet could affect an electric current. It is important that opposite poles face each other. If you make a map of the field of these magnets, you will find that, except at the edges, the field lines are all in the same direction (figure 18.11b).

Figure 18.11
a A "slab" magnet with poles on each face.
b The magnetic field pattern of a pair of slab magnets.

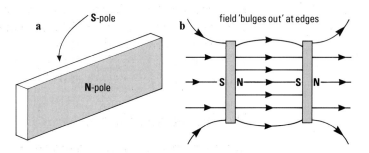

P18.4　Magnetism and electric currents

The experiments you did using Worksheet **P18B** showed that electric currents, as well as other magnets, are affected by magnetic fields. Using the apparatus shown in figure 18.2, you will have discovered that to get the best movement of the free wire, the magnets have to be arranged so that the direction of the magnetic field is at **right-angles** to the direction of the current in the free wire. Perhaps this result surprised you?

And what about the direction of movement of the free wire? You will have seen that this is at right-angles to both the direction of the current **and** the direction of the magnetic field.

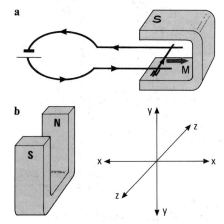

Figure 18.12

2a Give a brief description of the apparatus shown in figure 18.12a. Say what happens when the current is switched on. (The arrows on the wires show the direction of the current. The field direction is upwards, from N-pole to S-pole. The direction of motion of the free wire is to the right, shown by the arrow marked M.)
b What happens to the direction of motion of the free wire:
　i　if the magnet is reversed so that the N-pole is at the top
　ii　if the current direction is reversed　　iii　if **both** are reversed?
c What happens if you hold the magnets so that the field is in the same direction as the electric current in the free wire (figure 18.12b)?

The free wire moves because there is a force on it. We can show the force between the wire and the magnets by doing the experiment shown in figure 18.13. When no current flows through the wire loop, the top-pan balance shows only the weight of the magnets and the iron. When the current is switched on, the extra force between the wire and the magnets pulls the magnets up, decreasing the reading on the balance.

The force is greatest if the current flowing through the bottom of the loop is at right-angles to the direction of the magnetic field.

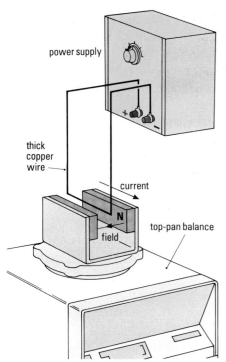

Figure 18.13
Using a top-pan balance to show the way the force can vary on a wire carrying a current in a magnetic field.

3a What happens to the reading on the top-pan balance if the direction of the current is reversed?

b (A hard question for you to think about.) Why can we be sure that it is only the current in the bottom of the loop that matters in making the force and not the current running up and down the vertical connecting wires?

Here are the important things to remember from these experiments.

- A magnetic field will produce a force on a wire carrying an electric current.
- The force will be greatest if the magnetic field is at right-angles to the direction of the electric current.
- The direction of the force is always at right-angles to both the magnetic field and the current (figure 18.14).

Making an electric motor

The diagram in figure 18.15 shows how we can use this force on a wire carrying an electric current to make an electric motor.

The magnetic field is provided by the slab magnets as before. The wire is wound into a flat coil, which is fixed to a rod so it can turn. The coil and the rod, together, are called the *armature* of the electric motor.

Try connecting the wires from the coil to a low-voltage d.c. power supply using some thin, flexible wire. If you start with the coil in the position shown in figure 18.15, you should find the coil moves almost quarter of a turn but then stops near the position shown in figure 18.16. Try turning the coil further in the same direction. What happens when you let go?

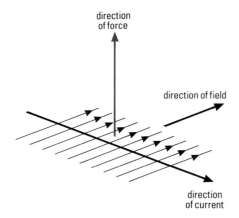

Figure 18.14
This diagram shows the direction of the force exerted by a magnetic field on a wire carrying a current.

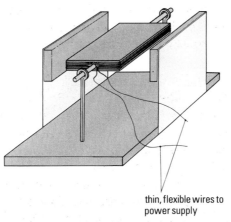

thin, flexible wires to power supply

Figure 18.15
A coil of wire in the magnetic field of a pair of slab magnets.

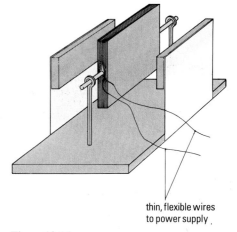

thin, flexible wires to power supply

Figure 18.16
The same coil turned through a right-angle.

If you try to turn the coil further you will find that a force acts to push it back to where it was in figure 18.16. The diagrams in figure 18.17 will help to explain why this happens.

In figure 18.17a, there is a **upwards** force on the wires marked A. The direction of this force is at right-angles to the magnetic field and the direction of the current. There is also a force on the wires marked B. The direction of this force is **downwards**. These forces turn the coil until it reaches the position shown in figure 18.17b.

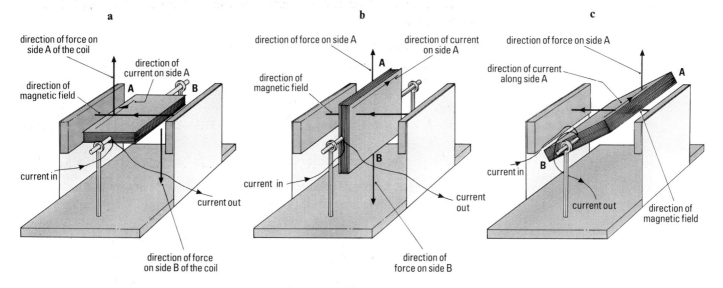

a   **b**   **c**

Figure 18.17
a The forces acting on a coil of current-carrying wire in a magnetic field.
b The direction in which the forces act after the same coil has been turned through 90°.
c In this diagram the same coil has been turned through almost a further 90°.

The forces on the wires in figure 18.17b are still in the same direction. This is because the current and the magnetic field are still in the same direction. But this is no longer any good for turning the coil.

You could use your fingers to push the coil to the position shown in figure 18.17c. The diagram shows the forces acting on the coil. The direction of the force on the wires marked A is **still** the same! But because these wires have "changed sides", the force is now trying to twist the coil back to where it came from.

4a In figure 18.17a, why is the direction of the force on the wires marked B downwards, which is opposite to the direction of the force on the wires marked A?
b In figure 18.17b, the direction of the forces is no longer any good for turning the coil. But what about the size of the forces? Do you think the forces will be weaker, stronger, or the same size as the forces in figure 18.17a? Explain your answer.
c Explain why the direction of the force on the wires marked A in figure 18.17c is the same as the direction of the force on the wires marked A in figure 18.17a.
d Explain why the coil will not keep turning when you pass a current through the wires.
e What would have to happen to the direction of the force on the wires marked A every half-turn of the coil, for the coil to go round and round?

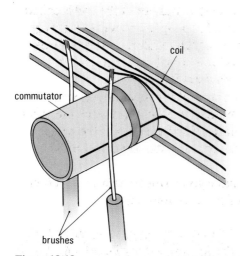

Figure 18.18
The commutator and brushes on a model motor.

To make a motor, we have to find some way of making the coil turn continuously. To do this, we have to find a method of changing the direction of the force on the wires every half-turn of the coil.

Figure 18.18 shows how this can be done in the model motor. The rod, on which the coil turns, is first covered with a piece of sticky tape to insulate it.

The ends of the wire which make the coil are stripped of their insulation and fixed on either side of the rod. The wires can be held down by tiny rubber bands made from cycle valve tubing.

The two bare ends of the wires from the power supply press against the wires from the coil. When the power supply is switched on, current will flow from the positive terminal of the supply through the wire marked + and along side A of the coil in figure 18.19a. As before, a force will pull the coil round a quarter of a turn. But because the coil and the rod on which it is mounted have turned, the connection between the coil and the supply has been broken.

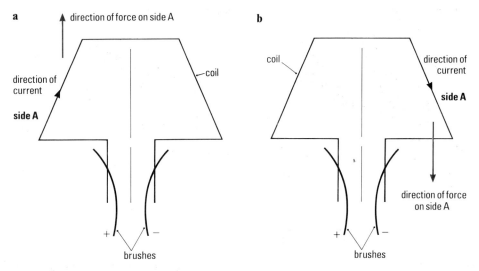

Figure 18.19
This shows how a commutator changes the direction of the current through a coil.

Although the current momentarily stops flowing, the coil carries on turning. This brings the wires alongside A into contact with the negative (−) terminal of the electricity supply (figure 18.19b). As you can see the current now flows in the opposite direction round the coil. The force on A is now downwards. This is just the direction in which it needs to be to keep the coil turning.

After another half-turn, the current again changes direction round the coil and the force on A is upwards. So it goes on, as the coil spins.

This "sliding switch" which leads the current in and out of the coil is called a *commutator*. (We use the same sort of word for people who work in a large city, yet live outside. "Commuters" are people who regularly go backwards and forwards to the city, just as a commutator is something that lets the current go backwards and forwards through the coil.)

Apart from changing the direction of the current through the coil every half-turn the commutator serves another useful purpose. It prevents the wires to the coil getting twisted up as the coil rotates. The bare ends of the wires which lead from the electricity supply to the commutator are called brushes (because they "brush" against the coil).

You can now use Worksheet **P**18C to make your own model motor. When you have done that, try answering some of the questions below.

5 Explain carefully in your own words why an electric motor needs a commutator, and how a commutator works.

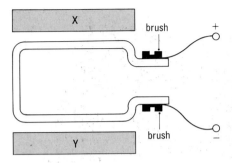

Figure 18.20
A simplified top view of a model electric motor.

6 When you made an electric motor, you connected the coil to the electricity supply through ''brushes''. Figure 18.20 is a very simple top view of a motor. Both brushes are marked in black.
a Copy the diagram. Colour one of the long sides of the coil red and the other long side blue. Put an arrow on each side to show the way the current flows.
b X and Y are the poles of a horse-shoe magnet. They are arranged to make a strong field in the gap. The side of the coil near X moves **up**. Which way does the side of the coil near Y move — up or down? Why does it go this way?
c Draw another sketch for when the coil has gone **half-way** round, so the red side is where the blue side was and the blue side is where the red side was. Put an arrow on each side of the coil to show which way round the current flows.
d Which way will the side near X move — up (as before) or down?
e Which way will side Y move?
f Why are brushes used?

7 Many real motors are made with a coil in a magnetic field, like your model motor.
a What changes could you make to your model to make it more powerful and efficient?
b In powerful motors, the coils are wound on an iron core. Why do you think that is?
c All electric motors need a magnetic field inside to make them work, but some don't have permanent magnets. What do they have instead?

8 A pupil decides to make a model motor at home. She saw that the model she made at school ran unevenly, in jerks. So she arranges a long axle which will take **two** coils, each fed by a commutator and brushes.
a Should she arrange the coils like **A** or **B** in figure 18.21?
b Give a good reason for your answer to part **a**.
c Picture **C** in figure 18.21 shows a short piece of wooden broom handle. Could it be used instead of the flat block of wood as a frame for the two coils? Copy the drawing and show the two coils on it.
d Now look again at the motor in an electric drill (figure 18.3). How has it been constructed so that it will run smoothly?

A   B   C

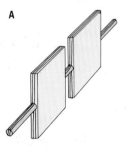
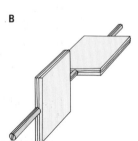
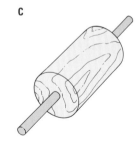

Figure 18.21
Possible arrangements of coils for a model motor.

    In real motors, the commutator is divided up into many *segments* connected to different coils. The current is led into the coils through brushes which are made from carbon. These are pressed down on the commutator by springs.
    Eventually the brushes wear out and have to be replaced. This is frequently a reason for electric motors failing to work properly. It is usually easy to replace the brushes, and you should expect to have to do this in domestic electric motors every so often.

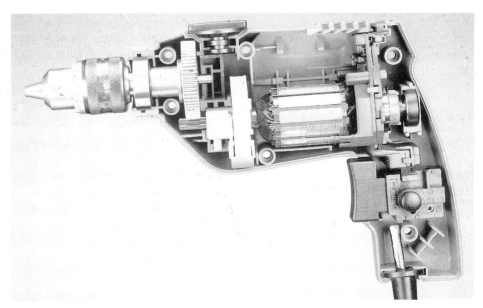

Figure 18.22
Where are the commutator and brushes in the electric motor in this drill?

P18.5 Electromagnets

To get a large force from an electric motor, we need to pass a large current through a coil of many turns of wire. But we also need to have a strong magnetic field. *Electromagnets* are used for this purpose.

We have seen that wires carrying electric currents are affected by a magnetic field. It will probably not surprise you to learn that electric currents themselves have a magnetic field around them. You may have seen that is so already. If you wind a piece of wire round an iron nail and place the end of the coil near a magnetic compass, you will see the end of the compass move when the current is switched on through the wire (figure 18.23).

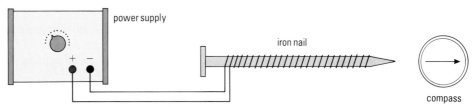

Figure 18.23
A simple electromagnet.

9a Why is the coil wound on an iron nail? Would the compass needle deflect without the nail there? (Try it and see.)
b What happens if the direction of the current through the coil is reversed?
c Is there a relationship between the way the current goes round the coil and the north and south poles of the coil?

It is easy enough to show that electric currents are surrounded by a magnetic field if someone tells you how to look for it. But suppose you are told no more than the fact that someone **suspects** there might be a magnetic field round a wire carrying a current – no more than that. How would you

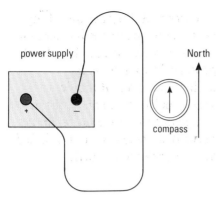

Figure 18.24
The compass needle is unaffected by the current in the wire if the two are side by side on a bench.

Figure 18.25
Hans Oersted (1777–1851) demonstrating the effect of an electric current on a magnetic compass needle.

Figure 18.26
Oersted's discovery of the magnetic field of a current-carrying wire.

start looking? You might bring a magnetic compass close to a wire carrying a current as in figure 18.24. What happens? Nothing! (Try it for yourself.) Perhaps the current isn't big enough. Try a bigger current. Still nothing happens to the compass needle.

These are the sort of experiments scientists were doing in the early years of the nineteenth century. They suspected a wire carrying an electric current was surrounded by a magnetic field, but no one was able to show that this was so until Hans Oersted made the discovery in 1820.

Hans Oersted

Hans Oersted was born in Denmark in 1777. He discovered the magnetic field around a wire carrying an electric current quite by accident while giving a lecture in Copenhagen. An electric current was being passed down a wire when Oersted noticed that a compass needle lying nearby was deflected (figures 18.25 and 18.26). Perhaps others had noticed this before, but Oersted was the first to realize the connection between the needle's deflection and the electric current.

Like many other scientists, he had suspected for some time that an electric current might have a magnetic field. But everyone had assumed the magnetic field would stick out from the wire like the spokes of a wheel from its hub. What Oersted found was that the magnetic field actually went in circles **round** the wire. No one had expected this.

You can see for yourself what Oersted saw by doing the experiment in Worksheet **P**18D. You can also "map out" the magnetic field round a current-carrying wire using iron filings.

The next few paragraphs are about scientists making discoveries. It is not essential to the rest of the chapter, and the passage and the question which follows are quite hard. Do it if you have time and are interested in these things.

Oersted's work tells us a lot about the way scientists may make discoveries. They are not necessarily the result of deliberate planning, but they are rarely due entirely to chance. Usually the scientist is looking for something similar to the "discovery". A well-known writer, Professor J. D. Bernal, has written about Oersted's discovery. Here is what he said:

"Oersted . . . had certainly been looking for the connection between electricity and magnetism for thirteen years, but his actual discovery was not the result of any deliberate planning. In this case, as there were so many people playing with electric currents and compass needles at that time,

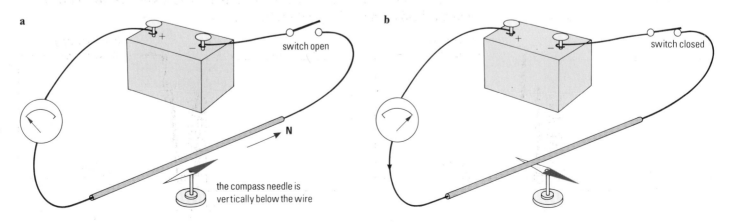

someone could hardly fail sooner or later to notice their interaction. Many probably did and thought no more of it. The difficulty in science is often not so much how to make the discovery but to know that one has made it. In all experiments there are a number of effects, produced by all kinds of extraneous causes, which are not in the least significant, and it requires a certain degree of intelligence or intuition to see which of them really mean anything. . . . Sooner or later, however, if enough people concentrate on the field, someone will be found sufficiently observant, sufficiently broadminded, and sufficiently critical or ignorant of orthodox theories to make the discovery.''

10a What do the following phrases mean?
   i ''The difficulty in science is not so much how to make the discovery but to know that one has made it.''
   ii ''all kinds of extraneous causes''
   iii ''sufficiently critical or ignorant of orthodox theories''
b Try to find another discovery that was made by accident.
c Some people say, ''If you have a problem in science all you have to do is put enough people on it. Someone is bound to come up with a solution sooner or later!'' Do you think this view is supported by discoveries like Oersted's?

*You can read some other views of scientific discoveries in section **C5.6** in your Chemistry book.*

Because Oersted's discovery was what so many people were looking for, it led immediately to many important developments. Within three years the electromagnet had been invented. This in turn led directly to the electric telegraph (used on the railways) and the electric motor.

*You can learn about the electric telegraph in Chapter **P21**.*

Using electromagnets

Worksheet **P18E** gives you an investigation to make into electromagnets. But before turning to the last section of this chapter, we will look at one application of electromagnets – the electromagnetic *relay*.

The relay is a switch that you can control with an electric current. The only sort of "relay" you may have heard of before is a team race in athletics. This use of the word "relay" is quite different. A diagram of a relay in use is shown in figure 18.27. The diagram in fact shows two circuits. On the righthand side is a mains lamp connected to the 240-volt mains and a switch. Normally the switch is held in the "off" position by a spring.

Figure 18.27
The relay is an electromagnetic switch.

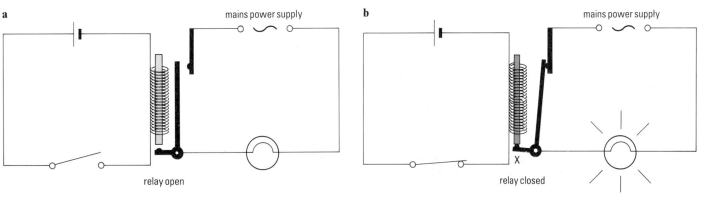

The switch is operated by the circuit on the left. This consists of a 6-volt battery, another switch that you can operate by hand, and a coil. When a current flows through the coil, it becomes an electromagnet. To make the electromagnet stronger there is some iron in its centre. The switch that controls the righthand circuit is made of a metal that is attracted to magnets. So when the coil is magnetized, the end of the switch marked X moves towards it and the switch closes.

As soon as the current through the coil is turned off, the spring in the relay opens the switch again. The advantage of a relay is that large and possibly dangerous currents can be controlled by currents and voltages that are not themselves large. It is also possible to switch such circuits on and off from a considerable distance away. You will find many uses for relays in Chapter **P20**.

P18.6   *Making electric currents from magnetism*

When you have completed your investigations with your model electric motor, do not take it to pieces at once. There is one more experiment you can do with it that gives a most surprising result. The diagram in figure 18.28 shows a model motor connected to an ammeter that will respond to very small currents. You will notice that the motor is not connected to any electricity supply.

If the armature is spun with your fingers, you will see that the ammeter shows that an electric current flows. Worksheet **P18F** gives some more experiments you can do to investigate this.

When Hans Oersted showed that an electric current could behave like a magnet, many scientists thought that this could only be half the story. Surely, they said, if an electric current can produce magnetism, then magnetism ought to be able to produce an electric current. But it was ten years after Oersted's discovery before somebody managed to show how such an electric current could be produced. That "somebody" was Michael Faraday.

Michael Faraday was one of the most remarkable scientists since Isaac Newton. In Newton's time many scientists had been doing experiments with forces and movement. But only Newton was able to "put it all together" and make sense of what we now call *dynamics*. Faraday did the same, in the nineteenth century, for electricity.

Figure 18.28 (below left)
A model motor connected to a galvanometer.

Figure 18.29 (below right)
Changing the strength of the magnetic field through a coil by switching an electromagnet on and off.

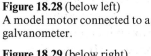

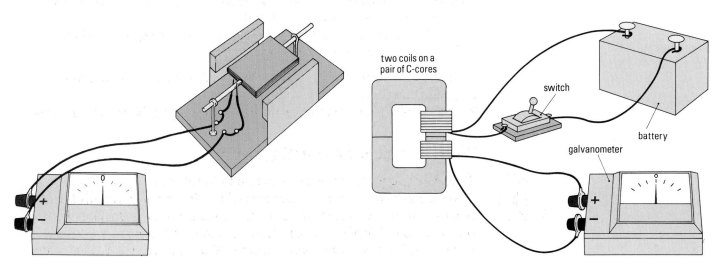

Oersted's discovery of the magnetic field around an electric current was an accident. Faraday's discovery of electromagnetic induction was not an accident; it was the result of carefully planned experiments. The reason it came so long after Oersted's discovery is because no one except Faraday realized that the wire carrying the current had to be **moved** through the magnetic field of a magnet – no movement, no current!

You should try to do at least some of the experiments on Worksheet P18F before reading any further.

In some of the experiments described in Worksheet **P**18F, you can make a current **without** moving either magnet **or** wire. This is when you **change** the strength of a magnetic field by using an electromagnet (figure 18.29).
   In each of the experiments there are three pieces of apparatus:

● a permanent magnet or an electromagnet (A)
● a wire or a coil of wire (B)
● an ammeter to show when a current is flowing (C).

After doing these experiments, ask yourself the following questions.

● Is any current produced when A and B are held near each other **without moving** (and without the electromagnet's current changing)?
● Is any current produced when the magnet A is moving?
● Is any current produced when the wire or coil B is moving?
● Is any current produced when the electromagnet is growing stronger or weaker because the current in it is changing?

Induced currents

An electric current can be made to flow in a circuit by simply putting an electric cell in it. The currents produced by moving or changing magnetic fields are produced in another way. They are often called *induced currents*. But they are no different from electric currents produced from a battery.
   Your answers to the questions above should show you that an induced current will only flow in a circuit if a magnetic field through it is somehow changed. This may be by moving the circuit, or the magnet, or by changing the strength of the magnetic field.
   If you take your investigation further you will find that the size of the induced current depends on how quickly this change in field is made. The faster the change, the bigger the current.
   All of this is summed up in *Faraday's Law of electromagnetic induction* which we can state simply as follows.

1 An induced current will only flow in a circuit if there is a change in a magnetic field inside it.
2 The size of the induced current depends on how quickly the field changes.

Direct current and alternating current

When you rotate the armature of your model motor by hand and produce a current, you have made a new sort of machine. It is not a motor any longer because you are not feeding it from a battery and making it do a job. Instead, **you** are doing a job in spinning it; and **it** is sending a current to the outside world. You have made a *dynamo* – a device that transfers energy electrically.

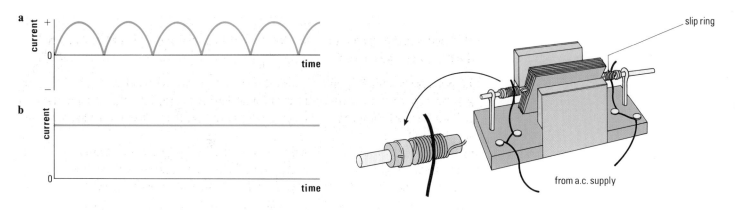

Figure 18.30 (above left)
a A graph of the way the current from a d.c. dynamo changes as its coil is rotated. The current is always in the same direction, but varies in size.
b The current from a battery does not vary in size in the way the current from a d.c. dynamo does.

Figure 18.31 (above right)
A model a.c. dynamo.

Notice what happens to the ammeter needle if you turn the armature of your model dynamo slowly. The current produced is not steady. It swings from high to low and back again as the armature rotates, but the current is always in the same direction.

When current always flows in the same direction it is called a *direct current*. The direct current from the model motor is different from the direct current from a battery. The battery current remains at a steady value (until the battery runs down) as shown in figure 18.30b.

Suppose we re-make the dynamo so that it hasn't got a commutator. Instead, each end of the coil is connected to a *slip ring*. The two slip rings are insulated from each other. Each is in contact with one brush (figure 18.31). The wires from the brushes are connected to an ammeter. What happens when the armature spins? You may be able to try this for yourself.

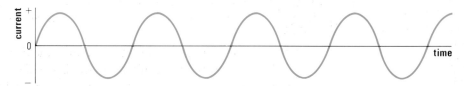

Figure 18.32
The way the current from an a.c. dynamo changes as its coil is rotated. The current surges first one way, then the other.

Provided the coil doesn't spin too quickly you should see that the galvanometer needle swings back and forth, showing the current goes first one way and then the other. A current like this is called an *alternating current* (figure 18.32). Alternating currents can drive motors and transfer energy to heaters to warm the surroundings just like direct currents. But as you can see in Chapter **P**11, currents that surge back and forth in this way have some special advantages. The electric current that flows from the "mains" supply is of this sort.

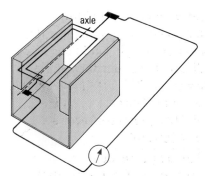

Figure 18.33
A model a.c. dynamo. Only one turn of the coil is shown.

11 Figure 18.33 is a sketch of a model a.c. dynamo, with only one turn of the coil drawn, for simplicity.
a Copy the diagram and label:
  i the slip rings   ii the brushes   iii the magnets.
b What happens if the coil is spun steadily and slowly?
c What happens if the coil is spun very fast?
d Why are slip rings used? (Think what would happen if you joined the brush to one end of the wire forming the coil.)

12 What would happen if you fixed the coil in the dynamo in question **11** and **rotated the magnet** round the coil?

13 Suppose you tried to run the a.c. dynamo in figure 18.31 as a motor.
a If you connect the brushes to a battery (or any other d.c. supply) what will happen?
b If you connect the brushes to a low voltage a.c. supply the machine will just buzz or vibrate. Explain why.
c The mains supply of a.c. is 50 hertz. (That is, the voltage and current switch forward-backward-forward-backward making 50 forward-backward ''cycles'' in each second.) An engineer tells you, ''If you could start the machine by spinning it **very** fast with your fingers, it would run.'' How fast (that is, how many revolutions per second) should it spin for it to work?
d Engineers usually give the speed of a motor in revolutions per **minute** (rev/min). Give your answer to part **c** in revolutions per minute.

P18.7   Dynamos and alternators

Until the dynamo was invented, batteries were the only source of electric current. It was impossible to make day-to-day use of electricity because a battery can only store a little energy.

The next few paragraphs show, by doing a few calculations, how unrealistic it is to depend on batteries for energy. You can omit this and go on to the cycle dynamo if you wish.

First of all we will work out how much energy a car battery can store. Such a battery can provide a p.d. of 12 V and drive a current of 20 A round a circuit for about 1 hour before running down (figure 18.34).

How many coulombs of charge flow round the circuit? A current of 20 A means that 20 coulombs pass round the circuit every second; 1 hour is equal to 3600 seconds. So in 3600 seconds, 20×3600 coulombs flow round the circuit. That is 72 000 coulombs in all.

The battery transfers 12 joules of energy for each coulomb that flows round the circuit (that is what 12 V means). So the battery can transfer 72 000 coulombs with 12 joules per coulomb. That is a total energy of $12 \times 72\,000$ joules $= 864\,000$ joules.

That may seem a lot of energy. Let us see how far it would go on a cold winter's night in one room! (Figure 18.35.)

Suppose the room is lit by a 60-watt lamp and warmed by a 2000-watt electric fire. This is a total energy transfer of 2060 joules every second. If this was provided by a car battery we could work out how long it would be before the battery would run down. Of course we shall have to assume that the light and the electric fire are specially constructed to run on 12 V, but that will not affect the energy the room needs for light and warmth. The battery will provide a total of 864 000 joules; the room needs 2060 joules per second.

So the time the battery would "last" $= \dfrac{864\,000 \text{ joules}}{2060 \text{ joules per second}}$
$= 420$ seconds (to the nearest 10 s)

420 seconds is just 7 minutes! You can see why the invention of the dynamo was necessary before there could be much day-to-day use of electricity!

Figure 18.34
A car battery.

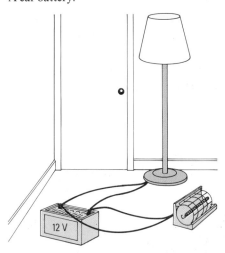

Figure 18.35
Using a car battery to light a lamp and power an electric fire. It would be only a matter of minutes before the battery "runs down".

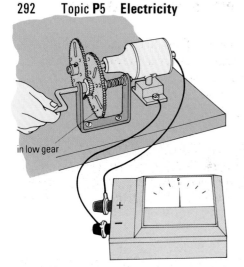

Figure 18.36
A bicycle dynamo. This dynamo has been mounted so that it can be turned by hand at fast and slow speeds.

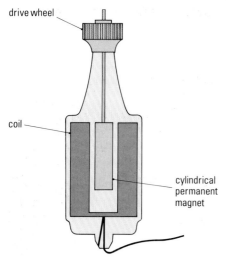

Figure 18.37
A cut-away diagram of a bicycle dynamo.

The cycle dynamo

You may be able to try operating a cycle dynamo, like the one in figure 18.36.

14 The cycle dynamo can be turned by hand and the current it produces can be made to light a lamp. Why is it so much easier to turn the handle of the dynamo when the lamp is disconnected than when the lamp is being lit? (Try this for yourself, if you can.)

See what happens if the dynamo is connected to a galvanometer and the handle turned very slowly. The needle goes backwards and forwards showing that the cycle dynamo produces an alternating current. The diagram in figure 18.37 shows the inside of a cycle dynamo. Compare it will your own model dynamo. You will see that it is an "inside-out" sort of dynamo. It is the permanent magnet which is rotated. The coils, in which the current is induced, do not move.

15 Can you think of any advantage in constructing a cycle dynamo in this way? (To answer this question, think first how the current is taken from the coil when it rotates. Then ask yourself how the current is taken from the coil in the cycle dynamo.)

Power station generators

Generators which produce alternating current are usually called *alternators*. All power stations transfer energy to electricity using alternators. As in the cycle dynamo, it is the magnet which is rotated. The current is drawn from fixed coils that surround the magnet. To produce the magnetic field, electromagnets are used in power station alternators.

Figure 18.38 is a photograph of the turbine hall at Sizewell. One of the two alternators can be seen in the bottom lefthand corner of the photograph.

Figure 18.38
The turbine and generator hall at Sizewell nuclear power station. It is so noisy in here that no one is allowed to stay in it for more than twenty minutes without ear protection. Power station workers operate from a sound-insulated room.

Sizewell is a nuclear power station. The energy from uranium is used to produce steam at high pressure. It is this steam that turns the alternators by using *turbines*. Each of the two alternators is capable of providing 250 megawatts of power at 17 500 V. There is more about the production and distribution of electrical energy in Chapter **P11**.

16 What current will an alternator deliver if its output is 250 megawatts and its voltage 17 500 V? (1 megawatt is the name for 1 000 000 watts.)

Summary

Figure 18.39 shows a coil made of a single turn of wire which can rotate in the magnetic field of the two magnets. An electric current passes around the coil via a commutator. The diagram shows the direction of forces acting on the coil the moment the current starts to flow.

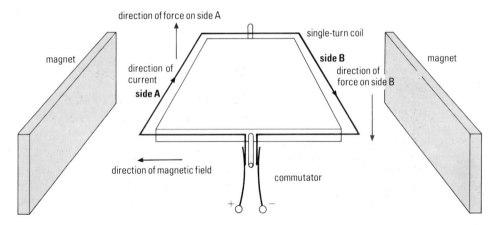

Figure 18.39
A diagram showing the forces acting on a one-turn coil in a magnetic field.

The sentences below explain why the coil rotates continuously. However they have been written down in the wrong order. Write out the sentences in an order that makes sense.

1 The coil rotates a little way and then side A breaks contact with the positive wire from the supply.
2 These forces act so that the coil continues to rotate in the same direction.
3 During the same time side B of the coil breaks contact with the negative wire from the supply and makes contact with the positive wire.
4 The moment the current starts to flow, the force on side A of the coil is upwards and the force on side B is downwards.
5 The force on side A of the coil is now downwards and the force on side B is upwards.
6 These forces make the coil start to rotate.

Suppose someone says to you "A dynamo seems to be a motor in reverse." Explain carefully what they mean.

Chapter P19 Making pictures with electricity
Electrons

This chapter introduces electrons and shows how they are used to make pictures on a television screen. The electron is of great importance in explaining many other things in physics and chemistry. You can learn more about its importance in Chapter C18 of your Chemistry book.

P19.1 Television

Have you ever seen inside a television set? Probably not – you are usually warned not to take the back off a television set as there are very high voltages inside. But if you do see inside one, you will notice that nearly all the space is taken up by a large glass bulb called the "television (or picture) tube". It has to be handled with care. It is made of glass, and it has a vacuum inside (that is, it contains no air or any other gas). Figure 19.2 is a diagram of a television tube that shows what it is like inside and outside.

Figure 19.1 (above left)
Watching television.

Figure 19.2 (above right)
A cut-away diagram of the picture tube in a television set.

When a television tube is switched on it shows a bright picture on the outside. You might expect to find a light source inside the tube. In fact there is no light, only electricity.

1 How many different electrical connections can you see that go into the television tube in figure 19.2?

How can electricity be used to make a picture? How can electricity travel through a vacuum? To answer these questions, we need to remind ourselves first about the nature of atoms.

What is an atom like?

In Chapter **P3**, we saw that the discovery of radioactivity led to a number of experiments which explored the structure of an atom. These experiments led to our present-day picture of an atom consisting of a nucleus (built from protons and neutrons) surrounded by a cloud of electrons. Both the nucleus and the electrons are electrically charged. The charge on the nucleus is positive and the charge on the electrons is negative. It is the force between these charges that holds the atom together.

If the charge carried by the electron cloud does not equal in size the charge on the nucleus, the atom will be electrically charged and form an ion. Atoms easily gain or lose electrons in this way.

We shall now see if this picture of an atom can help us understand how a television set works. In doing so, we shall look at some experiments that also help support the picture of the atom that has just been described.

P19.2   Electric currents in a vacuum?

As you have probably already guessed, it is electrons that are used to form the pictures in a television set. At the back of the tube in figure 19.2 there is an *electron gun*. The electrons that will form the picture on the front of the tube come from here.

How does an electron gun work? What evidence is there that it is producing negatively-charged particles? To answer these questions we shall do some experiments. It is easier to do experiments with specially constructed tubes than with a television tube itself. You may see some demonstrations with one or other of the special "electron tubes" shown in figure 19.3.

Both types of tube have a wire coil at one end which can be heated by passing an electric current through it. This wire is called the **heater**. Television tubes have the same sort of heater at one end of the electron gun.

We shall first look at some experiments that can be done with the tube shown in figure 19.3a. The large glass bulb shown in figure 19.3a is empty of air. It contains a metal plate at one end and a wire coil at the other. It is called

Figure 19.3a (below left)
A large diode valve.

Figure 19.3b (below right)
A fine-beam tube. The beam of electrons in a fine-beam tube collides with gas molecules, causing them to emit light. This is the way you can see the path of the electron beam in the tube.

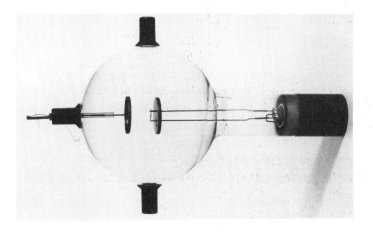

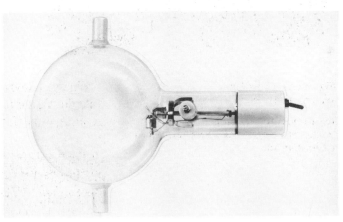

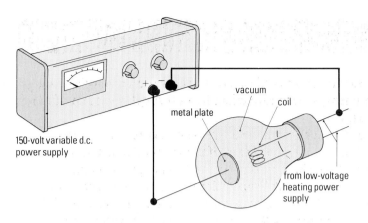

150-volt variable d.c.
power supply

vacuum

coil

metal plate

from low-voltage
heating power
supply

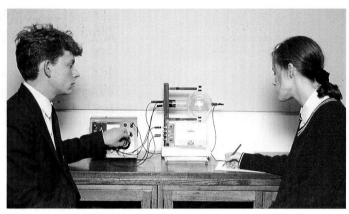

Figure 19.4 (above left)
A large diode valve in a circuit.

Figure 19.5 (above right)
Taking readings of current and voltage
using a diode valve.

a *diode*. The wire coil can be heated by passing a current through it from a
low-voltage supply. We shall refer to this supply as the "heating voltage".
When the diode is connected into the circuit shown in figure 19.4, the
ammeter shows a current is passing when the wire coil is made hot enough to
glow. You may see some experiments done with this circuit. If you do, you
should write down the observations you make using Worksheet **P**19A.

If you are unable to see the experiment yourself, look at the observations
two other people, Ian and Louise, made when they did the experiment (figure
19.5) and then try Worksheet **P**19A.

*This is not an experiment you should expect to do on your own. If you see the experiment, it will
probably be demonstrated to you.*

Two pupils made the following observations about the way a diode behaves
in a circuit.

- The galvanometer only shows a current to be flowing if the positive
  terminal of the high-voltage supply is connected to the cold plate, **and** the
  filament is hot enough to glow.
- If the temperature of the filament is reduced (by reducing the heating
  voltage) the current recorded by the galvanometer also goes down. If the
  filament was made hotter, the current recorded by the ammeter increases.
- The two experimenters then tried reducing the voltage of the high-voltage
  supply. They made sure that the heating voltage remained constant. They
  found that the current recorded by the galvanometer again went down.
- Next they tried increasing the high voltage. As a result the galvanometer
  reading went up. But when the voltage reached a particular value, the
  galvanometer reading did not go up any more, even if they continued to
  increase the voltage.

2a When Ian and Louise connected the high-voltage supply so that the **negative**
terminal was connected to the cold plate, no current was shown on the ammeter.
Another pupil said that might be because there was a fault in the circuit. After all,
that was the usual reason why no current flowed in circuits! What do you suggest
Louise should do to convince the other pupil there was no fault in the circuit?
b Why were Ian and Louise careful to see that the heating voltage did not change
when they were checking on the effect of changing the high-voltage supply?

You may return to Worksheet P19A later.

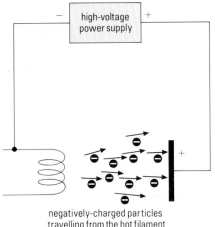

negatively-charged particles
travelling from the hot filament
to the positively-charged plate

Figure 19.6
Negatively-charged particles are attracted
to a positively-charged metal plate.

P19.3   The electron

In Chapter **P**16, we saw that an electric current in a wire is a flow of electric charge. In this experiment, an electric current flows through a vacuum. But it is still a flow of electric charge.

Ian and Louise's experiments with the diode (and maybe your own) showed that it would only conduct a current if the wire coil in it was made very hot. This suggests that whatever is carrying the charge across the vacuum (the "charge carriers" as they are called) comes from the hot wire.

You will remember that Ian and Louise found a current flowed only if the cold plate was connected to the **positive** terminal of the high-voltage supply. This suggests that the charge carriers carry a **negative** charge (figure 19.6).

3 *(For discussion)*
a What is the reason for thinking that the charge carriers only carry a negative charge?
b Can you suggest any other explanation for the results that Ian and Louise found in their experiment? If so, can you suggest how you would decide which explanation is the best?

One thing you might have suggested in answer to question **3b** is that the charge carriers are ions of metal atoms from the heated wire.

4 If the charge carriers **are** metal ions, what would you expect to find on the cold plate after a current had passed for some time?

In fact, no evidence has ever been found to support the idea that metal ions come off the hot wire to provide the current in the tube. Other experiments, which you may meet if you go on to do more work in physics, show that the charge carriers carrying the electric current through the tube are, in fact, **smaller** than atoms.

In Chapter **P**3, an atom is described as having a tiny, positively charged *nucleus* surrounded by a cloud of negatively charged *electrons*. It is suggested in that chapter that atoms become **ions** by gaining or losing one or more electrons.

The negatively-charged particles which carry the electric current in the diode are these same electrons. In fact, it was experiments such as the one you have just seen that led scientists to realize that atoms were not the unbreakable bits of matter they once thought they were. They realized that these small sub-atomic specks of negative charge must be a part of the atoms which go to make up the wire of the heater in the tube. Normally electrons cannot escape from the metal wire; but if the wire is made very hot, it becomes possible for them to "evaporate off" (figure 19.7).

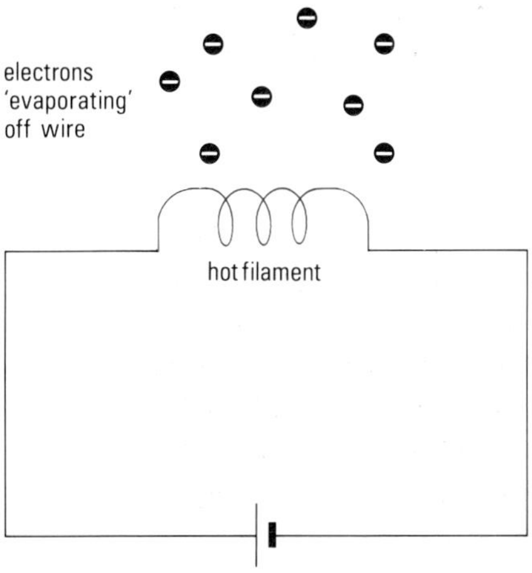

*You can now return to Worksheet **P**19A and try to answer the questions in the second part. These questions ask you to explain the observations you have made using the idea of electrons "evaporating" from the hot wire. However, it is not essential to do this part of the worksheet in order to understand the rest of this chapter.*

electrons
'evaporating'
off wire

hot filament

Figure 19.7
Electrons "evaporating" off a hot wire.

Using the "electron idea"

Theories become valuable when they can explain many **different** things. We will now try to see how "electrons" can help explain some other things.

Electric currents in wires

An electric current is a flow of charge. The charge carrier cannot be the metal atoms of the wire; they are packed too closely together to allow some of them to move. But the charge could be carried by electrons.

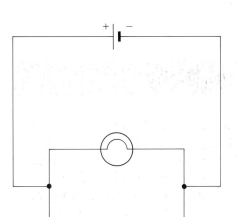

Figure 19.8
A lamp and resistor in parallel with a battery.

> **5** Look at the circuit in figure 19.8.
> **a** If the electric current was a flow of electrons, which way would it flow round the circuit?
> **b** What would happen to the electrons when they reached a junction?
> **c** What is the battery doing to the electrons?

Charging a plastic rod by friction

The plastic rod in figure 19.9 is given a negative charge by rubbing it with the cloth. Electrons are scraped off one object and given to the other.

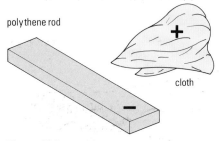

Figure 19.9
Charging a polythene rod by friction.

> **6a** Which object **loses** electrons – the cloth or the plastic rod?
> **b** Which object **gains** electrons – the cloth or the plastic rod?

You can find out more about the importance of electrons as parts of the atom in Chapter C18 of your Chemistry book.

An electron gun

We can now return to the "electron gun" that we saw first in the television tube. Suppose you drilled a hole in the cold positive plate in a diode (figure 19.10). The electrons "evaporated" off the hot wire are attracted to the cold, positive plate. The force of attraction to the positive plate makes them speed up as they cross the gap between the wire and the plate. Some of the charge carriers would reach the hole instead of hitting the plate, and they would go straight through. Now you have an electron "gun" which makes a stream of these carriers come out through the hole in the plate.

Figure 19.10
a The principle behind an electron gun. Electrons are attracted to a positively charged plate and some pass through the hole in the centre of the plate.
b An electron gun in a television tube. This is simplified as the gun also contains other electrodes (charged plates) as well, to focus the beam and vary its intensity.

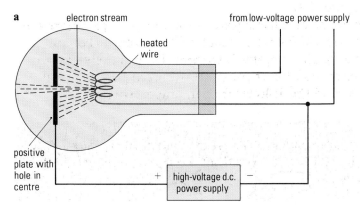

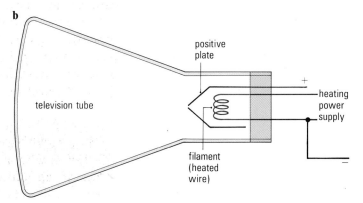

In the television picture tube the electrons make a bright spot on the screen by colliding with some special chemicals painted on the inside of the tube. You may be able to see this demonstrated in an electron tube like that shown in figure 19.3b. That tube also contains a low-pressure gas that makes the path of the electrons visible inside the tube.

P19.4   **The cathode-ray oscilloscope**

When scientists first started doing experiments with electron beams, they had not invented the name "electron". Instead they used another name for them. They called them "cathode rays". In the nineteenth century, Michael Faraday invented special names for positive and negative plates he had used in his work in electricity. He called the positive one the *anode* and the negative one the *cathode*. When in later years it was discovered that an electric current could travel in a vacuum, the charge carriers were called *cathode rays* because the charge carriers travelled from the negative plate (cathode) to the positive one. Although today we know these charge carriers are electrons, the old name has stuck. Perhaps a cathode-ray oscilloscope ought to be called an "electron-beam oscilloscope".

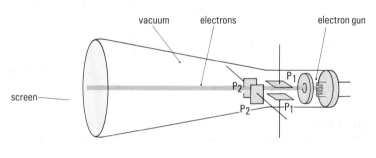

plates provide electric force to swing the electron stream up and down and across and back

Figure 19.11 (above left)
A cathode ray oscilloscope of the sort you may have in school.

Figure 19.12 (above right)
A cathode ray tube. The beam can be deflected by voltages across the plates P_1P_1 and P_2P_2.

The picture in figure 19.11 shows a cathode-ray oscilloscope (often shortened to CRO) of the sort you may have seen already. Inside it contains a glass bulb very like a television tube – in fact it works in the same way. Electrons are produced by an electron gun at the back of the tube. These hit the front of the tube and produce a bright spot on the special paint inside.

The electron beam can be moved up and down by attaching a battery to the terminals on the front of the CRO. To understand how this works, look at the cathode-ray tube in figure 19.12.

Inside the tube are two pairs of metal plates. Connecting the pair nearest to the electron gun (P_1P_1) to a high-voltage supply will cause one to become positively charged and the other negatively charged. The positively-charged plate will attract the electrons while the negatively-charged plate will repel them. The electron beam will be deflected from its original course.

7 Suppose that the top plate of the pair of plates P_1P_1 in figure 19.12 is connected to the positive terminal of a d.c. power supply. Explain the direction in which the electron beam is deflected.

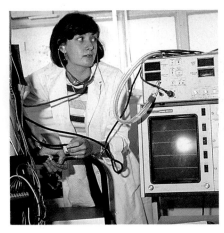

Figure 19.13
Using a cathode ray oscilloscope to monitor someone's heart beat.

If the voltage across the deflecting plates is increased, they become more highly charged and the beam is deflected more. The tube inside a cathode-ray oscilloscope has **two** sets of plates like this (figure 19.12).

One set (P_1P_1) will deflect the beam vertically and the other set (P_2P_2) will deflect the beam horizontally. The terminals on the outside of the oscilloscope connect a voltage to the vertical-deflection plates.

Because the electron beam deflection changes whenever the deflecting plate voltage changes, the cathode-ray oscilloscope can be used as a *voltmeter*. The usefulness of a cathode-ray oscilloscope lies in the fact that the electron beam responds **almost instantly** to a change of voltage on the deflecting plates. It can thus be used to follow very fast voltage changes, such as those which can be produced by a patient's heart beat (figure 19.13). In Chapter **P20** you can learn how changes in light, sound and temperature can all be turned into changes in electric voltages. Oscilloscopes can then be used to display these changes in voltage.

*Worksheet **P**19B describes some experiments you can do to learn to use a cathode-ray oscilloscope.*

P19.5   Making television pictures

The bright spot produced by the electron beam on the front of the electron tube in a cathode-ray oscilloscope is like a very simple television picture. Look at the newspaper picture in figure 19.14a using a magnifying glass. You will see that it is built-up from many tiny dots. The only difference between the dots is in their colour and how dark or light they are. An enlarged portion of the picture is shown in figure 19.14b. It is difficult to make much sense of this enlarged portion. The whole picture looks all right because the dots are very small and close together.

A television picture is built-up in the same way. The electron beam sweeps over the face of the tube producing dots of light. Each spot the beam produces is called a *pixel* (the word comes from an abbreviation of the two words "picture element"). Each dot is of a different brightness. If the picture is built-up quickly enough, the eye will see a complete picture on the screen.

Figure 19.14
a (left) A newspaper photograph.
b (right) An enlarged portion of the photograph in **a**.

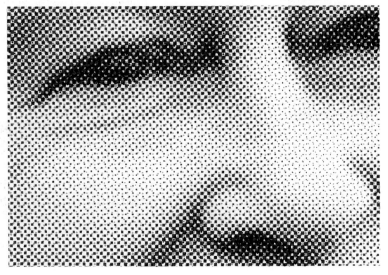

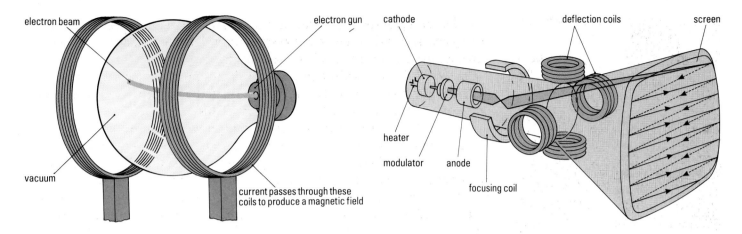

electron beam

electron gun

cathode

deflection coils

screen

vacuum

current passes through these coils to produce a magnetic field

heater

modulator

anode

focusing coil

Figure 19.15 (above left)
Deflecting an electron beam using a
magnetic field.

Figure 19.16 (above right)
The electron beam sweeps backwards and
forwards across the face of the television
tube. Each picture is built up from 625
lines, in $\frac{1}{25}$ of a second. The dotted lines
show the path of the electron beam from
the end of one line to the beginning of the
next. This is called flyback and is not part
of the picture.

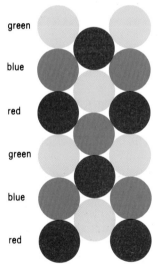

green

blue

red

green

blue

red

Figure 19.17
Colour television pictures are made up
from a pattern of red, green and blue dots.

Another way of deflecting an electron beam

There is a difficulty in deflecting an electron beam by charging up metal plates
inside the tube. First of all, for big deflections, the plates can get in the way of
the beam. Secondly, the plates need high voltages. The diagram in figure
19.15 shows another way of deflecting an electron beam. This time the beam
is deflected by the magnetic field produced by a current through the coils. The
bigger the current through the coils, the bigger the deflection of the beam.

This is the way the beam is deflected in a television tube. However, the
deflection coils are a different shape from those shown in figure 19.15. By
changing the current through the deflection coils steadily with time, the beam
can be made to sweep over the screen in the pattern shown in figure 19.16.

Building up a picture

As the beam sweeps over the face of the tube, the brightness of the spot
changes. The brightness of a spot on the screen is controlled by the number of
electrons hitting it. Inside the picture tube is a special plate in front of the
electron gun called the *modulator* (figure 19.16). The size of the voltage on this
plate controls the number of electrons travelling towards a particular spot on
the front of the tube.

The deflection coils swing the beam over the screen "painting" a picture as
it goes. It takes $\frac{1}{25}$ of a second to build up one complete picture, and then the
beam starts on another one. Our eyes cannot respond so quickly to such
changes, and so the pictures seem to blend smoothly into each other.

Colour television works in the same way, but it builds up three overlapping
pictures in red, green and blue dots (figure 19.17). As you will see in Chapter
P15, these colours can combine together to give the impression of every
colour in the spectrum.

Summary

Look at the diagram of the inside of the television picture tube shown in
figure 19.2. Explain the function of each of the following:

the electron gun
the grid in front of the electron gun
the deflection coils.

Chapter P20   Control

An introduction to electronics

In this chapter you will be able to see how the work you have done on circuits, current, voltage and magnetism can be put to good use. You will be applying the physics of electricity to an area called **electronics**.

The chapter starts by looking at some simple circuits, but introduces some new items which you can use to build them. As in Chapter **P**16, *we shall use the general name* **components** *to describe items we use in the circuits. In a very short time, you will be asked to put them to use to do some useful jobs.*

You will not be asked to understand the technical details of how the new components work. You can do this later if you decide to continue your interest in electronics. For the moment you should just concentrate on the application of principles you already know to produce new circuits that will enable you to control electricity in a useful way. By the end of the chapter you should have used a computer to control lights, motors and buzzers in ways that can, for example, improve the quality of life for a handicapped person.

P20.1   Switches

In the first part of this chapter we shall consider some switches which are different from the simple *on/off switch* you have used so far. These new switches play an important part in electronics.

The circuit diagram of the on/off switch is shown in figure 20.1a. Another switch you will be using is called a *push-button switch*. When the push-button is pressed, the switch is closed to complete the circuit. The circuit symbol and a picture of such a switch are shown in figure 20.1b.

A third useful type of switch is called the *reed switch*. This type of switch does not need to be pushed by you. It uses a different method of closing the contact and completing the circuit.

You should be able to remember from Chapter **P**18 that if a magnet is brought near a piece of soft iron, it causes the soft iron itself to become a magnet. One end of the iron becomes a south pole and the other a north pole.

The reed switch (figure 20.2a) has contacts made of soft iron. Without a magnet near it, the springiness of the metal keeps the contacts apart. Under a magnifying glass you would see something like the diagram in figure 20.2b.

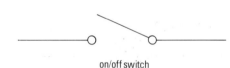

on/off switch

Figure 20.1a
The circuit symbol for a normal on/off switch.

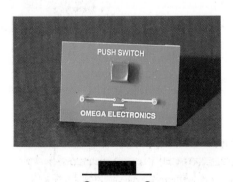

push button switch

Figure 20.1b
A push-button switch mounted on a board and its circuit symbol.

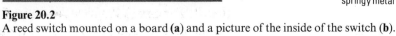

springy metal

Figure 20.2
A reed switch mounted on a board (**a**) and a picture of the inside of the switch (**b**).

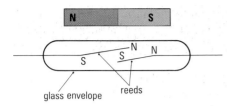

Figure 20.3
How a reed switch can be closed by a magnet.

To close the contacts we can bring up a magnet. The two contacts (called the "reeds") become magnetized (as shown in figure 20.3). They attract each other and close the switch.

1 What do you think would happen if the magnet in figure 20.3 were reversed?

2 The reed switch could be used as part of an alarm to warn when a door closes. Draw a diagram to show how you could use a reed switch that caused a lamp to light when a door was closed.

Detector switches: a light switch

You may have seen on television a thief setting off an alarm by walking through a light beam. To detect changes in light levels we use something called a *light dependent resistor* (*LDR* for short). A picture and circuit symbol for an LDR are shown in figure 20.4.

You came across the idea of *electrical resistance* in Chapter P17. The higher the electrical resistance of a conductor, the more difficult it is to "push" a current through it.

A switch can be thought of as something that has a very **high** resistance when it is "open" and a very **low** resistance when it is "closed". The LDR can be used as a switch because its resistance changes with the level of light falling on it. In very bright light its resistance is low. In the circuit shown in figure 20.5a, the LDR acts as a switch which is closed.

In the dark its resistance is very high. In the circuit shown in figure 20.5b, the LDR allows very little current to pass and so acts as a switch which is open.

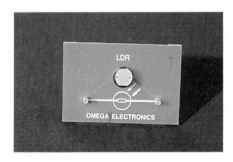

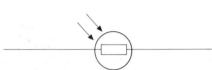

Figure 20.4
A light dependent resistor.

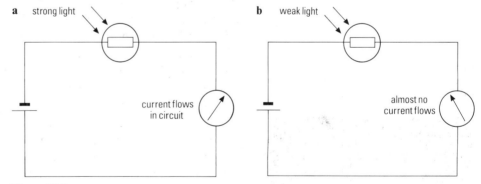

Figure 20.5
a A light-dependent resistor in strong light.
b A light-dependent resistor in weak light.

In earlier work with electrical circuits we have often used a lamp to show whether a current is flowing or not. Most components used in electronics do not carry large enough currents to light an ordinary filament lamp. For this reason we will often use another component called a *light emitting diode* (*LED* for short). There are two important differences between an LED and a filament lamp. First of all, the LED lights up in response to a much smaller current than the lamp – the sort of current electronic components can pass. Secondly, the LED will **only** work if it is connected the correct way round in a circuit. The circuit diagram for an LED is shown in figure 20.6. The arrow shows the direction in which a current **can** flow through it.

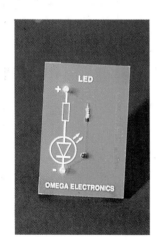

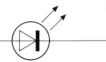

Figure 20.6
A light emitting diode.

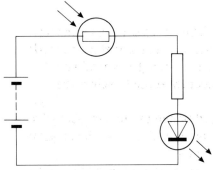

Figure 20.7
A light emitting diode in series with a light dependent resistor. In weak light the resistance of the LDR will be so high that the LED will not light.

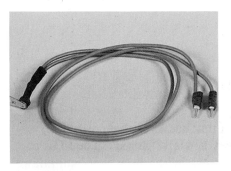

Figure 20.8
A thermistor.

Even in very bright light, an LDR allows only a small current to flow. Therefore it will be able to control an LED "lamp", but not an ordinary lamp in series with it (see figure 20.7).

Detector switches: a thermal switch

To detect changes in temperature we can use a device called a *thermistor* (figure 20.8). We shall call this a thermal switch. Its resistance changes with temperature and it can be used to control the current flowing in a circuit in a similar way to a light dependent resistor.

You should now try experiment 1 in Worksheet P20A.

P20.2   Control circuits

In a car the starter switch (usually operated by the ignition key) is on the dashboard. A starter motor may need a current as large as 300 A to be able to turn over the engine to start the car. 300 A is a very large current.

> **3** Using Ohm's Law (see Chapter **P17**) work out the total resistance in a circuit in which a 12-volt battery can give a current of 300 A.

To have a resistance as low as this, the wire needs to be very thick and as short as possible. The starter switch is some distance from the starter motor, so the starter switch is used to switch on a **small** current which can be used to control the **large** current needed by the starter motor. In this way the wire between battery and motor can be kept as short as possible. In a car, the device which allows this small current to control a large one is called a *relay*. (How a relay works is described in section **P18.5**.) The circuit controlled by the starter switch is a *control circuit* (figure 20.9).

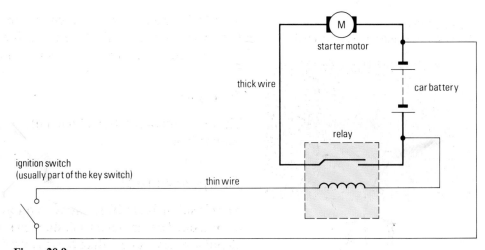

Figure 20.9
The starter motor circuits in a car. The high current needed by the motor can be controlled via the relay by a very small current passing through the ignition switch.

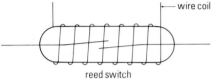

Figure 20.10
A reed relay.

Figure 20.12a
A small buzzer and its circuit symbol.

Figure 20.12b
A small motor and its circuit symbol.

Using a reed relay

You have already seen how a reed switch can be closed using a permanent magnet. Instead of using a permanent magnet, we can magnetize the reeds using the magnetic effect produced by a current through a coil of wire. We call this an electromagnet. The electromagnet can be used to close the contacts of the reed switch.

In practice the coil is wound round the reed switch but for simplicity its circuit symbol shows the coil to one side, as in figure 20.11. As the diagram shows, the reed switch links two **separate** circuits.

Using one circuit to control another plays an important part in electronics. What happens in the controlling part of the circuit is called the *input*. What happens (as a result) in the other circuit is called the *output*.

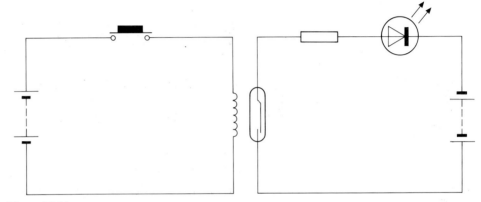

Figure 20.11
Using a reed relay to link two circuits.

Output devices

Now we will look at some of the devices we can control using control circuits. The simplest output device you might want to control is an LED "lamp", switching it on and off. Photographs and circuit symbols for two more useful output devices which you can use are shown in figure 20.12.

The buzzer

This device makes a sound when an electric current passes through it. The buzzer you use may only "work" if it is connected the right way round. It is marked with a " + " and a " − " sign to help you connect it up correctly.

The motor

The direction of rotation of the motor can be reversed by changing round the connections.

Relays in control

The circuit in figure 20.13a shows how an LDR can be used to switch a motor on and off. The ammeters will show that the current flowing in the **input circuit** is much smaller than the current flowing through the **output circuit**. By using a reed relay to link the two circuits, the low-current LDR can be used to control a high-current motor. You may see a demonstration of this.

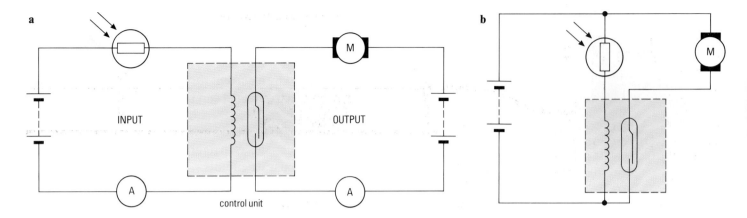

Figure 20.13
a Using a reed relay as a control unit.
b Another way of wiring up the circuit in **a**. This time only one battery is used.

Figure 20.13b shows how we can use **one** battery or power supply instead of two to do the same job. The motor and the relay coil share the same power supply. Electronic circuits often make one power supply do several jobs.

You can now make up some circuits using a reed relay. Experiment 2 on Worksheet P20A shows you some you can set up.

Use a thermal switch, a reed relay and an output device to tell you when the temperature of a liquid reaches a certain temperature. A similar device could be used by a blind person to warn when a pan of milk is warm enough to be used for a drink.

Design a circuit to tell you when it is raining outside so you can get the washing in. For this you will have to make your own detector. *Hint:* water with a little salt in it will conduct electricity.

Draw a circuit which would turn on the motor of a fan when the temperature of a room gets above a certain point.

The reed relay is not the only device that can link an input to its output. Electronic circuits can be built from other components to do the same sort of job as the relay does in linking circuits together. These circuits can be so small that they are no bigger than a single resistor. But they are all there to do the same job – to link an input to its output.

We shall use the term *control unit* to describe a device that links an input circuit to an output circuit. Figure 20.14 shows a control unit found in many homes and offices. It is a central heating thermostat. This control unit switches the central heating on and off in response to changes in room temperature.

Figure 20.14
A domestic central heating thermostat.

You will find out how some organs in the body act as "control units" to enable the body to function correctly in Chapter B12 of your Biology book. Body organs do not function in the same way as electronic control units, but the basic principles are the same. For example, both have inputs and outputs.

Making circuits containing control units

Complex arrangements, such as the control units in a washing machine, may have more than one input and more than one output circuit. All of these circuits need a supply of electricity. Often, as in your experiments, they use the same supply.

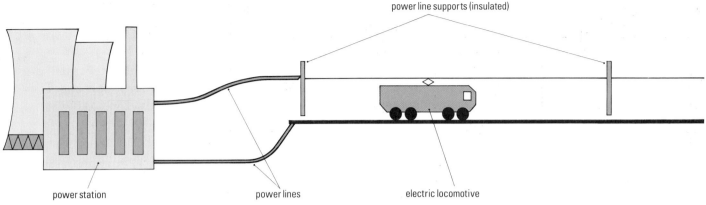

power line supports (insulated)

power station

power lines

electric locomotive

Figure 20.15
An electric train draws its current from the overhead wire. The rails form the other part of the circuit back to the power station. Many trains can run between the same overhead wire and rails.

Using control units

When an electric train needs electricity to run, it raises its supply contact until this touches the overhead electric cables. This completes the circuit, and current can flow through the electric motor to the track below. In electronics a similar arrangement is used to supply current to the components. One wire comes from the positive terminal of the power supply and is called the *positive line*. The other wire comes from the negative terminal and is called the *negative line*. You should be careful to connect your control units the right way round between these two lines. Not doing this might damage the control units.

Many trains use the same track and power lines. In the same way we can provide the voltage for many control units as well as for their inputs and outputs using just **two** "lines" – one positive and the other negative. You have already seen an example of this in figure 20.13b.

Figure 20.16
Setting the controls on an automatic gas cooker.

Gas	Cooking time	Warning light
OFF	OFF	ON
OFF	ON	ON
ON	OFF	ON
ON	ON	OFF

Figure 20.17
The behaviour of the control unit.

P20.3   Another type of control unit

Have you ever tried cooking a meal using an automatic timing control on a gas cooker? To make the cooker work properly, you have to remember to do several things! First you set the clock time for the cooker to start cooking. Most people remember to do that! But then you have to remember to switch on the gas **and** set the length of time for which the meal is to cook (figure 20.16).

Imagine you have to design a warning device to remind you to switch on the gas **and** to set the time for the meal to cook. The warning device could, for example, be a red light that only went out when both operations have been completed. Figure 20.17 shows a table which summarizes what such a control unit would have to do.

You need a new control unit to do this sort of job which requires two inputs. There are several different control units that use two inputs. If you go on to do more work in electronics, you will learn about them there. For now, we shall just look at one such control unit called a *NAND unit*. The word "NAND" comes from the two words "Not AND". It refers to a control unit like the one just mentioned. The warning light (which is controlled by the output of the control unit) must be **not** ON only if the gas tap is ON **and** the cooking time is set.

You can now try using a NAND control unit. You will find some instructions in Worksheet P20B. You should try to do experiment 1 before reading the next section.
The next section summarizes some of the things you will have discovered in your experiment.

A NAND unit has **two** inputs, A and B in figure 20.18. The output lamp can be switched on by connecting either A or B to the negative supply line. The lamp is only switched off if both A **and** B are connected to the positive supply line.

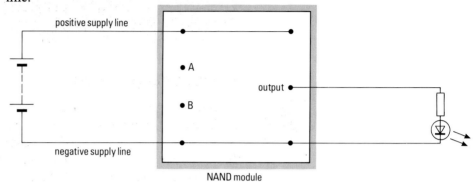

Figure 20.18
A NAND control unit. This unit could do the work of a gas cooker control unit.

We can show the results of your experiment with a NAND unit in a table. But first, here is a shorthand way of saying "on" and "off", or "connect to positive supply line" and "connect to negative supply line". Connecting an input to the positive line puts a **high** voltage on the input of the control unit. Electronic engineers often represent this with a "1". Connecting an input to the negative line puts a **low** voltage on the input. This can be represented by a "0". Similarly, if the lamp connected to the output is **on**, there is a **high** voltage across it – represented by the figure "1". If the lamp is **off** there is a **low** voltage at the output – represented by the figure "0".

We can now represent the results of your experiment with a NAND unit by the table in figure 20.19.

Input A	Input B	Output P
0	0	1
0	1	1
1	0	1
1	1	0

Figure 20.19
The behaviour of a NAND control unit.

4 How could you use a NAND unit to make a warning light that only went **off** if you switched on the gas and set the cooking time when using the cooker described earlier?

The NAND control unit enables us to turn an output device **off** when both the inputs to the NAND unit are **high**. To solve some of the problems you may meet, you will want to turn an output device **on** when both the inputs to

Figure 20.20
A control unit which uses two NAND units.

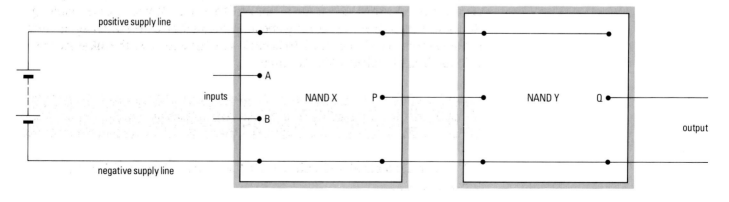

the NAND unit are **high**. Experiment 2 in Worksheet **P20B** shows you how we can do this using two NAND units.

*You can now try experiment 2 in Worksheet **P20B**.*

> **5** Look at the circuit in figure 20.20. Make a table similar to the one in figure 20.19, to show all the inputs to NAND unit X and the corresponding output from NAND unit Y. This output is marked Q in figure 20.20.

Making a burglar alarm

If a burglar enters a house he could be detected if he crosses a light beam. This can be used to operate an alarm. But a good alarm needs to continue to sound even if the burglar steps out of the beam. How can we design a burglar alarm that will operate and **stay on** when someone crosses a light beam? Look at figure 20.21. This shows two NAND units linked together.

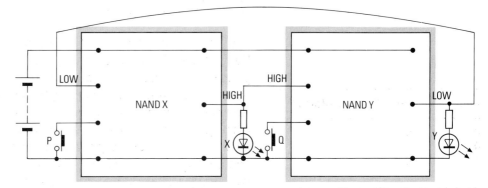

Figure 20.21
A bistable unit.

You have already experimented with two linked NAND units (figure 20.20). In the circuit in figure 20.21, the output from NAND unit Y is taken back to the input of NAND unit X.

*To see how two NAND units connected together in this way behave, you should now use Worksheet **P20C** to help you set up such a circuit.*

You will have found from your experiment that when the circuit is switched on, one LED is on and the other is off. Look again at figure 20.21. In the diagram LED X is ON and LED Y is OFF. By pressing switch Q, the lights change over. Now LED X is OFF and LED Y is ON. If you release switch Q, the lights stay in their new arrangement. Pressing that same switch again does nothing more. To change the LEDs back, you have to press the **other** switch, P. This circuit is called a *bistable* circuit.

> **6** Explain why a circuit such as this is referred to as a "bistable" circuit.

You can use a bistable circuit to solve the burglar alarm problem on Worksheet **P20C**.

P20.4   Solving problems

This chapter has shown you how electronics can be used for control. Industry is increasingly using electronics to provide solutions to problems. So far in this chapter you have been given problems to solve. Now it is your turn to find a problem! You are a member of a small team. Imagine that your team has been asked by an industrial manager to show how electronics can be used to help his company.

1 Your group has to think first of some simple problems in a factory of their choice that may be able to be solved using the components you have met in this chapter. Agree on one problem.
2 Before trying out a solution to the problem using your electronic components, you should "talk it through" with your group. One successful way this can be done is for each of you to think up some ideas which are then discussed by the group. The group must then decide on one possible solution.
3 Now use the electronic components to try out the solution.
4 You will be very lucky if the group's first ideas work! If they don't, the group has to go back to *2* and select another solution.
5 The group should finally write a short report for the manager.

P20.5   Microelectronics

The rest of this chapter deals briefly with how it is possible to solve more complicated problems using more control units.

From television, books and magazines you will have heard about *microelectronics* and the so-called "chip". Microelectronics is the technology which enables the building of very small electronic circuits. It is possible to put many circuits (such as NAND and bistable units) together in a very small space by making them on thin layers of silicon (the "chip"). A magnified view of a silicon chip is shown in figure 20.22. You will be able to see one under a microscope.

Another name for a silicon chip containing many circuits is an *integrated circuit*, or IC for short. An integrated circuit can now contain as many as 100 000 circuits, similar to the ones you have been using, in the space of a 5-mm square.

Although you will have used one of these circuits at some time you may not have been aware of it. Your calculator, "digital" watch, the television at home or even the washing machine, toaster or microwave cooker has one or more "chips" at the "heart" of its **control** unit.

Certain complex control units use integrated circuits called *microprocessors*. Microprocessors are at the heart of the machines illustrated in figure 20.23. Once they have been set up, it is difficult to change the tasks they will perform. They are wired up to respond in a fixed way to certain inputs. For example, when buttons are pressed on the washing

Figure 20.22
A tiny integrated circuit. A unit like this may contain thousands of circuits linked together.

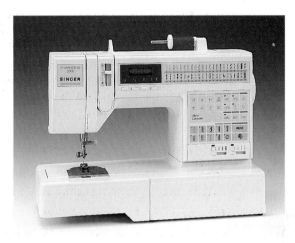

Figure 20.23
Two microprocessor-controlled machines.

machine it will go through all the sequences in a particular wash cycle. **You cannot change the sequence in the washing cycle.**

Microprocessors are also at the heart of *microcomputers* (figure 20.24). The main difference between the microprocessors in a microcomputer and those in the machines in figure 20.23 is that microcomputers can be given new instructions to change the sequence of operations they carry out.

Figure 20.24
A school microcomputer.

For example, to solve the problems set for you earlier you had to wire up special circuits using your control units. To solve a different problem, you had to make a different circuit. A computer can be used to solve many different problems by simply giving it new *instructions*. These instructions will control how the microprocessor behaves as a control unit.

Giving a computer instructions is called *programming*. The set of instructions called a program can be put into the computer in a number of ways:

- from magnetic tape
- from a magnetic disc
- from a keyboard, similar to a typewriter's.

Suppose we want to use a computer to control a set of traffic lights. The first thing we have to do is to write down what the traffic lights are to do. You might start off with:

"**1** Switch on red light and switch off yellow and green lights.
2 Keep red light on for two minutes.
3 ..."

7 Continue writing down the list of instructions until you have gone through one complete cycle (so that you are back to instruction 1 again). Write down a similar list for two sets of traffic lights at a junction.

This series of instructions must now be given to the computer.

Interfaces

Outputs from the computer to operate traffic lights are connected through a circuit called an *interface*. This must be used to protect the computer circuits from damage.

Figure 20.25 shows you a picture of an interface that can be connected to a school microcomputer. You will see that this interface has four outputs. These outputs are controlled by the computer so that they will switch **on** or **off** other devices connected to them.

The diagram below shows the arrangement to light one LED from switch A.

Figure 20.25
An interface unit that enables a computer to control a variety of output devices, such as lamps and motors.

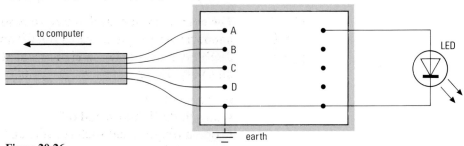

Figure 20.26
How a computer might be connected to an output interface and used to light a light-emitting diode.

Once the computer has been connected by an interface to some traffic lights, the set of instructions you have written can be used to control them. However the computer can only work using a *language* of its own. The instructions have to be turned into this special language before they can be used to control the traffic lights. Worksheet **P20D** explains how you can use a school computer and an interface to control some lights and even make the lights behave in the way traffic lights would do.

If you are able to do this, you can try solving the next problem.

Use the computer to switch on or off a single LED at each of the four switches.

Try to use the program to build the traffic lights we talked about earlier. You will use three LEDs as the lights, so you will need three of the output lines.

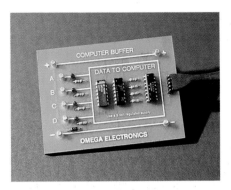

Figure 20.27
An interface unit that can be connected to a computer to allow it to use inputs from sensors.

Inputs to the computers

So far you have used a computer to follow a set of instructions **you** have provided. But what if you wanted to use a computer to control, say, the temperature in a number of rooms in a house? The "instructions" would have to come from something that could measure the temperature of the rooms – something we call a temperature *sensor*. To make computers respond to instructions of this sort, we use another sort of interface.

This interface also has four circuits that can be used. The computer can recognize whether the outputs of the interface are **high** or **low**. The outputs to the computer can be changed by connecting a switch, or any of the switch **sensors** that you have used earlier in the chapter, to the output of the interface.

You can find out more about the input interface on Worksheet **P20D**. Use an input interface to help you solve the next problem.

Make the traffic lights change when an input goes high from a light beam being broken. This would happen in reality when a sensor on the "lights" detects a car approaching. You will see the sensor on the top of traffic lights at quiet junctions or at road works. It helps avoid delays.

We now have a control system that can be used to undertake many different tasks if it is programmed by you correctly.

Computers and the handicapped

The microcomputer and microprocessor can also be used to help handicapped people to lead a full life and to cope with tasks that their disability makes difficult. Handicapped people have very different degrees of disability. For example they may find it difficult to:

● open curtains
● switch the lights on and off
● operate equipment such as radio and television
● control the temperature of the room.

Many of these tasks can now be undertaken by controlling the input to a microprocessor.

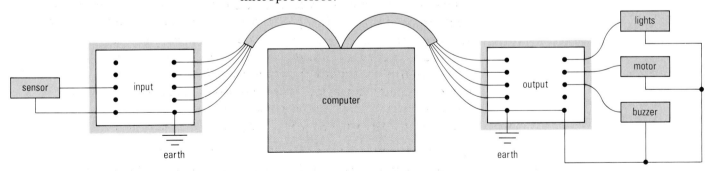

Figure 20.28
A block diagram of an aid for a handicapped person.

Design a control system that a handicapped person could use for some task that might normally be difficult for him or her to do. If you want to, you can use a computer with an input and output interface in your design.

Chapter P21   Communication
Transferring information electrically

P21.1   Introduction

We often write down messages and send them to each other through the post. Even today this is a slow process. In this chapter we are going to consider quicker means of communication. Simply by lifting a telephone receiver and dialling the right set of numbers, you can talk to someone on the other side of the world. In the process, your conversation may well be "beamed" to a satellite and then back to Earth. To understand something of how modern communication systems work we must look at the story of their invention and at the scientific principles used. Finally we will see how the basic technology has been developed in response to demand.

Some history

Until modern times, the distance over which communication could take place was limited to how far a person could see or hear. Communication using sight achieved greater distances than methods that relied on hearing. For example, in Chapter **P**13 you saw how signal beacons were used to warn of the approach of the Spanish Armada.

---

1 Figure 21.1 shows four kinds of primitive communication.
a Explain how each method works.
b The method of communication shown in figure 21.1d has a number of limitations (this means that it cannot be used in every situation). Describe two limitations it suffers from.

Figure 21.1
Four kinds of primitive communication.

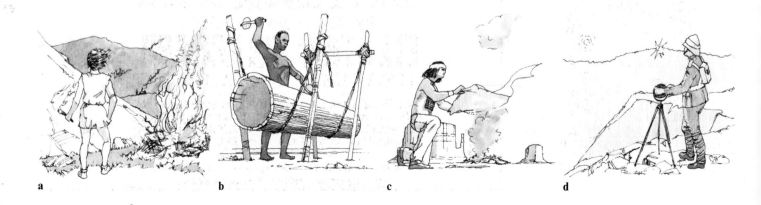

a   b   c   d

Now try to work out this message:

Figure 21.2
The semaphore code.

Messages could be sent using a code. *Semaphore* makes use of arm or flag positions to send messages which can be seen from a kilometre or so (figure 21.2). However, long messages take both time and skill to send. It also takes skill to decode the message at the other end.

P21.2   Communication using electricity

As you saw in Chapter **P**18, Hans Oersted discovered that an electric current produces a magnetic field which can in turn affect nearby magnets. This led to the earliest form of electrical signalling called the electric *telegraph*.

2 Look at the picture in figure 21.3a. Find out how the operator makes the needles on the telegraph move.

Figure 21.3a (below left)
An early electric telegraph.

Figure 21.3b (below right)
An advertisement inviting people to see the electric telegraph in operation when it was first introduced.

When a person at one end (usually called the *sender*) wants to get in touch with someone at the other (the *receiver*), he or she closes a switch. This causes a current to flow in the wires. At the receiving end, the current causes a needle to move one way or the other.

Under the Special Patronage of Her Majesty

And H. R. H. Prince Albert

GALVANIC AND MAGNETO
ELECTRIC TELEGRAPH,
GT. WESTERN RAILWAY.

The Public are respectfully informed that this interesting & most extraordinary Apparatus, by which upwards of 50 SIGNALS can be transmitted to a Distance of 280,000 MILES in ONE MINUTE,

May be seen in operation, daily, (Sundays excepted,) from 9 till 8, at the
Telegraph Office, Paddington,

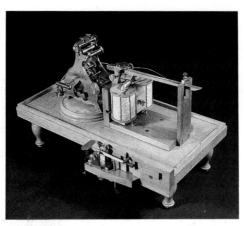

Figure 21.4
A Morse code transmitter.

Figure 21.5
An early telephone.

An American inventor, Samuel Morse, invented a special code for sending messages by electric telegraph. The electrical "signal" that passes along the wire is used to operate a buzzer. On its own, the sound of a buzzer does not tell the receiver much more than the fact that the sender wants to get in touch, so Morse used a series of long and short "buzzes" to represent the letters of the alphabet. These "dots and dashes" became known as the Morse code. It is still in use today for some communications over long distances.

You may have seen "cowboy" films in which this telegraph system is used. The system replaced the "pony express" as the fastest way of sending messages over the thousands of miles from the East to the West coast of America. The problem with the system is the speed at which the operators can "code" the messages into Morse and then "decode" them at the other end. Using Worksheet **P21A**, you can send messages across the laboratory using Morse code. You might also try sending messages in Morse using a mirror to flash "dots" and "dashes".

In 1876, there was a further advance in electrical communication when Alexander Bell demonstrated his invention of the *telephone* (figure 21.5). The telephone enables sender and receiver to talk directly to each other. This is now such an important means of communication that it is worth investigating how the telephone works.

Sound, as you have seen in Chapter **P15**, causes vibrations in the air. These can be turned into electrical signals using a *microphone*. Several sorts of microphone are in use. One of the simplest is shown in figure 21.6.

Carbon particles are packed behind a flexible metal sheet called a *diaphragm*. As the sound vibrations make the diaphragm vibrate, the carbon particles are squeezed and released. This changes their electrical resistance. An inwards movement on the diaphragm of the microphone in figure 21.6 will squeeze up the carbon particles. This makes their resistance low and a larger-than-normal current flows in the telephone wires.

In a similar way, an outwards movement of the diaphragm makes the resistance high and a smaller-than-normal current flows in the telephone wires. Thus the current flowing in the wires varies in time with the vibrations of the diaphragm.

Another form of microphone is shown in figure 21.7. In this type the movement of the diaphragm causes the magnetic field in a coil to change. If you studied the last part of Chapter **P18** you will understand that this causes an *induced current* to flow in the coil. The induced current will vary in time with the vibrations of the diaphragm.

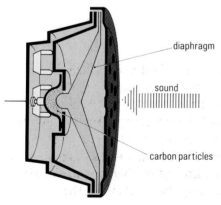

diaphragm

sound

carbon particles

Figure 21.6
A carbon microphone.

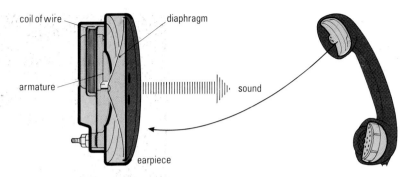

coil of wire   diaphragm

armature

sound

earpiece

Figure 21.7 (above left)
A "moving coil" microphone. Such microphones are often referred to as dynamic microphones.

Figure 21.8 (above right)
A telephone handset. This uses a moving coil microphone and a moving coil earpiece.

3 (Only try this question if you have done the experiments on electromagnetic induction in Chapter **P18**.) Explain why the induced current in the microphone illustrated in figure 21.7 varies with the vibrations of the diaphragm.

When the small electrical signals from the microphone reach the *receiver* (or *earpiece*) at the other end of the cable, they must move another diaphragm in order to make the sounds. The changing currents pass through a coil which is wrapped around a permanent magnet. The magnetic field changes in time with the changing current (figure 21.8). The result is that a soft iron diaphragm fixed just in front of the magnet moves backwards and forwards. This causes the air in front of it to vibrate and a sound is heard.

Worksheet **P21A** gives you an experiment which shows you how speech can be transmitted along wires.

The sounds of your voice or of a musical instrument are quite complex. You saw in Chapter **P19** how we can use a cathode-ray oscilloscope to look at the output from a microphone and see the way its output follows the patterns of the sound falling on it (figure 21.9). If you did not have time to do the experiment in Worksheet **P19B**, you might like to try it now.

*Many organisms use electrical signals for communication. This is the way messages are sent from one part of the organism to another along nerve fibres. You can learn more about nerve fibres in Chapter **B11** of your Biology book. You will see that nerves are likened to complex telephone cables.*

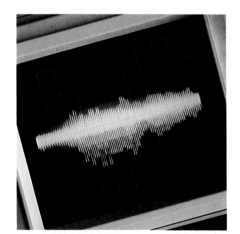

Figure 21.9
The pattern produced on a cathode ray oscilloscope screen by the output from a microphone when someone speaks into it.

Analogue signals

The currents that flow between sender and receiver in the simple telephone system we have just looked at vary in almost exactly the same way as the sound vibrations producing them (figure 21.10, on the next page). Systems that transmit information in this way are called *analogue* systems. We use the same sort of word when we describe one thing as being an "analogy" of something else. We mean the two things are alike in many ways. An analogue system is one in which changes in one thing (more often than not an electric current or voltage) imitate changes in something else (in this case the vibrations produced by a sound wave).

4 A music record or a tape cassette are often parts of an analogue system.
a What is imitated on the record or tape?
b How does each make its imitation?

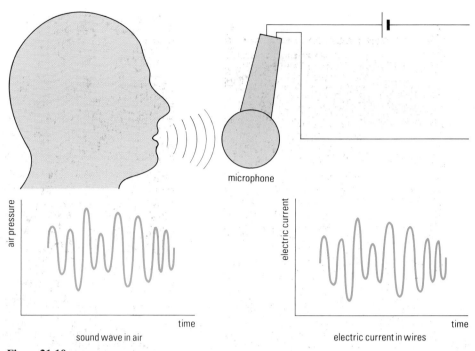

Figure 21.10
The pattern of the variations in current produced by a microphone is exactly like the pattern of the sound wave falling on the microphone.

The telephone system

Although the "sender" and "receiver" also have to be connected together by wires, the telephone has great advantages over the telegraph.

5 What are the advantages of the telephone over the telegraph?

In 1877 the first telephone exchange was opened in Britain which allowed many different people to be connected by telephone *operators*, using complex switching circuitry.

Soon after this, different telephone exchanges were themselves linked together. The cables connecting different exchanges have to carry many different signals. These cables are called *trunk lines*. Nowadays, links between telephone users (still referred to as *subscribers*) are mostly made automatically. The system which allows subscribers to be connected automatically along trunk lines is referred to as *subscriber trunk dialling* (usually shortened to STD).

The telephone system has not been bettered as a communication system which enables two people to talk to each other over a long distance. But for some purposes, the telephone system we have just described does have one major disadvantage; the "sending" and "receiving" equipment still have to be connected together by wires. It is called a point-to-point communication system.

6 What disadvantages are there in having to connect the sending and receiving equipment by wires?

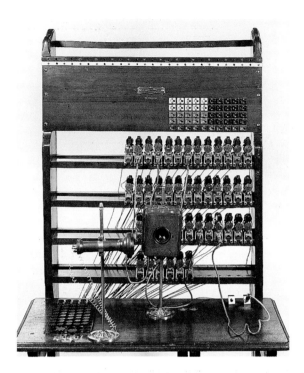

Figure 21.11a (above left)
An early telephone exchange. This one was designed to connect 50 telephones.

Figure 21.11b (above right)
The sort of equipment in use in a modern telephone exchange.

In the next section we shall look at another analogue communication system.

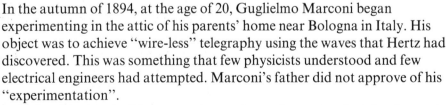

P21.3 Radio

In 1888, Heinrich Hertz discovered that a spark between two spheres sent out an electromagnetic wave that could be picked up some distance away. The first person to use this discovery for sending messages was Guglielmo Marconi, an Italian physicist. Until his invention, the fastest way to send messages was down the electric telegraph, using wires. So his new invention was called "wireless" telegraphy, which soon became shortened to "the wireless". It is known today as radio-wave transmission.

Marchese Guglielmo Marconi

In the autumn of 1894, at the age of 20, Guglielmo Marconi began experimenting in the attic of his parents' home near Bologna in Italy. His object was to achieve "wire-less" telegraphy using the waves that Hertz had discovered. This was something that few physicists understood and few electrical engineers had attempted. Marconi's father did not approve of his "experimentation".

At first his signals did not carry more than a few metres but then he read about a device that would detect a wave by causing iron-filings to stick together. These acted as a conductor and so a current could be sent through them to sound a bell. This device, called a "coherer", was much more sensitive than other receivers he had used to detect the waves, but he experimented until he had improved it even further. Marconi, working his transmitter from the attic of his home, was able to use his receiver further and further away in the field around his home. The sign that his waves had been

Figure 21.12
A spark transmitter. Sparks are produced across a small gap in the centre of the aerial rods. They can be picked up by a similar aerial up to 1 m away and detected by a sensitive ammeter.

Figure 21.13
Guglielmo Marconi (1874–1937) shortly after his arrival in England from Italy in 1896.

received was the waving of a white flag on a pole. Eventually he showed that the waves would pass over a hill. A hunting rifle had to be fired to signal success.

His family approached the Italian Ministry of Posts and Telegraphy to see if they were interested in the idea of "wireless" telegraphy. They were not, as they had already established a working telegraphic system of their own, using wires.

Marconi then moved to England where experiments with the system by the Royal Navy were a great success. In 1897, Marconi established a company called "The Wireless Telegraphy and Signal Company Limited". Marconi received £15 000 on the launch of the company together with some shares.

During the next few years he developed his equipment and extended its range, particularly with the Navy. His "sets" were priced at about £100 but the Navy thought this too expensive. By 1900 the company was almost out of funds due to lack of orders.

At this point Marconi announced that he was going to build two powerful stations with the aim of communicating across the Atlantic ocean. All the advice he received said this was impossible, because, due to the curve of the Earth, there was a "mountain" of water 200 km high for the radio waves to go over. If he was successful, Marconi would be able to undercut the operators of the submarine cables who used the telegraph system.

On 13 December 1901, Marconi confirmed that he had picked up the Morse letter "s" at a range of 3500 km. The age of long distance wireless communication had begun.

Marconi made a great contribution to science by taking the lecture-room novelty of "Hertzian waves" and turning them into a central feature of our everyday lives. On the day he died all radio transmissions throughout the world were stopped for two minutes as a tribute to his work. He was undoubtedly one of the great technologists of this century.

Figure 21.14a
An early radio receiver.

Figure 21.14b
A modern portable radio receiver.

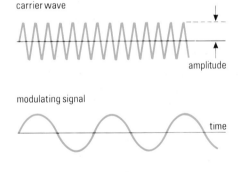

carrier wave

amplitude

modulating signal

time

amplitude modulated
carrier wave

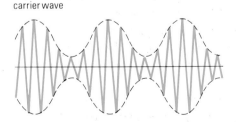

Figure 21.15
Modulating an electromagnetic carrier
wave with another wave representing the
sound that the carrier wave is to transmit.

Radio transmissions

At first radio could only be used to send messages in Morse code. But the invention of radio made it possible to communicate with many people at the same time. Now it is possible to send speech, music and even pictures by radio all over the world. Even a cheap radio receiver can be used to pick up signals (or *broadcasts* as they are called) from around the world.

7 Why do you think that radio and television transmissions have been given the general name "broadcasts"?

The next section explains in more detail how radio transmission and reception work and gives you the chance to make your own radio. Only do this however if you have time. You could omit this section and go straight on to the section "Some uses of radio communication" on page 323.

Radio transmission

Worksheet P21B gives you instructions on how to make your own radio. If you have time, either in class or outside, you may like to do this.

If you look at your chart of the electromagnetic spectrum that you made when reading Chapter **P15**, you will see that radio waves are a part of the electromagnetic spectrum. They cover a very wide band of wavelengths. Radio 4 in Britain is broadcast on an electromagnetic wave of wavelength 1500 m in what is called the *long wave band*. At the other end of the "radio spectrum" Radio 4 is also broadcast on an electromagnetic wave of wavelength of approximately 3 m. This is part of the *VHF wave band*.

8 Electromagnetic waves travel at a speed of 300 000 km per second. What are the frequencies corresponding to wavelengths of 1500 m and 3 m? (It may help to refer to Chapter **P14** to see how to do this calculation.)

The frequency of the sound waves that we hear ranges from about 30 Hz to 20 000 Hz. You may have measured this range of hearing in your work in Biology (see Chapter **B**11). In question **8** you should have found that the frequency of radio waves used to broadcast sound is very much higher than this: about 1000 times higher. So how is sound broadcast by radio waves which have a frequency 1000 times higher?

The answer is that the vibrations produced by a sound wave are first turned into electrical oscillations. These can then be "added" to a radio "carrier" wave (figure 21.15). Then, when the radio wave is transmitted it carries the sound pattern "on its back".

Your radio set is able to pick up the carrier wave from the radio transmitter that you tune in to. The tuning of your radio is done using a circuit that will only pick up vibrations of a certain frequency. A diagram of such a circuit, containing a device called a "capacitor" and a coil of wire, is shown in figure 21.16 on the next page. (A capacitor is a device that will store up electric charge when connected to a battery.) You saw a similar circuit in figure 15.27. The circuit is "tuned" to respond to the frequency of the carrier wave by altering either the capacitor or the coil.

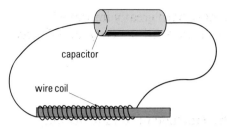

an electric circuit that can oscillate

Figure 21.16
The tuning circuit in a radio or television.
This picks up the carrier wave carrying the
signal you want to receive.

Modulation

When, as in figure 21.15, the sound wave pattern is added to the radio wave,
the *amplitude* of the radio wave varies in time with the sound wave pattern.
This process of adding a changing electrical signal to a much faster-varying
radio wave is called *modulation*. When the amplitude of the radio wave
follows the pattern of the other signal, the process is called *amplitude
modulation*.

To illustrate amplitude modulation you may see the experiment illustrated
in figure 21.17. It is a slow-motion imitation of how a radio wave can "carry"
another wave.

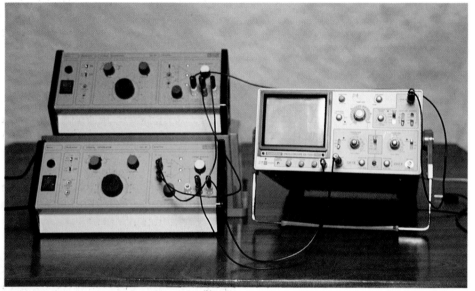

Figure 21.17
This experiment demonstrates how carrier waves can be modulated.

In this experiment, one alternating voltage is modulated by another, more
slowly varying, one. The result can be seen on the CRO. Of course, in a real
transmitter, all this is done electrically.

There is another way that radio waves can be modulated. This is by having
their *frequency* varied so that it follows the variation in the amplitude of the
slower signal. This process is called *frequency modulation*. It has the
advantage that it is less easily upset by things like electrical machinery and car
ignition systems which frequently interfere with amplitude modulation.

9 Some radio broadcasts use frequency modulation and some use amplitude
modulation. Broadcasts using frequency modulation are marked "FM" on your radio
tuning dial. Broadcasts using amplitude modulation are marked "AM".
Find out which broadcast wavebands use FM and which use AM. (Remember there
are four sound wavebands – called *Long, Medium* and *Short wave* and VHF – as well
as the television band called UHF. Find out what VHF and UHF stand for.)

By 1906, signals carrying speech and music could be sent thousands of
kilometres. Unfortunately these were often distorted when received, and also
picked up what is called "noise" on the way from sender to receiver. Morse
code was still used to send accurate messages over very long distances.

Today, radio transmission and reception have been greatly improved. Better design of radio receivers and the introduction of frequency modulation have both helped.

Some uses of radio communication

Using radio transmission is the most practical method of communicating over large distances. Radio waves are now used to transmit not only speech and music, but also pictures. Television pictures are transmitted using radio waves.

As technology allowed us to send spacecraft from Earth, first to the Moon and then to other planets in the Solar system, so communication systems also developed. The pace of that development has been remarkable. In 1957, the Russian "Sputnik" satellite (the first satellite to be launched into space) did no more than send out "bleeps" to the listeners below. In 1969, when the first footstep was taken on the Moon, pictures and conversation were being transmitted back to Earth.

In 1974, the spacecraft Mariner 4 sent back 22 pictures from the planet Mars. The signals from which the pictures were built up were transmitted by the spacecraft over a period of nine days. These signals were recorded back on Earth. When they had all been received, the pictures were re-made from the signals.

In 1980, the Voyager spacecraft (figure 21.18) was sending back pictures of Saturn. By then it had become possible to send back all the details for one picture in a time of only 48 s.

10 At its closest, Mars is about 80 million km from the Earth (80 × 10⁶ km). The planet Saturn is about 1280 million km from the Earth. Radio waves travel at 300 000 km/s. Calculate how long it will take a radio signal to travel these distances.

Figure 21.18
The Voyager spacecraft, and one of its pictures of Saturn.

Figure 21.19a (above left)
Intelsat V. This satellite is already in
service. It can relay 12 000 two-way
telephone calls, two colour television
channels and two maritime channels
simultaneously.

Figure 21.19b (above right)
Intelsat V on top of its launching rocket in
May 1983.

In 1986, pictures and other data were received from the same spacecraft as
it flew past Uranus. During the six years of Voyager's journey from Saturn to
Uranus, the computers on board the spacecraft were re-programmed using
radio transmission from Earth. Repairs were also made to some of the
mechanism by using radio signals to operate remote control mechanisms. All
of these radio signals were crossing 1000 million km of space – an incredible
technological achievement.

People on opposite sides of the Earth can now communicate by telephone
using radio waves relayed by Earth satellites. The satellite Intelsat V (figure
21.19) carries 12 000 telephone channels at the same time.

Using satellites we can now send pictures as well as information stored in
computers to any part of the Earth. People can even receive television
programmes directly from other countries via satellite. Some of the ways we
can communicate by radio waves are shown in figure 21.20.

Figure 21.20
The uses of radiocommunication.

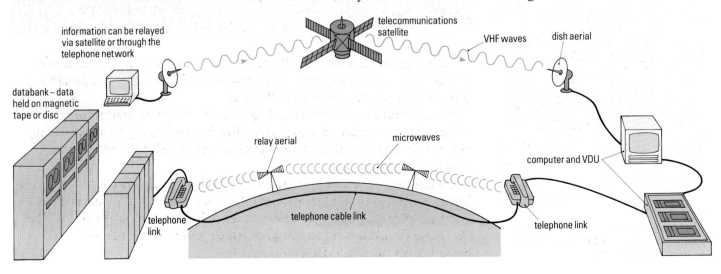

P21.4 Digital communication

The advantage of Morse code is that messages can be transmitted with great accuracy. "Dots and dashes" can be easily distinguished from background "noise".

In recent years scientists and engineers have extended this idea of "coding" messages. But instead of using trained operators to do the coding and decoding, they use electrical circuits to do it instead. The process they use is called *digital communication*.

Digital communication uses only two electrical signals: a high voltage pulse and a low voltage pulse (figure 21.21). These represent two digits. The high voltage represents a "1" and the low voltage represents a "0". You may already know how only two digits can be used to represent any number you like using *binary coding*. Figure 21.22 shows the number "26" coded in binary and then represented by a sequence of high and low voltage pulses. The number "26" in binary is given by 11010. This means:

$$1 \times 16 + 1 \times 8 + 0 \times 4 + 1 \times 2 + 0 \times 1$$

This becomes high–high–low–high–low when transmitted as a series of voltage pulses.

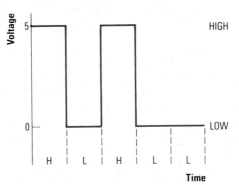

Figure 21.21
A digital signal. This consists only of a sequence of "high" and "low" pulses.

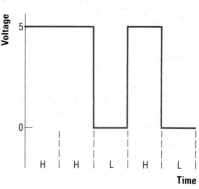

Figure 21.22
Coding the number "26" as a digital signal.

11 What is the **decimal** number represented by the sequence of voltage pulses shown in figure 21.21?

Letters of the alphabet can also be given a binary coding. This code can also be turned into a sequence of voltage pulses. Thus it becomes possible to transmit any written messages in this way.

Microprocessors use binary coding. So it is a very easy matter for computers to communicate with each other by sending digital signals along wires. This they do with great speed and accuracy, using the telephone network for the purpose.

Computers are connected to the telephone lines by a device that turns their binary output into suitable pulses for the telephone lines. The same device converts telephone line signals back to the pulses the computer can use. The thing that does this is called a *modem*, which stands for **mo**dulator/ **dem**odulator (figure 21.23).

Figure 21.23
A computer modem. This device enables computers to be linked to each other via the telephone network.

Sending sound signals by digital coding

Communication by digitally-coded signals has been found to be so reliable that ways have been found to extend it to sound itself. In this way it has proved possible to transmit and record speech and music with great accuracy. But how can this be done?

You have already seen how the vibrations produced by sound can be turned into a varying electrical voltage. This is done using a microphone. If the output of a microphone is shown on a CRO, a pattern is produced on the screen. This pattern shows the way the microphone's output is varying with time (figure 21.24).

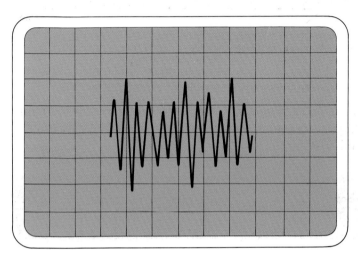

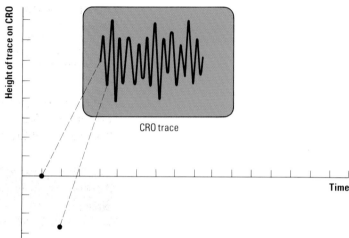

Figure 21.24 (above left)
The output from a microphone as it would appear on a cathode ray oscilloscope.

Figure 21.25 (above right)
Plotting the CRO trace on graph paper. The trace has been divided up into equally-spaced time steps. The height of the trace at each step is plotted on to the graph paper.

Suppose you were asked to make a copy on paper of figure 21.24. How would you set about it? You might just try to make a rough sketch. But here is a more accurate way you could do it.

You could take a piece of graph paper and draw a scale to correspond to those in the screen. You could then divide up the time-axis (which is the horizontal one) into small steps (figure 21.25). Now you could ask a friend to read off the heights of the pattern on the CRO screen at each of the times you have marked on your graph. All you have to do is to plot them on your graph and join up the dots!

But what you have done is to turn the wave pattern into a sequence of numbers. Anyone could now draw the pattern, provided they knew the time intervals at which you had made your measurements.

This is exactly how the varying voltages that are produced by a microphone, for example, are turned into a sequence of numbers which can then be stored or transmitted in binary code. Of course all the work you and your friend might do with pencil and paper is done by electrical circuits. Reading voltages in time-steps like this is called *sampling*. The more frequent the sampling, the more accurate will be the wave copy that is eventually produced (figure 21.26).

*Worksheet **P21C** shows you how to do some sampling for yourself on graph paper. It also gives you some idea of how many samples have to be made in order that the numbers can be turned back into a good copy of the original wave. It is not however essential to do this worksheet in order to understand the rest of the chapter.*

Special circuits are needed to turn the electrical signals produced by a microphone into a sequence of binary numbers. These circuits are called

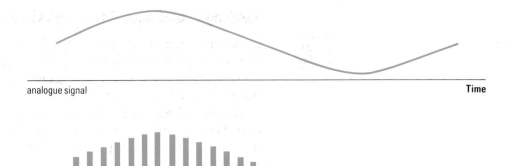

analogue signal   **Time**

pulse samples of analogue signal   **Time**

Figure 21.26
This diagram shows the output from a microphone picking up sound from a chorus and orchestra. The output was stored digitally in an instrument called a VELA before being fed into a chart recorder.

analogue-to-digital converters. (When they work the other way at the receiving end they are called "digital-to-analogue converters".) These names are often shortened to ADC and DAC circuits.

12 Why are the two words "analogue" and "digital" used in the names for these circuits?

Using digital coding

Digitally coded information signals can be transmitted with great accuracy and at great speed. For this reason increasing use is being made of digital coding to relay information.

It might at first seem strange to suggest that digital signals increase the speed of communication. No information can be sent at a faster speed than that of light! The answer is that the increase in speed comes from the way information can be packed together.

13a Read some lines from this book out loud and measure how long you take.
b Now count the number of letters in the passage you have read.
c Work out the number of letters you "transmit" per second using speech.

What answer did you get to part **c** of question **13**? A typical answer might be 12 letters per second. Using binary coding, each letter can be represented by a code of eight binary digits. So 12 letters could be represented by about 100 binary digits.

When these are turned into voltage pulses, it is possible to transmit them at up to 48 000 pulses per second. This means that messages can be transmitted in a time approximately $\frac{1}{500}$ the time it would take to say them. Very much higher "transmission speeds" are already technically possible and will eventually be used.

Compact disc players also use digital coding. The ordinary plastic record is an analogue recording. The "ups and downs" along the grooves are a copy of

Figure 21.27
A modern "stereo system" which contains both a conventional record player and a compact disc player.

the original sound signal. This is picked up by the *stylus* which again copies the movement of the original sound waves. Eventually this gets passed to the loudspeakers. A lot can go wrong with the sound signal on such a hazardous journey.

To try to improve the reproduction of music, the original sound can be turned into binary numbers which are "coded" onto a disc. The "coding" takes the form of tiny patches which will reflect light (the "1"s) and tiny patches that do not (the "0"s). These patches are turned back into electrical pulses by directing a light beam on to the disc and picking up the reflections using a photodetector.

This digital signal is turned back into the original sound by electrical circuits. Many people think this gives much better music recording.

Optical communication systems

You have seen in Chapter **P**13 how optical fibres are replacing copper cables in communication systems. You saw that optical fibres had several advantages over copper cables. Here is another advantage they have.

As you have already seen, the time taken to transmit information using binary coding is limited only by the number of "high" and "low" voltage pulses that can be sent down a cable each second. This number is greatly increased if light is used instead of electrical pulses.

If you have not already completed it, now would be a good time to do Worksheet **P***13B "Optical fibres and telecommunications".*

Summary

This chapter has been concerned with communication. Modern communication systems have been developed using ideas and theories in physics. In learning about them you have had to use a great deal of your knowledge of physics that you have gained in earlier chapters.

Make a table showing as many **different** ideas in physics as you can find that have been used in this chapter and where each was used. Figure 21.29 gives an example to help you. Copy out this table and fill in as many more entries as you can.

PHYSICAL PROPERTY OR IDEA	APPLICATION
1. Light travels further in air than sound.	Using semaphore enabled communications to take place over greater distances than before.
2.	

Figure 21.29

Index